Rationality, Religious Belief,
and Moral Commitment

Rationality, Religious Belief, and Moral Commitment

New Essays in the Philosophy of Religion

Robert Audi and William J. Wainwright

Cornell University Press, Ithaca and London

First published 1986 by Cornell University Press.

International Standard Book Number (cloth) 0-8014-1856-9
International Standard Book Number (paper) 0-8014-9381-1
Library of Congress Catalog Card Number 85–48200

Printed in the United States of America

Librarians: Library of Congress cataloging information appears on the last page of the book.

The paper in this book is acid-free and meets the guidelines for permanence and durability of the Committee on Production Guidelines for Book Longevity of the Council on Library Resources.

TO WILLIAM P. ALSTON

Contents

Preface

The field of philosophy of religion is probably more vital today than at any other time in this century. This volume is intended to reflect that vitality, and it contains original papers by many of the leading writers in the field. For the most part the papers are systematic studies that exhibit both the philosophical depth and the wider implications of the issues they address. As a group, the essays bear significantly on most of the major problems in the philosophy of religion, but they approach these problems in quite different ways. Some take up a leading issue, such as the problem of evil, independently of any particular works in which it has received philosophical treatment; others critically examine historically influential texts. Some of the papers assess the implications, for the philosophy of religion, of a major philosophical position, such as coherentism in epistemology or naturalism as a metaphysical view of the world. Others explore the meaning of important religious doctrines, for instance that of total devotion to God.

A number of important developments in recent philosophy are also reflected in the papers. These developments are extensive, and we can mention only a few. The past decade or so has produced much important work in epistemology and the theory of rationality. For instance, the classical rivals in the theory of knowledge, foundationalism and coherentism, have each been clarified and defended more carefully than ever before. Some of the papers directly pursue the relevance of

9

these positions to the rationality of belief in God. In modal logic and possible-worlds semantics, there has also been significant progress in recent years. Some of the papers apply concepts drawn from these fields. Some of them also explore historically important texts in the light of current issues, particularly in epistemology. And some of them bring to bear concepts and distinctions that have lately received much philosophical attention in metaphysics, ethics, the philosophy of mind, or epistemology.

This collection differs from much other work in the philosophy of religion in another respect. The traditional arguments for the existence of God are kept entirely in the background. To some extent, this aspect of the book reflects the authors' sense that those arguments have been disproportionately emphasized in the literature and their awareness of many other important problems in the philosophy of religion. But there is at least one other, perhaps deeper reason for keeping the traditional arguments for the existence of God in the background in a collection in the philosophy of religion produced at this time. The epistemological discussions of the past decade strongly support the conclusion that certain beliefs (such as simple perceptual beliefs) can be justifiably held even if they do not in any sense rest on arguments and perhaps even if the believer in fact could not produce an argument in support of them. If this conclusion is correct, then it may well be a mistake to approach the question of the justification of belief in God as philosophers often have done—and still commonly do—entirely in relation to the arguments that apparently support it. A similar point may be made about rationality. Recent work both in epistemology and in the general theory of rationality suggests that the rationality of holding a belief is not entirely a matter of its epistemic justification, for example of the believer's evidence for it. If this view is sound, then questions of rationality are not wholly reducible to questions of epistemic justification, and there is some reason to doubt the commonly held view that the rationality of belief in God depends on the arguments that believers can marshal in support of it.

We may further characterize the intent of this collection by comparing it with an earlier book that exercised considerable influence, *New Essays in Philosophical Theology*, edited by Antony Flew and Alasdair MacIntyre and published in 1955. Like that volume, this one ranges over a number of the main problems in the philosophy of religion and brings recent philosophical advances to bear on them. But in places, at least, that collection exhibited a perhaps excessive preoccupation with ordinary language, a somewhat cavalier attitude toward formal logic, and, at times, an insufficiently critical acceptance of a positivistic view of meaningfulness. On that view, a sentence that purports to be about the world, such as 'God exists', is meaningful only if it expresses a verifiable proposition, that is, one testable by observations in the way appropriate to verifying scientific hypotheses. This collection has none of those characteristics. There is, however, a more profound difference. For the most part, the papers gathered here more strongly represent systematic philosophical thinking. Where they are not themselves systematic treatments of a major topic, they at least form part of the author's overall position. They can thus be read not only for the views—often far-reaching and controversial ones—that they defend, but also as parts of a larger position in the philosophy of religion, in metaphysics, in epistemology, in ethics, or in other major philosophical areas.

The division of the papers into the volume's three parts is natural, but it is not meant to suggest that those in a given part concentrate only on the overall topic of that part. A number of the papers bear significant relationships to at least several others, including some of those in one or both of the other parts. Nor is there any simple division between the historical papers and those that simply pursue their topic with little explicit attention to its history. The former tend to pursue their own philosophical direction as well as to explicate the texts under study, and the latter are often consciously developing a historically important view.

The essays also differ in the background that they presuppose on the part of the reader. All are professional papers intended to contribute to advancing the field, and several may be difficult for non-philosophical readers. Most of the papers, however, should be quite accessible to students of the philosophy of religion, particularly those who have mastered the materials in some basic philosophy courses or are guided by an instructor.

All of the papers were presented at a Research Conference in the Philosophy of Religion held at the University of Nebraska, Lincoln, in April 1984. None has been previously published (except Pike's paper, which also appears in *Religious Experience and Religious Belief: Essays in the Epistemology of Religion*, edited by Joseph Runzo and Craig Ihara and published by University Press of America). The authors greatly benefited from discussions at the conference and from critical studies presented by a very able group of commentators: David Conway, Laura Garcia, Joshua Hoffman, Jonathan L. Kvanvig, Robert McKim, Thomas V. Morris, Gary Sol Rosenkrantz, Eleonore Stump, Edward Wierenga, David E. White, Stephen J. Wykstra, Keith Yandell, and Linda Zagzebski. The editors are also grateful for a grant from the National

Endowment for the Humanities; this support made the conference possible. The advice and help of John G. Ackerman and the staff of Cornell University Press have also aided us greatly. We owe special thanks to William P. Alston. Over a period of many years, as a philosopher writing in the field, as a critical respondent to the authors' ideas, and, more recently, in his contributions to the conference as commentator at large, he has done a great deal to make this collection what it is.

ROBERT AUDI

Lincoln, Nebraska

WILLIAM J. WAINWRIGHT

Milwaukee, Wisconsin

PART ONE

Rationality and Religious Belief

John of the Cross on the Epistemic Value of Mystic Visions

NELSON PIKE

That mystic visions and locutions have value as potential sources of information is a theme that is clearly detectable in Augustine's *Literal Commentary on Genesis* and in that portion of the *Summa theologica* devoted to a discussion of what Aquinas refers to as "prophecy."[1] It is a view that governs thinking about mystic apprehensions[2] in most modern manuals of Christian mysticism as well. Furthermore, that some of the information conveyed in this way consists of propositions of importance to the Faith is, again, a commonplace thesis in the literature of Christian mysticism. For example, when cataloguing the kinds of information that can be (as he says) "prophetically revealed," in addition to descriptions of mundane facts such as those revealed to Solomon concerning the kinds of beasts and fishes indigenous to the lands surrounding Israel, Aquinas lists some that (in his words) "surpass human knowledge," such as the mystery of the Trinity that was revealed in the vision of

I am indebted to a host of people who have read and commented on earlier versions of this essay. Those to whom I am especially grateful include David White (St. John Fisher College), Paul Draper (University of California, Irvine), M. Pabst Battin (University of Utah), and Steven Payne (Discalced Carmelite Friars, Washington, D.C.).

1. II of II, q. 171–74.
2. The term "apprehension" is used by St. John to cover both visions and locutions. As a general remark, visions are visual or visual-like experiences while locutions are auditory or auditory-like experiences. (Cf. *Ascent of Mount Carmel*, II, ch. 23, sec. 3.) Within the Christian mystical tradition, apprehensions constitute one of two broad classes of mystical experiences and are usually referred to as "Gratuitous Graces" (i.e., special gifts from God). The other broad class of mystical experiences is referred to as the "states of infused contemplation" or, more colloquially, the "states of mystic union."

the seraphim described in Isaiah II (4:3). On this same topic, in chapter 18 of perhaps the most widely respected modern treatise on Christian mystical theology, namely, *The Graces of Interior Prayer*, Anton Poulain writes as follows concerning the vision of the Trinity that not uncommonly accompanies the state of mystic contemplation called "rapture": "Even if we did not know by the Church's teaching how many persons there are in God, and how they proceed One from the Other, we should come to know it, and, by experience, through seeing it (in rapture)."[3] Similar remarks can be found in most of the classical and modern texts that constitute the center of the Christian mystical literature.

The renegade nature of the dominant thesis advanced by St. John of the Cross in Book II of his celebrated work *The Ascent of Mount Carmel* can best be appreciated when it is viewed in the context of this tradition. In this source, although there are passages that suggest a contrary (that is, more traditional) view,[4] John's principal claim seems clearly to be that the private experiences of individual mystics have no value whatsoever as sources of information. John insists on this point with respect to the visions and locutions recorded in the Bible, and on the question of whether the experiences of mystics can serve as a basis for accepting truths already revealed to the Church (for example, the mystery of the Trinity), John's remarks also carry a heavily negative verdict. Furthermore, not only does John claim that mystic apprehensions are useless as information bearers; his position is that to treat them as such is to risk a variety of pitfalls of considerable threat to the spiritual life. As regards the latter, before one can accept a given apprehension as a source of genuine knowledge, one must make what is traditionally referred to as a "discernment of spirits." In other words, one must determine whether the apprehension is a communication from a reliable source (for example, God) as opposed to an unreliable informant (for example, the devil). And according to John, since this is an especially subtle and complicated task, the receiving mystic must be prepared to suffer not only the distraction of making the relevant calculations, but the anxiety that goes with the possibility of making a mistake. These disturbances, plus the fact that if error is made the mystic could be led to embrace a false belief injurious to his faith, make the project precarious in the extreme.[5] But of course, in spite of the dangers, one

3. Ch. 18, par. 23. This passage taken from the 1910 English edition translated by Leonora York Smith (London: Kegan Paul, Trench Trubner).

4. Two passages in particular seem to fit this category, viz, pt. II, ch. 22, secs. 2 and 3; and ch. 26, secs. 12 and 13.

5. *Ascent*, II, ch. 17, sec. 7. See also ch. 16, sec. 14; ch. 21, sec. 7; ch. 29, sec. 11; and ch. 30, sec. 5. Throughout this essay I quote from the 1964 English edition translated by Kieran Kavanaugh and Otilio Rodriguez (New York: Doubleday).

must allow that in some cases the visionary will succeed in discovering that his vision is from a reliable source and thus can be trusted to convey only truth. The center of St. John's negative stance regarding the epistemic value of mystic apprehensions is that, even in this optimal case, the apprehension in question cannot be taken as a legitimate source of propositional knowledge. It is with respect to this last thesis that John parts company with virtually the whole of the classical as well as with modern Christian theological opinion on this topic. It is this that leads him to declare in the end that mystics ought not to busy themselves with the discernment of spirits. With respect to apprehensions generally, one ought not to seek them or (once they have been given) to "accept them or keep them." John says that, whether they be true visions or false, the best thing to do is to "reject them all."[6]

In the first two sections of the present paper, I review and then critique a theory concerning the nature of mystic apprehensions that is advanced by St. John in Book II, chapters 18–20, of the *Ascent* and that has as a consequence the negative thesis just identified. The third section is then offered as an expansionary interlude in which attention focuses on an account proposed by the contemporary Protestant theologian Emil Brunner of what he calls "the revelation in creation." I argue that, although Brunner's theory of revelation differs importantly from the one formulated by St. John in chapters 18–20, both embody the same incoherent theological thesis. The point of the interlude is to display this thesis in its most general form, by first identifying and then discounting variations in its content as it appears in the two contexts studied. In the fourth and final section of the paper, I return to Book II of the *Ascent* in an effort to piece together a second argument for John's negative position on the epistemic value of mystic apprehensions which does not make use of the deficient thesis inherent in the first. I should add that the argument developed in this concluding section rests on a theory concerning the nature of mystic apprehensions which is constructed rather than simply lifted from John's remarks on this subject. Though much of the relevant material is taken from chapter 17, essential ingredients are imported from scattered discussions in later portions of the text—in particular, from chapters 21, 22, 24, 27, and 29. For this reason, some readers may protest that the theory suggested is, at best, Sanjaunian rather than John's own view. Be this as it may (and I shall leave this question for others to decide), I am anxious that the theory be injected into the serious philosophical discussion of mysticism that is just now getting under way. It is one that has prompted me (at least) to rethink my presuppositions

6. *Ascent*, II, ch. 17, secs. 6–9. Cf. also ch. 16, secs. 10–14.

regarding what we as students of the mystical literature should be looking for when attempting to estimate the epistemic value of mystic apprehensions or, for that matter, mystical experiences more generally.

ON THE MEANING OPACITY OF MYSTIC APPREHENSIONS

I can know that a given string of symbols expresses a proposition and understand the proposition but not know whether the proposition in question is true. That situation is commonplace. Correlatively, I can know that a given string of symbols expresses a proposition and know that the proposition is true but not understand the proposition in question. This last possibility is exemplified by the case in which Paul Revere is expecting a message from the bell tower concerning the course of the British advance but, after receiving the signal from his trusted comrade, realizes that he never did have it straight whether it is one if by land and two if by sea or two if by land and one if by sea. Here Revere knows that the glimmer from the tower is an information bearer and knows that the information contained in the message is true but does not know what the propositional content of the message is supposed to be.

With this thought in mind, consider the case of Abraham, who, after being brought to the land of Canaan, was told by God: "I will give you this land." Abraham was led to believe that he would someday rule this land. Imagine his astonishment (as well as that of those around him) when he found himself old and enfeebled without ever having ruled in Canaan.[7] What went wrong? The most obvious conclusion would appear to be that the message contained in the words spoken to Abraham was false. However, neither John nor any other traditional mystical theologian would allow this as a possibility. Within the Christian mystical community, it is held as an axiom that if a given mystic apprehension is produced by God (is "from God" or is "divine"), whatever revelation (message) is contained in that apprehension is true.[8] Well, then, what did go wrong in the case of Abraham? John claims that in this case the revelation contained in the divine locution was not that Abraham himself would rule in Canaan, but that Abraham's descendents would possess that land someday in the distant future. Abraham simply mis-

7. *Ascent*, II, ch. 19, sec. 2.
8. Cf. Aquinas's *Summa theologica* (hereafter *STh*), II of II, q. 171, art. 6. St. John concurs, e.g., *Ascent*, II, ch. 19, sec. 1 (first sentence); ch. 19, sec. 14; and ch. 20, sec. 1 (first sentence).

understood the words. He thus did not receive the message therein contained.

Using this and a number of other cases taken mostly from Old Testament sources,[9] John arrives at the following general account: As a rule, when God attempts to communicate via direct verbal symbols (locutions), the words he employs are not used in their ordinary senses. There are passages in which John suggests that this is not just true as a general rule but holds in every case.[10] God speaks in a kind of code. Unlike Revere's comrade, however, God uses symbols that are the same as those used in everyday language. It is the meanings attached to the symbols that are different. It is thus not surprising that, in some instances, even though the message contained in a given locution is true, because the words are taken literally they convey a message that is false. John maintains that there have been cases in which "the ideas [expressed] in God's words are so different from the meanings men would ordinarily derive from them" that even prophets such as Jeremiah and Christ's own disciples were led to hold false beliefs as a result of receiving divine communications.[11]

Why should it be that, when God communicates by way of locutions, he uses words carrying meanings other than those attached to them when used by men in ordinary discourse? On John's account, the answer to this question has something to do with the nature of the messages God attempts to communicate. He says: "God's chief objective in conferring these revelations is to express and impart the elusive spir-

9. Some other cases given in *Ascent* II, ch. 19 are these: (1) Sec. 3: Jacob is told by God that he should go to Egypt and that when the time comes, he (God) will lead him out again. Jacob dies in Egypt. Real message: God will lead Jacob's descendents out of Egypt. (2) Sec. 7: Jeremiah is told by God: "Peace will come to you." However, only wars and trials fall on Jeremiah and the people of Israel. Real message: The Messiah is coming sometime in the future. (3) Secs. 7–8: David is told by God that the Messiah will reign and free the people from bondage. The Messiah is born of humble state and is, himself, persecuted and slain by those who oppress Israel. Real message: Christ reigns in heaven and frees the people from the devil. (4) Sec. 12: A devout man is told by God: "I will free you from your enemies." His enemies prevail against him and kill him. Real message: "I will give you salvation." (5) Sec. 13: A devout man who wants to be a martyr is told by God: "You shall be a martyr." He dies peacefully in his sleep. Real message: "I will give you the love and peace that goes with being a martyr." I should point out that some of the cases that John cites in this connection are not of this form and do not support the generalization I am about to formulate. For example, ch. 20, sec. 1: Jonah is told by God that he will destroy the city of Nineveh in forty days. He does not. In the interim, the people repent and God does not follow through. In this case, it is not that Jonah misunderstood what he heard; it is rather that the condition "unless the people repent" was not explicit in the original formulation.
10. *Ascent*, II, ch. 19, secs. 5, 7, and 11.
11. *Ascent*, II, ch. 19, secs. 7 and 9.

itual meaning contained in the words. This spiritual meaning is richer and more plentiful than the literal meaning and transcends those limits."[12] Apparently, ordinary language is simply not an adequate tool for expressing the "elusive spiritual meanings" that God wants to impart. In some passages John says that these meanings are simply not available to our understanding. The truths expressed are "hidden truths" that are quite beyond our powers of comprehension.[13] There are other passages, however, in which this position is softened. Sometimes John says that the meanings in question can never be *completely* comprehended—suggesting, perhaps, that they may be understood in part.[14] At other times he tells us that the meanings expressed in the words used by God are only very difficult to understand—implying (I should think) that there is nothing here that is incomprehensible, but only meanings that we must work very hard to grasp.[15] But whether John is claiming that the meanings expressed in the words used by God are incomprehensible, only partially comprehensible, or just very difficult to understand, he seems clearly to be saying that they cannot be expressed in sentences using words carrying the meanings they have in ordinary human discourse.[16]

If God's messages are coded, how shall we proceed when trying to uncover the revelation contained in a particular locution? John holds that there is no codebook, no translation formulas. There simply is no safe procedure by which one can begin with an understanding of the literal meaning of the words and emerge in the end with an understanding of the message therein contained. John writes: "Let it be realized, therefore, that there is no complete understanding of the meanings of the sayings and things of God, and that this meaning cannot be decided by what it seems to be without great error and, in the end, grievous confusion."[17] The conclusion is that, with respect to any given divine locution, one can never be sure that one has grasped the message carried by the words: "Evidently, then, even though the words and revelations be from God, we cannot find assurance in them, since in our understanding of them we can easily be deluded and extremely so. They embody an abyss and depth of spiritual significance and to want to limit them to our interpretation and sensory apprehension is like wanting to grasp a handful of air, which will escape the hand entirely and leave only a particle of dust."[18]

---

12. *Ascent*, II, ch. 19, sec. 5. Cf. also ch. 19, sec. 1.
13. *Ascent*, II, ch. 20, sec. 5.
14. *Ascent*, II, ch. 20, sec. 6.
15. *Ascent*, II, ch. 19, sec. 7 (first line) and sec. 9 (first line).
16. *Ascent*, II, ch. 19, secs. 5 and 11.
17. *Ascent*, II, ch. 20, sec. 6.
18. *Ascent*, II, ch. 19, sec. 10. Cf. also ch. 19, sec. 9: and ch. 19, sec. 1.

So far we have dealt exclusively with experiences in which words are apprehended (locutions) and have as yet said nothing about visual experiences (visions), which may or may not be accompanied by locutions. However, it is clear in John's text that he intends the conclusion just reached to apply to visions as well as to divine locutions. In the opening paragraphs of both chapters 19 and 20 he claims that, although the messages contained in both locutions and visions from God are true, in no case can one assume that one understands the messages in question. Why? In the case of locutions, the explanation rests in the fact that God uses words in extraordinary senses. But, of course, this explanation will not apply to visions in which there are no verbal symbols and thus no ordinary or extraordinary senses of words to consider. Inasmuch as John nowhere addresses himself separately to visions, there is something of a hiatus in the reasoning. Let me here risk a suggestion as to how the argument might be completed.

Let us suppose that a small angel appears holding a spear with a hot iron tip.[19] Let us assume that the apprehension is from God and that it is a meaning bearer that contains a message having a positive truth value. What is the message—that is, what is the revelation contained in the vision? Even if one assumes that there is one and only one such revelation, the question remains as to what the specific content of that revelation is. I think John would say that there is just no way to answer this question. Though we assume that the various elements of the visual presentation (the size of the angel, the hot iron tip of the spear, and so forth) are symbols that jointly embody some propositional message, there is no way to be sure that whatever meaning we assign to it is the one that is actually intended. There is no way to start with the symbols and arrive at the meaning they presumably contain.

The upshot, then, is that neither divine locutions nor divine visions can be taken as sources of knowledge—neither religious knowledge such as that codified in the doctrines of the Church (the mystery of the Trinity) nor mundane knowledge concerning, for example the beasts and fishes indigenous to the lands surrounding Israel. And most interesting here, I think, is not that this conclusion is urged by one of the most important spokesmen for the Christian mystical tradition (a fact already surprising in the extreme) but that the argument for his negative position proceeds without challenging any element of the epistemic apparatus routinely used in Christian mystical sources for determing the reliability of mystic apprehensions.[20] Since, for John, any message

19. Such a vision was reported by St. Teresa of Avila in her *Life*, ch. 29.
20. I review and discuss the elements of this apparatus in an article "Mystic Visions as Sources of Knowledge," in *Mysticism and Philosophical Analysis*, ed. Steven Katz (London: Sheldon Press, 1978).

contained in a divine apprehension is (by hypothesis) true, the issue here has nothing to do with lack of assurance concerning reliability. John's claim is that, even if we grant that the message is true (since the apprehension is divine), there is no safe way to determine precisely what it is. Mystic apprehensions are, we might say, *opaque* as regards their meaning. It is this opacity that renders them useless as potential sources of propositional knowledge.

CRITIQUE

The conclusion just reached concerning the meaning opacity of mystic apprehensions is presumably based on a study of biblical cases in which God (allegedly) tried to communicate truths to selected individuals and because the truths in question were deep (at best, very difficult for us to understand), God found it necessary to formulate them in symbols carrying meanings other than the ones they have in ordinary discourse. Because the recipients interpreted the symbols in standard fashion, they failed to receive the intended message. However, let us look again at these biblical cases. John tells us that the real message intended for Abraham in the words "I will give you this land" was "I will give this land to your descendents." John identifies the precise nature of Abraham's mistake by identifying and then comparing the real message with the apparent message. This pattern is repeated for each of the cases treated in the text. But what is so difficult to understand about the sentence "I will give this land to your descendents"? It looks straightforward enough. Indeed, it is only because we can readily understand it that we can readily understand John's analysis of Abraham's mistake. Had the import of the real message been as opaque as John's conclusion would lead us to believe, we (and he) should have had difficulty understanding it and thus should have had equal difficulty understanding what John was telling us about the nature of Abraham's mistake. And note, too, that John has apparently formulated the real message contained in the divine locution using only standard words carrying their ordinary meanings. If John were not using the words "I will give this land to your descendents" with standard meanings attached, since he provides no glossary to which we might refer, he could not assume that we would understand the real message, and thus he could not assume that we would understand the point he is making when he identifies the specific nature of Abraham's mistake. Thus the cases used by John to support his generalization about the meaning opacity of mystic locutions do nothing to warrant his final conclusion. If anything, they pull in the opposite direction: they look more like counterexamples than like cases meant to support his position.

This criticism seems to me to be decisive. However, it is decisive not against John's position concerning the meaning opacity of divine apprehensions but against the procedure he uses when attempting to show that that position is correct. It is one of those special cases in which the import of the theory undermines the argument used in its support. In the next few pages I will argue that, from the point of view of one committed to a more or less standard medieval picture of the nature of God, there is something wrong with the theory itself and not just with John's particular way of supporting it. I offer the argument as one that might be advanced by, for example, Thomas Aquinas in response to John's challenge of the traditional view concerning the epistemic value of mystic apprehensions.

God is omnipotent if he has unlimited productive power, that is, if he has productive power greater than which cannot be conceived, that is, if it is within God's power to bring about any state of affairs S where "God brings about S" describes a logical possibility. Second, God is onmiscient if he knows all things knowable. According to Aquinas, the class of things knowable includes future events and circumstances, that is, so-called future contingents.[21] Last, allow that God counts as having communicated a given proposition R to a particular person P if God brings it about that P understands R. Now, with these three assumptions in mind, suppose that God exists and is both omnipotent and omniscient. I want to consider a case in which a person P does not understand a proposition R. And with respect to this case, there would appear to be three possibilities vis-à-vis God and his communicative activities, namely, (1) it was not possible for God to communicate R to P; (2) though it was possible for God to communicate R to P, God made no effort to do so; and (3) though it was possible for God to communicate R to P and God made an effort to do so, that attempt failed. I will look at each of these three possibilities separately.

I am not sure that I can provide a fully convincing illustration of the first possibility, but the following will perhaps at least suggest how one might look. R is the Special Theory of Relativity, and P is a severely retarded person suffering from Down's syndrome. R is thus such as to be beyond the range of P's powers of comprehension and our notion of personal identity is such that any person having powers of comprehension sufficient for the understanding of R would fail to count as the person P. But of course, if it were not possible for P to understand R, God (being omniscient) would know this. That P should be brought to understand R would then not be something that God might try to do. One can be described as *trying* to communicate R to P only if one

---

21. *STh*, I, q. 14, art. 13.

undertakes an action that one knows, thinks, or at least suspects will, or at least might (as far as one knows to the contrary), bring it about that P understands R. But if God knew that it was not possible for P to understand R, he would also know that any action he might undertake to communicate R to P would fail to do so. Hence, in this circumstance, God could not be described as having *tried* to communicate R to P. The reason is that in this circumstance, God could not be described as having undertaken an action that he knew, thought, or even suspected would, or even might (so far as he knew to the contrary), bring it about that P understands R. If we assume alternative 1, therefore, it would appear that God could not have tried to communicate R to P. Alternative 1 and alternative 2 thus seem to collapse into a single case, namely, one in which God made no attempt to communicate R to P. With respect to some person who does not understand a given proposition, therefore, our options concerning God's communicative activities reduce to two. Either God made no attempt to communicate R to P, or God made such a attempt and the attempt in question failed.

Consider a case in which it was possible for God to communicate R to P and God (allegedly) made an effort to do so, but the attempt failed. Let us suppose that the means of communication employed was a mystic locution or vision. Since it was possible for God to communicate R to P, we must assume that some other means of communication at God's disposal would have succeeded had it been employed. But God, being onmiscient, would have known that the means of communication chosen was going to fail. He would also have known that some other means of communication would have succeeded. Under these conditions, the conclusion would again appear to be that God did nothing that would count as an attempt to communicate R to P. As I suggested above, one makes an attempt to communicate a given proposition to a given person only if one undertakes an action that one knows, believes, or at least suspects will, or at least might (so far as one knows to the contrary), result in that person's understanding the proposition in question. But in the case before us, God undertook an action that he knew would not lead to understanding—and thus could never have thought that it might result in P's understanding R. This, by itself, is enough to assure that God made no effort to communicate R to P. This conclusion is reinforced when we add that God specifically opted against some alternative mode of communication that he knew would have resulted in P's understanding R. Alternative 3 thus appears to be incoherent. If a particular person fails to understand a given proposition, the reason cannot be that God tried but failed to communicate that proposition to the person in question. At this point, a note of clarification should be added.

According to St. Thomas, an act of assent involves choice. The act of accepting a revelation from God thus involves an act of will on the part of the one receiving the revelation.[22] If we now assume that the intelligent agents to whom revelations are given have free will, I could imagine someone arguing as follows: it makes perfectly good sense to suppose that God might try to get P to accept R and that the attempt might fail. P does not count as having accepted R unless he does so freely. Thus God could not *make P accept R*. To do so would involve making P do something freely. Of course, P does not count as having done something freely if he is made to do it by another. Hence, God can invite, command, or demand that P accept R. He might also want or hope and thus encourage or cajole P to accept R. But these efforts might fail. P might reject R regardless of God's efforts to the contrary, however persistent and skilled they might be. I cite this argument in order to make clear the following point of contrast.

Whatever connections there may be between the concept of assent and the concept of choice, *understanding* does not appear to be something one can choose (not choose, choose not) to do. I can choose (not choose, choose not) to take steps that lead (or may lead) to understanding. I can thus choose (not choose, choose not) to bring myself to a point where understanding occurs. But understanding itself seems best described not in the language of action but in the language of occurrences, happenings, or events. Thus, even if one grants that God could not make a given individual assent to a given proposition (on the grounds that assent requires an act of choice), I see no reason to deny that God could effect the corresponding case of understanding. As far as I can see, the claim that God might try but fail to communicate a given proposition to a given individual can receive no shelter by appeal to the peculiarities of the notion of choice. Inasmuch as God is both omnipotent and omniscient, any communicative effort he makes must, of necessity, succeed.

EXPANSION

According to Emil Brunner in *Revelation and Reason*, God created the universe in order to provide a "manifestation of his (own) power and wisdom" and thus to reveal himself to rational creatures. Brunner elaborates this idea as follows:

> God's will and nature are such that he creates in order to reveal himself. That which is created bears the stamp of its Maker through His will as Creator and through His act of creation. Therefore, the doctrine of

22. *STh*, II of II, q. 2, arts. 1 and 2.

analogia entis, which has been such a controversial topic of late, is not peculiar to the Catholic Church, but it has been part of the common Christian inheritance of belief from the earliest days of the Church; for it simply expresses the fact that it has pleased God so to create the world that in and through it His "everlasting power and divinity" may be made known.[23]

Brunner makes clear that this is a comment about what he calls the "objective process of revelation," that is, about the content communicated as well as the means employed by the one whose intention it is to communicate. Concerning the other side of the equation, that is, "the subjective reception of the revelation on the part of man," Brunner comments: "The works of God in creation are placed before the eyes of all, and reason is the endowment common to all men, and that which places them on a higher plane than that occupied by all other creatures. The objective process of revelation, or the objective means of revelation, and the subjective capacity to receive the revelation are thus made for each other."[24] But, if so, a question must surely arise as to why not all men have received the message contained in the divine revelatory act of creation. Brunner replies that the reason is the corruption inherent in man's sinful nature. The idea that man is a sinner is not just the idea that man is corrupt in "heart and will." Brunner insists: "It is an integral part of the sin of man that the the knowledge of God which begins to dawn upon him through revelation is suppressed by him, so that the revelation which God gives him for knowledge of Himself becomes the source of the vanity of idolatry. God gives the revelation in order that man may know Him, but man turns this into an illusion."[25] Shall we then conclude that the divine act of creation is not an act of communication after all? Brunner says: "As the Bible, just as it is, is an objective means of God's revelation—whether men understand it as God's word or not—so also the creation is a means of divine revelation whether men see it as such or not."[26] The point is that, although God's self-disclosure in the act of creation is (in Brunner's words) "communicated to" and is "meant" or "intended" for all men, man is afflicted with an "incomprehensible blindness" that prevents detection of what Brunner refers to as "the meaning" of God's revelation. Using a variation on the analogy introduced in the first section of this essay, we can say that the message is being beamed from the tower, and receiving

23. Emil Brunner, *Revelation and Reason: The Christian Doctrine of Faith and Knowledge* (Zurich, 1941), trans. Olive Wyon (Philadelphia: Westminster Press, 1946), pp. 68, 67.
24. Ibid., p. 68.
25. Ibid., p. 65. See also p. 66.
26. Ibid., p. 68.

equipment (reason) has been amply provided. The problem is that the equipment has fallen into disrepair. Brunner concludes: "The result is that man either does not perceive this evident, divine revelation, or, if he thinks he perceives it, he falls into gross error and misunderstanding."[27]

Regarding the credentials of the position just reviewed, Brunner says that it is a doctrine very clearly advanced in the works of the Reformers (principally Calvin) and is also in harmony with the teachings of the Bible. In both sources (Brunner assures us) we find insistence on the truth of the message contained in what he calls "the general revelation" or "the revelation in creation" coupled with the claim that there can be no "natural knowledge of God," that is, that natural theology is not a possibility. Brunner insists that, in both sources, too, the explanation of this somewhat surprising circumstance rests on the recognition of (in Brunner's words) "the cognitive significance of sin, that is, the fact that it prevents the knowledge of God. As one who *knows*, man stands in just as much opposition to the truth of God as he does in the sphere of action: his knowledge is no better than his practical relation to God; his knowledge is as corrupt as his heart."[28]

Brunner makes clear that the act of creation is only one of several "forms" or "methods" that God employs when attempting to communicate knowledge to men. Another, of course, is the Bible and there will be yet a third used in the final days.[29] Thus I do not want to suggest that what I have just reviewed is the whole or even a major part of what Brunner has to say about God's revelation to men. However, I have said enough for present purposes. I now want to return to the theory advanced by St. John to note some points of comparison.

A difference between Brunner and John regarding the vehicle by which revelation is conveyed is obvious. For Brunner it is the whole of creation, while for John the message is contained in more localized phenomena, such as words spoken on a specific occasion. However, more interesting differences are to be found in what Brunner and John have to say about the content of revelation, that is, about what God attempts to convey via whatever vehicle is involved. First, let me say that I have not been able to discover whether or not for Brunner we are to regard the content of the revelation in creation as a piece of information that is (or might be) cast in propositional form, for example, *that* God is wise and powerful or *that* the creator of the universe is wise and powerful. The fact that Brunner speaks of God's message as

27. Ibid., pp. 63 and 67, 84 ("meant," "intended"), 77, 84 (also see p. 77), 68.
28. Ibid., p. 65.
29. Ibid., pp. 58–59.

being available to reason and makes clear that he is (at least in part) concerned in this portion of the text with the question of whether natural theology is a real possibility would suggest that the revelatory content is propositional. Still, when he speaks of the revelation contained in the Bible, Brunner insists that the relevant content is God himself and not information of one sort or another.[30] Exactly what this statement means and whether it is intended to hold for the "revelation in creation" as well as for the biblical revelation is not very easy to determine. However this may be (and I shall not pursue it further), for Brunner the content (whether propositional or otherwise) appears to be singular (God's power and wisdom), is projected in a single communicative action (the act of creation), and is intended for a multiple audience consisting of all human beings. For John, on the other hand, what is revealed (clearly propositional in nature) consists of separate messages, separately delivered to each of a number of specifically targeted receivers. From an epistemological point of view, however, a further difference would appear to be more salient than any of these. According to Brunner, the meaning that God attempts to communicate by way of the act of creation is "manifest" and "evident" and is also readily available to man's natural powers of comprehension. On this last point, we may recall, he insists that the "objective" elements (the message and the means of communication) and the "subjective" element (man's capacity to receive the message) are well coordinated, (in his words) "made for each other." Thus on Brunner's theory, the fact that men fail to grasp the meaning contained in the divine communication cannot be traced to some feature of the message, to the medium, or to the natural receiving equipment. For him, the trouble is located in a kind of maintenance failure: the receiving apparatus has fallen into a deplorable state of corrosion. Of course, this view contrasts with the explanation offered by John. For him the communication failure stems from the fact that the messages involved are not well suited to man's natural intellectual capabilities and thus cannot be framed in the language men use to communicate thoughts to one another. God must then resort to a code. Communicative failure results when the code is misunderstood by the intended receivers.

Though these differences are interesting, I have stressed them not for their own sake but in order to isolate a thesis that is common to the theories advanced by Brunner and John and in relation to which each can be seen as a variation on a theme. The thesis in question is: "God attempts to communicate something or other (φ) to some one or more

30. Ibid., pp. 25ff.

of his intelligent creatures (ψ) but for one reason or another God's attempt to communicate φ to ψ does not succeed." I argued above that given a standard medieval theological context in which God is held to be omnipotent as well as omniscient and in which the doctrine of divine omniscience is held to entail foreknowledge of future contingents, the reasoning John offers in support of his negative position concerning the epistemic value of mystic apprehensions is incoherent. I now want to suggest that in any theological system that encompasses these same doctrinal elements (as those of Brunner and Calvin do),[31] any argument utilizing some version of the general thesis just formulated will be incoherent as well. As a general principle, God succeeds in communicating whatever it is that he attempts to communicate. As far as I can see, the theological assumptions operating in our discussion simply will not tolerate the contrary view.

ILLUMINATION

If I have been right in the preceding two sections, John's theory concerning the epistemic value of mystic apprehensions involves two incompatible claims, namely, (1) God's purpose (intention, objective) in conferring mystic apprehensions is to convey information to selected receivers; and (2) mystic apprehensions have no value as information bearers. Of course, it is the second of these claims that constitutes John's stand against mainstream theological opinion on this topic. The first claim is strictly in accord with traditional thinking as evidenced in the writings of Augustine and Aquinas. Framed in the light of this last observation, my criticism of John's theory might be put as follows: John rejects part of the traditional account, but he also accepts part. Unfortunately, the part that John accepts *entails* the part that he rejects. As a result, John's theory as a whole is stretched between two incompatible poles. Considerations of consistency would thus suggest that John should make a choice. Either he can retreat from the contratraditional position expressed in claim 2 above, or he can depart the tradition even more severely than he already has and deny the claim formulated in statement 1. John must either go the distance or return to the fold: the halfway house is simply not viable. I shall focus below on a theme that runs through much of the discussion in Book II of the *Ascent* and involves the denial of claim 1, that is, a theme that centers on the idea that God provides mystic apprehensions for purposes other than to

31. It is interesting to note that in book I, ch. 6, sec. 3 of the *Institutes*, Calvin maintains that God foreknew that the message contained in what Brunner calls the "revelation in creation" would not be understood by sinful men.

convey information. This is the theme of major concern in the present paper. In my opinion, it not only furnishes a consistent ground for his negative theory concerning the epistemic value of mystic apprehensions (that is, claim 2) but also is the most provocative of John's many interesting reflections on this general topic.

Speaking of apprehensions that are produced by God, in section 6 of chapter 24, John says: "The effects these visions produce in the soul are: quietude, illumination, gladness resembling that of glory, delight, purity, love, humility, and an elevation and inclination toward God. Sometimes these effects are more intense, sometimes less. The diversity is due to the spirit that receives them and to God's wishes." Mystic apprehensions that are produced by the devil (or one of his henchpeople) can be used for clarifying contrast. In the next section of the same chapter, John describes them so: "The devil's visions produce spiritual dryness in one's communications with God and an inclination to self-esteem to admiring them and to considering them important. In no way do they cause mildness of humility and love of God. . . . The memory of them is considerably arid and unproductive of the love and humility caused by the remembrance of good visions." Teresa of Avila said much the same thing in various passages throughout her writings. On her account, divine apprehensions usually result in happiness, joy, and a sense of peace. Even if they are fraught with pain and remorse, they result in a sense of humility, a sense of one's own sinfulness, an inclination toward virtue, and an awareness of one's own need for God. Teresa emphasized, too, that demonic visions and locutions have precisely the opposite effects. One so afflicted is "troubled, disturbed and restless; [one] loses that devotion and joy [that one] previously had and cannot pray at all."[32]

Note, first of all, that relative to the preceding discussion, the focus of attention has changed. Above, when we were dealing with a given apprehension, the generative question was "What does it mean?" Here, we are asking instead, "What does it *cause?*"—that is, what *effects* does it have primarily as regards the production of certain attitudes, feeling states, and behavioral dispositions on the part of the receiving individual visionary? Of course, the answer varies, depending on whether the relevant apprehension is of the divine or demonic variety. But note, second, that the answer in each case does not presuppose that the visionary has somehow arrived at a correct understanding of something called "the meaning" of the apprehension. John makes clear that

32. See Teresa's *Life*, ch. 20, para. 33; ch. 21, para. 10; ch. 25, para. 5; ch. 28, para. 19. The last-quoted passage is from the *Life*, ch. 28, para. 15. See also Poulain, *Graces of Interior Prayer*, ch. 22, para. 16 and 49–50.

any effects produced by a given apprehension are produced quite independently of any effort made on the part of the visionary to understand it.[33] With this thought in mind, we can immediately identify a clear value that attaches to divine apprehensions whether or not they are effective as meaning bearers. Visions and locutions from God are causally efficacious as regards a range of attitudes, feeling states, and behavioral dispositions that facilitate what John refers to as "spiritual growth" of the receiving mystic.[34] They work on the soul as a dose of vitamins might work on the body. They effect a kind of spiritual tune-up that results in easy commerce between the visionary and God. *Question:* Why does God confer mystic apprehensions? *Answer:* In spite of the danger of error and confusion, they are given in order to enhance the "spiritual growth" of the individual receiver.

This answer, I believe, signals a promising turn in the discussion. However, if we were to leave it at that, while divine apprehensions would then be portrayed as having value for the spiritual life, we would have no reason to think of them as having anything identifiable as cognitive, that is, *epistemic*, value, since the benefits so far mentioned have only to do with what might be called "conative" factors such as the occurrence of certain attitudes, feeling states, and behavioral dispositions. This would omit from consideration one of the themes running through John's discussion, namely, that divine apprehensions are vehicles by which (as he says) "the spirit is *instructed*."[35] They are means by which the individual visionary receives a special kind of *knowledge*— something that John describes as "supreme knowledge" and that he refers to alternatively as "spiritual wisdom" and "illumination."[36] Using an example of my own, I now want to suggest a way of understanding this idea that keeps us on the same track but introduces a reason why God confers apprehensions that relates to the cognitive side of the spiritual life. It also allows additional perspective as to why John is as firm as he is when advising against the traditional way of understanding the potential epistemic value of mystic visions and locutions.

I have in mind a man whose mother died when he was a boy. Some of his memories of her are vivid, but most are very dim. Partly because he can remember some of the relevant events, but mostly because he was told by others long after her death, he knows that his mother had a

33. *Ascent*, II, ch. 15, sec. 2; and ch. 16, sec. 10.
34. *Ascent*, II, ch. 17, sec. 6.
35. *Ascent*, II, ch. 17, sec. 4. Italics added.
36. Cf. *Ascent*, II, ch. 17, secs. 3 and 4. The term "illumination" is used in the passage quoted above from ch. 24, sec. 6.

very special attachment to him as a child. As an adult, the man has a dream. In the dream, he is a boy again, running up the walk on his way home from school. He stumbles and bruises his knee. Looking up, he sees his mother bending over him wearing a brightly colored scarf. He hears her say: "There, there, my little boy." He feels the peace of her presence. The dreamer then awakens and finds himself thinking, "My mother loved me deeply." Of course, that is something he had known for years, but I am supposing a case in which, via the dream, something new is added. There is a distinction between just knowing something and really getting it, that is, between correctly believing with evidence and grasping something at the base of the mind as something more than just correct information. That which was only known before now resonates more as a kind of cognitive feeling than as an ordinary thought. The new understanding—the depth grasp—that is what I want here to suppose has been added in this case.

I have three comments to make about the case described in this story. As I proceed, I shall weave in some of John's remarks concerning the way we should think about mystic apprehensions.

First, if a question were to arise about the evidence the dreamer has for thinking that his mother loved him deeply, it would consist of his memories from his childhood together with things told to him over the years by others in a position to know. These are the reasons the dreamer has for thinking that his belief about his mother is true. Furthermore, it is clear, I think, that whatever else might be said about the epistemic relevance of the dream I have described, it could not be included in the list. One does not verify a proposition about the affections of his mother by citing the content of a dream experience. Even when one's dream is true, or when one's dream prompts an investigation that later yields knowledge, he cannot support the proposition that it is true or that it is knowledge by pointing to the fact that he dreamed it. The point here is that a dream experience, unlike an ordinary, waking-life visual or auditory experience is simply not accepted as a legitimate source of knowledge.

Claiming first that there are no more articles of the Faith to be revealed to the Church, in Book II, chapter 27, section 4 of the *Ascent* John comments as follows on revelations of religious truths received via mystic apprehensions:

> In order to preserve the purity of his faith, a person should not believe already revealed truths because they are again revealed, but because they were already sufficiently revealed to the Church. Closing his mind to them, he should rest simply on the doctrine of the Church and its faith which, as St. Paul says, enters through the hearing (Rom. 10:17).

And if he wants to escape delusion, he should not adapt this credence
and intellect to those truths revealed again, no matter how true and
conformed to the faith they may seem.[37]

John is saying that a mystic apprehension ought not to be taken as a
reliable source of religious information. Even in the case where what is
revealed in the apprehension is true, it ought to be believed not *because*
it is given in the apprehension but because it is an item of faith already
specified in Church doctrine. The issue here concerns not what is
believed but what is to count as a legitimate ground for believing it. In
this regard, a mystic apprehension is like a dream experience. Whatever its specific content may be, it cannot be cited as a reason for
thinking that what one believes is true.

Returning to the dream, let us ask, second, why the dreamer came
away from the dream harboring the specific idea that his mother loved
him deeply. After all, in the dream his mother did not actually say so.
All she said was "There, there, my little boy." Then perhaps the proposition "my mother loved me deeply" was somehow deciphered from
the visual content—from the look on his mother's face or the scarf
around her neck. But how can the dreamer be sure that his "translation" of these sensible images is correct? Where is the codebook? What
do these things really mean? I will pause here for a moment to explain
why I think that this inquiry is irrelevant.

Suppose that, after awakening, the dreamer in my story had assumed that the dream was a vehicle by which some message was being
communicated to him—by God, by his mother, or perhaps by the local
telepathist who tends to be something of a prankster. He then sets out
to determine the message. Treating the auditory and visual dream
content as symbols, he assigns them a meaning and arrives at the message for the dream. *Now* we can raise the skeptical questions posed
above. They indicate that, in the scenario just sketched, the dream
contents were treated as data subject to something that would count as
an *interpretation*. But this is not the case that I meant to be describing in
the original story. In the latter, while the dream was described as having cognitive impact, I purposely omitted an interval in the telling
where the dreamer busied himself with the intellectual occupation of
deciphering symbols. In my case, the dream is not treated as a communication subject to interpretation. If it is a communication at all (and I

37. That there are no more articles of the Faith to be revealed is emphasized again by
John in *Ascent*, II, ch. 22 (see esp. secs. 3, 5, and 7). In *Ascent*, II, ch. 21, sec. 4, John again
stresses that an item should be believed because it is revealed to the Church and not
because it is revealed in an apprehension.

would not want to exclude this possibility), it works more like a piece of subliminal advertising than like a James Joyce novel. What I mean to be emphasizing here is that in the case as I intend it, the relationship between the dream and the cognitive state that results is *causal*. What is important, then, is not whether the *dream* is properly understood. As long as via the dream the dreamer comes to understand *that his mother loved him deeply*, the case remains the same for my purposes even if it is added that the dream, itself, is not understood at all.

This point leads to a more general observation: in the case we have been discussing, the dreamer dreamed about his mother. It was she whom he saw bending over him; it was she who said; "There, there, my little boy." Appropriately enough, the cognitive state that the dream occasioned was also about his mother—what he came to understand was that his mother loved him deeply. But given the remarks made in the preceding paragraph, one can see, I think, that the coincidence of content was in no way essential to the case. We could have imagined a case in which the dreamer dreamed a sequence in which he saw only the homestead and heard only a low melodious hum coming from the kitchen. He might still awake with a depth realization that he expresses in the sentence: "My mother loved me deeply." In the same way, we could imagine a case in which the auditory and visual content of the dream was the same as in the one described but in which the dreamer awoke from the dream experience harboring a very different cognitive feeling—perhaps one that he expresses in the sentence: "My father did not love my mother" or in the sentence: "Honey is sweeter than wine." If there are regularities here (and I suppose that there are), they will not be captured in translation rules—rules that tell us how to "read" symbols or how otherwise to determine something called "the mean-ing" of a dream. What rules there are will be (broadly) causal princi-ples—perhaps principles of association or something of the sort.

In Book II, chapter 26 of the *Ascent*, John discusses the specific kinds of "knowledge" communicated to the individual visionary by way of (so-called) "intellectual" visions and locutions. In section 16 he makes the following general comment about these knowledge states as well as those obtained from other kinds of divine apprehensions:

> These kinds of knowledge, as well as the other, come to the soul pas-sively, and thereby exclude any active endeavor of the soul. For it will happen that, while a person is distracted and inattentive, a keen under-standing of what he is hearing or reading will be implanted in his spirit, an understanding far clearer than that conveyed through the sound of

words. And although sometimes he fails to grasp the sense of the words—as when expressed in Latin, a language unknown to him—this meaning is revealed without his understanding the words themselves.

The "keen understanding" (as John calls it) is "implanted" via the apprehension quite independently of any effort made on the part of the visionary. In particular, the keen understanding does not result from any effort made on the part of the receiver to interpret the visual or auditory materials making up the apprehension. Is it Latin? No matter that one cannot understand it. What is understood is understood *by way* of the apprehension even if whatever it is that one hears or sees is not, *itself,* understood. The point, I think, is that, although the apprehension is here being thought of as a means of communication, the relationship between the vehicle and the message delivered is *causal.* In this respect, then, the cognitive value of a given apprehension is on precisely the same footing with what I earlier called the "conative" benefits. Like the latter, the former are what John calls "effects" that come to the individual "passively" and are "fixed in the soul without its having need for effort of its own."[38] We can see, then, that the auditory or visual content of the apprehension is of no special importance. What is important is the cognitive state that is causally effected. The content of the latter may or may not coincide with what is actually heard or seen in the apprehension itself.

Third, and last, let us go back for a moment to the reasons John gives for advising that mystic apprehensions be greeted by the visionary with an air of intellectual indifference, even rejection. When they are given, one ought not to bother deciphering them. Regardless of how keen the "keen understanding" they afford may be, they ought not to be taken as a ground for religious conviction.[39] If I am right in my estimate of how John is thinking about the way in which divine apprehensions are intended to work, these maxims make a lot of sense. In the case of a dream, why set about to determine what it means? In the first place, to do so would require a lot of energy that might better be used elsewhere. In the second place, since there are no translation rules with which to work, it cannot be done. In the third place, if you try to do it and take the results seriously, you may make a mistake and may thus be led to embrace a false belief. And in the fourth place, if you try to do it and take the results seriously, even if you are not led to embrace a false

38. *Ascent,* II, ch. 16, secs. 10–11; ch. 17, secs. 7–9.
39. *Ascent,* II, ch. 26, secs. 11 and 17.

belief, you will be deceived if you think (as you likely will) that you have thereby added to your store of knowledge. Of course, this is not to say that a mystic apprehension is devoid of interest for the epistemologist. It, like a dream, can have an important effect on what might be called the "mode" rather than on the content of the knowledge state. The point is, however, that like a dream, it ought not to be regarded as an information bearer. Any epistemic value that it has comes in the form of a cognitive wallop rather than in the form of a proposition.

POSTSCRIPT

John's cognitive-wallop theory of mystic apprehensions requires the assumption that there is a body of truth to which the individual mystic has access by means other than mystic visions and locutions. Without this assumption, John could not claim that the depth understanding caused by an apprehension is the depth understanding of a *truth*. And without this, it is hard to see how John could say that the mystic apprehension makes some contribution to something that would count as a knowledge state of the experiencing mystic. John's specific version of the needed assumption consists of the claim that there is a body of truth that has been revealed to the Church—the one codified in Church doctrine. The individual mystic thus has access to the relevant truths not by way of mystic apprehensions but by the ordinary instructional devices used by the Church for disseminating doctrine. But what shall we say about the means by which the truths in question were originally revealed to the Church? Reference to the Bible and to the interpretative deliverances of various Church councils would no doubt be relevant. But what about these materials? Shall we suppose that the truths involved were revealed by God to certain individuals—for example, those who composed the books of the Bible, individual members of the various Church councils, or the Pope? And if we do suppose this, shall we then allow that the relevant divine communications were mystic apprehensions such as the one given to Abraham? But, of course, that would not do. According to John's theory, mystic apprehensions cannot be taken as source of propositional knowledge. Their function presupposes that the receiver is already in possession of the truths to which they relate. Is this a difficulty for John? I am not sure—I have not thought it through far enough to tell. But whether or not it proves to be a difficulty for the theory, John's cognitive-wallop analysis of visions and locutions presupposes a view concerning the origin of what

John sometimes calls the "Public Revelation" that does not depend on the idea that it was delivered by God to individual receivers via anything classifiable as a mystic apprehension. John's finished mystical theology will require an account of the Public Revelation that does not derive it from God-given visions or locutions.

2

The Migration of the Theistic Arguments: From Natural Theology to Evidentialist Apologetics

NICHOLAS WOLTERSTORFF

Scarcely anything has been more characteristic of the modern Western intellectual than the conviction that *unless one has good reasons for one's theistic beliefs, one ought to give them up.* In the dialogue between belief and unbelief, belief is assumed guilty until it proves its innocence by evidence. In various essays Alvin Plantinga has inquired into the tenability of this thesis; in one place I have done so as well.[1] Here I want to consider the earliest articulate formulation of this conviction, so as to discern the framework of belief that made it seem plausible, even compelling, and the social situation that evoked it.

I suggest that, after the demise of antiquity, the evidentialist challenge to religious belief first became part of the mind-set of Western intellectuals at the time of the Enlightenment.[2] It belongs to the men-

1. "Can Belief in God Be Rational If It has No Foundations?" in *Faith and Rationality*, ed. A Plantinga and N. Wolterstorff (Notre Dame: University of Notre Dame Press, 1983).

2. One may be an evidentialist with respect to either rational belief, or knowledge, or *scientia*, and perhaps with respect to some other phenomena as well. Furthermore, two concepts of rational belief should be distinguished: a purely evaluative concept, in which rationality consists simply in certain merits, and a normative concept, in which rationality consists in fulfilling certain obligations. When I speak of *evidentialism* in the text, I have in mind evidentialism with respect to rationality, where rationality, in turn, is understood as grounded in obligations. It should also be noted that evidentialism is always relative to a certain set of propositions—though in principle that could include all. In the text I have

tality of the *Aufklärung*. Specifically, I suggest that the proto-Enlightenment figure John Locke first articulately issued the evidentialist challenge to the religious believer, doing so as himself a Christian who thought that he could meet the challenge.

The most obvious rejoinder to the claim that Locke was the first to issue the evidentialist challenge in articulate fashion is that long before Locke the medieval philosophers and theologians were engaged in attempting to meet the challenge with their project of natural theology. In the second part of my paper I shall reply to this rejoinder, arguing that the medieval project of natural theology was profoundly different from the Enlightenment project of evidentialist apologetics. It had different goals, presupposed different convictions, and was evoked by a different situation. It is true that some of the same arguments occur in both projects; they migrate from the one to the other. But our recognition of the identity of the émigré must not blind us to the fact that he has migrated from one 'world' to another.

In his *Church Dogmatics* (II/1, p. 93), Karl Barth says that in natural theology faith presents itself as deserting "its own standpoint" and pretends to take up the contrary "standpoint of unbelief." Barth seems to mean that, when the believer engages in natural theology, he presents himself to the unbeliever as having resolved that if the arguments fail, he will give up the faith. But Barth thinks that if the believer is true and faithful to his Lord, this will be mere pretense on his part. He will not give up the faith even if the arguments fail, and it is deceptive for him to give this impression that he would. I shall contend to the contrary that for the most part, anyway, the medieval theologian/philosopher who engaged in natural theology did not "appear to engage in the dialectics of unbelief." Barth's comments are relevant to the Enlightenment project of evidentialist apologetics; they are not relevant to the mainline medieval project of natural theology. They are a vivid man-

---

in mind evidentialism with respect to theistic propositions—propositions that entail God's existence. Naturally it is also possible to be an evidentialist with respect only to a limited set of these—that is, with respect to some theistic propositions but not all. When I speak of *evidentialism*, then, I have in mind this double thesis: (a) if one is rationally to believe some theistic proposition, one must believe it on the basis of others of one's beliefs that constitute good evidence for it; and (b) one is overall justified in believing some theistic proposition only if it is rational for one to believe it. In my terminology, someone who holds evidentialism with respect to theistic propositions issues the evidentialist *challenge* to whoever holds such propositions, and if he furthermore holds that a given person or group of persons fails to meet the challenge, he is lodging the evidentialist *objection* to their belief. A person conducts an evidentialist *apologetic* when he attempts to meet the evidentialist challenge by providing the requisite arguments.

ifestation of the regular failure to distinguish between these two very different projects.

I

Locke was vexed by the *enthusiasts*—people claiming private revelations from God without (to his mind) having any good evidence thereof. It was to these people that he issued his challenge; it was they that he accused of not meeting it. So vexed indeed was he by the presence of those who unwarrantedly "flattered themselves with a persuasion of an immediate intercourse with the Deity, and frequent communications from the Divine Spirit" (*Essay concerning Human Understanding* IV, xix, 5)[3] that most of his reflections on faith and reason occur within the context of his attempt to deal with this social ill.

Locke did not deny, indeed he affirmed, that God can and sometimes still does "enlighten men's minds in the apprehending of certain truths, or excite them to good actions by the immediate influence and assistance of the Holy Spirit" (*Essay* IV, xix, 16).[4] But in the case of the enthusiasts, he thought one could be confident that it is not God's enlightenment or excitement that accounts for their convictions but a disordered psyche, a "warmed or overweening brain" (*Essay* IV, xix, 7). The people susceptible to enthusiasm are those "in whom melancholy has mixed with devotion," along with those "whose conceit of themselves has raised them into an opinion of a greater familiarity with God, and a nearer admittance to his favor, than is afforded to others" (*Essay* IV, xix, 5). "Their minds being thus prepared, whatever groundless opinion comes to settle itself strongly upon their fancies, is an illumination from the Spirit of God, and presently of divine authority: and whatsoever odd action they find in themselves a strong inclination to

3. My citations from Locke's *Essay concerning Human Understanding* will be from the edition by Peter H. Nidditch (Oxford: Oxford University Press, 1979). I have, however, modernized spelling and capitalization.

4. In this way Locke's concern is fundamentally different from that of more recent philosophers and theologians who question whether there can be a word from outside our existence. Such a word would have to be received into the traditions of our interpretations of reality, into our construals of experience. But such traditions and construals cannot be grounded in our apprehension of unveiled uninterpreted reality. The purportedly revelatory phenomena, to be accessible to us, must become part of our way of life. But then they no longer communicate a word from outside our existence. The supposedly revelatory phenomenon is a component in reality as construed by us; it is part of our history. It may be for us an 'eye-opening' component, but it cannot be a word from outside. This hermeneutic skepticism concerning a word from outside our existence had not yet arisen at the time of Locke. Locke is concerned only with locating the occurrence of revelation.

do, that impulse is concluded to be a call or direction from heaven, and must be obeyed" (*Essay* IV, xix, 6). The religious consensus characteristic of medieval Europe had long been disrupted by Locke's time. Religion was well on the way to becoming a personal choice that one makes rather than a social role into which one is born. But the enthusiasts were departing even from any consensus that remained. For in locating revelation, they pointed beyond the prophets and apostles to private contemporary experiences. In other times and places the way of dealing with religious dissidents such as these would have been oppression and persecution. But Locke had written his *Letter concerning Toleration*. He could not now recommend their forceful suppression. His evidentialism was formulated when he was in the situation of being compelled to find some means other than governmental oppression of dealing with what he took to be the social evil of enthusiasm.

He charged the enthusiasts with irresponsibility. If one is to believe responsibly that God revealed so-and-so on such-and-such an occasion, one must believe it rationally. On a matter such as this, irrationality carries everthing before it. No merit or combination of merits in the belief can compensate for its lack of rationality—not its giving comfort to the believer, not its yielding him a sense of security, *nothing*. And if one is to believe rationally that God revealed so-and-so on such-and-such an occasion, one must believe it on the basis of good evidence— and indeed, believe it with a firmness not exceeding that warranted by the strength of the evidence. No rationality here without evidence. But the enthusiasts have no good evidence. The conclusion follows: they are irresponsible in their believings. They ought to give up their claim to revelation.

Is it really clear, though, that the enthusiasts lack good evidence for their claims of revelation? Does not their religious experience supply them with the evidence demanded? Locke thinks not. For when we interpret their metaphors, we see that to the question why they believe that God has spoken to them, their answer is just that they believe it strongly. "They see the light infused into their understandings, and cannot be mistaken . . . ; they feel the hand of God moving them within, and the impulses of the Spirit, and cannot be mistaken in what they feel. This is the way of talking of these men: . . . their persuasions are right, only because they are strong in them. For when what they say is stripped of the metaphor of seeing and feeling, this is all it amounts to" (*Essay* IV, xix, 8–9). But "if they believe it to be true because it is a revelation, and have no other reason for its being a revelation but because they are fully persuaded, without any other reason, that it is true, they believe it to be a revelation only because they strongly believe it to be a revelation; which is a very unsafe ground to proceed on, either in our tenets or actions" (*Essay* IV, xix, 11).[5]

Locke's analysis will leave even the sympathetic believer uneasy at a certain point. Is not God's power and freedom such that he might well reveal something to some person without providing good evidence for his having done so? Might he not simply effect in the person the firm conviction that he has said such-and-such? Locke himself affirms that God may well speak yet today. What reason is there for thinking that he cannot or will not sometimes do so in the absence of good evidence? But if we agree that he could and might, and also accept Locke's rule for belief, we are then in the curious position of admitting that God may speak in the absence of evidence while resolving never in the absence of evidence to *believe* that he has done so. Does not following Locke's advice put us in risk of sometimes not believing that God is speaking to us when he is? True, in general there is nothing paradoxical about the position that there are states of affairs of such a sort that it is both causally possible that they occur and not causally possible that one be in a situation where it is permitted to believe that they occur. But the case before us seems special: why would God speak to us if he did not want us to *believe* that he was speaking to us? And if he wants us to believe, are we not at least *permitted* to believe?

Locke never explicitly considers this matter. He just assumes without argument that as a matter of fact God *would not* speak into an evidential void. "God, when he makes the prophet, does not unmake the man," says Locke.

> He leaves all his faculties in their natural state, to enable him to judge of his inspirations, whether they be of divine original or no. When he illuminates the mind with supernatural light, he does not extinguish that which is natural. If he would have us assent to the truth of any proposition, he either evidences that truth by the usual methods of natural reason, or else makes it known to be a truth which he would have us assent to by his authority, and convinces us that it is from him, by some marks which reason cannot be mistaken in. Reason must be our last judge and guide in everything. [*Essay* IV, xix, 14]

5. Above, Locke says that they believe *that P has been revealed* because they strongly believe *that P has been revealed*. In another part of this same passage he suggests, without pointing out that this is a different analysis, that they believe *that P has been revealed* because they strongly believe *that P*—and in turn, they believe *that* P because it has been revealed: "Their confidence is mere presumption; and this light they are so dazzled with, is nothing: but an *ignis fatuus*, that leads them continually around in this circle: *It is a revelation, because they firmly believe it; and they believe it, because it is a revelation*" (*Essay* IV, xix, 10).

Locke is confident that God will play by the rules of evidence. The Creating Ground of our existence may indeed break through the crust of that existence to speak to us. But we must demand that if It does so, It authenticate to us that this is what It is doing. Locke adds that our demanding of God that he authenticate his speech is something that God demands of us. Our demanding that any word from outside our existence be authenticated for us is something demanded of us by him who is outside our existence. God is not merely the ground of our existence but exists with us in a society in which he asks this of us. Presumably, then, God will oblige; any speech of his that did not meet these conditions would be idle chatter on his part to which he wants us not to listen.

But why does Locke think *anything* has to be done about the enthusiasts? Why not leave them alone, on the ground that religion is a matter of individual taste? Or, more boldly, why not encourage them on the ground that they add richness and variety to the English religious scene?

Locke's reasons are important. Enthusiasm is socially pernicious. Irrational convictions such as those that the enthusiasts display have as their "constant concomitant" the arbitrary exercise of "an authority of dictating to others, and a forwardness to prescribe to their opinion." Dogmatism in religion has authoritarianism in society as its companion. One can see why, says Locke: "How almost can it be otherwise, but that he should be ready to impose on others' belief who has already imposed on his own? Who can reasonably expect arguments and conviction from him in dealing with others whose understanding is not accustomed to them in his dealing with himself?" (*Essay* IV, xix, 2). Only by following the voice of reason within will we walk the way of freedom without.

Locke has a second reason, even more resonant of what lies deep in modern Western conviction. To act as the enthusiasts do is to violate one's dignity as a human being, and to do so in that very domain of life which ought especially to manifest our dignity—namely, in religion. "To this crying up of faith in opposition to reason, we may, I think, in good measure, ascribe those absurdities that fill almost all the religions which possess and divide mankind. . . . religion, which should most distinguish us from beasts, and ought most peculiarly to elevate us as rational creatures above brutes, is that wherein men often appear most irrational, and more senseless than beasts themselves" (*Essay* IV, xviii, 11). Reason sets us above the brutes; this is the locus of our dignity. Thus to flout one's reason is to violate one's dignity. It is to degrade oneself.

In these two reasons we discern, I think, some of the deepest reasons for the grip of the evidentialist challenge on the minds of modern Western intellectuals. Whereas Locke explicitly issued the evidentialist challenge to the conviction that a revelation has occurred, most would now issue it to religious belief generally: only if a person's religious beliefs are held rationally is he permitted to hold them, and only if he holds them for good reasons does he hold them rationally. The alternative, so it is thought, is *dogmatism,* and the social authoritarianism that is presumed characteristically to accompany dogmatism.[6] A prerequisite of life together in our highly pluralistic societies is that we each submit our thought and actions to the common court of reason. In such submission is our freedom. In addition, to be a believer in the absence of evidence is to violate one's *dignity* at a most fundamental point. Reason is our most precious possession. To be a believer without good reasons is to stand bent in the world, to comport oneself in a manner unworthy of an adult human being. It is—this is the modern assumption—to exhibit a psychic disorder, not perhaps that of a "warmed or overweening brain," but that of arrested development. It is to fail or refuse to be a "man come of age." One can combine belief with maturity, faith with dignity, only by believing on good evidence.[7]

Most modern intellectuals believe that the evidence is missing. They believe that the evidentialist challenge has not been met. And many, it is clear, do not want it to be met. For if it is met, their dignity is wounded at a new point. To assent to the existence of God is to be confronted with the challenge to acknowledge the *claims* of God. Can a person of dignity humble himself before another?

6. For example, the association of intellectual 'dogmatism' with social authoritarianism (and of liberation from the one with liberation from the other) runs throughout the writings of the contemporary theologian Wolfhart Pannenberg. Here is just one passage: "For men who live in the sphere in which the Enlightenment has become effective, authoritarian claims are no longer acceptable, in intellectual as little as in political life. All authoritarian claims are on principle subject to the suspicion that they clothe human thoughts and institutions with the splendor of divine majesty" ("Response to the Discussion," in *Theology as History,* ed. J. M. Robinson and J. B. Cobb, Jr. [New York: Harper & Row, 1967], p. 226).

7. Compare this passage from Pannenberg, selected again from many such passages: "The question concerning the revelation of God, as it has been reformulated on the basis of the Enlightenment, is not seeking for some authoritarian court of appeal which suppresses critical questioning and individual judgment, but for a manifestation of divine reality which meets the test of man's matured understanding as such" (ibid., p. 229). Surely we also touch here on the root of the Marxist and Freudian critiques of religion: Religion degrades us. Religion emerges from the dark recesses of the soul. It is 'unscientific'. The very thing—belief in God—that the tradition saw as putting us in touch with the transcendent and thus elevating us far above the 'brutes' is in Marx and Freud seen as unworthy of us. It is of course Kant who most profoundly connects rationality, freedom, and dignity.

But something is missing here. *Why* is it assumed that faith in the absence of arguments is a violation of rationality? One might also question whether rationality is indeed at the core of our dignity. One might even ask whether dignity has the significance we typically assign to it; the ancients and medievals concerned themselves hardly at all with dignity, concerning themselves instead with happiness. For our purposes in this paper, however, we must set all but the first of those fundamental questions to one side and simply ask why it is assumed that the believer is violating his rationality if he does not believe for good reasons. For the answer, let us return to Locke.

Locke was persuaded that the only alternative to insisting on evidence in these matters is to allow that 'anything goes' in religion, and if there, why not elsewhere? "How shall any one distinguish between the delusions of Satan, and the inspiration of the Holy Ghost?" he asks. He "that will not give himself up to all the extravagancies of delusion and error, must bring this guide [that is, reason] of his light within to the trial. . . . Every conceit that thoroughly warms our fancies must pass for an inspiration, if there be nothing but the strength of our persuasions whereby to judge of our persuasions. If reason must not examine their truth by something extrinsical to the persuasions themselves, inspirations and delusions, truth and falsehood, will have the same measure, and will not be possible to be distinguished" (*Essay* IV, xix, 13–14).

But why, we ask in turn, does Locke assume this stark *either/or:* either accept the evidentialist challenge or allow that anything goes? The answer is that Locke was presupposing a certain epistemology, specifically, a certain way of understanding rationality. He was, furthermore, fully conscious of doing so. He explicitly issued the evidentialist challenge within the context of an articulate theory of rational belief. But we cannot understand his theory of that without glancing first at this theory of knowledge.

In the famous opening of Book IV of his *Essay,* Locke says that the mind has "no other immediate object but its own ideas." Accordingly, he says, "it is evident that our knowledge is only conversant about them" (*Essay* IV, i, 1). Knowledge, on Locke's (official) view, is then "nothing but the perception of the connexion and agreement, or disagreement and repugnancy, of any of our ideas" (*Essay* IV, i, 2).

A crucial step seems missing here. Even if we grant the fateful assumption that the mind has no other immediate object for any of its acts than its own ideas, why must we concede that knowledge is only conversant about ideas? The key to Locke's thought is his identification of *the known* with *the certain.* In his letter to Edward Stillingfleet, bishop of Worcester, Locke says that "with me to know, and to be certain, is the same thing; what I know, that I am certain of; and what I am certain of, that I know. What reaches to knowledge, I think may be called 'certainty'; and what comes short of certainty, I think cannot be called knowledge."[8]

It is now easy to surmise how Locke was thinking: Given that the immediate object of our awareness is our ideas, it seems obvious that one thing we can do is notice the *relations* among those ideas. We can, for example, notice that the 'ideas' of *two* and *plus* and *equals* and *four* are so related that $2 + 2 = 4$. In such noticing, there is no room for mistake and error. We are certain. For everything is right there before the mind's eye. All one has to do is inspect one's ideas. But when we go beyond our ideas to what cannot be inspected, we enter regions of uncertainty. So the noticing of what is there before the mind's eye is what Locke (officially) identifies as knowledge. To know is to notice some relation among one's ideas. Locke's discussion makes it clear that what he has in mind here is primarily, if not exclusively, *necessary* relations.

The classical twentieth-century view of knowledge is that it consists of a certain type of assent: to know is to believe some proposition, provided that the proposition be true and the believing be justified. Locke's view is different. He adopts what might be called an *inspectionist* view of knowledge: To know is to *notice that.* There are some indeed who deny that Locke's theory of knowledge has anything at all to do with propositions.[9] That view seems to me mistaken. After all, what is it to notice some specific connection among one's ideas other than to notice *that* those ideas are connected in that way? The difference between Locke and our classical contemporaries is not that the contemporary holds a propositional view of knowledge whereas Locke held a nonpropositional view. The difference is that our contemporaries hold a *noninspectionist,* pure *assent* (belief) view of knowledge, whereas Locke held an *inspectionist* (noticing) view of knowledge. Locke himself by no means avoids speaking of propositions in connection with knowledge. In *Essay* IV, i, 8, to take but one example, he remarks, "A man is said to know any proposition."

But though one can see why Locke repetitively states, as his official view of knowledge, that knowing is noticing that one's ideas are related in certain ways, one can also see why he regularly departs from that view by expanding the scope of things knowable. Again and again he finds himself forced to admit that we are certain of more than the

8. From Locke's second letter to Edward Stillingfleet, bishop of Worcester, in *The Works of John Locke* (London: Thomas Tegg and others, 1823), vol. 4, p. 145.
9. See, for example, Richard Rorty, *Philosophy and the Mirror of Nature* (Princeton: Princeton University Press, 1979).

(necessary) connections among our ideas. He acknowledges that we are certain that we ourselves exist (*Essay* IV, ix, 2; and passim in IV). He acknowledges, as one would expect, that we are certain as to *which* ideas are before our minds. And he even acknowledges that we are certain of the propositions that we once 'perceived' and now, on that account, remember (*Essay* IV, i, 8–9). All these are of course departures from his official view of knowledge.

The first and third departures are such that Locke, to be consistent, would have to surrender either his inspectionist view of knowledge or his 'way of ideas' conviction that the mind "hath no other immediate object but its own ideas." In view of these departures, he cannot hold that certitude (as he understands it) is the telltale mark of knowledge and then also hold both that knowing is noticing-that and that what is available as objects for *noticing-that* is ideas in their relationships. But which of these three assumptions he would in fact prefer to surrender is left thoroughly unclear. He never acknowledges their tension.

When Locke has firmly in mind his conviction that the only immediate objects of the mind's awareness are its own ideas, then he is inclined to say that knowing is just noticing how these ideas are connected.[10] But when that conviction recedes from his attention and he lets himself be carried along by his conviction that certitude is a telltale sign of knowledge, then he radically expands the scope of knowledge beyond his official declaration.[11] Obviously this expansion produces chaos in his theory of knowledge. The only order in the chaos is his conviction that certitude comes in degrees; "there are different degrees and ways of evidence and certainty," he says (*Essay* IV, ii, 14). Thus his official declaration gives us what, on his view, is knowledge at its highest pitch of certitude,[12] whereas his departures from that official declaration inform us as to his view regarding the full scope of certitude in all its intensities—and thus, regarding the full scope of knowledge.

One point remains to be made about Locke's theory of knowledge.

10. "If we will reflect on our own ways of thinking, we shall find that sometimes the mind perceives the agreement or disagreement of two ideas immediately by themselves, without the intervention of any other: and this, I think, we may call *intuitive knowledge. . . .* A man cannot conceive himself capable of a greater certainty, than to know that any idea in his mind is such as he perceived it to be; and that two ideas wherein he perceives a difference, are different, and not precisely the same" (*Essay* IV, ii, 1).

11. For example, when Locke considers whether we have "sensitive knowledge of particular existence" and not merely knowledge of 'sensitive ideas,' he remarks in favor of his affirmative answer that "here, I think, we are provided with an evidence that puts us past doubting" (*Essay* IV, ii, 14).

12. He says, for example, about intuitive knowledge of the agreement or disagreement of our ideas, that "this kind of knowledge is the clearest and most certain that human fraility is capable of" (*Essay* IV, ii, 1).

Locke held that we can know propositions by demonstration as well as knowing them immediately. He regularly called the former type of knowledge *demonstrative,* the latter, *intuitive.* Apparently he held that in a demonstration we not only come to know all the links in the proof, thus coming to know that the proposition has been demonstrated (he recognizes that normally this latter knowledge involves memory—*Essay* IV, ii, 7); he also held that we come to *know* the *proposition demonstrated.* Often he speaks of this too as a case in which we notice the agreement or disagreement of ideas; he says that demonstration occurs "where the mind perceives the agreement or disagreement of any ideas, but not immediately" (*Essay* IV, ii, 2). Apparently his thought is that sometimes just by contemplating a proposition itself we notice that its constituent 'ideas' are connected in such a way as to make it a necessary truth,[13] whereas in other cases we notice or discern this only by contemplating a proof with this proposition as its conclusion. In any case, he does not shrink from saying that "in demonstration the mind does at last perceive the agreement or disagreement of the ideas it considers" (*Essay* IV, ii, 4). So he says that demonstrated propositions are known, though he adds that the demonstrative is a lower degree of knowledge than the intuitive. Our assent is not "so ready," and "the evidence of it is not altogether so clear and bright" (*Essay* IV, ii, 4). Though "the perception produced by demonstration is also very clear; yet it is often with a great abatement of that evident lustre and full assurance that always accompany that which I call intuitive" (*Essay* IV, ii, 6).

Locke is thus a foundationalist concerning knowledge. Some of the propositions that we know to be true are known immediately, in the sense that we notice that our ideas are connected, in the manner exhibited by the proposition, without going through a process of inference. Our knowledge of everything else that we know is by demonstrative inference from what we know immediately. And as to *what* we know immediately, Locke's official view is that the only things we know immediately are those necessary truths that are self-evident for us, whereas his unofficial view is that we know immediately whatever we are

---

13. Locke here gives a classic formulation of the traditional concept of a proposition's being self-evident for a person. The notions of certitude, of irresistible belief, and of 'luminosity', are all woven together. In addition to these phenomenological notions he is of course presupposing the epistemic component of the traditional concept of the self-evident; namely, what is self-evident for a person is known by that person to be true. He says: "This part of knowledge is irresistible, and like bright sunshine, forces itself immediately to be perceived as soon as ever the mind turns its view that way; and leaves no room for hesitation, doubt, or examination, but the mind is presently filled with the clear light of it" (*Essay* IV, ii, 1). Cf. IV, vii, 2.

certain of without inference. In either case, knowledge is grounded in certitude.[14]

But Locke is convinced that for the conduct of his life, if not for "speculation," man cannot live by knowledge alone. He "would be at a great loss if he had nothing to direct him but what has the certainty of true *knowledge*" (*Essay* IV, xiv, 1). We human beings must sometimes "take" or assume certain of our ideas to agree or disagree without being certain that they do. This "taking to agree" is *assent* or *belief* or *opinion* or *judgment:* "Judgment is the presuming things to be so without perceiving it." It is "the putting things together, or separating them from one another in the mind, when their certain agreement or disagreement is not perceived, but *presumed* to be so" (*Essay* IV, xiv, 4).

Now, Locke regards *believing* that one's ideas are connected in a certain way (as contrasted with *noticing* that they are thus connected) to be subject to the will. We can *govern* our assent.[15] Accordingly, he inquires into the norms for belief governance. His conclusion is that we are permitted to believe something only if, on the basis of the available evidence, it is more probable than not. And the firmness with which we believe it must not exceed what is warranted by the strength of the evidence.[16]

A question that comes to mind is whether we must believe it *on the basis of* the evidence, or whether, regardless of what (if anything) one's belief is actually based on, the requirement is just that the available evidence support the belief. Locke nowhere (to the best of my knowledge) raises this issue. Yet I think it clear from the course of his discussion that, on his view, we must believe it *on the basis of* the evidence. We must actually *weigh* the probabilities and believe accordingly. The only exception to this rule occurs in those cases where we did once believe a proposition in this way and now *remember* that we did. Whether or not we remember the evidence, this too is justified belief (*Essay* IV, xvi, 1–2). Apart from this exception, for one to be justified in believing *P*, the available evidence must support *P*, and one must believe *P* on the basis of that evidence. Justified belief is always inferential, never immediate.

14. The core idea of foundationalism with which I work in this paper is this: a person is a foundationalist with respect to rationality (or knowledge or scientia) if he holds that a belief can be a rational belief (or knowledge or scientia) only if it is grounded in certitude, whether immediately or mediately.

15. For a most interesting discussion of belief and the will, see *Essay* IV, xx.

16. "For the evidence that any proposition is true (except such as are self-evident) lying only in the proofs a man has of it, whatsoever degrees of assent he affords it beyond the degrees of that evidence, it is plain all that surplusage of assurance is owing to some other affection, and not to the love of truth" (*Essay* IV, xix, 1).

To believe in this manner is to conform to our duties qua rational creatures, to conform to the duties of rationality. Believing rationally is believing on the basis of good arguments—albeit not demonstrative but probabilistic arguments. "The mind, if it will proceed rationally, ought to examine all the grounds of probability, and see how they make more or less for or against any probable proposition, before it assents to or dissents from it; and upon a due balancing the whole, reject or receive it with a more or less firm assent proportionably to the preponderancy of the greater grounds of probability on one side or the other" (*Essay* IV, xv, 5).[17]

And what, ultimately, are we allowed to take as evidence in the governance of our beliefs? To the best of my knowledge, Locke never explicitly addresses this question. But we can surmise what his answer would be: that which we *know*. A belief, to be rational, must be grounded in the bedrock of certitude. Thus Locke's full picture of knowledge and justified belief is this: some things we know intuitively. They are immediately certain for us. On the basis of this immediate knowledge we can, by the construction of demonstrative argument, come to know certain additional propositions. In addition we can make inferences that are probabilistically cogent from what we know. The beliefs we thus arrive at will be ones that we are *justified*, or *rational*, in holding. Locke is a foundationalist with respect both to justified belief and knowledge.

It is worth reemphasizing that, on Locke's view, we have the *duty* to regulate aright our assent. It is a duty that belongs to us as rational creatures. And it is a duty we owe to God our Maker. All this Locke never argues. He takes it entirely for granted. His attention focuses entirely on the *specification* of the duty: "He that believes, without having any reason for believing, may be in love with his own fancies; but neither seeks truth as he ought, nor pays the obedience due to his Maker. . . . He . . . misuses those faculties which were given him to no

17. Cf. IV, xv, 3: "Probability is likeliness to be true; the very notation of the word signifying such a proposition, for which there be arguments or proofs to make it pass, or be received for true. The entertainment the mind gives this sort of propositions is called *belief, assent,* or *opinion,* which is the admitting or receiving any proposition for true, upon arguments or proofs that are found to persuade us to receive it as true, without certain knowledge that it is so. Herein lies the difference between probability and certainty, faith and knowledge, that in all the parts of knowledge there is intuition; each immediate idea, each step has its visible and certain connexion; in belief not so. That which makes me believe, is something extraneous to the thing I believe; something not evidently joined on both sides to, and so not manifestly showing the agreement or disagreement, of those ideas that are under consideration."

other end, but to search and follow the clearer evidence and greater probability" (*Essay* IV, xvii, 24).

I trust it is now clear that in saying we must never believe without good reason, Locke is not maintaining that our 'commerce' with propositions is to be limited to believing on the basis of reasons. There are also propositions whose truth we *notice* (as opposed to *believe*) immediately. But they are *known* rather than *believed*. Duty enters the picture when we leave knowledge behind and move forward to belief. Our duty there is so to govern our assent as to believe only on good reason. Locke realizes that following this duty will sometimes yield falsehood and, conversely, that truth is sometimes netted while disobeying it. He sees clearly that one may well be justified in believing what is false and unjustified in believing what is true. But whether the proposition believed be true or not, if we have regulated our assent right, we have the satisfaction of knowing that we have done our duty to God as rational creatures.[18]

Locke's discussion of religious faith is set solidly within the context of his theory of justified belief. Faith, he says, "is nothing but a firm assent of the mind" (*Essay* IV, xvii, 24). And at once he adds, in accord with the theory, that "if it be regulated, as is our duty," it "cannot be afforded to anything but upon good reason." For Locke the decisive consideration establishing that faith is belief (assent) rather than knowledge is that faith lacks the certitude requisite to knowledge. In his letter to the bishop of Worcester he says that "the 'certainty of faith,' if your lordship thinks fit to call it so, has nothing to do with the certainty of knowledge. And to talk of the 'certainty of faith,' seems all one to me as to talk of the knowledge of believing—a way of speaking not easy to me to understand."[19] Locke does speak in the same passage of "the assurance of faith," and he says, of his assenting to an article of the faith, that "I steadfastly venture my all upon it."[20] Nonetheless, he insists that "Faith stands . . . upon grounds of its own," different from those of

18. He that does not govern his assent right, "however he sometimes lights on truth, is in the right but by chance; and I know not whether the luckiness of the accident will excuse the irregularity of his proceeding. This at least is certain, that he must be accountable for whatever mistakes he runs into: whereas he that makes use of the light and faculties God has given him, and seeks sincerely to discover truth by those helps and abilities he has, may have this satisfaction in doing his duty as a rational creature, that though he should miss truth, he will not miss the reward of it. For he governs his assent right, and places it as he should, who, in any case or matter whatsoever, believes or disbelieves according as reason directs him" (*Essay* IV, xvii, 24).

19. Locke, *Works*, p. 432.

20. Ibid.

knowledge. "Their grounds are so far from being the same, or having anything common, that when it is brought to certainty, faith is destroyed; it is knowledge then, and faith no longer."[21]

Locke stands in that long line of Christian reflection according to which *faith* is the correlate of *revelation:* "*Faith* . . . is the assent to any proposition . . . upon the credit of the proposer, as coming from God, in some extraordinary way of communication. This way of discovering truths to men we call *revelation*" (*Essay* IV, xviii, 2). Locke does not regard the holding of theistic beliefs in general as a matter of faith. He explicitly argues that God's existence is a matter of *knowledge,* not faith, though of *demonstrative* knowledge, it should be noted, not intuitive. Any knowledge we have of God's existence is based on inference (see *Essay* IV, x, 1–3). But faith goes beyond knowledge. Faith enters the picture when we acknowledge that the God whose existence we know by demonstration has revealed things to us. Faith is believing that which is taken to be revealed.[22]

We must distinguish two types of revelation. In *original revelation* an impression "is made immediately by God, on the mind of" the person (*Essay* IV, xviii, 3). *Traditional revelation* occurs when someone communicates to another what has been originally revealed to someone. Faith, in response to this latter type of revelation, consists of accepting as revealed by God what that person communicates as having been (originally) revealed to someone.[23]

We can be certain that whatever God reveals is true. This we can know immediately. "Whatever God hath revealed is certainly true" says Locke, "no doubt can be made of it" (*Essay* IV, xviii, 10). But that God did in fact reveal something on some occasion cannot be known, nor can it be known *what* he revealed; these can only be believed. That God

---

21. Ibid.

22. Cf. *Essay* IV, xviii, 6: "Faith . . . has to do with no propositions but those which are supposed to be divinely revealed." Accordingly, "it is a matter of faith, and not of reason, to believe that such or such a proposition, to be found in such or such a book, is of divine inspiration"—unless, Locke adds, "it be revealed that that proposition, or all in that book, was communicated by divine inspiration. Without such a revelation, the believing or not believing that proposition or book to be of divine authority can never be matter of faith, but matter of reason."

23. It is interesting that, in *The Reasonableness of Christianity,* Locke takes for granted that the biblical writers were faithful communicators of the original revelation given to them and of the confirmatory miracles. He has no worries on this score. There is severe tension between Locke's analysis of original revelation and his insistence that beliefs concerning the location and content of revelation must be held on adequate evidence. Indeed, the only thing that saves him from plain contradiction is the (odd) possibility that both God causes the belief immediately and the believer holds it on the evidence that God revealed it.

revealed *P* always lacks for us the certitude requisite for knowledge. We can never with certitude identify the occurrence or content of revelation.

And just as we can never be certain *that God has revealed* P, so *P* itself can never be fully certain for us, when accepted on the ground of its having been revealed by God. "Whatsoever truth we come to the clear discovery of, from the knowledge and contemplation of our own ideas, will always be certainer for us, than those which are conveyed to us by *traditional revelation.* For the knowledge, we have, that this *revelation* came at first from God, can never be so sure, as the knowledge we have from the clear and distinct perception of the agreement, or disagreement of our own ideas" (*Essay* IV, xviii, 4).

In deciding whether to accept *P,* on the ground of its having been revealed by God, we must weigh up the evidence pro and con the proposition *that* P *has been revealed by God.* Only if this latter proposition is probable, on the evidence available, are we justified in accepting *P* itself—unless, of course, we have some additional ground for accepting it than that it has been revealed. Locke makes clear that he is not insisting that we need evidence in favor of *P* itself—in favor of the content of the purported revelation—to be justified in accepting it. Quite to the contrary: the very genius of revelation is that by this means God can present to us for our belief things that we could not justifiably believe by the unaided use of our faculties.[24] What is required is not independent evidence in favor of *P* but evidence in favor of the proposition *that* P *has been revealed.*

Nonetheless, there are important connections between content and presentation. For one thing, if the purportedly revealed proposition *P* is one that (self-evidently) contradicts something of which we are intuitively certain, then we must reject the proposition *that God has revealed* P. "Since no evidence of our faculties by which we receive such revelations can exceed, if equal, the certainty of our intuitive knowledge, we can never receive for a truth anything that is directly contrary to our clear and distinct knowledge. . . . *no proposition can be received for divine revelation,* or obtain the assent due to all such, *if it be contradictory to our clear intuitive knowledge,* because this would be to subvert the principles and foundations of all knowledge, evidence, and assent whatsoever" (*Essay* IV, xviii, 5).[25]

24. Cf. *Essay* IV, xix, 4.
25. Cf. *Essay* IV, xviii, 10: "Whatever God hath revealed is certainly true; no doubt can be made of it. This is the proper object of faith: but whether it be a divine revelation or no, reason must judge; which can never permit the mind to reject a greater evidence to embrace what is less evident, nor allow it to entertain probability in opposition to knowl-

One would expect Locke to go on from here to say that, if on the evidence available it is probable *that God revealed* P, whereas *P,* judged on its own merits, is improbable, then we must weigh up this probability with this improbability, and only if the former is stronger may we proceed to believe *P.* But though he is not entirely lucid on the matter, Locke's view seems to be that if *P* does not contradict some intuitive certitude, then we need no longer consider its own independent probability but can look exclusively to the probability of its having been revealed—with the consequence that sometimes we may believe what is highly improbable. When the content of a purported revelation does not violate some certitude, then, says Locke, "an evident revelation ought to determine our own assent even against probability. For where the principles of reason have not evidenced a proposition to be certainly true or false, there clear revelation, as another principle of truth and ground of assent, may determine" our belief (*Essay* IV, xviii, 3). There is another connection between content and presentation. Though Locke regularly speaks of the assurance of faith, apparently this is to be a tempered assurance. Apparently the firmness with which we believe *P* is not to be in excess of that with which we are entitled to believe *that God has revealed* P. Indeed, in one passage he says that as a matter of fact we *cannot* believe the content of a revelation with more firmness than that with which we believe the event of revelation: "the natural ways of knowledge" give us "the greatest assurance we can possibly have of any thing, unless where God immediately reveals it to us; and there too our assurance can be no greater than our knowledge is, that it is a revelation from God" (*Essay* IV, xviii, 5).[26]

It should now be clear why Locke demands arguments from the enthusiasts. The conviction that such-and-such has been revealed by

---

edge and certainty. There can be no evidence that any traditional revelation is of divine original, in the words we receive it, and in the sense we understand it, so clear and so certain as that of the principles of reason. And therefore *nothing that is contrary to, and inconsistent with, the clear and self-evident dictates of reason, has a right to be urged or assented to, as a matter of faith, wherein reason hath nothing to do.*"

26. The matter is not entirely clear, however. Consider Locke's waffling in the following passage, in which it remains unclear whether the content as well as the fact of revelation is to be held tentatively: "Besides those we have hitherto mentioned, there is one sort of propositions that challenge the highest degree of our assent, upon bare testimony, whether the thing proposed agree or disagree with common experience and the ordinary course of things or no. The reason whereof is, because the testimony is of such an one as cannot deceive nor be deceived, and that is of God himself. This carries with it assurance beyond doubt, evidence beyond exception. This is called by a peculiar name *revelation,* and our assent to it, *faith;* which as absolutely determines our minds and as perfectly excludes all wavering, as our knowledge itself; and we may as well doubt of

God is never a matter of certitude—is never something *known*. If it is nonetheless to be justifiably believed, it must be inferred from what is known and must be probable with respect to that. Locke issues the evidentialist challenge on the basis of his foundationalist theory of justified belief.

And so it is, I suggest, for our modern intellectuals in general. Evidentialism has its home in our modern situation. Outside a situation of religious pluralism it would lack social urgency, if not relevance. And in its generalized form, where religious belief in general is put on the defensive and not just identification of revelation, it can be seen as a natural accompaniment to the increase of secularization in our society. But evidentialism also needs a tacit epistemology for its acceptance. Such epistemology was given birth in the seventeenth century at the hands of Descartes and, especially, Locke. Its form is foundationalism, with its characteristic insistence that beliefs, to be justified, must be grounded in the certain. If we surrender the demand that our beliefs be thus grounded, then we shall have to concede that 'anything goes' in our beliefs, says Locke. Foundationalism or antinomianism: that gaunt *either/or* has seemed obviously true to most reflective modern intellectuals. The alternative to grounding is thought to be arbitrary dogmatism.

Significant alterations in our social or intellectual situation will make evidentialism seem irrelevant or implausible or unimportant. Those alterations are taking place. Less and less does foundationalism seem a plausible epistemology. Thereby evidentialism is losing its traditional intellectual underpinnings. And the old worry is surfacing: Does anything go? Must dogmatism reign?

---

our own being, as we can whether any revelation from God be true. So that faith is a settled and sure principle of assent and assurance, and leaves no manner of room for doubt or hesitation. Only we must be sure that it be a divine revelation, and that we understand it right: else we shall expose ourselves to all the extravagancy of enthusiasm, and all the error of wrong principles, if we have faith and assurance in what is not divine revelation. And therefore in those cases, our assent can be rationally no higher than the evidence of its being a revelation, and that this is the meaning of the expressions it is delivered in. If the evidence of its being a revelation, or that this is its true sense be only on probable proofs, our assent can reach no higher than an assurance or diffidence, arising from the more or less apparent probability of the proofs" (*Essay* IV, xvi, 14). What is clear from this is that we can know that whatever God reveals is true. What is also clear from this and other passages is that we can never know with certitude, but only believe with a firmness tempered to the strength of the evidence, *that God revealed* P. But what then about *P* itself? It is not certain. But may we believe it with a firmness exceeding that to which we are entitled for *that God revealed* P? If the answer is "No," it is hard to see why Locke would say that faith "leaves no manner of room for doubt or hesitation." But to repeat, the matter is not clear.

Of course all along the argument could have gone either way: if according to foundationalist canons much religious belief is not rational, then one can scrap either the beliefs or the canons. A striking fact about our Enlightenment mentality is that though science no more fits the foundationalist canons than religion, we have religiously clung to the conviction that it does, and so, while saying, "So much the worse for religion," we have continued to embrace our science. The religious believer has been challenged to display the grounding for his beliefs, but few have challenged the scientist to show that his beliefs are grounded in certitude. Many have struggled to *show* that they were, but few have concluded from the failure that then we ought to give up on science. Instead, the reluctant acknowledgment that our science does not fit the foundationalist canons has, in recent years, contributed to the demise of foundationalism. Until the work of Kuhn and his colleagues, science was assumed to be a paradigm of embodied rationality, even though the foundationalism supposedly embodied therein could never be extracted. No such benefit of the doubt has been extended to religion. And now that we have come to see that science is not foundationalism embodied, we have given up on foundationalism. When religion did not fit our canons of rationality we threw out religion, whereas when science proved not to fit them we threw out the canons. But giving up on foundationalism leaves our evidentialism dangling.

II

Did not the medievals reach this point long before Locke? Were they not implicitly answering the evidentialist challenge with their natural theology? Is not Locke merely carrying on the tradition of his medieval predecessors? Was not evidentialism at home already in the medieval situation? Here we cannot survey the medievals generally. I shall be content to explore one mainline tradition, taking Aquinas as representative.

Aquinas's project of natural theology was as much embedded in his view regarding the end of man as in his views on epistemology. For Aquinas, every human being imparts to his life a certain structure—the structure of a life lived in pursuit of a certain goal. A human life is a goal-directed life. Furthermore, the goal is the same for every human being: happiness—not dignity, not freedom, but happiness. To be a human being—indeed, to be an intellectual creature of any sort whatever—is to live in pursuit of happiness "as an ultimate end, and for its own sake alone" (*SCG* IIIa, 25, 14).[27]

27. I shall be citing *Summa theologica* (hereafter *STh*) in the Dominican translation (New York: Benzinger Bros., 1947). I shall be citing *Summa contra gentiles* (hereafter *SCG*) in the translations of the Image Books edition (Garden City, N.Y.: Doubleday, 1956).

But of course human beings disagree as to the content of happiness and as to the means for achieving it. Aquinas contends that ultimate happiness for every human being is to be found nowhere else than in the contemplation of God. Ultimate happiness for each of us consists in an act of the intellect, for that is what is 'proper' to us as intellectual creatures.[28] And specifically, it consists in contemplating that which is most perfect—namely, God. Hence "to know God by an act of understanding is the ultimate end of every intellectual substance" (*SCG* IIIa, 25, 3).[29] It may be added that such knowledge is properly called *wisdom* (*SCG* I, 1; *STh*, I of II, q. 57, art. 2).

And how can we attain this knowledgeable contemplation—or contemplative knowledge—of God? The first thing to notice is that in practically all human beings there is a "common and confused knowledge of God" (*SCG* IIIa, 38, 1). His own view, says Aquinas, is that this indigenous knowledge of God has its origins in the fact that, "when men see that things in nature run according to a definite order, and that ordering does not occur without an orderer," they generally come to believe that "there is some orderer of the things that they see" (ibid.). But this knowledge of God, though indeed common, remains 'confused', for it is not yet grasped "who or what kind of being" this orderer is, or "whether there is but one orderer of nature."[30] Accordingly, this common indigenous knowledge of God is thoroughly inadequate for ultimate human felicity. It is found amid vast errors and confusions concerning the nature of God, something that surely is not true to the sort of knowledge of God that constitutes our ultimate felicity (*SCG* IIIa, 38, 3). It may be added that those relatively few who, as atheists, lack this knowledge of God, are blameworthy for that lack,

28. One could even say that "all other human operations seem to be ordered to this one, as to an end. For, there is needed for the perfection of contemplation a soundness of body, to which all the products of art that are necessary for life are directed. Also required are freedom from the disturbances of the passions—this is achieved through the moral virtues and prudence—and freedom from external disorders, to which the whole program of government in civil life is directed. And so, if they are rightly considered, all human functions may be seen to subserve the contemplation of truth" (*SCG* IIIa, 37, 7).

29. Though the contemplation of God is man's *ultimate* beatitude, "man's beatitude does consist somewhat in the right use of creatures, and in well-ordered love of them: and this I say," says Aquinas, "with reference to the beatitude of a wayfarer" (*STh*, II of II, q. 9, art. 4, ad 3).

30. In *STh* I, q. 2, art. 1, ad 1, Aquinas speaks of a different sort of "general and confused" knowledge of God's existence "implanted in us by nature"—namely, a knowledge we have just "inasmuch as God is man's beatitude. For man naturally desires happiness, and what is naturally desired by man must be naturally known to him. This, however, is not to know absolutely that God exists; just as to know that someone is approaching is not the same as to know that Peter is approaching, even though it is Peter who is approaching."

whereas someone who lacks felicity is scarcely blameworthy on that account (*SCG* IIIa, 38, 5).[31]

May it then be that our human felicity consists in the knowledge we have of God by way of demonstration from principles that we 'see' to be true? Well, certainly this form of knowledge is higher than the preceding; for when we follow a demonstration of some proposition from premises seen to be true, we also come to 'see' that that conclusion is true, and certainly such is not the case for what is known in that indigenously human manner. And lest there be doubts on the matter, let it be said that we can in fact demonstrate various things about God. Demonstration, says Aquinas, "shows that God is immutable, eternal, incorporeal, altogether simple, one, and other such things" (*SCG* IIIa, 39, 1).

Furthermore, such demonstrations belong to authentic sciences. In Aquinas there is as yet no Kantian skepticism concerning the ability of the metaphysician to grasp the transcendent—though indeed the teachings of Plotinus on the simplicity of God have cast a discernible chill over the enterprise. Science consists of that body of propositions which have been (deductively) demonstrated from premises that are (or were) evident to some intellectual being or other.[32] Of course science is a community enterprise, and it may well be that a given person, working in a corner of science, begins from premises that he has not himself traced out deductively from propositions evident to himself. He may take it on good authority that this has been done by someone else and may proceed from there. He would then be in a less than ideal state with respect to those propositions; the ideal would be to proceed from premises each of which he 'sees' to be true and by arguments each of which he 'sees' to be deductively valid. Nonetheless, authentic science will customarily emerge from the endeavors of a community.

Aquinas tacitly distinguishes, then, among these three things: the propositions belonging to objective science at a given time, the propositions that a given person correctly and justifiably believes to belong to objective science at a certain time, and those propositions which that person has himself 'seen' to be demonstrated from what was self-evi-

31. It is striking how similar these remarks of Aquinas on our indigenously human knowledge of God are to the remarks of John Calvin on the same topic, in the opening chapters of his *Institutes*. The common assumption of a vast gulf between Calvin and such medievals as Aquinas on this matter will have to be discarded for a more tempered view of the differences.

32. "Science," as Aquinas uses the term, does not include what is self-evident or evident to the senses of some intellectual creature but includes only what has been demonstratively *inferred* from that. In *STh*, I of II, q. 57, art. 2, he says that in science, what is known is known through another, whereas that 'habit' whereby we know a proposition in itself is *understanding*.

dent for him or evident to his senses. Science, as an objective communal enterprise, has a foundationalist character: it is grounded in the certitude of what is self-evident or evident to the senses of someone or other,[33] and the grounding is confined to deductive arguments. In contrast, a given person's *apprehension* of the contents of objective science may not have an entirely foundationalist character. At several junctures he may take someone's word for it that something has been demonstrated without himself 'seeing' that it has been.

We were considering the fact that various things have been demonstrated about God by deductive arguments beginning from what is evident to us in our natural condition. We added that there is, accordingly, a science of 'natural' theology. Aquinas sees this science of natural theology as the apex of that portion of the scientific enterprise which appeals solely to our natural reason. It is that in a double way: natural theology is the science of that being which is most perfect, namely, God; and it brings to a climax the process of 'natural' scientific inquiry whose overall pattern is from creatures up to God.[34] The science of natural theology is the highest scientific attainment of which we human beings are capable by unaided nature.

33. I interpret Aquinas as holding that (objective) science begins from what has been 'seen' to be true and that "those things are said to be seen which, of themselves, move the intellect or the senses to knowledge of them" (*STh*, II of II, q. 1, art. 4, resp.). Indeed, he says that "the object of science is something seen" (ibid., art. 5, ad 4). There are, though, a number of passages in which he seems to limit the foundation of scientia to what is self-evident, thus not allowing what is evident to the senses. He says, for example, that "all science is derived from self-evident and therefore *seen* principles" (*STh*, II of II, q. 1, art. 5, resp.), and he says that "those things are said to be self-evident which are known as soon as the terms are known" (*STh* I, q. 2, art. 1, obj. 2; cf. *SCG* I, 10, 2). From this it seems clearly to follow that what is evident to the senses is not included in the basis of (objective) science. Furthermore, he says that "science demands that its object should be deemed impossible to be otherwise" (*STh*, II of II, q. 1, art. 5, ad 4), and this will scarcely be true of immediate perceptual knowledge. Again, he says that "the intellect cannot be infallibly known in conformity with things in contingent matters, but only in necessary matters, therefore no speculative habit about contingent things is an intellectual virtue, but only such as is about necessary things" (*STh*, I of II, q. 57, art. 5, ad 3). And he cites science, along with wisdom and understanding, as an intellectual virtue. Yet, when he introduces his arguments for God's existence in both the *Summa contra gentiles* and the *Summa theologica*, he says it is "evident to our senses" that some things are in motion (*STh* I, q. 2, art. 3, resp.; *SCG* I, 13, 3), and he speaks of these proofs as demonstrations. Furthermore, he clearly says that the demonstrations in a science may either be "apriori," proceeding from our grasp of some essence, or "aposteriori" (*STh* I, q. 2, art. 2, resp.) demonstrations quia (*SCG* I, 12, 8–9), proceeding from effects to the cause thereof; and in the latter case, these will usually be propositions evident to the senses. My conclusion, then, is that he is speaking imprecisely when he says that the basis of (objective) science must be what has been self-evident to someone. What he really means is that it must have been *evident* to someone—must have been 'seen'.

34. See *Commentary on the Trinity of Boethius*, q. 5, art. 1

Already the contrast between the Thomistic enterprise of natural theology and the project of evidentialist apologetics begins to emerge. The enterprise of natural theology, for Aquinas, occurs within the overlapping projects of the development of science and the contemplation of God. It is not a response to concern about the rationality of religious belief. Though Aquinas believes that theism is indigenous to humanity, he never worries whether those who hold to that indigenous theism are responsible (rational, justified) in so doing. And most emphatically his natural theology is not a response to such a worry. Accordingly, whereas the evidentialist apologist presupposes that the religious believer may believe only on the basis of good arguments, Aquinas nowhere suggests that the pursuit of natural theology is obligatory for all theists. It does indeed mark a significant step toward ultimate felicity, yet there may be very good reasons for a given person not to pursue it. The goal of natural theology is not to protect our dignity as rational beings but to enhance our happiness as creatures whose felicity is to be found in the contemplation of God.

But we do not fully understand the import of natural theology for Aquinas unless we approach it from above as well as from below. Not only can natural theology be approached from the side of the sciences erected on the basis of the natural light of reason; it can also be approached from the side of *faith*.

In spite of all the praise that we may rightly render to natural theology as a fulfillment of our intellectual natures, it has some serious defects when measured against that goal of the felicity that consists in the knowledgeable contemplation of God. For one thing, relatively little can be demonstrated about God. And when we scrutinize what *can* be demonstrated about God, we see that it all has an important deficiency: it tells us what God is *not* like. He is *not* changeable, *not* temporal, and so forth. The method of demonstration proves to be a "method of remotion" (*SCG* I, 14, 3). In full-orbed knowledge of a thing we grasp the essence of the thing, its what-it-is-as-such, and we proceed to unravel that essence. But we are not "able in this life to see the divine essence" (*SCG* IIIa, 47, 1); we do not know 'what God is as such'. Our access to him is only by way of his effects; "throughout this life God can be known in no higher way than that whereby a cause is known through its effect" (*SCG* IIIa, 47, 9).[35] And what is demon-

---

35. Cf. *SCG* I, 3, 3. The point is not just that in *natural theology* there is no other way of knowing God than through his effects; rather, our situation is that *in general* there is no other way of knowing him in this life. Revelation, it must be remembered, is one of his effects, as is faith in the content of revelation. "Although we cannot know in what consists the essence of God, nevertheless in this science we make use of His effects, *either of nature or of grace*, in place of a definition, in regard to whatever is treated of in this science concerning God" (*STh* I, q. 1, art. 7, ad 1; emphasis added).

strated of him, starting from his effects, proves to be negations. More specifically, we learn that God *transcends* his effects in various ways. Now, we need not doubt that this is "proper knowledge" (*SCG* IIIa, 39, 1) of God; a proper knowledge of a thing involves knowing in what ways that thing differs from others.[36] Yet to know only how God differs from other things and not to know *what he is* is less than the best. But it is the entire extent of "the proper knowledge that we have of God through demonstrations" (*SCG* IIIa, 39, 1).[37]

There are other defects as well. Since the demonstrations are relatively complex, only a few people can arrive at a knowledge of God in this way. The reasons for this are various: it takes a good deal of intelligence to follow the proofs, and not everyone has that much intelligence. It takes a good deal of intellectual training to follow them, and not everyone has the time for that training. And it takes an industrious, nonindolent character and not everyone has such a character (*SCG* I, 4). Second, because of the lengthy intellectual training required for the comprehension of the proofs, those who do acquire knowledge of God in this manner acquire it rather late in life (ibid.). And last, it is easy to make mistakes in the attempt to construct such proofs, with the result that some who think they have arrived at knowledge of God in this way have in fact not done so (*SCG* IIIa, 39, 4). Furthermore, we all *know* that it is easy to make such mistakes. Thus a certain shakiness and uncertainty invades the minds of those who pursue divine knowledge in this way exclusively (*SCG* IIIa, 38, 5; cf. *STh*, II of II, q. 2, art. 4, resp.). For all these reasons, "man's ultimate felicity does not lie in this [demonstrative] knowledge of God" (*SCG* IIIa, 39, 4).

What, then, is to be done? Or are we destined forever to remain alienated from our ultimate felicity? There is abroad in the world yet another mode of attaining knowledge of God—or at least, apprehension of truths about God—apart from those we have yet canvased.

36. Cf. *SCG* I, 14, 2–3: "Now, in considering the divine substance, we should especially make use of the method of remotion. For, by its immensity, the divine substance surpasses every form that our intellect reaches. Thus we are unable to apprehend it by knowing *what it is*. Yet we are able to have some knowledge of it by knowing *what it is not*. Furthermore, we approach nearer to a knowledge of God according as through our intellect we are able to remove more and more things from Him. For we know each thing more perfectly the more fully we see its differences from other things; for each thing has within itself its own being, distinct from all other things. . . . Finally, there will then be a proper consideration of God's substance when He will be known as distinct from all things. Yet, this knowledge will not be perfect, since it will not tell us what God is in Himself."

37. It is not at all clear why Aquinas thinks that knowledge of God gained by way of demonstrations from his effects is *negative* knowledge. Is not the knowledge that God is a mover, a cause, itself a bit of *positive* knowledge? Is there not a middle terrain between knowing things about God by way of knowing his essence and knowing what God is not like?

That additional mode is faith. Could it be that our ultimate felicity is to be achieved by way of that knowledge of God which is attained by faith? Faith consists in assenting to something that is proposed by God to us for our belief, and *as* proposed to us by God. Faith and revelation are correlatives in Aquinas, as they were in Locke.[38] Now, the apprehension of truths about God that we gain by way of faith has (at least) one clear advantage over that which we get by way of demonstration: the content is more ample. "In comparison with the knowledge that we have of God through demonstration, this knowledge through faith surpasses it, for we know some things about God through faith which, because of their sublimity, demonstrative reason cannot attain" (*SCG* IIIa, 40, 1). Yet when judged by reference to our ultimate felicity, which consists in the knowledgeable contemplation of God, faith too displays some striking inadequacies.

Its principal shortcoming is that, to repeat, it consists in accepting something on testimony, and as a general truth, when one accepts something on testimony, one does not 'see' that it is true. If one 'saw' that it was true, one would no longer accept it on testimony. Yet the highest form of knowledge consists precisely in 'seeing' something to be true: our ultimate felicity consists in grasping the essence of God and thereby 'seeing' various things to be true of him. One may accept a mathematical theorem in two fundamentally different ways: one may 'see' that it is true by way of demonstration or self-evidence, or one may take someone's word for it. It is obvious that the former mode of apprehension is superior. Yet "faith has a knowledge that is more like hearing than vision." For the "one who believes gives assent to things that are proposed to him by another person, and which he himself does not see" (*SCG* IIIa, 40, 4).[39]

It is important to remark, however, that faith is not to be regarded as just a species of opinion. Rather, it is midway between science and opinion. When we 'see' that such-and-such a proposition is true, either by way of its being immediately evident to us or by way of our having followed a demonstration, there is no act of the will involved in our

---

38. Faith "does not assent to anything, except because it is revealed by God" (*STh,* II of II, q. 1, art. 1, resp.).

39. Cf. *SCG* IIIa, 40, 2: "In the knowledge of faith, there is found a most imperfect operation of the intellect, having regard to what is on the side of the intellect, though the greatest perfection is discovered on the side of the object. For the intellect does not grasp the object to which it gives assent in the act of believing. Therefore, neither does man's ultimate felicity lie in this kind of knowledge of God." Cf. *SCG* IIIa, 40, 5: "Every man desires to see what he believes." And *SCG* IIIa, 40, 6: "An item of belief is not made perfectly present to the intellect by the knowledge of faith."

assent. The known proposition grips us; we irresistibly assent.[40] But when we assent to some proposition that we do not 'see' to be true, then an act of will is involved. In this case, "the intellect assents to something, not through being sufficiently moved to this assent by its proper object, but through an act of choice, whereby it turns voluntarily to one side rather than to the other" (*STh*, II of II, q. 1, art. 4, resp.).[41] Now, if this act of the will "be accompanied by doubt and fear of the opposite side, there will be opinion, while if there be certainty and no fear of the other side, there will be faith" (ibid.). So with respect to the fact that faith "cleaves firmly to one side," it "has something in common with science," but with respect to the fact that "its knowledge does not attain the perfection of clear sight," "it agrees with doubt, suspicion, and opinion" (*STh*, II of II, q. 2, art. 1, resp.).

Is faith then arbitrary, in its voluntary assent to propositions about God which it does not 'see' to be true? Is there a "leap of faith"? Is it *foolishness*, asks Aquinas, to give one's assent to the truths of faith that are above reason? Not at all. For "the divine Wisdom itself, which knows all things to the full" (*SCG* 1, 6, 1), has revealed these things, and there can be no more reliable basis for belief than that. "Other things being equal," says Aquinas, "sight is more certain than hearing; but if [the authority of] the person from whom we hear greatly surpasses that of the seer's sight, hearing is more certain than sight; thus a man of little science is more certain about what he hears on the authority of an expert in science, than about what is apparent to him according to his own reason; and much more is a man certain about what he hears from God, Who cannot be deceived, than about what he sees with his own reason which can be mistaken" (*STh*, II of II, q. 4, art. 8, ad 2).

But of course this response only answers our question by raising a new one: what assurance do we have that it is indeed God who revealed something? Well, in the first place, we must keep in mind that "a man would not believe in things that are unseen but proposed to him by another man unless he thought that this other man had more perfect knowledge of these proposed things than he himself who does not see

---

40. In this case the mind is "moved to assent by its very object, which is known either by itself (as in the case of first principles, which are held by the habit of understanding), or through something else already known (as in the case of conclusions which are held by the habit of science)" (*STh*, II of II, q. 1, art. 4, resp.). "Now the assent of science is not subject to free-will, because the scientist is obliged to assent by the force of the demonstration" (*STh*, II of II, q. 2, art. 9, ad 2).

41. "But in the knowledge of faith the will takes priority; indeed, the intellect assents through faith to things presented to it, because of an act of will and not because it is necessarily moved by the very evidence of the truth" (*SCG* IIa, 40, 3). "*To believe* is an act of the intellect, in so far as the will moves it to assent" (*STh*, II of II, q. 2, art. 2, resp.).

them" (*SCG* IIIa, 40, 4). Or if that is not quite accurate, given that one may believe something on the testimony of someone whom one believes to have heard it from someone else in turn, at least we must believe that the *chain* of believing-on-testimony ends with someone who has a different and better mode of access to the proposition in question than that of believing it on testimony. In the case of faith, specifically, if the believer was not (justifiably) convinced that behind the whole chain of human testimony was something better than testimony, "the assent of faith would be foolish and without certitude."

So what lies back of the chain of witnesses whom we interpret as communicators of revelation? What "higher knowledge" stands at the far end of this chain of testifiers? Either Christ, who himself "sees the truth immediately," or the apostles and prophets, who, though they do not themselves 'see' the truth that they propose for faith, nonetheless "take it immediately from one who does see," namely God (ibid.).

And what reason do we have for supposing that Christ *did* see those truths about God immediately and that God *did* plant immediately in the minds of the prophets and apostles these truths which they deliver to us? The answer given by Aquinas, and by the whole medieval tradition, is that miracles confirm the event of revelation and thus bring it about that faith is not mere "foolishness." The presence of miracles breaking through the ordinariness of existence makes faith a responsible act (*SCG* I, 6); the intellect of the believer is "moved by the authority of Divine teaching confirmed by miracles" (*STh*, II of II, q. 2, art. 9, ad 3).[42]

It should be added that in the case of faith it is *God* who actually moves the will, though in the presence, indeed, of testimony to the occurrence of a revelation confirmed by miracles. "The act of believing is an act of the intellect assenting to the Divine truth at the command of the will moved by the grace of God" (*STh*, II of II, q. 2, art. 9, resp.). Faith involves the interconnected factors of God, acknowledged as speaking with authority, moving the will to assent to certain propositions as revealed by him, with the presence of miracles confirming the occurrence of revelation. "The believer . . . is moved by the authority of Divine teaching confirmed by miracles, and, what is more, by the

---

42. "Faith has not that research of natural reason which demonstrates what is believed, but a research into those things whereby a man is induced to believe, for instance that such things have been uttered by God and confirmed by miracles" (*STh*, II of II, q. 2, art. 1, ad 1); "the authority of Scriptures—an authority divinely confirmed by miracles" (*SCG* I, 9, 2).

inward instinct of the Divine invitation; hence he does not believe lightly" (*STh,* II of II, q. 2, art. 9, ad 3).[43]

It is when Aquinas asks whether faith is foolish that he addresses himself to the concerns Locke had in mind when he formulated his evidentialist challenge and issued it to the enthusiasts. Presumably Aquinas's question as to whether it is foolish to assent to the articles of faith is the same as Locke's question as to whether such assent is a violation of our duty as rational creatures. And for both Locke and Aquinas, the rationality of identifying an occurrence of revelation is secured by the presence of miracles—though whether Aquinas holds that our belief that God revealed something must be *based on* the evidence of the miracles or merely that one's awareness of the miracles enters into the justifying circumstances is not clear. In any case, it is striking that Aquinas spends only a short time on the very issue that so gripped Locke. Having identified the issue, he passes right on. Nothing in his social and intellectual situation made it an issue of any urgency whatsoever. Guarding against foolishness was profoundly subordinate to the search for happiness. Furthermore, his project of natural theology was not at all addressed to this issue. In natural theology, as practiced by Aquinas and the other medievals, one takes various propositions that are components in the *content* of revelation and tries to demonstrate them. In evidentialist apologetics, as proposed by Locke, one assembles evidence for the *occurrence* of revelation.[44]

43. "As regards . . . man's assent to the things which are of faith, we may observe a twofold cause, one of external inducement, such as seeing a miracle, or being persuaded by someone to embrace the faith; neither of which is a sufficient cause, since of those who see the same miracle, or who hear the same sermon, some believe, and some do not. Hence we must assert another internal cause, which moves man inwardly to assent to matters of faith. The Pelagians held that this cause was nothing else than man's free-will. . . . But this is false, for since man, by assenting to matters of faith, is raised above his nature, this must needs accrue to him from some supernatural principle moving him inwardly; and this is God. Therefore faith, as regards the chief act of faith, is from God moving man inwardly by grace" (*STh,* II of II, q. 6, art. 1, resp.). "Science begets and nourishes faith, by way of external persuasion afforded by science; but the chief and proper cause of faith is that which moves man inwardly to assent" (ibid., ad 1). For further development of these points see *SCG* III, 6; 89, 5; 146, 3–4, and 152, 2.

44. Actually, Aquinas says something much stronger than that faith is not foolishness—that the believer is *permitted* to believe what God reveals. He says that all propositions such that "it is clear to him that they are contained in the doctrine of faith" are ones that "he is bound to believe . . . explicitly" (*STh,* II of II, q. 2, art. 5, resp.). Aquinas says that, for any believers whatever, this obligation includes "the primary points or articles of faith" (i.e., the Apostles' Creed). "Man is bound to believe them, just as he is bound to have faith." But as to other points of faith, "man is not bound to believe

Not only is faith not a piece of foolishness. Aquinas goes beyond this view to contend that the contents of the faith constitute a science, or, more strictly perhaps, the *basis* of a science. He calls it *sacred doctrine* or *divine science*. But how can faith possibly be that? we ask. A science, in Aquinas's sense, consists of a body of propositions that have been deduced from others that are evident to someone or other. Yet Aquinas has emphatically said that, when it comes to faith, we do not 'see' to be true the propositions that we accept. They are not evident to us. How, then, can these propositions serve as the basis of a science?

We must remember the distinction made between objective science and a given person's (warranted) apprehension of some segment of objective science. I may take it on someone's word that a certain body of propositions has been demonstrated and I may go on from there in my own work, without myself tracing those demonstrations. The practitioners of a whole branch of science may characteristically proceed in this way, taking as first principles various propositions that they themselves do not demonstrate but that they justifiably believe to have been demonstrated by others. We may call this a 'lower' or 'subordinate'

---

them explicitly, but only implicitly, or to be ready to believe them, in so far as he is prepared to believe whatever is contained in the Divine Scriptures" (ibid.). In short, "the direct object of faith is what whereby man is made one of the Blessed" (ibid.), which are "those things . . . the sight of which we shall enjoy in eternal life and by which we are brought to eternal life" (*STh*, II of II, q. 1, art. 8, resp.); "while the indirect and secondary object comprises all things delivered by God to us in Holy Writ, for instance that Abraham had two sons, that David was the son of Jesse, and so forth" (*STh*, II of II, q. 2, art. 5, resp.). Aquinas fully realizes that an implication of this is that the specific obligations of faith very much depend on our situation: "Men of higher degree, whose business it is to teach others, are under obligation to have fuller knowledge of faith, and to believe them more explicitly" (*STh*, II of II, q. 2, art. 6, resp.). Furthermore, not only ought the believer to accept the articles of faith but the believer *understands* that he ought to accept them: "The faithful . . . know them, not as by demonstration, but the light of faith which makes them see that they ought to believe them" (*STh*, II of II, q. 1, art. 5, ad 1). What the believer cannot do, on Aquinas's doctrine, is 'see' that the contents of the faith are true; seeing and believing are in that way incompatible. Yet Aquinas is confronted with the fact that St. Paul says, "We see now through a glass in a dark manner" (1 Cor. 13:12). His solution is to say that the contents of the faith are "seen by the believer" "under the common aspect of credibility." "For he would not believe unless, on the evidence of signs, or of something similar, he saw that they ought to be believed" (*STh*, II of II, q. 1, art. 4, ad 2). His thought seems to be that the miracles ("the evidence of signs") put the believer in the position where he sees that he ought to believe that God has revealed something and that he ought to believe whatever God has revealed. He may not, in the usual sense of "understand," understand fully the things that are "proposed to be believed," yet he understands that he "ought to believe them," and that he "ought nowise to deviate from them" (*STh*, II of II, q. 8, art. 4, ad 2).

science, in contrast with a 'higher' science in which the basic principles are not taken over from some other science.[45] Divine science is of this subordinate sort. It "does not argue in proof of its principles, which are the articles of faith, but from them it goes on to prove something else" (*STh* I, q. 1, art. 8, resp.).

But how, you ask, does this aid in showing that it is a science? If divine science is a subordinate science, what is the higher science in which those principles that it takes for granted are demonstrated or in which they were evident to someone? Aquinas answers that 'sacred science' is a science because it proceeds "from principles established by the light of a higher science, namely the science of God and the blessed" (*STh* I, q. 1, art. 2, resp.). Those truths about God that we accept on faith are in fact self-evident to God and the blessed. God and the blessed see the essence of God and accordingly see how these various truths flow forth from that. "Hence, just as the musician accepts on authority the principles taught him by the mathematician, so sacred science is established on principles revealed by God" (ibid.).

This appeal to God and the blessed takes most of us modern readers aback. We moderns do not believe as firmly as did Aquinas and the medievals that human beings living on earth do not constitute the totality of intelligent persons. But given that belief, it is not a large step to hold that God and the blessed also belong to the "community of scientists."[46] We have it on faith, says Aquinas—faith being reasonable, not foolish—that what is now dark and hazy for us is 'seen' by those who enjoy beatitude. And the deliverances of faith thus constitute (the basis of) a science.

The person who wishes to engage in this divine science has two tasks confronting him at once. He can "meditate . . . on the truth belonging to the first principles [of this science] and . . . teach it to others," and he can "refute the opposing falsehood" (*SCG* I, 1, 3). Wisdom has both an articulative-pedagogical dimension and an apologetic-polemical dimension. We shall shortly see that it has a third dimension as well.

In carrying out the former task, the theologian will of course in part be concerned to determine the precise content of revelation. In this, *sola scriptura* is the ultimate principle. The sacred theologian "properly

---

45. *STh* I, q. 1, art. 2, resp. Cf. *Division and Methods of the Sciences*, 59.

46. There is, nonetheless, some incoherence in Aquinas's thought or terminology here. Science for him consists entirely of beliefs arrived at by demonstration. But God knows what he knows immediately on Aquinas's view; and perhaps on his view the knowledge of the blessed about God is also immediate. But then God and the blessed have no science.

uses the authority of the canonical Scriptures as an incontrovertible proof, and the authority of the doctors of the Church as one that may properly be used, yet merely as probable. For our faith rests upon the revelation made to the apostles and prophets, who wrote the canonical books, and not on the revelations (if any such there are) made to other doctors" (*STh* I, q. 1, art. 8, ad 2). Having determined the contents of revelation, the theologian will work out the implications of what is revealed. Naturally he will use arguments in this; but "the reasons employed by holy men to prove things that are of faith, are not demonstrations; they are either persuasive arguments showing that what is proposed to our faith is not impossible,[47] or else they are proofs drawn from the principles of faith, i.e., from the authority of Holy Writ" (*STh*, II of II, q. 1, art. 5, ad 2).[48] "As other sciences do not argue in proof of their principles, but argue from their principles to demonstrate other truths in these sciences: so this doctrine does not argue in proof of its principles, which are the articles of faith, but from them it goes on to prove something else" (*STh* I, q. 1, art. 8, resp.).

But here it is of indispensable importance to distinguish between *the articles of faith*, as Aquinas has just called them, and the *preambles of faith*. If we look at the contents of revelation, in Scripture, we see that various truths about God that are there affirmed or presupposed can in fact be demonstrated—that is, proved from what is evident to us.[49] For example, Scripture teaches God's immutability, and this, says Aquinas, is something demonstrable. Now "the existence of God and other like truths about God, which can be known by natural reason, are not articles of faith, but are preambles to the articles" (*STh* I, q. 2, art. 2, ad 1). So when we said above that the sacred theologian does not offer demonstrations, it was of the *articles* of faith that we were speaking. In support of these, he either appeals to Scripture or offers arguments that he frankly concedes to have only the force of probability.

But things are different with respect to the *preambles*. The calling of the sacred theologian is to offer demonstrations of the preambles. Why? Why would the theologian bother to do that? Here we come to the second dimension of the theologian's task—the apologetic-polemi-

---

47. In another place he speaks of this as "setting forth the truth of faith by probable arguments" (*SCG* I, 9, 3).

48. He adds: "Whatever is based on these principles is as well proved in the eyes of the faith, as a conclusion drawn from self-evident principles is in the eyes of all. Hence, again, theology is a science."

49. "The distinction to be made is that certain things, of themselves, come directly under faith, because they surpass natural reason . . . whereas other things come under faith, through being subordinate in one way or another, to those just mentioned, for instance, all that is contained in Holy Scriptures" (*STh*, II of II, q. 8, art. 2, resp.).

cal dimension. The theologian is well aware that there are those who do not accept the contents of revelation, even those who have objections to it. Now, if the person in question accepts the authority of Scripture, no special problem is posed. But suppose he does not. Suppose, for example, that the Christian theologian is confronted by Muslims who do not accept the authority of the Old and New Testaments (*SCG* I, 2, 3). What does he do in this case? There is no alternative but to "have recourse to the natural reason, to which all men are forced to give their assent" (ibid.). By natural reason he will demonstrate those elements and presuppositions of revelation that can be demonstrated, which is by definition, those that are preambles of faith (*SCG* I, 9, 3).[50] And second, when it comes to the *articles* of faith, he will, in addressing the opponent who "believes nothing of divine revelation," engage in "answering his objections—if he has any—against faith. Since faith rests upon infallible truth, and since the contrary of a truth can never be demonstrated, it is clear that the arguments against faith cannot be demonstrations but are difficulties that can be answered" (*STh* I, q. 1, art. 8, resp.).

And what about a third strategy, the one already mentioned of constructing *probable* arguments in *favor* of the articles of faith? Well, this is quite acceptable in the theologian's address to believers—that is, in the implementation of his articulative-pedagogical task. But he should beware of offering such arguments to the unbeliever, lest the unbeliever "imagine that our acceptance of the truth of faith was based on such weak arguments" (*SCG* I, 9, 2).[51] And in any case, probable arguments

50. It is of course very odd that Aquinas did not propose, in dialogue with the Muslims, appealing to the Koran. Most if not all of the preambles of the Christian faith could be established in that way.

51. "Now, to make the first kind of divine truth known, we must proceed through demonstrative arguments, by which our adversary may become convinced. However, since such arguments are not available for the second kind of divine truth, our intention should not be to convince our adversary by arguments: it should be to answer his arguments against the truth; for, as we have shown, the natural reason cannot be contrary to the truth of faith. The sole way to overcome an adversary of divine truth is from the authority of Scripture—an authority divinely confirmed by miracles. For that which is above the human reason we believe only because God has revealed it. Nevertheless, there are certain likely arguments that should be brought forth in order to make divine truth known. This should be done for the training and consolation of the faithful, and not with any idea of refuting those who are adversaries. For the very inadequacy of the arguments would rather strengthen them in their error, since they would imagine that our acceptance of the truth of faith was based on such weak arguments" (*SCG* I, 9, 2). Aquinas then describes his procedure in *Summa contra gentiles* as follows: "We shall first seek to make known that truth which faith professes and reason investigates. This we shall do by bringing forward both demonstrative and probable arguments, some of which were drawn from the books of the philosophers and of the saints, through which truth is

have no place in *science*, properly understood.[52] They will not occur in divine science.

Seeing that a good deal of the content of revelation can either be demonstrated or probabilistically established, and recalling that faith is an act of the will, some might insist on having good reasons for that part of the content of the faith before assenting to it. But this would be a serious mistake, says Aquinas; it would lessen or destroy the merit of faith. "When a man either has not the will, or not a prompt will, to believe, unless he be moved by human reasons," then "human reason diminishes the merit of faith" (*STh*, II of II, q. 2, art. 10, resp.). The situation is entirely different for the person who has in faith accepted the contents of revelation and now seeks reasons for the content. Since this person's "will is ready to believe" and since he "loves the truth he believes," he now "thinks out and takes to heart whatever reasons he can find in support thereof; and in this way human reason does not exclude the merit of faith but is a sign of greater merit" (ibid.).[53] Of course it is true that when certain of the *preambles* are *demonstrated*, then the person no longer takes them on faith. He then 'sees' them to be true, and thereby the "measure of faith" is diminished (*STh*, II of II, q. 2, art. 10, ad 2). But the *merit* is not diminished. For the merit of faith does not reside in how much we actually accept on faith and how little we 'see' to be true. It resides rather in our willingness to believe that God reveals himself and in our willingness to accept *what* he reveals even if we do not 'see' it to be true.[54] Seeking reasons for the faith that is already within us need not reduce that willingness.

---

strengthened and its adversary overcome. Then, in order to follow a development from the more manifest to the less manifest, we shall proceed to make known that truth which surpasses reason, answering the objections of its adversaries and setting forth the truth of faith by probable arguments and by authorities, to the best of our ability" (*SCG* I, 9, 3).

52. See Commentary on Boethius's *De Trinitate*, q. 6, art. 1; in Armand Maurer, *St. Thomas Aquinas: The Division and Methods of the Sciences* (Toronto: Pontifical Institute of Medieval Studies, 1953), p. 52.

53. This is strikingly similar to what Calvin says in *Institutes* I, 8.

54. "Gregory is referring to the case of a man who has no will to believe what is of faith, unless he be induced by reasons. But when a man has the will to believe what is of faith, on the authority of God alone, although he may have reasons in demonstration of some of them, e.g. of the existence of God, the merit of his faith is not, for that reason, lost or diminished" (*STh*, II of II, q. 2, art. 10, ad 1). "The reasons which are brought forward in support of the authority of faith, are not demonstrations which can bring intellectual vision to the human intellect, wherefore they do not cease to be unseen. But they remove obstacles to faith, by showing that what faith proposes is not impossible; wherefore such reasons do not diminish the merit or the measure of faith. On the other

We have now carried out the task we earlier set for ourselves, of approaching the enterprise of natural theology from above as well as from below—from the side of faith and sacred science as well as from the side of the sciences of natural reason. As he engages in the task of sacred science, the theologian discovers that revelation contains truths of two quite different orders: those accessible to our natural reason and those not so accessible. He proceeds then to demonstrate the former; he constructs deductive proofs from premises evident to at least some of us in this our natural condition. And this is just the enterprise of natural theology—occurring now for a different purpose from that of seeking to share in the scientific enterprise of humanity. The sacred theologian engages in natural theology for apologetic and polemical purposes—that is, for the purpose of quieting the unbeliever's objections to what is revealed and of getting him to accept as much of it as he can.

But along the way we saw glimmerings of a third reason for engaging in natural theology, a third "project of natural theology." And thereby we saw glimmerings of yet a third task of the sacred theologian, in addition to his articulative-expository and apologetic-polemic tasks. We saw Aquinas saying that the believer, loving the truth he believes, "thinks out and takes to heart whatever reasons he can find in support thereof"; and this, said Aquinas, is "a sign of greater merit." The enterprise of natural theology is not only addressed to the unbeliever and is not only addressed to all who are interested in the pursuit of science. It is also addressed to *the believer*. It represents an *advance* for the believer, and that in the most fundamental way: an advance toward ultimate felicity. Our ultimate happiness lies in 'seeing' truths about God. And when we in this life manage to demonstrate some of the things that we unseeingly took on faith, so that now we 'see' them to be true, that is a step up the road toward felicity. It will be recalled that such demonstrations as are available to us do not involve our grasping God's essence; indeed in this life we have no access to his essence. Nonetheless, a proposition about God is better demonstrated than taken on faith—better in the precise sense that 'seeing' something to be true is always better than taking it on testimony.

---

hand, though demonstrative reasons in support of the preambles of faith, but not of the articles of faith, diminish the measure of faith, since they make the thing believed to be seen, yet they do not diminish the measure of charity, which makes the will ready to believe them, even if they were unseen; and so the measure of merit is not diminished" (ibid., ad 2).

Of course we are here presupposing, as we have all along that "it is impossible that one and the same thing should be believed and seen by the same person. Hence it is equally impossible for one and the same thing to be an object of science and of belief for the same person" (*STh,* II of II, q. 1, art. 5, resp.).[55] The implication is clear: in demonstrating the preambles, we leave faith behind with respect to those preambles, we advance toward 'seeing'. We *transmute* believing into seeing, faith into vision. And this advance represents an advance toward our ultimate felicity. In ultimate felicity, faith will be entirely left behind, entirely transmuted into sight.

So the enterprise of natural theology, when approached from above, is not only to be a polemic/apologetic project addressed to unbelievers but also a transmutation project addressed to believers. Participation in this transmutation project is by no means obligatory for all Christians; the press of other duties forecloses that to some. Yet it is a key component in the pursuit of the contemplative life. And the contemplative life, in turn, is the highest form of human life. "There is nothing in this life so like this ultimate and perfect felicity as the life of those who contemplate truth, to the extent that it is possible in this life" (*SCG* IIIa, 63, 10).[56] It remains true that "the slenderest knowledge that may be obtained of the highest things is more desireable than the most certain knowledge obtained of lesser things" (*STh* I, q. 1, art. 5, ad 1). Yet more desirable than slender knowledge of higher things is *firm* knowledge of higher things.

By virtue of his affirmation of the transmutation project of natural theology, the project of transmuting what is believed into what is seen, Aquinas stands in the great Augustinian/Anselmian tradition of *fides*

55. The passage continues: "It may happen, however, that a thing which is an object of vision or science for one, is believed by another: since we hope to see some day what we now believe."

56. The passage continues: "In fact, the contemplation of truth begins in this life, but reaches its climax in the future; whereas the active and civic life does not go beyond the limits of this life." Aquinas takes it for granted that the contemplative life in its highest form available to us will take the form of engaging in the science of sacred theology. For a description of a very different medieval understanding of the contemplative life—the *monastic* understanding—see the fascinating book by Jean Leclercq, *The Love of Learning and the Desire for God* (New York: Fordham University Press, 1977). In their meditations on the Scriptures and the articles of faith, the monastics and scholastics alike were vividly aware of standing in a tradition of such meditation—of joining the fathers and doctors of the church. The presence of *disputes* within the tradition (and between those within and those outside the tradition), however, was far more vivid to the scholatics than to the monastics. Accordingly, scholastic meditation, much more than monastic, was focused on sifting through the disputed questions. Meditation for the medievals was never simply staring. It was always informed meditation. The mind of the medieval meditator was a wondering mind, in our double sense of that: filled with wonder and filled with questions. In the monastics, however, the former dominated, in the scholastics, the latter.

quaerens intellectum. But before we confirm this fundamental continuity amid differences, we should consider an objection that might be lodged against my interpretation of the project of "natural theology from above." I have represented Aquinas as holding that natural theology is a gain for the believer. It transmutes his taking the preambles on faith into his seeing them to be true. Someone might note, however, that, according to Aquinas, faith is more certain than natural knowledge, subsequently objecting that surely Aquinas would not regard moving from the more certain to the less certain as a gain. So this cannot be a reason for the scriptural theologian to participate in natural theology, whatever other reasons there may be.

But here we must be clear, as Thomas himself is, on the *way* in which faith is more certain. Certitude can be regarded in two ways. It "may be considered on the part of the subject, and thus the more a man's intellect lays hold of a thing, the more certain it is. In this way," says Aquinas, "faith is less certain, because matters of faith are above the human intellect, whereas the objects of [wisdom, science, and understanding] are not" (*STh,* II of II, q. 4, art. 8, resp.). But certitude can also be regarded from the standpoint of its cause, "and thus a thing which has a more certain cause, is itself more certain. In this way, faith is more certain than those three virtues, because it is founded on Divine truth, whereas the aforesaid three virtues are based on human reason" (ibid.).[57] Now, probably what Aquinas calls "certitude" in this second sense would more naturally be called "reliability" by us. His point in this last passage can then be put as follows: in faith God himself moves the will of the person to assent to what he himself has revealed. When this occurs, there is reliability; for when this happens, we will not be found assenting to falsehoods. In science, by contrast, what evokes assent is our disposition to believe certain propositions upon grasping their terms and our disposition to believe certain propositions upon having certain sensations, plus demonstration. And this is less reliable than God's speech.[58] But as Aquinas himself observes, this point about

57. Cf. *STh,* II of II, q. 4, art. 8, ad 3: "But in so far as science, wisdom and understanding are intellectual virtues, they are based upon the natural light of reason, which falls short of the certitude of God's word, on which faith is founded."

58. There is something perplexing about the contrast that Aquinas draws here, however. He says that faith is more certain than science and understanding, because it is "founded on Divine truth," whereas those are "based on human reason." And quite clearly it is comparative reliability that he has in mind. For he speaks of "the natural light of reason, which can err," and he contrasts this with "the light of the divine knowledge, which cannot be misled" (*STh* I, q. 1, art. 5, resp.). But what does he mean, when he says that the natural light of reason can err? Does he mean that false propositions can be self-evident for us? If this is what he does mean, he nowhere makes a big point of it. Perhaps what the Russell Paradoxes show is just exactly this: that falsehoods can be self-evident to us (assuming that *that* p *is self-evident to* S does not entail *that* S *knows* p). But Aquinas

reliability is fully compatible with the claim that the way in which the mind entertains a proposition in science is more certain than the way in which the mind entertains it in faith. It is more certain because in the former case, the mind 'sees' the proposition to be true, and in the latter case, not. But of course I had in mind exactly this contrast when I said

knew nothing of the Russell Paradoxes! Furthermore, Aquinas defends the thesis "that the truth of reason is not opposed to the truth of the Christian faith" (*SCG* I, 7). Now perhaps we should view this passage as addressed to the theory that reason may yield truths which contadict the truths of faith (the "two-truth" theory) rather than to the theory that the deliverances of reason may contradict the deliverances of faith, with the consequence that one is false. Yet he does say that "that with which the human reason is naturally endowed is clearly most true" (para. 1). And he concludes his discussion by saying that "whatever arguments are brought forward against the doctrines of faith are conclusions incorrectly derived from the first and self-evident principles imbedded in nature. Such conclusions do not have the force of demonstration: they are arguments that are either probable or sophistical" (para. 7). It seems reasonable to conclude from these passages that, on Aquinas's view, though falsehoods will never be self-evident to us, we may in some cases *think* that a proposition is self-evident to us when it is not. And perhaps it is this that he has in mind when he says that the natural light of reason can err. That would seem the natural interpretation of this other passage from *Summa contra gentiles* (I, 4, 5): "The investigation of the human reason for the most part has falsity present within it, and this is due partly to the weakness of our intellect in judgment, and partly to the admixture of images. . . . With the many truths that are demonstrated, there is sometimes mingled something that is false, which is not demonstrated but rather asserted on the basis of some probable or sophistical argument, which yet has the credit of being a demonstration. That is why it was necessary that the unshakeable certitude and pure truth concerning divine things should be presented to men by way of faith." But have we now not lost all contrast between the reliability of faith and of science? We can think that something is self-evident to us when it is not, but can we not also think that God has revealed something that he has not and that he has not revealed something that he has? Aquinas is strikingly reluctant to admit this latter. He does concede that it is possible not only for the "simple" but also for "the learned to err" and to "stray from" "the Divine truth that is the rule of faith" (*STh*, II of II, q. 2, art. 6, obj. 3 and ad 3). Yet he also says that "by the habit of faith, the human mind is directed to assent to such things as are becoming to a right faith, and not to assent to others" (*STh*, II of II, q. 1, art. 4, ad 3). And in response to the objection that "it is dangerous for man to assent to matters, wherein he cannot judge whether that which is proposed to him be true or false," he says that "just as man assents to first principles, by the natural light of his intellect, so does a virtuous man, by the habit of virtue, judge aright of things concerning that virtue; and in this way, by the light of faith which God bestows on him, a man assents to matters of faith and not to those which are against faith" (*STh*, II of II, q. 2, art. 3, obj. 2 and ad 2). I do not know what Aquinas's full thought on this matter is. It may be added here that Aquinas shares none of our characteristic modern worries over the reliability of the *witnesses* to revelation—over the reliability of the prophets and apostles. When he raises the question of whether it is "foolish" to accept the faith, his answer focuses on the dual claim that what God reveals is true and that accompanying miracles confirm the event of revelation. The reliability of the recipients of primary revelation in discerning what was revealed and in accurately reporting that plus the accompanying miracles is no concern of his. He does, in *STh* I, q. 1, art. 8, ad 2, speak of "the authority of those to whom the revelation has been made," and he says that we "ought to believe" on that authority. But this is highly uncharacteristic.

that the pursuit of natural theology by the believer, whereby faith is transmuted into sight, is a gain. It secures "the intellect's arrival at the stage of perfection that comes with the certitude of sight" (*STh*, II of II, q. 2, art. 1, resp.).

III

Aquinas of course differs at many points from his great predecessors Augustine and Anselm. Yet in his affirmation of natural theology for transmutation he stands squarely in their tradition of fides quaerens intellectum. Often this Augustinian motto has been interpreted as an affirmation of "liberal learning in Christian perspective." It was nothing of the sort. It was an affirmation of the project of seeking to understand that which already we believe, thus transmuting faith into knowledge. Such transmutation was a key component in their understanding of the practice of Christian contemplation.

Here we shall have to content ourselves with looking at Anselm.[59] In the preface to his *Proslogium*, Anselm remarks that he wrote his earlier *Monologium* as "an example of meditation on the grounds of faith" and that in fact he originally titled it accordingly. The preface to the *Monologium* itself makes clear how he understood his project. Certain of his brothers, he said, had urged him to set down some of the thoughts about God that he had expressed in conversation. He had acceded to this wish, he says, "in order that nothing in Scripture should be urged on the authority of Scripture itself, but that whatever the conclusion of independent investigation should declare to be true, should, in an unadorned style, with common proofs and with a simple argument, be briefly enforced by the cogency of reason, and plainly expounded in the light of truth."

Accordingly, Anselm asks us to imagine a person who, "either from ignorance or unbelief, has no knowledge of the existence of one Nature which is the highest of all existing beings." He then says that such a person, though ignorant of what Anselm and the brothers "believe regarding God and his creatures," "still believes that he can convince himself of these truths in great part . . . by the force of argument." And so, says Anselm, he will present his arguments "so that, as reason leads the way and follows up these considerations, he advances rationally to those truths of which, without reason, he has no knowledge."

It is clear, then, that the *Monologium* is addressed to the unbeliever. Natural theology is here addressed not to the believer, with the intent

59. I shall be quoting from the translations of *Proslogium* and *Monologium* by Sidney Norton Deane (La Salle, Ill.: Open Court, 1954).

of assisting him to transmute faith into sight, but to the unbeliever with the intent of carrying him along by reason to assent to much, at least, of what Anselm and his brothers already accept on faith. Of course it is a hypothetical unbeliever to whom it is addressed. Did the brothers want to give the book to actual unbelievers? Did they want to use its contents in their own address to unbelievers? Or did they see other benefit in having in hand this address to unbelief? All that remains obscure. The project of natural theology that we find in the *Proslogium* is profoundly different. Anselm tells us, in the preface, that on reflection he felt that the argument of the *Monologium* was too complex. So he began to search for "a single argument which would require no other for its proof than itself alone; and alone would suffice to demonstrate that God truly exists." In his discovery of the ontological argument he felt that he had found what he was looking for. So he proposes to set out his discovery. Yet the context in which he embeds this new argument is as different from the old as is the argument itself.

Anselm does not now address himself to a (hypothetical) unbeliever. He addresses himself to himself ("Up now, slight man!") and to God ("O Lord, my God"). And he says that he has written his "treatise in the person of one who strives to lift his mind to the contemplation of God, and seeks to understand what he believes." Indeed, he tells us that he had originally intended to title his book "Faith Seeking Understanding."

In chapter 1, before he begins his proofs, Anselm plaintively characterizes his "exile" from God. His language is rich and varied. But again and again it is the language of vision and of sight. "Never have I seen thee," he says. "Do I know thee?" "I was created to see thee, and not yet have I done that for which I was made." Thy servant, he says, "pants to see thee." "Why do I not see thee present?"

What is the cause of this departure from our "native country into exile, from the vision of God into our present blindness?" The cause is sin. We were created in the image of God, so that we would be "mindful" of him, "conceive" of him and "love" him. "But that image has been so consumed and wasted away by vices, and obscured by the smoke of wrong-doing, that it cannot achieve that for which it was made," except God "renew it, and create it anew." This he has done, by granting us faith. Without the gift of faith, the understanding for which we long is impossible; "unless I believe, I should not understand."[60]

60. The characteristically Augustinian insistence that faith must cleanse and purify our hearts so as to make natural theology possible is foreign to Aquinas's thought. Aquinas does stress that *faith* becomes possible only if God cleanses the heart and intellect

But faith does not end our exile; it does not by itself give us the understanding and sight for which we long. "I long," says Anselm, "to understand in some degree thy truth, which my heart believes and loves. For I do not seek to understand that I may believe, but I believe in order to understand." And so Anselm prays to God, who "dost give understanding to faith," that God may give him, "so far as thou knowest it to be profitable, to understand that thou art as we believe; and that thou art that which we believe." Anselm then presents his ontological arguments, in which at no point is there an appeal to matters taken on faith. ("It is so evident, to a rational mind, that thou dost exist in the highest degree of all.") And at the conclusion of the arguments he makes clear that, with respect to God's existence at least, his exile has been ended. The vision he longed for has been attained. His faith has been transmuted into understanding: "I thank thee, gracious Lord, I thank thee; because what I formerly believed by thy bounty, I now so understand by thine illumination, that if I were unwilling to believe that thou dost exist, I should not be able not to understand this to be true."

There is no more elegant statement of the project of natural theology as transmutation, set within the context of the practice of Christian contemplation, than this of Anselm.

IV

But even a faith whose preambles have been transmuted into *scientia* does not represent for Aquinas that knowledge of God in which our ultimate felicity consists. It is true that, "in so far as a man gives himself to the pursuit of wisdom, so far does he even now have some share in true beatitude" (*SCG* I, 2, 1). But no more than a *share*. The root of the deficiency is that we still do not know *what God is*. We know him only through his effects, and what we know thereby is well short of knowing his essence. The conclusion is unavoidable:

> If ultimate felicity does not consist in the knowledge of God, whereby He is known in general by all, or most, men, by a sort of confused appraisal, and again, if it does not consist in the knowledge of God which is known by way of demonstration in the speculative sciences, nor in the cognition of God whereby He is known through faith . . . ; and if it is not possible in this life to reach a higher knowledge of God so as to know Him through His essence . . . ; and if it is necessary to identify

---

(*STh*, II of II, q. 8, art. 7, resp.), but natural theology, he seems to think, can be done by anyone.

human felicity with some sort of knowledge of God . . . ; then it is not possible for man's ultimate felicity to come in this life. [*SCG* IIIa, 48, 1]

"Man's ultimate felicity will lie in the knowledge of God that the human mind has after this life" (*SCG* IIIa, 48, 16).

But now it must be observed that faith has a double function in God's economy: not only do we, by faith, come to know various propositions about God that transcend the reach of natural reason. God also rewards the virtue of faith with a vision of his essence in a life after this life. "In order that a man arrive at the perfect vision of heavenly happiness, he must first of all believe God, as a disciple believes the master who is teaching him" (*STh*, II of II, q. 2, art. 3, resp.). The reward of faith is that vision of God which is our ultimate happiness.

V

We have uncovered not one but three projects of natural theology in Aquinas—three purposes for engaging in a theology erected on the foundations of natural reason. One may approach natural theology from below, engaging in it for a purpose shared in common between believer and unbeliever: the purpose of developing *scientia* as far as our natural reason will carry us. This is the project of *natural theology as metaphysics*. But one may also approach natural theology from above, as Aquinas himself did for the most part, engaging in it for purposes unique to the believer. One may do so for the purpose of getting the person who does not accept the authority of revelation nonetheless to accept a good deal of its content. This I have called the project of *natural theology as apologetic-polemic*. And one may engage in natural theology for the purpose of enabling the believer to transmute into sight some of what already he believes, the project of *natural theology as transmutation*.

In Aquinas all three of these projects were embedded in his vision of authentic human existence: to be human is to seek happiness and to find that happiness ultimately only in the vision of God. One might, of course, ask which of these various purposes for engaging in natural theology makes sense in one or another alternative vision of human existence. Here I have asked only within what vision these purposes were embedded by Aquinas.

Locke was different. The project of evidentialist apologetics is a project entirely from above; a project whose purpose is unique to believers. The believer may not neglect it, whereas the unbeliever has no reason for engaging in it—though in principle the project might be carried out so successfully that he is bound to sit up and pay attention. It is the project of securing the rationality of one's faith by argument. The vision that nourished this project was a vision of us human beings as having obligations of rationality—duties to govern our beliefs in accord with the norms for believing. Evidentialist apologetics is a strategy not for the believer's ascent toward fulfillment in contemplation but for the construction of supports beneath his feet. It is a movement not within faith but beneath faith. Its concern is not to promote the fulfillment of faith but to assure the legitimacy of faith. Instead of gazing ahead and telling us wherein lies our fulfillment, Locke peers at us now and tells us what is permitted.

Though Locke himself mentioned the connection of our duties of rationality to our dignity and freedom, it awaited later writers to stress these connections. Our dignity and freedom reside at bottom, so many have argued, in carrying out our duties of rationality. To follow the way of reason rather than the way of passion and impulse is to guard one's dignity as a human being and to act freely rather than being put upon. Hence the believer is obliged to meet the evidentialist challenge on pain of violating his dignity and freedom. Belief, unlike unbelief, constitutes a threat to our dignity and freedom. The threat can be met only by believing on evidence. There is a presumption in favor of atheism. Some of the very proofs that the believer once used to attain his felicity are now used to fend off the charge that he is violating his dignity. Though Locke believed that *knowledge* of God's existence could be attained only by demonstration, the demonstrations he offered are hasty and ill considered. It is evident that he never really doubted. Later, God's existence would become as much a matter of anxiety as his revelation. It was then that the medieval arguments for God's existence were lifted from their context of natural theology and transported into this new context of evidentialist apologetics.

Happiness as something to be attained, dignity as something to be guarded: do we not see in this contrast a reflection of the change from the hierarchical solidarity of medieval society to our pluralistic society of individual freedoms?[61]

Between Aquinas and Locke a vast change of mentality occurred. The telic vision of all humanity aimed toward happiness in the contemplation of God decayed. In John Calvin and the Reformers gener-

61. For an interesting discussion on the replacement of the medieval ideal of honor with our modern ideal of dignity, see Berger, Berger, and Kellner, *The Homeless Mind* (New York: Random House, 1973), pp. 88–90. A tracing of the change from the pursuit of happiness to the guarding of dignity and honor would no doubt also have to take account of Pico della Mirandola's famous "Oration on the Dignity of Man."

ally it is subordinate to the vision of a life of obedient and appreciative gratitude to God. In such a life there is no urge to move beyond faith to vision; indeed, faith, seen now as trust more than propositional assent, is never to be superseded. But Calvin is also not Locke. The life of obedient and appreciative gratitude to God is not yet the life of guarding one's dignity and freedom as a rational being. And indeed, on many of the issues we have canvassed, Calvin is closer to Aquinas than to Locke. Neither he nor Aquinas attached foundationalist conditions to Christian faith—nor indeed to theistic belief. Though Calvin has no interest in the theistic proofs as a means for attaining our felicity, he also has no interest in them as a means for guarding our dignity.

One other change of mentality was necessary before evidentialist apologetics could replace natural theology. In both Aquinas and Locke one finds the foundationalist vision of grounding one's beliefs in certitude. But in Aquinas such grounding was a condition of authentic science; in Locke, of rationality. The grounding that in Aquinas was a duty of the scientist qua scientist was spread out in Locke to the duty of all of us in all of our lives. Aquinas's telic view of the end of man was paired off with a foundationalist view of science. Locke's concern to guard the freedom and dignity of man was paired off with a foundationalist view of rationality.

In consequence, the believer was put on the defensive in the dialogue between belief and unbelief. Aquinas was of course deeply convinced of the success of the project of natural theology as polemic (and apologetic). But even if the polemic of belief with unbelief should fail because the arguments all prove to lack the force of demonstration, its failure would imply nothing whatsoever as to the acceptability of the believer's faith. Indeed, a striking feature of the Thomistic picture is that the failure of the theistic arguments makes no difference whatsoever to the believer other than that his longing to 'see' the truth about God will lack fulfillment in his earthly existence. In contrast, in Locke the failure of evidentialist apologetics implies that the believer must surrender his faith. And so at last it is clear why Karl Barth, in the passage cited near the beginning of this paper, misinterprets natural theology, construing it as if it were evidentialist apologetics. Barth's argument is with the Enlightenment, not with the medievals.[62]

62. A more accurate understanding of the medieval project of natural theology is to be found in Etienne Gilson. Describing fides quaerens intellectum as the method of Christian philosophy, he says, in *The Spirit of Medieval Philosophy* (New York: Scribner, 1936), that "this effort of truth believed to transform itself into truth known, is truly the life of Christian wisdom, and the body of rational truths resulting from the effort is Christian philosophy itself. Thus the content of Christian philosophy is that body of rational truths discovered, explored or simply safeguarded, thanks to the help that

Of course Aquinas briefly considered the question of whether faith is
"foolish." But that which he just briefly mentioned became for Locke
the preoccupying focus of attention, made so by the decay of the medieval vision of our human existence, the rise of religious pluralism in
society, and the emergence of a foundationalist understanding of rationality. Perhaps today we are living through the decay of the Enlightenment vision as well. Perhaps that which nourished the evidentialist challenge is today fading for many into the oblivion of implausi-
bility, as that which nourished natural theology faded for many centuries ago.[63]

---

reason receives from revelation. . . . There is no question of maintaining—no one has
ever maintained—that faith is a kind of cognition superior to rational cognition. It is
quite clear, on the contrary, that belief is a succedaneum of knowledge, and that to
substitute science for belief, wherever possible, is always a positive gain for the understanding. For Christian thinkers the traditional hierarchy of the modes of cognition is
always faith, understanding, and vision of God face to face" (pp. 34–35). See also the
remainder of the chapter. Barth himself seems to take a different position with respect to
the natural theology of Anselm than he does with respect to natural theology generally.
Or more strictly, he exempts Anselm from his strictures against natural theology because
he does not regard him as doing natural theology. See his *Anselm: Fides Quaerens Intellectum,* trans I. W. Robertson (London: SCM Press, 1960).
   63. And why do I not ascribe to Descartes the dubious honor of first issuing with
clarity the evidentialist challenge to the religious believer? Because he nowhere does issue
it. Of course, the challenge may be an implication of his general epistemology. But even
that is not clear. The issue hangs on whether Descartes, like Locke, was a foundationalist
with respect to justified (rational) belief or whether he was a foundationalist only with
respect to scientific knowledge. And on that issue, the evidence seems to me
contradictory.

3

Faith and Evidentialism

KENNETH KONYNDYK

"Now faith is the assurance of things hoped for, the conviction of things that are not seen," according to the writer of the Epistle to the Hebrews (11:1). This writer goes on to add that "without faith it is impossible to please God, for he that comes to God must believe that he is, and that he is rewarder of those who seek after him" (Heb. 11:6). These words have long been a touchstone for Christian philosophers and theologians. One is not a Christian without having faith that certain beliefs are true.

Yet numerous Christians, philosophers and theologians, also maintain that Christianity's central beliefs are rational. They admit that these beliefs are not always clear; there are mysteries, to be sure, but embracing the salvation God offers does not offend reason. It is rational at least in the sense of not committing one to any noetic improprieties and requiring no abuse of one's intellectual equipment.

Some of these Christians, from popular writers to philosophers of religion, have tried to do more. They have tried to bring forward evidences and proofs of various doctrines and articles of the Christian faith. These evidences and arguments are not theologians' arguments;

I am grateful to Robert Audi, Arvin Vos, and my colleagues at Calvin College, especially Stephen Wykstra, for their help at various stages in the writing of this paper.

they do not presuppose acceptance of the authority of Scripture or the Magisterium. These proofs are supposed to find a basis in the experience and intelligence of any unbiased observer who takes the trouble to examine these matters. A passionate debate about these evidences has continued for many centuries now. For several of these centuries it was obvious to nearly all clear-thinking philosophers that God's existence, his simplicity, his eternity could be demonstrated without appealing to any data a rational infidel could refuse. Nowadays the prevailing opinion is that such proofs and such confidence were buried with the publication of Hume's *Dialogues concerning Natural Religion,* although lively ghosts have appeared occasionally since then. There no longer seem to be any universally convincing proofs.

It would be a mistake to suggest that the debate about arguments for the articles of the Christian faith has played itself out. Quite the opposite is true. More writing, learned and otherwise, is being produced on such arguments nowadays than since the close of the Middle Ages. Why? What rides on these arguments? What inspires the zealous analysis, dissection, and evaluation of these arguments? In a word, it is evidentialism—the view that, unless one has adequate evidence for one's theistic beliefs, it is rationally improper to hold them. It is the common assumption in the background of much modern argumentation back and forth about proofs of God's existence and their value. Atheists and agnostics are busy refuting every alleged theistic proof so as to remain rationally justified in their atheism or agnosticism. Theists produce, rehabilitate, and refurbish theistic proofs to assure themselves and unbelievers of the epistemic propriety of their theistic beliefs.

Regardless of which way the evidentialist principle actually cuts, I want to observe that it has been adopted by Christians and non-Christians alike. W. K. Clifford, Antony Flew, and John Mackie are well-known examples of non-Christians who endorse evidentialism. John Locke, on the other hand, is a Christian who enthusiastically embraces this principle, and it is endorsed by many contemporary Christian writers as well. The principle is not without its detractors, however. One thinks immediately of William James's assurances that it is proper to exercise the "will to believe." In more recent years, Alvin Plantinga and Nicholas Wolterstorff have launched attacks against it.[1] Plantinga has raised a few eyebrows with his contention that belief in God, by which he means belief that there is a God, can be rational and yet not be based on the evidence of any other beliefs. It can be a basic belief. But it is not

1. See especially their papers in *Faith and Rationality,* ed. Alvin Plantinga and Nicholas Wolterstorff (Notre Dame: University of Notre Dame Press, 1983).

a basic belief in most of the senses sanctioned by standard versions of foundationalism. As a result, Plantinga has rejected these usual versions of foundationalism.

David Hume displays a curious ambivalence toward evidentialism. On the one hand, he cites with approval a broad and sweeping version in section X of his *Enquiry concerning Human Understanding:* "A wise man, therefore, proportions his belief to the evidence." He goes on to employ his principle in his argument against accepting the veracity of reports of miracles. Earlier in the same *Enquiry,* however, Hume argues forcefully that causal inferences are inadequately supported by rational and experiential evidence, without concluding that the wise man will reject, or will perhaps tentatively accept, such inferences. Instead he says that, fortunately for us, rejecting these beliefs is not within our power and that our nature is not purely rational. We accept these inferences out of custom or habit, even though doing so violates evidentialist principles. While it is not clear that Hume rejects evidentialism as untrue, it seems clear that he thought no human could or should try to live by it.

Here I do not directly challenge the evidentialist principle. I want to claim rather, that it is a surprising principle for a traditional Christian to adopt. Christians have traditionally held that "without faith it is impossible to please God." My thesis is that a traditional view of the nature of faith (not just its content) is incompatible with the adoption of the evidentialist principle, at least in some of its stronger forms. I will try to substantiate my thesis by examining the concepts of faith articulated by St. Thomas Aquinas and John Calvin, two of the most important and influential theologians in Western Christendom and two theologians who might be supposed to take rather different attitudes toward evidentialism. I will explain Aquinas's view of faith, showing how natural theology fits in with it. Calvin's view of faith will be seen to be remarkably similar to Aquinas's, although Calvin takes a far dimmer view of natural theology.

Turning to the evidentialist principle, I distinguish and consider a number of versions, showing that the nature of faith is incompatible with the bolder versions of this principle. Yet neither Aquinas nor Calvin thought that it was noetically improper or irrational to be a Christian believer without the sort of evidence typically demanded nowadays for "rational belief." The idea that the Christian faith is irrational derives from skeptical fideists of a later period.[2] Our examination of Aquinas's and Calvin's views makes it clear that their views of

---

2. For an account of this, see Richard Popkin, *The History of Skepticism from Eramus to Spinoza* (Berkeley: University of California Press, 1979). See also T. Penelhum, *God and Skepticism* (Dordrecht: D. Reidel, 1983).

faith are compatible only with more subtle, nuanced versions of evidentialism.[3]

AQUINAS ON FAITH

Faith is a virtue, the first of the three theological virtues, according to Thomas Aquinas. This way of understanding the nature of faith is influenced by the fact that the Scriptures commend faith, hold up for emulation a number of "heroes of faith," and teach that God both desires faith and is pleased by it. Faith makes certain actions good. Faith is classified as a theological virtue because of its object—God. This is *Christian* **faith,** which is virtuous. Faith in the more generic sense is not always virtuous. St. Thomas describes this latter kind of faith as "that by which we are said to believe that about which we have an opinion which we hold tenaciously, or to believe on the testimony of some man."[4] The cultivation of such a habit seems unlikely to guarantee an intellectually respectable result. In general, faith is not a virtue. I wish here to examine the nature of Christian faith, partly to see what in its nature makes it virtuous.

Virtues are habits. A habit is a disposition toward some good end effected by repeating some appropriate acts over and over. Two of the most important good ends in human life are contemplating the truth and being happy. The intellectual virtues make their possessor apt to discover and contemplate the truth, while practicing the moral virtues, or cardinal virtues, produces happiness. While the moral virtues aim at a good in accord with human nature, God has seen fit to offer us an even higher, supernatural happiness. This happiness is a good beyond human nature, achievable only with God's help and ultimately terminating in God himself—an eternal life of loving contemplation of God. This is the end of the theological virtues.

Virtues, like all habits, are known by their acts, says Thomas. The act of faith, its inner act, is belief. There is also an outward act, confession, but it does not necessarily have to be performed in order for a person to have faith. Belief he defines as "thinking with assent," following the authority of St. Augustine (*De veritate* XIV, 1; *STh*, II of II, q. 2, art. 1). The kind of thinking involved in belief, and hence in faith, differs

3. The second and third sections of this paper deal with Aquinas's views of faith and natural theology. They overlap with section 2 of Wolterstorff's paper in this volume. I emphasize more than he does the *act* of faith, but the reader who has studied his paper may be able to skip these two sections of the present paper.

4. St. Thomas Aquinas, *Truth*, a translation of *Quaestiones disputate de veritate* by James V. McGlynn (Chicago: Regnery, 1953), vol. II, q. 14, ch. 2. Hereafter references to this volume will be indicated parenthetically in the text as *De veritate*, followed by the question and chapter numbers. References will also be made to Thomas's *Summa theologica* (*STh*) and *Summa contra gentiles* (*SCG*).

from that involved in knowing, which correlates with Aquinas's view that belief and knowledge are mutually exclusive. The thinking that takes place when we know is an act of having some proposition present to the mind. But this is not thinking, more properly speaking, says Aquinas. Properly speaking, thinking is weighing, pondering. Believing involves deliberation, an examination aimed at making up one's mind. The thinking that characterizes belief is a thinking over of things that culminates in firm assent.[5] Belief involves the resolution of some indecision and inquiry. Knowledge, on the other hand, involves no indecision or inquiry in the relevant sense. When we know, the intellect is moved directly to assent by its clear grasp of the object of knowledge. The assent of the knower is the result of a clear vision of the truth.

Belief's assent is due to an act of the will. This assent is firm and unwavering, unlike the tentative assent of opinion or suspicion, but it is not brought about by direct evidence as is the assent of knowledge.[6] How does this firm assent of the will come about? The will is moved by a desire for the good. Assent may seem "good or fitting" (*De veritate* XIV, 1). In the case of Christian faith, the will moves the intellect to assent and is prompted by a desire for God and eternal life, the reward promised for faith.

In a properly meritorious or virtuous act of faith, the assent to the truths about God must come from "a free will that is moved by God through his grace" (*STh*, II of II, q. 2, art. 9). The will's consent is free of coercion; it is not forced either by the weight of evidence or by threats. Herein lies its merit—not merely that it effects assent but that it does so from a loving desire for God. This is clear from Aquinas's contrast between the belief of the faithful and the belief of the devils described by St. James (2:19).

> Now the will's influencing the intellect towards assent can come about from either of two sources. The first is the will's own relationship toward the good, and it is on this basis that belief is a praiseworthy act. The second source is the mind's being convinced, even though not on the basis of internal evidence, to the point of judging that what is proposed ought to be believed. . . .
>
> The belief of Christ's faithful is praiseworthy in being of the first kind indicated. The devils have no such faith, but only one of the second sort. They see many clear signs on the basis of which they perceive that the Church's teaching is from God. . . .
>
> Hence: The devil's faith is, so to speak, forced from them by the

5. I should add that these "things being thought over" in the kind of thinking found in faith are universal concepts (*intentiones universales*). These are general intellectual concepts, not particular sensory concepts (*STh*, II of II, q. 2, art. 1).

6. Thomas holds that the will has no role in scientific knowledge, that the "intelligible object" brings about the assent of the intellect either immediately, as when the object is self-evident, or mediately, when the object is demonstrated (*De veritate* XIV, 1).

evidence of signs. That they believe, then, is in no way to the credit of their wills. [*STh*, II of II, q. 5, art. 2]

Christian faith, the "belief of Christ's faithful," requires that the assent of the will come about as result of a loving trust and not be caused by evidences. There is no denial that there is evidence, but it is denied that the believer's will is moved to belief by it.

Thomas further clarifies his view of how this assent comes about in *STh*, II of II, q. 6, art. 1, in the question about the cause of faith. There he identifies two types or causes of assent. "One is a cause that persuades from without, e.g., a miracle witnessed or a human appeal urging belief." But such causes are not sufficient causes, as is shown by the fact that they do not always work when they are present. It can happen that two persons may witness a miracle or hear a sermon and only one believes. So an internal cause is required, "one that influences a person inwardly to assent to the things of faith." Because in faith a person assents to something beyond anything human nature can aspire to or attain, it must have a supernatural source—God. "The assent of faith . . . , therefore, has as its cause God, moving us inwardly through grace."

We can summarize Aquinas's view of faith in his definition. We have just seen that faith is belief, "an act of mind fixed on one alternative by reason of the will's command" (*STh*, II of II, q. 4, art. 1), and that the will is moved by the grace of God. Aquinas spends some time explaining how the apparent definition of Hebrews 11:1 satisfies the criteria for a good definition and is in fact equivalent to the definition given by him and the other medieval authorities. His "official" version is this: "Anyone interested in reducing the text to definitional form can say that faith is that habit of mind whereby eternal life begins in us and which brings the mind to assent to things that appear not" (*STh*, II of II, q. 4, art. 1; *cf. De veritate* XIV, 2). This definition identifies the object of faith as "things that appear not." So far we have concentrated on the act; let us turn to the object.

Because faith is an act of the intellect, it has an intellectual object. The object of the intellect is the truth and the object of faith is the first truth. Now, of course, the first truth is God. But God is not in human intellects; the thing is in the intellect according to the mode of the knower. Since human knowledge comes in the form of propositions, the human intellect's apprehension of the Divine Truth takes the form of assent to propositions.

What is the source of these propositions that we must know in order to have our highest happiness? Basically they come from God, through Christ or the biblical authors. God has seen to it that these propositions have been revealed to human beings. God rewards the trusting belief in these propositions with an eternal life of happiness in which Christians will know what they had accepted by faith in this life. Knowledge of some of these propositions in this life by a believer constitutes a beginning of the beatific vision that is the proper supernatural end of man. Aquinas notes that this vision in the final analysis consists in a knowledge higher than our 'natural knowledge', scientific knowledge (that is, natural theology) and faith. Such knowledge will come only after the soul has been freed from the limitations on its ability to know that are imposed by its need to obtain its concepts through the senses. In the afterlife, the soul will enjoy the perfection of vision now enjoyed by God and the blessed.

The act of faith is a single act describable in at least three different ways: *credere Deum, credere Deo,* and *credere in Deum. Credere Deum* describes faith as a belief in God, that is, holding various Christian beliefs *about* God. This also involves holding any given Christian belief in a different way from that of the unbeliever.[7] *Credere Deo* refers primarily to the belief or trust placed in God as the source of the articles of faith. We rely on God. The beliefs and promises held in faith are believed because they come from God.[8] Finally, *credere in Deum* refers to the desire for God that characterizes faith. So this third description characterizes faith from the point of view of the will. Desire for God and his reward of eternal happiness prompts the will to move the intellect to assent. It is this third way of characterizing faith that is used in the creed (symbolum) when the believer confesses, "Credo in unum deum."[9]

As a kind of belief, faith has a place in the hierarchy of intellectual activities between scientific knowledge and opinion. Scientific knowledge is the highest act of the intellect. It is certain assent, given without fear or even thought of contradiction, brought about by the intellect's clear vision of the truth. The will is not involved in this act of scientific knowing. Faith is likewise a certain assent, but in the act of faith the certitude is the product of an unshakable will. It is not prompted by the clear vision of the truth. Indeed, in faith the clear vision of the truth is lacking; the object of faith is "unseen" and hence the certitude cannot come about in this way. Below faith is opinion. Here also the evidence is

7. St. Thomas observes that both a believer and an unbeliever can believe that God exists. But, says Thomas, they do not believe in the same way (*STh,* II of II, q. 2, art. 3, ad 3).
8. In scholastic terms, *credere Deo* characterizes faith by specifying the formal object of the intellect, while *credere Deum* specifies the material object of the act of faith.
9. Interestingly, the language of the creed shifts to the mode of "belief that" as the believer professes to believe "unam sanctam Catholicam et apostolicam ecclesiam," and so on for the remainder of the creed.

not conclusive; the vision of the truth is not clear and the assent is not certain. Suspicion and doubt rank lower yet because of the lack of full conviction (see *De veritate* XIV, 1, 2 and 9; *STh*, II of II, q. 4, art. 1). So knowledge is the highest state of the highest part of us, followed by belief (including faith), opinion, and doubt. But the object of belief in the case of faith is higher than the object of scientific knowledge can be in this life.

NATURAL THEOLOGY

Before trying to relate Aquinas's view about faith to evidentialism, we must also consider his views about natural theology, since natural theology is concerned with evidences and proofs for various articles of faith. Here I must concentrate on the nature of natural theological knowledge and its relationship to the articles of faith and to the need for faith.

Natural theology is the branch of philosophy in which various truths about God are "proved demonstratively by the philosophers, guided by the light of natural reason" (*SCG* I, 3, 2). God is its material object, to use the Aristotelian terminology, but God is not its formal object. The assent one gives to propositions about God in natural theology is the assent of knowledge, which is elicited from intellect automatically, so to speak, by its clear vision of the truth. Such knowledge proceeds from that which is self-evident and deducible from the self-evident. It is a purely natural and scientific knowledge. As scientific knowledge, it is a higher state than faith. Can natural theology then replace faith?

In one sense it sometimes does replace faith. When a believer comes to understand an article of faith by means of natural demonstration, there is scientific knowledge of it. It is no longer assented to in faith, for science and faith are mutually exclusive (*STh*, II of II, q. 1, art. 5, ad 4; *De veritate* XIV, 9). However, this scientific knowledge of God is difficult to obtain. It takes considerable intellectual ability and a long period of training. In addition to these problems, which only a few people can overcome, there is the problem of our human propensity to make mistakes, as an examination of the works of the various philosophers illustrates (*SCG* I, 4; *STh*, II of II, q. 2, art. 4). The student of natural theology, Thomas implicitly suggests, should not suspend belief in the articles of faith nor even withhold assent from those articles that can be expected to become items of knowledge. "That science capable of proving God's existence and other matters about him is last to be studied, many other sciences being presupposed to it. Consequently, without faith a person would come to a knowledge [cogitatio] about God only late in life" (*STh*, II of II, q. 2, art. 4). Natural theologians should not wait for scientia but should have faith and pursue the broader knowledge (cogitatio) of God before they have scientia.

Furthermore, the knowledge that one gains by means of natural theology is not very ample, and it is negative. Our method of demonstration in natural theology is a *via negativa;* it uses the way of remotion (*SCG* I, 14). It provides us with a vision not of what God is but only of what he is not. Not that this knowledge is worthless; it is worth a great deal. It tells us much about how God differs from other things and as such is proper knowledge. But it affords an inadequate conception of God and falls far short of what a person must believe to obtain eternal happiness. A faith that goes beyond natural theology remains necessary in this life, but both will be superseded in the life to come.

> The final perfection toward which man is ordained consists in the perfect knowledge of God, which, indeed, a man can reach only if God, who knows himself perfectly, undertakes to teach him. Early in life, however, man is not capable of receiving perfect knowledge. So, he has to accept certain things on faith and by means of these he is led on till he arrives at perfect knowledge.
>
> Now, some of these things are such that they can never be perfectly known in this life, for they wholly transcend the power of human reason. These we must believe as long as we are in this life. However, we shall see them perfectly in heaven. [*De veritate* XIV, 10; cf. *STh*, II of II, q. 2, art. 3]

This beatitude is one of the primary purposes of natural theology. The natural theologian engages in the required learning for the greater happiness that his scientific knowledge produces. Natural theology is a pursuit of wisdom, a more perfect pursuit "because, in so far as a man gives himself to the pursuit of wisdom, so far does he even now have some share in true beatitude" (*SCG* I, 2, 1). Aquinas also cites from Aristotle several considerations that make it "clear that even the most imperfect knowledge about the most noble realities brings the greatest perfection to the soul" (*SCG* I, 5, 5).

This positive benefit of natural theology for the believer seems to me to be the primary purpose for making known "the truth that the Catholic faith professes" (*SCG* I, 2, 2), but it is not the only purpose. Although when we discuss Christianity with Jews, we share the Old Testament as an authority, and in arguments with heretics we have the New Testament in common as well, when we deal with Mohammedans and pagans, no such appeal is effective. "We must, therefore, have recourse to the natural reason, to which all men are forced to give their assent"

(*SCG* I, 2, 3).[10] Not only can natural theology provide a way to demonstrate articles of the Christian faith to unbelievers, it also gives a way of refuting many errors. There are apparently two different sorts of things to be done. The natural theologian, having demonstrated the omniscience of God or the immateriality of God, is then in a position to refute some common misconceptions about the nature of the deity. And second, he may use his insight and arguments to refute arguments and objections raised against these articles of the faith.

The proofs of natural theology are sometimes called the motives of credibility. That is to say, they give some credibility to the articles of faith that come after, even though they provide no direct evidence for them. St. Thomas also refers to those truths proven by natural theology as the preambles to faith (*STh* Ia, q. 2, art. 2, ad 1). For anyone who has obtained demonstrative knowledge of these opening articles of the faith, the articles are no longer believed but known. Thus they are no longer properly regarded by that person as articles of his faith. In such a person, these truths now constitute preambles, a kind of introduction, to the articles he holds by faith.

CALVIN ON FAITH

The name of the great Reformation theologian John Calvin is not among those that first come to mind when one thinks of rational defenses of theism. The Reformed stream of Protestantism, of which Calvin is the fountainhead, has been outspoken in its criticism of proofs of God's existence and other natural theological arguments. One of the best known and most vociferous of such critics in the twentieth century is Karl Barth. In philosophical circles, Alvin Plantinga, also a Calvinist, has presented to the American Catholic Philosophical Association "The Reformed Objection to Natural Theology."[11]

In spite of criticisms of natural theology, theology, and "scholasticism" among Calvinists, Calvin himself is regarded as one of the more intellectual Protestant theologians. According to Edward Dowey, "Calvin's theology exalts the category of knowledge."[12] It might be interest-

---

10. Interestingly, St. Thomas goes on to add immediately that "it is true that in divine matters the natural reason has its failings."

11. *Proceedings of the American Catholic Philosophical Association* 54 (1980): 49–62. Plantinga there provides references to a number of Calvinists' objections to natural theology in general and proofs of God's existence in particular. (Some of these later Calvinists may have been guilty of the very confusion about the role of the theistic arguments that Nicholas Wolterstorff's paper tries to dispel.)

12. *The Knowledge of God in Calvin's Theology* (New York: Columbia University Press, 1952), p. 3.

ing, then, to see how Calvin's views compare with those of Aquinas on the subject of faith.

Calvin's presentation is not as subtle, as detailed, or as refined as St. Thomas's, partly because he is not interested in giving an account of faith for the sake of having a true, accurate, articulate, theoretical account. Calvin wants an account that will conduce more directly to piety on the part of believers. Yet, as I will try to show, Calvin's view of faith, when unpacked a bit, is remarkably similar to that of Aquinas. Calvin defines faith as "a firm and certain knowledge of God's benevolence toward us, founded on the truth of the freely given promise in Christ, both revealed to our minds and sealed upon our hearts through the Holy Spirit" (*Institutes* III, ii, 7).[13] Calvin's apparent location of faith in the category of knowledge is initially eye-catching, but he subsequently makes it clear that "the knowledge of faith consists in assurance rather than in comprehension" (*Institutes* III, ii, 14). This statement should not be taken to mean that Calvin implicitly retracts his claim that faith is a form of knowledge. Rather, I think it means that faith is knowledge in a popular and common sense of knowledge, even though faith might not turn out to be knowledge in a more technical or scientific sense of knowledge. Aquinas also sanctions this usage in *De veritate* XIV, 2, ad 15, as a popular usage, but he uses his more technical and precise terms consistently in his exposition. Calvin prefers biblical terminology, and the Bible is full of references to the "knowledge" of God. The characterization of the knowledge of faith as assurance should not be taken as implying that faith's certitude is merely psychological, however. The believer is justifiably confident, possessing a confidence that results from a kind of illumination.

Calvin is clearly concerned with the kind of faith that theologians call "true" or "saving" faith. He rails at the scholastic notions of "implicit" faith and "unformed" faith.[14] But unlike Aquinas, Calvin offers no theory of the operation of the intellect in order to flesh out his account of the intellectual component of faith. Far from denying that there is an intellect component, however, Calvin insists on an explicit em-

13. John Calvin, *Institutes of the Christian Religion*, trans. Ford Lewis Battles, Library of Christian Classics (Philadelphia: Westminster Press, 1960). Hereafter, references to this work will be incorporated into the text, indicating the book, chapter, and section referred to.

14. *Institutes* III, ii, 2 and 3. This does not, I believe, put him at odds with Aquinas, because Aquinas is careful to hold that we must explicitly believe some things in order to be saved (*STh*, II of II, q. 2, art. 5) and clearly rejects "implicit" faith as having any merit (*STh*, II of II, q. 4, art. 4). Although Aquinas holds that these aberrant varieties of faith still deserve the name faith, at least in some degenerate sense, he also holds that they do not constitute the sort of faith a Christian must have.

ployment of it, criticizing the Roman Catholics for allowing this requirement to be weakened by accepting overly permissive forms of "implicit faith." In what little description of the operation of the intellect he gives, Calvin's view resembles Aquinas's.

There is a kind of comprehension by which we have a grasp of sensible things, our knowledge of "earthly things." The human mind, even the minds of pagans, can achieve a great deal here. Although he does not produce a theoretical account of how it happens, Calvin seems to think that in this area of human thought, such certainty as we have is produced by the clarity of our comprehension. In a vague form, Calvin's view parallels Aquinas's view about science and how in science the intellect achieves certitude.

Like Aquinas, Calvin thinks that the clarity of comprehension that we can have in our knowledge of earthly things is not the source of faith's certitude. What the believer knows (that is, the content of faith) goes beyond the capacity of the senses to deliver certitude. Calvin says: "When we call faith 'knowledge' we do not mean comprehension of the sort that is commonly concerned with those things which fall under human sense perception. For faith is so far above sense that man's mind has to go beyond and rise above itself in order to attain it. Even where the mind has attained, it does not comprehend what it feels" (*Institutes* III, ii, 14). He says elsewhere that "there is one kind of understanding of earthly things; another of heavenly" (*Institutes* II, ii, 13). Thus Calvin agrees with Aquinas that the grasp of what is believed by faith differs from the grasp of scientific knowledge.

For Calvin, faith must be "firm and certain." We have now seen that the source of this certainty is not the clarity of ordinary comprehension. The certainty is the work of the Holy Spirit. The Spirit illuminates our understanding of God's truth and applies it to our hearts: "But our mind has such an inclination to vanity that it can never cleave fast to the truth of God; and it has such a dullness that it is always blind to the light of God's truth. Accordingly, without the illumination of the Holy Spirit, the Word can do nothing. From this, also, it is clear that faith is much higher than human understanding. And it will not be enough for the mind to be illumined by the Spirit of God unless the heart is also strengthened and supported by his power" (*Institutes* III, ii, 33). Two sections later Calvin cites the Apostle Paul as teaching that "faith does not depend upon men's wisdom, but is founded upon the might of the Spirit" (*Institutes* III, ii, 33). This I take to be Calvin's explanation of what happens when, in St. Thomas's words, faith is "infused into us" by the grace of God.

Calvin emphasizes more than Aquinas the way in which faith must become the activity of the person as a whole, not just an act of the intellect. If it is only intellectual, it is not faith. "For the Word of God is not received by faith if it flits about on the top of the brain, but when it takes root in the depth of the heart" (*Institutes* III, ii, 36). But although in Calvin there is a difference in emphasis and an extensive attempt to draw out more pastoral implications, the teaching is the same as Aquinas's. Mere assent is not meritorious faith, the faith that brings salvation. The will must love and trust God.

Calvin trusts man's native intellectual powers far less than Aquinas does. Nevertheless he readily agrees that people are rational, that there is a great deal we can know, that there is in fact a natural knowledge of God (arising from the *sensus divinitatis* innate in us), and that there are rational evidences that the Scriptures are veracious and come from God. Calvin does not want us to make any of these evidences the source of our confidence and trust in God. There may be many indications of God, more than enough to justify our assent to the claim that God exists, but such things are not the ultimate source or ground of our belief that God exists. Although there are ample evidences of the reliability of Scriptures available independently of the work of the Spirit, these evidences must never be the basis of our confidence.

In the opening chapter of Book I of his *Institutes*, Calvin repeatedly claims that "there is within the human mind, and indeed by natural instinct, an awareness of divinity [*divinitatis sensum*]" (I, iii, 1). But God "not only sowed in men's minds that seed of religion . . . but revealed himself and daily discloses himself in the whole workmanship of the universe" (I, v, 1). Calvin never advances any of the many considerations he brings forward as arguments or demonstrations in any rigorous logical or scientific sense.[15] But he obviously thinks that there is some evidence (in a broad sense) for the existence of God available to everyone. Here again, it seems that Aquinas may agree. Consider the following passage from Aquinas:

> For there is a common and confused knowledge of God which is found in practically all men; this is due either to the fact that it is self-evident that God exists, just as other principles of demonstration are . . . or, what seems indeed to be true, that man can immediately reach some sort of knowledge of God by natural reason. For, when men see that

15. I am not sure that we should make too much of this. Although Calvin was trained in law and philosophy, his humanistic training was apparently most influential. His erudition was in the fields staked out by the humanists. This suggests that Calvin would be unlikely to offer his evidence in the form of a rigorous argument, and this may be the reason why he did not, rather than because he took belief in God to be basic.

things in nature run according to a divine order, and that ordering does not occur without an orderer, they perceive in most cases that there is some orderer of the things that we see. But who or what kind of being, or whether there is but one orderer of nature, is not yet grasped in this general consideration. [*SCG* I, 38, 1][16]

Perhaps the knowledge of which Calvin speaks is an account of what Thomas here distinguishes as the "immediately" reached knowledge of God, except that Calvin adds that there is also an "awareness of divinity." Calvin might be willing to accept the arguments for God's existence in natural theology as refinements of these evidences.

Calvin attaches little or no value to this information about God, not because the evidence is so bad or inadequate or unclear, but because it is not the kind of knowledge of God that conduces to the saving love of God. This "natural" knowledge has no value, or perhaps some instrumental value in so far as it might open us up to the knowledge of "the truth of the freely given promise in Christ: sealed upon our hearts through the Holy Spirit." The knowledge naturally available to us is not sufficient to generate love of God; but that is the point of knowledge of God for both Calvin and Aquinas.

The additional knowledge of God, according to Calvin, must come from the Scriptures. Knowing that there is an eternal supreme being or an omniscient, omnipotent first mover is of little value by itself. We must come to know (be assured) that God is our creator and redeemer, and the only way we can acquire this knowledge is from the Scriptures—from the Word of God.

But how do we discover that the Scriptures are credible? We might do so by means of human reason, according to Calvin. The title of chapter 8 of Book I of the *Institutes* claims that, "so far as human reason goes, sufficiently firm proofs are at hand to establish the credibility of scripture." The "proofs" turn out to be from a more or less standard list, many items from which are cited by Aquinas as well: the superiority of scriptural wisdom to human wisdom, the antiquity of Scripture, miracles, the fulfillment of prophecy, the acceptance of Scripture by the Church, and the testimony of the martyrs.[17]

Although the credibility of the Scriptures may be reasonably established, Calvin clearly teaches that the Christian must rely not on such reasons but upon the testimony of the Holy Spirit. "And the certainty it deserves with us, it attains by the testimony of the Holy Spirit. For even

---

16. This passage contains a few interesting anticipations of Hume's criticisms of the argument from design.

17. See *SCG* I, 6.

if it wins reverence for itself by its own majesty, it seriously affects us only when it is sealed upon our hearts through the Spirit" (*Institutes* I, vii, 5). Why does Calvin proceed this way? Calvin believes that our reason is always suspect. If we start with the arguments and evidences, basing our trust on them, there will always be some doubt. "Unless this certainty, higher and stronger than any human judgment, be present, it will be vain to fortify the authority of Scripture by arguments. . . . For unless this foundation is laid, its authority will always remain in doubt" (*Institutes* I, viii, 1). The proper order, Calvin says, is to trust Scripture first and then to consider the evidence. "Conversely, once we have embraced it devoutly as its dignity deserves, and have recognized it to be above the common sort of things, those arguments—not strong enough before to engraft and fix the certainty of Scripture in our minds—become very useful aids" (*Institutes* I, viii, 2). To sum up Calvin's point here, the credibility of Scripture and the Christian's reliance on it should not be based on evidence, even though there is ample evidence. The basis is the internal working of the Holy Spirit.

For both Calvin and Aquinas, the sufficient cause of faith must lie beyond the evidence for two reasons. First, the believer's certainty, which is part of faith, does not and can not be accounted for in terms of the arguments and evidences, and, second, there is a large group of persons possessing these same evidences who do not come to have faith. The proper explanation is the one taught by Scripture—that faith is given of God through the work of his Spirit.

AGREEMENT OF AQUINAS AND CALVIN

Before I turn to evidentialism it might be useful to summarize some of the main points about the nature of faith that are relevant to the evidentialist thesis and on which Calvin and Aquinas agree.

First, both of these theologians agree that faith is necessary for salvation. It is indispensable; no one, not even the most brilliant natural theologian, can be without it. Second, faith is a virtue.[18] It is desirable and extends our noblest and highest desires. It brings us closer to what we were made for. Indeed, for Calvin, without faith we have no virtue. Not only is it not noetically improper or substandard for us to have faith, faith fits right in with our noetic capacities, complementing them,

---

18. It is not clear that Aquinas and Calvin understand virtue in the same way, however. See Robert M. Adams, "The Virtue of Faith," *Faith and Philosophy* 1, no. 1 (1984): 1–17, for an illuminating reflection on how faith can be a virtue.

extending them, and correcting them.[19] Yet, as both Aquinas and Calvin insist, faith goes beyond any evidence and insight of which we are capable in this life. The object of faith, that which is believed and must be believed, is "unseen." Both men take this declaration to mean that all in this present life and in this present state possess an inadequate evidential case for the overall content of faith.

Yet there are ample evidences for the truth of the faith. Both Aquinas and Calvin agree that belief that there is a God is ordinarily rational, something for which there are evidences, although they may disagree on how that belief may arise from the evidence. Both of these men agree that the holding of articles of faith is not based on and does not rely on any evidences for its certitude. Their accounts of how and why are somewhat different, but the conclusion is the same. And finally, each holds that faith requires a certainty that cannot be rooted in sensory experience because of the nature of what must be believed.

One potentially interesting area of disagreement between Aquinas and Calvin is Calvin's view that we are blinded to the truth by wickedness and the consequences of wickedness. While Aquinas seems to think we must catch the vision of higher happiness, Calvin holds that there are impediments to be removed that cannot be moved simply by additional information, evidence, or rational argumentation.[20]

EVIDENTIALISM

Now it is time to see how the evidentialist challenge comports with Aquinas's and Calvin's view of faith. Nicholas Wolterstorff argues that Aquinas and Calvin wrote in an intellectual climate that preceded the evidentialist challenge,[21] and I agree with his conclusion. Because they antedate the challenge, it may not always be possible to derive from their writing a clear response to the varieties of evidentialism that could be considered. These two theologians give an orthodox picture of faith as it was understood prior to the skeptical challenges of the early modern era and prior to the evidentialism of the enlightenment. Only later, and perhaps as a consequence of these challenges, do we see a wider spectrum of views of faith.

Evidentialism may come in many forms, and I have neither the time nor the ability to examine them all. In this section, I will exhibit some

19. Cf. Aquinas, *SCG* I, 7.
20. This idea of "epistemic blindness" is being explored by Mark Talbot in a doctoral dissertation for the University of Pennsylvania.
21. See Wolterstorff's paper in this volume.

forms of evidentialism drawn from claims to be found in philosophical writing and based on distinctions that need to be made. Then I suggest the reaction of the Thomist or Calvinist. Here I will construe evidentialism as a principle that applies to theistic beliefs, more specifically to beliefs that comprise Christian theism. However, I believe that what I and others are calling evidentialism is the application to religious beliefs of a more general philosophical position. Many formulations of it appeal to general epistemological claims, and unless that is the case or some other explanation is forthcoming, it is hard to construe these objections as something more than an ad hoc objection to religious belief. There are some other issues that I cannot resolve here. I shall not try to say to what extent, if any, our beliefs are under our direct control. I simply assume that we can do things to acquire beliefs and to prevent ourselves from acquiring beliefs, and therefore it is sensible to hold persons responsible for at least some of their beliefs. Likewise I will not try to say what constitutes adequate evidence. That issue must be settled by the particular epistemological theory being conjoined with the evidentialist principle. However, I do assume that adequate evidence must be evidential support bearing on the truth of the belief it is supposed to support. And I assume that this evidence is inferential, although I am prepared to construe "inference" broadly, meaning "based on" some other belief or beliefs.

If we initially construe evidentialism as the thesis that unless one has adequate evidence for one's theistic beliefs, those beliefs are irrational, then we must make a further distinction. When we call a person's belief irrational, we may mean that in acquiring the belief or in holding it this person violated some intellectual duty.[22] Such a person has done something he ought not have done; he has violated a duty. Presumably if a person finds that he has acquired a belief in some illicit fashion, he should abandon it unless he can find a proper way of holding it. The word "irrational" as thus applied to someone's belief is a normative term.

In the second sense, to call a person's beliefs irrational need not imply that they have been acquired illegitimately or in violation of some epistemic or moral duty. To call a belief irrational in this sense is simply to make a judgment about the place it has in a structure of beliefs in which some beliefs support others. An irrational belief lacks the kind or

22. For a more detailed description of this sense, see Alvin Plantinga, "Reason and Belief in God," pp. 29–39, and Nicholas Wolterstorff, "Can Belief in God Be Rational?" pp. 141–45, in *Faith and Rationality*, ed. Plantinga and Wolterstorff.

amount of evidential support in a person's belief structure that is necessary to render it well founded. Epistemic rules are here taken to be descriptive of a properly formed structure of knowledge and are not statements of duty. A person might come to hold such an irrational belief in a way that is neither morally nor epistemically censurable. This person would not be irrational in the first sense, but he would be in the second sense.

David Hume may be an example of someone who uses this distinction. According to Hume, our belief in the causal principles we hold is irrational in the second, descriptive sense, in that such beliefs lack proper evidential support. And Hume seems to accept the structural evidentialism, that these beliefs would not be part of a rational noetic structure. But he does not recommend that any of us give them up. Of course, he would regard that as idle advice, since we are incapable of following it. Hume apparently holds that we do not have an obligation to give up these admittedly defective beliefs and thus he appears to reject the first kind of evidentialism, the kind I have called normative. I do not know whether evidentialist objectors have often made this distinction, but I shall use it here. Accordingly, we will distinguish two versions of each form of evidentialism, a normative version and a structural version.

It is also important to keep in mind that foundationalist theories of evidence distinguish between basic and nonbasic beliefs. Nonbasic beliefs presumably rest upon, that is, draw their evidential support from, other beliefs. Basic beliefs lack evidence in this sense, although in an extended sense of evidence, there may be evidence for them, too (for example, having had a certain kind of experience or thought). Accordingly, we shall have to be alert to the kind of evidence an evidentialist objector might claim is lacking.

Many of the recent discussions of evidentialism and of the rationality of theism (for example, by Plantinga, Wolterstorff, Alston, and Mackie) focus on the rationality of belief in God. But, of course, believing that there is a God is only the barest beginning toward believing in God, according to Aquinas and Calvin. There are quite a number of things to be believed, which are summarized, let us say, in the Nicene Creed. Accordingly, we can ask (1) are Aquinas's and Calvin's views about belief in God incompatible with the evidentialist principle, and (2) would they think that such a principle could be correctly applied to one's acceptance of the further extended list of the articles of the faith as found in the Nicene Creed?

Cliffordian evidentialism. This takes its name from W. K. Clifford, author of those immortal words, "it is wrong always, everywhere, and for anyone, to believe anything upon insufficient evidence."[23] This is a form of evidentialism that perhaps merits Stephen Wykstra's description "extravagant" evidentialism.[24] Fortunately, people find themselves incapable of carrying out Clifford's advice and so *do* trust each other beyond what they have evidence for, *do* believe in their ability to perform tasks and feats the evidence suggests are not possible, and *do* accomplish hosts of other things without which human life would be poorer. Cliffordian evidentialism requires every person, regardless of age, intelligence, skills, education, and so forth, to have adequate evidence for all his or her beliefs. All beliefs are guilty until proven innocent.

Following the distinction made earlier, we can divide Cliffordian evidentialism into two types, depending on whether we take the word "wrong" in the above-cited quotation from Clifford to be pointing out a violation of a duty or a defect in structure (or breaking a rule). So we may distinguish a normative version

> (C1) If a person holds a set of beliefs S on the basis of inadequate evidence, then that person has violated an epistemic (or moral) duty and, ceteris paribus, ought to give up some or all the beliefs in S,[25]

from a structural version,

> (C2) If a person holds a set of beliefs S on the basis of inadequate evidence, then that person's belief structure is defective.

We remind ourselves that one can hold structural evidentialism without implying that the person with defective beliefs has any kind of obligation to give them up. Also I have slipped a ceteris paribus clause into (C1) to acknowledge that epistemic obligations are prima facie and may be overridden. Of course, one could be a "hardnosed" Cliffordian

23. W. K. Clifford, "The Ethics of Belief," in *Lecture and Essays* (London: Macmillan, 1877), p. 186, and reprinted in numerous anthologies. Historical accuracy to Clifford's view is not my point here. Clifford may not have wanted this unvarnished version to be taken as seriously as I take it.

24. Stephen Wykstra, "Plantinga versus Evidentialism: Relocating the Issue" (paper read at the Eastern Regional Meeting of the Society of Christian Philosophers, held at the University of Notre Dame, March 9, 1984).

25. A person ought to give up these beliefs until he or she acquires adequate evidence and holds the beliefs on the basis of adequate evidence.

evidentialist and hold that everyone has this epistemic obligation *simpliciter*.

Are either of these versions of Cliffordian evidentialism compatible with the Thomist and the Calvinist conceptions of faith? Consider (C1), where the set of beliefs *S* consists of the belief that God exists. Aquinas and Calvin both believe there is evidence that God exists,[26] enough to lead most people to entertain the belief, although not enough to *compel* everyone who entertains the belief to hold it. Calvin thinks the fact that not all believe shows how strong our sinfulness is rather than how weak the evidence is. However, not every believer believes on the basis of evidence, and those believers who do have adequate evidence have in addition a certitude that is independent of the evidence. If a Plantinganian were temporarily confused by reading J. L. Mackie and no longer accepted the ontological argument, according to Aquinas, then if she is one of the faithful she should continue to believe as confidently as ever that there is a God. Even though God's existence can be known "scientifically," not everyone can, does, or should hold it that way. Furthermore, Aquinas and Calvin think we have a duty to believe that there is a God. This duty derives ultimately from our love of and desire for the Truth, the First Truth—God himself. It is hard for me to believe that they think we could have an epistemic duty which could conflict with this.

Both Calvin and Aquinas insist that there is a knowledge of God that goes beyond anything proofs or evidences can produce. There is a knowledge that there is God that is not of faith. To say "I know that God exists" is not the same as saying "I know that my Redeemer liveth" (Job 19:25). Aquinas can be read as holding that there are degrees of articulateness and insight in various persons' belief in God. In a passage quoted earlier, Aquinas suggests that there is a simple and immediate knowledge of God. Knowledge that God exists in this somewhat confused and inchoate sense amounts to little more than the belief that there is an orderer of the universe. Even the natural theologian's grasp of God's existence is as a first mover, first cause, necessary being, and so on. But the person who has faith goes beyond these to believe that there exists one who is his creator and redeemer (cf. *SCG* I, 5, 3). The distinction here is perhaps not unlike Pascal's contrast between the God of the philosophers and the God of Abraham, Isaac, and Jacob. The content of the simple man's belief that God exists and of the natural theologian's belief both fall short of what the faithful mean when they

---

26. This evidence need not be some other belief; it may be some kind of experience.

say there is a God. The conclusion is that the belief in God required in faith includes a degree of adherence and a connectedness to the whole of Christian belief that violates (C1); Aquinas's and Calvin's views of faith thus conflict with (C1).

This conclusion is compatible, however, with holding that there is and must be adequate evidence for the "minimal" belief that there is a God. It seems that Aquinas and Calvin might accept a Cliffordian evidentialism applied to this minimal sense of the claim that there is a God, provided that an appropriate account of adequate evidence were given or that the possibility that such a belief is basic were not ruled out. Yet it remains the case that the Christian believer's adherence goes beyond what the evidence "allows" on both of their accounts.

The case is equally clear where the set S mentioned in (C1) is the set of basic Christian articles of faith as found in the Nicene Creed. There seems to be no question in the minds of Calvin and Aquinas that many parts of such belief go far beyond any evidence we have. Again, both think that *some* evidence is available: it is to be found in the Scriptures. And there is some evidence, both testimonial and internal, that the Scriptures are the Word of God. This evidence, although it is sufficient to show that belief is not foolish and although it is capable of increasing one's confidence, is not sufficient to compel assent by all rational persons. That it is not compelling is shown by the fact that persons can listen seriously and fail to be persuaded.[27] Besides, these evidences, miracles, fulfillment of prophecy, the exalted character of the message, and so forth, do not meet Aquinas's standard for a "scientific" demonstration. In the final analysis, it rests on something else for the believers—on what Aquinas calls the grace of God or Calvin the "testimony of the Spirit." "Since for unbelieving men religion seems to stand by opinion alone, they, in order not to believe anything foolishly or lightly, both wish and demand rational proof that Moses and the prophets spoke divinely. But I reply: the testimony of the Spirit is more excellent than all reason" (*Institutes* I, vii, 4). Such a basis for belief is not surprising, since these articles of the faith are "unseen," beyond our comprehension, and beyond our powers of evidence gathering and knowing. Principle (C1), where S is the set of articles of the Christian faith, is incompatible with the Thomistic and Calvinistic concepts of faith.

27. Aquinas and Calvin tend to explain this is different ways. For Aquinas, the fact that honest hearers are not persuaded shows that the "case" is not scientifically and rationally airtight. Calvin, however, sees the failure of hearers to believe as evidence that the barriers to belief are deep and subtle, often subconscious, and rooted in human sinfulness.

Principle (C2) is a milder form of Cliffordian evidentialism. It carries no necessary implication that the person with a defective belief is obliged to give up that belief. The question becomes whether St. Thomas or John Calvin might hold that a person's belief in God or belief in the articles of faith (which are "above reason") is epistemically defective if not based upon adequate evidence.

This question is a bit more subtle. Aquinas holds that the simple believer, the natural theologian, and the faithful in this life all have an inferior apprehension of their belief that there is a God. Their apprehension is inferior to what he calls the "Science of God and the blessed" (*STh* Ia, q. 1, art. 3), and it is inferior to scientific knowledge of physical things. It is inferior in the sense that it is neither as clear nor as full as the understanding that God and the blessed have. But it need not be inferior in the sense of lacking the best evidence available in this life. And far from generating a defective belief structure, the beliefs of faith help us anticipate the ideal belief structure of God and the blessed, and they help us get our beliefs into a more perfect kind of alignment.

Calvin may be construed as claiming something even stronger: that any belief structure that fails to include belief in God (including the love and fear of God) and to include it in a primary position is defective and in need of revision. Calvin sounds this theme at the very beginning of the *Institutes,* where he claims that a proper knowledge of oneself is impossible without the knowledge of God (*Institutes* I, i, 2). Both Aquinas and Calvin, it seems clear, hold views about the nature and purpose of faith that are incompatible with (C2).

Lockean evidentialism. Clifford says that if one lacks adequate evidence for a belief, that belief should be given up. Locke and others propose something a bit different—proportioning one's degree of assent to the amount or weight of the evidence. Locke claims this is the mark of genuine lovers of truth: "The not entertaining any Proposition with greater assurance than the proofs it is built upon will warrant."[28] This view is endorsed by Blanshard when he advises us: "Equate your assent to the evidence."[29] This is perhaps a less extravagant form of evidentialism than Clifford's, where one must reach the level of adequate evidence or one is denied a right to the belief.[30]

28. John Locke, *An Essay concerning Human Understanding* (Oxford: Clarendon Press, 1975), p. 697.
29. Brand Blanshard, *Reason and Belief* (New Haven: Yale University Press, 1975), p. 401. Blanshard's version implies that we also have a duty not to believe with *less* assurance than the evidence allows.
30. Locke permits highly probable beliefs to be overridden by revelation, provided that we have adequate reason to believe that the revelation in question is from God.

As before, we may distinguish two forms of this type of evidentialism: a normative form, (L1), and a structural form, (L2):

(L1) If a person holds a set of beliefs S with a degree of assurance exceeding the evidence that person has for S, then that person has violated an epistemic (or moral) duty and, ceteris paribus, ought to reduce the degree of assurance with which he or she believes.

(L2) If a person holds a set of beliefs S with a degree of assurance exceeding the evidence that person has for that belief, then that person's belief structure is defective.

The preceding discussion of the views of faith has made it clear that Aquinas and Calvin call for wholesale violations of these principles. Even where they think there is evidence besides scriptural revelation for the articles of faith, they maintain that these articles should be held with a certitude which exceeds that warranted by such evidence and which would be unaffected by the loss of that evidence. It is safe to conclude that (L1) and (L2) also are incompatible with their concepts of faith.

Communal evidentialism. The forms of evidentialism considered so far, even though seriously proposed, may be thought extravagant and unacceptable on their own merits. William P. Alston has argued against a principle similar to the two just discussed, declaring that it "expresses an unwarranted 'imperialism' of reason." It errs, he says, in that "it takes one sufficient condition for the rationality of belief and inflates it into a necessary condition."[31] So we should look for something more likely to be correct. One suggestion is that it is too strong to require each individual to possess adequate evidence for the beliefs that individual has or to proportion assurance to the amount of evidence available. A more reasonable evidentialist might hold that a person's belief can be rational when his or her community, which there is some reason to trust, teaches that belief to the individual and when the community itself possesses adequate evidence. A belief acquired this way might still be rational if the person in question does not know how or where to discover this evidence or could not understand the evidence if he or she did find it. As with the previous types, I formulate this communal evidentialism in two versions.

31. "The Role of Reason in the Regulation of Belief," in *Rationality in the Calvinian Tradition*, ed. H. Hart, J. van der Hoeven, and N. Wolterstorff (Lanham, Md.: University Press of America, 1983), p. 138.

(CE1)   If the members of a community hold a set of beliefs *S* for which no subset of members of that community possesses adequate evidence, then, ceteris paribus, the members of that community are not rationally entitled to their beliefs and ought to give up some or all the beliefs in *S*.

(CE2)   If the members of a community hold a set of beliefs *S* for which no subset of members of that community possesses adequate evidence, then each member of that community has a defective belief structure.

These formulations are an attempt to begin to capture the way we acquire many of our scientific beliefs, our beliefs about what is happening in the world far away from us, and many other beliefs that we derive by interacting with people around us and trusting what they tell us. Sometimes an "authority" passes the belief on to us—our schoolteacher tells us or we read it in the the *National Enquirer* or whatever. Somebody, we may suppose, has the evidence or knows where and how to get it.

Aquinas and Calvin both seem to allow, if not endorse, the view that belief in God may be properly basic (that is, rationally permissible without being based on evidence). But if it is possible for everyone's belief that there is a God to be properly basic—and I think Calvin would allow that this is possible, and perhaps Aquinas would as well—then they would reject (CE1) as applied to belief in God.

Matters may be a bit different with (CE2). Belief that there is a God might be a belief that everyone is *entitled* to hold without basing one's belief on another belief, and yet belief that there is a God might at the same time be the sort of belief that requires justification or evidence in a nondefective belief structure. Aquinas's arguments for God's existence might be seen as an attempt to show that such evidence can be supplied and to show that some in the community *do* have the evidence and that therefore the believing community cannot be accused of this latter kind of irrationality.

Calvin, on the other hand, may hold that belief in God is immediately justified, and not epistemically based on evidence. If he does, he would reject (CE2). But clearly he also thinks that certain considerations, certain kinds of evidence, are relevant to belief in God. If he thinks that belief in God would not be rational in the absence of these evidences, then he may accept a principle like (CE2). Considering (CE2) with respect to the rest of the beliefs expressed in the creed, it is clear that (CE2) is not rejected. The articles of the faith are derived from and evidentially depend on a variety of sources.

Sensible evidentialism. In a recent paper Stephen Wykstra has suggested another form of evidentialism, which he regards not only as more plausible but also as more accurately expressing the insight that leads people to subscribe to principles of the sort that we have been formulating. He suggests that we have an intuition that some of our beliefs stand in need of inferential justification and others do not. To introduce a piece of his terminology, some of our beliefs are "evidence-essential" while others are not. That is to say, "we consider it essential that there be a good evidential case . . . *available* to the *community*." This means that "if we were to learn that the evidential case . . . is bankrupt . . . , we should take our belief . . . to be in big doxastic trouble."[32] He does not take this to imply that any given believer must hold a given evidence-essential belief on the basis of adequate evidence; some person's belief may be basic in the sense of not being in fact based on any other belief. Nor does it mean that a given believer must be able to produce or discover the evidence for the belief in question. But it does mean that there must *be* a good evidential case, and, according to Wykstra, it must be "available."

Wykstra's candidate for an evidence-essential belief is the belief that there is a God. We may assume that he would say the same for the other beliefs that are part of the Nicene Creed. Sensible evidentialism, it should be noted, makes an important concession; it does not require that a person actually have evidence in order to hold one of these religious beliefs rationally. Rather it claims that religious beliefs, like many other beliefs, are a type of belief that depends on others for justification.[33]

Setting aside the large question of how to understand some of the crucial concepts here, let us speculate about the responses of Aquinas and Calvin. I believe that it cannot be shown that Aquinas's view of faith rules out this sort of evidentialism with respect to the belief that there is a God. With Calvin there is some likelihood that he would reject it, since it is arguable that he thinks that belief in God is not evidence-essential but basic.

The situation seems clearer with respect to other creedal beliefs.

32. Wykstra, "Plantinga versus Evidentialism," unpublished manuscript.

33. The idea of evidence-essentiality seems similar to (although not exactly the same as) an idea Robert Audi introduces in his essay "Direct Justification, Evidential Dependence, and Theistic Belief" in the present volume—that of a belief being "justificatorily dependent." My belief is justificatorily dependent if its justification (and rationality) depends on my having or having had one or more justified (or rational) beliefs whose justification (or rationality) is or was essential to grounding the current justification (or rationality) of the belief in question.

Here it appears that Aquinas and Calvin take these beliefs to be evidence-essential, in some sense at least. The evidence, however, usually consists primarily of other beliefs accepted only by believers. Consider, for example, the confession that "Christ was crucified for us under Pontius Pilate." That Christ was crucified and that Pontius Pilate was the responsible official are understood as historical claims. Extra-biblical evidence is certainly relevant, if not essential. But to affirm that Christ was crucified *for us* is a claim that goes beyond historical evidence and that requires other Christian beliefs as evidence. Aquinas and Calvin both accept the Scriptures as normative for determining theological beliefs, and Calvin holds that unless a doctrine is supported by Scripture, it need not be accepted.

It must be added that this present sense of evidentialism is polemically weaker than the earlier versions, although how weak it is will depend finally upon the theory of justified belief added to it. It does not follow from this version that the person or community that lacks an evidential case ought to give up its belief on pain of being irrational. It is not clear what a person or community ought to do when it finds itself unable at a given moment to give an adequate account of a key belief. Therefore it is not immediately clear how this variety of evidentialism is to be used to press the evidentialist challenge as described in the beginning of this essay.

EPILOGUE

Nothing we have seen suggests that Aquinas or Calvin eschew evidence for belief in God or reject it. Both welcome evidence for Christian beliefs, as well as rational reflection on the Christian faith. For Aquinas, evidence is capable of turning belief into knowledge. Finding evidence, reasons, and arguments can deepen one's insight into the content of the faith and is a positive aid in writing theology. Evidence is desirable and often necessary in dialogue with unbelievers. But Calvin, especially, insists that one's faith is not to be made to depend on arguments and evidences. And both of these theologians reject the idea that faith somehow must rest on evidence to be held justifiedly, unless the "evidence" includes the testimony of the Spirit.

The modern era is filled with people who concluded that evidentialism conflicted with the traditional conception of faith and then tried to adjust their belief structures. Locke is utterly convinced of the truth of a strong form of evidentialism and so he makes adjustments in the concept of faith, subordinating it to the evidentialist principle. The believer must have evidence for the existence of God and evidence that any putative revelation is from God before that revelation is acceptable as an article of faith.[34] Locke's view is that the Christian believer can and must meet the evidentialist challenge. Others hold that believers have no obligation to meet the evidentialist challenge, for a variety of reasons, either because evidence plays no role or need play no role in Christian belief or because the challenge itself is ill founded. Still others, sometimes called skeptical fideists, accept the claim that evidentialism is at the core of rational belief and that Christian beliefs cannot satisfy such a standard, and therefore "reason" is to be rejected in favor of faith.[35] Still others, including some Wittgensteinians, for example, have taken a noncognitivist view of Christian beliefs and evade the evidentialist challenge in that fashion.

Our discussion suggests that it is not as easy as it might seem initially to produce a plausible version of evidentialism. The more plausible the versions become, however, the less obviously incompatible they seem to be with Aquinas's and Calvin's views of faith. I favor the approach being pursued by Plantinga, Wolterstorff, and others, which is to examine the philosophical credentials of the evidentialist challenge and to pursue the accompanying theories of evidence. I think Aquinas and Calvin, too, would favor that approach, if my accounts of their views of faith are correct.

34. As Nicholas Wolterstorff points out in his chapter in this volume, the arguments for God's existence play a different and more crucial role in justifying Locke's faith than they do in the case of Aquinas.

35. Cf. Kierkegaard's discussions of the absolute paradox and of faith as involving the "setting aside" of reason in his *Philosophical Fragments* and in *Fear and Trembling*.

4

Coherentism and the Evidentialist Objection to Belief in God

ALVIN PLANTINGA

According to the evidentialist objection to theistic belief, belief in God—the belief that there is such a person as God—is unreasonable or irrational or intellectually irresponsible or somehow noetically below par.[1] Why so? Because, so the claim goes, there is *insufficient evidence* for it; and there is something improper or defective about believing a proposition for which one has insufficient evidence. In "Reason and Belief in God"[2] and elsewhere, I claimed that the evidentialist objection to theistic belief is typically rooted in *classical foundationalism;* I went on to argue that classical foundationalism is self-referentially incoherent and thus hoist on its own petard. By way of response, William Alston points out that the evidentialist objection need *not* be rooted in classical foundationalism.[3] The fact is, he says, it need not be rooted in founda-

1. Among those who have urged this objection are Brand Blanshard in *Reason and Belief* (London: Allen & Unwin, 1974), pp. 400–433; Antony Flew in *The Presumption of Atheism* (London: Pemberton, 1976), pp. 22–30; Michael Scriven in *Primary Philosophy* (New York: McGraw-Hill, 1966), pp. 87–107; and Bertrand Russell in *Why I Am Not a Christian* (New York: Simon & Schuster, 1957), pp. 3–23. Even more important than these published versions of the evidentialist objection is an enormous oral tradition; this objection is widely popular at nearly any major or minor university.
2. In *Faith and Rationality: Reason and Belief in God,* ed. A. Plantinga and N. Wolterstorff (Notre Dame: University of Notre Dame Press, 1983), pp. 16–93 (hereafter R&BG).
3. "Plantinga's Epistemology of Religious Belief," in *Alvin Plantinga,* ed. James Tomberlin and Peter Van Inwagen (Dordrecht: D. Reidel, 1985).

tionalism of any sort, whether classical or otherwise; it could, for example, be rooted in *coherentism*. Why could not the evidentialist objector raise his evidentialist objection, not from the standpoint of foundationalism, but from a coherentist stance? Indeed, one of the objectors I cited in R&GB is Brand Blanshard, as doughty a coherentist as one will easily find. Of course Alston is right in noting that my treatment of evidentialism suffers from a certain incompleteness. In what follows I shall try to put things right; I propose to explore coherentism, to see whether it offers the resources for something like a viable evidentialist objection to theistic belief. First, I shall briefly delineate the evidentialist objection;[4] in the next two sections I shall try to characterize coherentism by contrasting it with foundationalism; then I shall argue that coherentism does not in fact offer a viable means of mounting an evidentialist objection; and finally I shall argue that in any event coherentism ought to be rejected.

THE EVIDENTIALIST OBJECTION

The evidentialist objector's central claim is that belief in God without evidence—even if in fact there is such a person as God—is wrong, improper, defective, or in some way deplorable. He therefore holds that correct or proper belief in God, if indeed such belief in God is possible, requires evidence; he holds that one who accepts the belief that there is such a person as God but has no evidence for that belief is, so far forth, unjustified, intellectually irresponsible, or in some way unreasonable. Thus Flew: "It is by reference to this inescapable demand for grounds that the presumption of atheism is justified. If it is to be established that there is a God, then we have to have good grounds for believing that this is indeed so. Until or unless some such grounds are produced we have literally no reason at all for believing; and in that situation the only reasonable posture must be that of either the negative atheist or the agnostic."[5]

But how, exactly, are we to understand the evidentialist objector? What, precisely, is his complaint? Here there are several possibilities. Those who state this objection most explicitly—Blanshard, Clifford, and Scriven, for example—appear to be *deontological* evidentialists; they apparently hold that there are intellectual or epistemic duties or obligations, and that the theist without evidence is guilty of flouting

---

4. For a fuller account of the evidentialist objection, see R&GB pp. 17–39.
5. Flew, *Presumption of Atheism*, p. 22.

these obligations.[6] From this point of view, there is at least a prima facie obligation not to accept belief in God without evidence—that is, not to accept belief in God in the absence of other beliefs that evidentially support it.

A crucial problem for the deontological evidentialist is that belief is not for the most part directly within our voluntary control.[7] It is not within my power, for example, to divest myself of the belief that I have a social security number. If you offer me $1 million to stop believing that I have a social security number, it is hard to see how I could collect. (Of course there may be radical procedures—a coma-inducing drug, for example—that would rid me of this belief (as well as of the rest of my beliefs); but I don't need the $1 million *that* badly.) My belief in God, however, is no more within my direct control than is my belief that I have a social security number; how, therefore, could I fulfill this alleged obligation to withhold belief if I have no evidence? Can I have a duty—intellectual or otherwise—to do what it is not within my power to do? I should think not.

Now perhaps the deontological objector is not without reply at this point; but there is (as I see it) a much more promising direction for him to take here. The evidentialist objector, I think, should desert deontological evidentialism for something else—something, barbarism aside, we could call "axiological evidentialism," or more simply "value evidentialism." What she should hold is not that the theist without evidence has flouted some intellectual duty; perhaps he cannot help himself. Nonetheless, his structure of beliefs is in some way *flawed* or *defective*. Consider someone who believes the earth is flat on the basis of an outrageously bad argument. Such a person need not have evaded any obligations (prima facie or otherwise); nevertheless his structure of beliefs reveals a certain unhappy condition, a fault, a flaw, a deficiency, something like such physical deficiencies as, say, astigmatism or tone deafness. One who suffers from astigmatism violates no duty in so suffering and deserves sympathy rather than censure. Still, this condition is unhappy and deplorable; we ought to do what we can to prevent or cure it in ourselves and others. Now the evidentialist objector's best

---

6. Blanshard, *Reason and Belief*, pp. 401–33; and Scriven, *Primary Philosophy*, pp. 103–7. For a fuller characterization of deontological evidentialism, see R&GB, pp. 25–34. I use here the term "deontological" to highlight the fact that evidentialist objectors of this stripe put their objection in terms of *duty* or *obligation*. I do not mean to attribute to them any specific view as to the *nature* of duty or obligation; in particular I do not mean to attribute to them any view about the connection or lack thereof between *duty* and *value* or *the good.*

7. See R&GB, pp. 34–38.

hope, I think, is to hold that belief in God without evidence is just such a flaw or defect. And if belief in God without evidence *is* a noetic defect or deficiency, then (all else being equal) we ought to do what we can to divest ourselves and our students of it and prevent its occurrence in our children.

Suppose we agree that a structure of beliefs can in fact be flawed or defective in the way the value evidentialist objector says it can: why does he credit a theist who has no evidence with this sort of defect or blemish? The answer, I think, is to be seen in the fact that the evidentialist objection is typically rooted in some form of classical foundationalism. According to the classical foundationalist, rational belief has a certain structure.[8] Some beliefs can be rationally held without the evidential support of other beliefs; a self-evident belief such as 2 + 1 = 3 would be an example. A person is rational in accepting or believing such propositions even if he does not believe them on the basis of any other propositions at all; such propositions, we may say, are *properly basic*. Other propositions, however, are not properly basic, and if I am rational in believing one of *those* propositions, then I will believe it only on the basis of beliefs that support it.

A crucial component of classical (or any other) foundationalism is a specification of the sorts of propositions that *are* properly basic. Roughly speaking, according to the ancient and medieval foundationalism of Aristotle and Aquinas, it is self-evident propositions and propositions "evident to the sense," as Aquinas says, that are properly basic; according to modern foundationalism—Descartes, Malebranche, Locke, Leibniz, Berkeley, Hume—it is self-evident propositions together with certain propositions directly about one's experience that deserve this accolade.[9] The belief that there is such a person as God, however, is neither self-evident nor evident to the senses nor about one's own immediate experience; according to classical foundationalism, therefore, it is not properly basic and cannot rationally be accepted without evidence.

FOUNDATIONALISM

If classical foundationalism were correct, the evidentialist objector would be right: a theist without evidence is in some kind of trouble. Of course it is not correct, and she is wrong—or so, at any rate, I argued in

---

8. See R&GB, pp. 48–59. One can be a classical foundationalist with respect to *rationality* (taken as nondefectiveness) but also with respect to *certainty, justification*, and *knowledge*.

9. See R&GB, pp. 55–59.

R&GB. Our present concern, however, is with coherentism. Suppose we agree that classical foundationalism does not offer a viable basis for an evidentialist objection; does coherentism have more to offer? Our first problem, naturally enough, is to characterize coherentism. This problem is not wholly trivial: there is no generally accepted account of the relevant coherence relation. But perhaps we can make some initial progress in explaining coherentism by contrasting it with foundationalism. So suppose we begin by giving a partial account of foundationalism, focusing on those features most relevant to the contrast between coherentism and foundationalism. And since the coherentist is often accused of endorsing *circular reasoning*, we shall pay special attention to the foundationalist's rejection of such reasoning.

Basis and Support

We may see the foundationalist as beginning with the observation that we accept some beliefs as *basic*. If I believe a proposition *p* but do not believe it on the evidential basis of other beliefs I hold, then *p* is basic for me. (It does not follow, of course, that *p* is certain, incorrigible, unrevisable, maximally warranted, or believed more firmly than any belief that is not basic for me.) Many beliefs about one's own immediate experience—the sort of belief I might express by such sentences as "I am feeling tired" or "It seems to me that I see something red" or even "I am being appeared to greenly"—are typically basic for one. It would be difficult, if not impossible, for me to believe the proposition that I seem to see something red on the evidential basis of *other* propositions; such beliefs are basic for me. Many beliefs that we accept a priori are also typically basic for us. For example, I believe such propositions as the corresponding conditional of *modus ponens* and a host of other obvious truths of mathematics and logic in this basic way. Many of these propositions will be apparently self-evident for me; they will display the "evident luster" of which Locke speaks in this connection; a self-evident proposition, he says, displays a kind of "clarity and brightness to the attentive mind." Descartes speaks here of "clarity and distinctness"; each, I think, is referring to the same phenomenal feature. And indeed there *is* a phenomenal, experiential aspect to our apprehension of self-evident truths; but ordinarily, at least, such truths are not believed on the evidential basis of other beliefs detailing this phenomenal aspect.

The above two sorts of beliefs are typically basic for us; according to the modern classical foundationalist, they are also *properly* basic. We may add that many other sorts of belief are typically basic for us—ones with respect to which the modern classical foundationalist will not be quite so indulgent. For example, suppose I seem to see a tree: I have that characteristic sort of experience that as a matter of fact goes with seeing a tree. I may then form the belief that I see a tree. In the typical case, that belief will be basic for me; in the typical case I will not believe the proposition that I see a tree on the basis of other beliefs I hold. In particular, I will not ordinarily accept this proposition on the basis of the proposition that I have that special seeming-to-see-a-tree experience, for I will not ordinarily believe this latter proposition at all. In the typical case I will not be paying any attention to my experience; I will be concentrating on the tree. I will, indeed, *have* the experience in question, but I will not *believe* that I have it. Nor, of course, will I believe I *do not* have it; I will not have any belief on that topic at all. Of course I *could* turn my attention to my experience, notice how things look to me, and acquire the belief that I seem to see something that looks like *that;* and if you challenge my claim to see a tree, perhaps I *will* thus turn my attention to my experience. But ordinarily when I perceive a tree I do not believe (or entertain) any proposition about my experience. Hence I do not believe that I see a tree on the basis of such propositions; I take that proposition as basic; I believe it in the basic way. Here the modern classical foundationalist will disapprove. He need not deny, of course, that we do *in fact* accept such perceptual beliefs in the basic way, but in his view such beliefs are not *properly* basic. The ancient and medieval classical foundationalist, on the other hand, will have no such scruples; perceptual beliefs of this sort, as he sees things, are typically taken as basic and furthermore are properly basic.

A final example: I believe I had breakfast this morning. Once more, I do not believe this proposition on the basis of some belief about my experience—for example, that I *seem to remember* that I had breakfast this morning. Of course there *is* the characteristic sort of experience that goes with remembering that I had breakfast, an experience that involves a felt inclination to believe the proposition in question, together with what we can only call a certain feeling of *pastness.* But ordinarily I will not have considered the question of whether I am having that experience; I will not have a belief on that question at all. I will simply believe that I had breakfast, not believing it on the evidential basis of any other proposition; I take it as basic. Here again the modern classical foundationalist may concede that in fact we often do accept memory beliefs in the basic way; he will deplore this tendency on our parts, however, for in his view—his official view, at any rate—memory beliefs are not properly basic. On the other hand, things are less clear for the ancient and medieval classical foundationalists; many of them seem to regard memory as a special kind of *sense,* and memory beliefs as a special kind of perceptual belief.[10] Still other foundationalists—Thomas Reid, for example—would regard memory beliefs as properly basic, whether or not they are to be considered as a special sort of perceptual belief.

According to the foundationalist view, then, some of my beliefs are basic for me. The rest, naturally enough, are nonbasic for me; and a belief is nonbasic for me just in case I hold that belief and accept it on the basis of other beliefs I hold. Thus I believe that $42 \times 3 = 126$; I accept this belief on the basis of such other beliefs as that $2 \times 3 = 6$ and $3 \times 40 = 120$. If I am rational, of course—if my structure of beliefs is *nondefective*—I will not believe a given proposition on the basis of just *any* proposition; I will instead believe A on the basis of B only if B *evidentially supports* A. How shall we understand this "evidential support" relation? Here different foundationalists, naturally enough, make different suggestions. Descartes seemed to think that the only support worth its salt is deductive support. Locke added inductive evidence, of which a paradigm is the statistical syllogism. (The facts that Feike is a seventeen-year-old Frisian and that nineteen of twenty seventeen-year-old Frisians can swim evidentially support the proposition that Feike can swim.) Peirce added *abductive* evidence: the sort of evidence provided (for example) for the special theory of relativity by the null result of the Michelson-Morley experiment, by muon decay phenomena, and by the Hafele-Keating experiment involving jet transport of cesium clocks.[11]

I believe we can understand foundationalism more fully if we introduce the idea of a *noetic structure*. A person's noetic structure is the set of propositions he believes, together with certain epistemic relations that hold among him and these propositions. As we have seen, some but not all of my beliefs will be based upon others; an account of a person's noetic structure, then, will specify which of his beliefs are basic and which nonbasic. Of course it is abstractly possible that none of his beliefs is basic; perhaps he holds just three beliefs, A, B, and C, and believes each of them on the basis of the other two. We might think this improper or irrational, but that is not to say it could not be done. And it is also possible that all of his beliefs are basic; perhaps he believes a lot of propositions but does not believe any of them on the basis of any others. In the typical case, however, a noetic structure will include both basic and nonbasic beliefs. Second, an account of a noetic structure will

10. See, for example, Thomas Aquinas, *Summa theologica* I, q. 78, art. 4.

11. J. S. Hafele and Richard Keating, "Around-the-World Atomic Clocks: Predicted Relativistic Time Gains and Observed Relativistic Time Gains," *Science* 177 (July 14, 1972): 166–70.

include something like an index of degree of belief. Some of my beliefs are much stronger or firmer than others. I believe that I once visited the village of Oban in Scotland; I believe much more firmly that I have visited Scotland: and perhaps I believe more firmly still that there is such a country as Scotland. Third, an account of a noetic structure will include, for any belief B that is a member of it, an account of which beliefs (and which sets of beliefs) *support B,* and the degree of support they provide for it. Fourth, an account of a noetic structure will include an epistemic *history* of each belief: under what conditions was the belief formed and how has it been sustained? Still further, *belief* must be distinguished from *acceptance* (R&BG, pp. 37–38); and an account of a noetic structure will include an index of degree of acceptance. Still other properties of a noetic structure are important and relevant, but I shall ignore them for now.

Now, foundationalism is a normative thesis about noetic structures; more exactly, it is a connected group of such theses. Our present concern is with only some of these theses: those relevant to the presence or absence of the defect the evidentialist objector claims to find in the theist who believes without evidence. A noetic structure free from this defect is, so far forth, healthy or well formed—or, as we have been putting it, *rational.* And a noetic structure is rational, says the foundationalist, only to the degree that the beliefs it contains are either properly basic or believed on the basis of propositions that support them.[12] So, according to the foundationalist,

(1) A rational noetic structure will have a foundation: a set of beliefs not accepted on the basis of other beliefs.

Next, the foundationalist accepts some theses about the supports relation and the believed-on-the-basis-of relation (the *basis relation,* for short).

(2) The supports relation is irreflexive.

Although every proposition entails itself, no proposition provides evidential support for itself. From this perspective, the term "self-evident" is something of a misnomer. A self-evident proposition is not one for

---

12. This condition is not logically sufficient for rationality (i.e., nondefectiveness) as presently construed. Suppose I believe A on the basis of B (alone) and suppose B supports A; suppose further that I believe B does *not* support A and, indeed, believe that it supports the denial of A. A situation like this seems possible; but in such a situation A would not, for me, be free of the defect in question.

which the evidential support is provided, oddly enough, by *itself;* it is rather a proposition for which no evidential support is needed.

(3) The basis relation is irreflexive in a rational noetic structure.

It may be doubted that anyone is so benighted as to believe a proposition *A* on the basis of *A;* but even if it could be done, it clearly should not be.
The supports relation and the basis relation coincide on irreflexivity; they diverge on asymmetry. For:

(4) The supports relation is not asymmetrical

and

(5) The basis relation is asymmetrical in a rational noetic structure.

The supports relation, clearly enough, is not asymmetrical. Relativity theory provides evidential support for muon decay phenomena, and muon decay phenomena also provide evidential support for relativity theory. For one who is convinced of the Axiom of Choice, that axiom could serve as his evidence for the Hausdorff Maximal Principle, for the former entails the latter. But someone else already convinced of the latter could properly use it as his evidence for the Axiom of Choice, for the latter also entails the former. A person might find it obvious that there are no nonexistent objects and use this truth (as I see it) as his evidence for his view that proper names in fiction ("Captain Marvel," "Hester Prynne") that do not name existent objects, do not name any objects at all. On the other hand, someone who held that such names name nothing could properly take that fact as part of his evidence for the claim that there are no nonexistent objects.

But even if the supports relation is not asymmetrical, the basis relation, in a rational noetic structure, is. If my belief that *A* is based upon my belief that *B*, then my belief that *B* must not be based on my belief that *A*. More exactly, suppose *N* is a rational noetic structure. Then if the belief that *A* (in *N*) is based upon $B_1 \ldots B_n$, none of the B_i will be based upon *A*. So, for example, if I am rational and my belief that life arose in antediluvian tidepools is based on, among others, my belief that the probability that life would arise in a given tidepool in a hundred-year period (under the conditions that then obtained) is $1/n$, then my belief that that probability is $1/n$ will not be based on the proposition that life arose in this way, and there were n tidepool/100-year pairs available. If my evidence for special relativity is, say, the muon decay phenomena and the Hafele-Keating experiment, then if I am rational it will not also be the case that my evidence for muon decay is special relativity.

Circularity and Warrant

According to the foundationalist, therefore, the basis relation, in a rational noetic structure, is asymmetrical. More generally,

(6) The basis relation, in a rational noetic structure, is noncircular.

That is, a rational noetic structure will not contain a belief A_0 which is based on a belief A_1, which is based on A_2, ..., which is based on A_n, which is based on A_0. Suppose I believe

(7) Life originated in tidepools during an n-year stretch some m years ago

on the basis of my beliefs that

(8) Conditions C then obtained

and

(9) The probability that life would arise on earth during an n-year stretch when condition C obtained is high.

Suppose I believe (9) on the basis of my belief that

(10) The probability that life would arise in a single tidepool during a 100-year stretch under condition C is $1/p$;

and suppose finally that I believe (10) on the basis of my belief that life did indeed arise in tidepools during an n-year stretch and that this would be improbable on any assignment significantly less than $1/p$ to the probability that life would arise, under condition C, in a single tidepool during a 100-year stretch. That is, suppose I believe (10) on the basis, among other things, of (7). Then my noetic structure is defective by virtue of containing a circle in the basis relation.

Now, why exactly does the foundationalist object to circular reasoning? Why do *we* object to it? It is not easy to say. Of course if the basis relation (in a rational structure) were *transitive*, then we could see why circular reasoning would be objectionable. For suppose this relation were transitive: then if there were a circular path in my noetic structure, there would be some proposition *A* which I believe on the basis of *A* itself, and this is wholly objectionable. The fact is, however, that the basis relation need not be transitive in a rational noetic structure; I can be entirely rational in believing *A* on the basis of *B* and *B* on the basis of *C* without believing *A* on the basis of *C*. Perhaps things are different for an *ideal* reasoner; for perhaps a person who is *aware* of believing *A* on the basis of *B* and *B* on the basis of *C* and who is appropriately nondefective will also believe *A* on the basis of *C*. But there is no reason to think rationality requires transitivity for us ordinary mortals.

We are therefore without an answer to our question about the unacceptability of circular reasoning. I think we can make progress if we turn to another property a belief may have; we could call it 'acceptability' or 'justification'; or we could take a page from Roderick Firth and call it 'warrant'.[13] Warrant is a *normative* or *evaluative* property; to say that a belief has warrant for a person *S* is to make an appraisal, an evaluative judgment. It is to make a *positive* appraisal; it is to say that the belief in question has *positive epistemic status* for *S;* it is to say that the way in which this belief is held and sustained, in *S*'s noetic structure, measures up to the appropriate norms or standards for holding that sort of belief in *S*'s circumstances. It is to say that *S*'s noetic structure suffers from no defect or blemish or malfunction by way of *S*'s holding this belief in the way he does. More particularly, it is to say there is no defect or blemish in *S*'s noetic structure by virtue of the way this belief is related to *S*'s other beliefs and to *S*'s experience.

An important feature of warrant is that it comes in degrees; at any rate one proposition may be more warranted for a given person at a given time than at another. And here again we had best resort to examples. A proposition that seems self-evident—$2 + 1 = 3$, for example, or the corresponding conditional of *modus ponens*—will have a high degree of warrant for me, a higher degree than, say, that of my belief that arithmetic is incomplete. The belief that it looks from here as if that peak is triangular will have a higher degree of warrant, for me, than the proposition that it really is triangular. The belief that I had breakfast this morning—the memory is still fresh—is more warranted for me than the belief, also based solely on memory, that I once visited

---

13. "Epistemic Concepts and Ethical Concepts," in *Values and Morals,* ed. A. Goldman and J. Kim (Dordrecht: D. Reidel, 1978), p. 216.

a certain university in northern England. A proposition for which I have a lot of evidence has more warrant, for me, than one for which my evidence is flimsy. If I believe propositions A, B, and C, which strongly support D, but do not believe D on the basis of those propositions, then if D has no other source of warrant, it has no warrant for me; and if I believe D on the basis of those propositions but believe that they do *not* support D or that they do support the denial of D, then, once more, D has no warrant for me—or, more conservatively, it has less warrant than it would have in the absence of the offending beliefs.

Now according to the foundationalist, a proposition can have or acquire warrant in at least two ways. On the one hand, it can be properly basic; on the other, it can acquire warrant by virtue of *warrant transfer:* by virtue of being believed on the basis of some other proposition that already has warrant. The *degree* of warrant enjoyed by a non-basic belief will depend on at least two factors: the degree of warrant enjoyed by the propositions on the basis of which it is believed and the strength of the supports relation holding between it and them. In the extreme case, a proposition B believed on the basis of a proposition A may have as much warrant as A itself—perhaps where A obviously and self-evidently entails B. If you tell me that you are thirty-five years old, my belief that you are over thirty, even if based only on my belief that you are thirty-five, may enjoy as much warrant, for me, as does the belief that you are thirty-five. In other cases the warranted proposition may display much less warrant than the warrant-conferring propositions; but in no case will the warrantee enjoy *greater* warrant than the warrantor. If my warrant, for a given proposition, arises from my believing it on the basis of other propositions, then my warrant for that proposition cannot exceed my warrant for any of those others.

Here two caveats are necessary. First, I am not claiming that if A's warrant, for me, arises from my believing it on the basis of $B_1, \ldots, B_n$, then my warrant for A cannot exceed my warrant for the conjunction of the B_i. This would be a natural further suggestion; and surely for some sorts of propositions believed on the basis of others—conjunctions of those others, for example—it would be no more than the sober truth. But for present purposes, we need not saddle the foundationalist with this affirmation. Second, a proposition believed on the basis of others may have a higher degree of warrant than those others by virtue of deriving some of its warrant from other sources. Suppose I have a relatively dim or vague memory of having seen Paul at the New Year's Eve party two months ago; you tell me that you distinctly remember seeing Eleanor at the party, and I know that Eleanor seldom attends parties without Paul. Then my belief that Paul was at the party is based partly on my beliefs that you saw Eleanor there and that she seldom attends parties without Paul; for my warrant for believing the proposition in question is greater than it would have been had I had only my memory to go on. It therefore receives part of its warrant from being believed on the basis of the propositions that Eleanor was there and that she never goes to parties without Paul. Nevertheless, it may have a higher degree of warrant, for me, than is enjoyed by either of those propositions; it also receives some warrant, for me, from my memory of having seen Paul there, dim and vague as that memory may be. The foundationalist need not hold, therefore, that if A is believed on the basis of $B_1, \ldots, B_n$, then the warrant of A cannot exceed that of any of the B_i; he holds instead that, if A's warrant for S is derived *entirely* from its being based on the B_i, then its warrant cannot exceed any of theirs. (Perhaps he will add that, if A's warrant is partly derived from its being based upon the B_i, then A cannot receive more warrant from them than is possessed by the least warranted of the B_i.)

In sum, when a belief B enjoys an increase or access of warrant by being believed on the basis of other propositions, we have *warrant transfer* from a belief that already has it to another; and according to the foundationalist,

(11) Warrant does not increase just by virtue of warrant transfer.

We are now in a position to see more clearly why circular reasoning is objectionable from a foundationalist point of view. For the sake of simplicity, suppose we confine our attention to the special case where A_0 is believed solely on the basis of A_1, A_1 solely on the basis of A_2, . . . , A_{n-1} on the basis of A_n, and A_n on the basis of A_0; and let us add that none of the A_i receives any warrant from any source other than its being believed on the basis of A_{i-1}. (The application to the more general case is easy enough to make.) Say that B is *directly warranted* by A if B is believed on the basis of A and gets all of its warrant by virtue of being believed on the basis of A. Then what we have here is a *circular chain* (a chain circular with respect to the *directly warrants* relation): a finite set of propositions A_0 to A_n (ordered by the *directly warrants* relation) such that for any A_i, A_i is directly warranted by A_{i+1}, and A_n is directly warranted by A_0. Say further that, for any member A and B of the chain, A *gets all its warrant from* B if and only if A is directly warranted by B or A is directly warranted by some proposition that gets all its warrant from B. It is clear, first of all, that if a proposition gets all its warrant from *itself*, then it gets no warrant at all; a proposition that gets all its warrant from itself has no warrant. It is clear, second, that this relation—the gets-all-its-warrant-from relation—is transitive. For suppose C gets all its warrant from B and B gets all its warrant from A. If C is directly warranted by B, then it follows immediately that C gets all its warrant from A; so suppose C is not directly warranted by B. Consider the segment of the chain from B to C (inclusive). Clearly $B + 1$, the proposition that is directly warranted by B, gets all its warrant from A; but then the same will go for $B + 2$, the proposition directly warranted by $B + 1$, and so on all the way to C. Thus C gets all its warrant from A. The relation in question, therefore, is transitive. But then it follows that, in the circle in question, A_0 will get all its warrant from itself. As we have seen, in that case A_0 has no warrant at all; and the same will go for each of the other members of the circular chain. We can therefore see why, according to the foundationalist, a noetic structure that displays a circle in its basis relation displays a defect—a warrant defect.

Returning to the central idea of foundationalism, we recall that (as the foundationalist sees the matter) warrant accrues to a proposition in a rational noetic structure in either of two ways: either by virtue of transfer from some other proposition that already has warrant or by virtue of proper basicality. Now suppose we think a bit further about this second way. First, a proposition is properly basic in a noetic structure if and only if it is basic in that noetic structure and receives none of its warrant by virtue of being believed on the basis of some other propositions. We may therefore say that proper basicality, in contrast to the basis relation, is a *source* of warrant. What sorts of propositions, according to the foundationalist, *are* properly basic? As we have already seen, different foundationalists give different answers. According to the ancient classical foundationalism of Aristotle and Aquinas, a proposition is properly basic if and only if it is either self-evident or "evident to the senses," as Aquinas says. According to the modern classical foundationalism of Descartes, Locke, Malebranche, Leibniz, Berkeley, and Hume, a proposition is properly basic for me if and only if it is either self-evident for me or appropriately about my own mental states. According to Thomas Reid, there is nothing but an arbitrary partiality in favor of awarding this status only to propositions of those two sorts; he proposed that certain beliefs acquired by way of perception (Aquinas's propositions 'evident to the senses') are also properly basic, as are beliefs acquired by way of memory, what he calls "sympathy," what he calls "induction," and still others. According to John Calvin, as I understand him, certain beliefs about God are also properly basic (R&GB, pp. 65–73); the *sensus divinitatis* takes its place along with perception, reasons, memory, and introspection as a source of properly basic belief.

In seeing these beliefs as properly basic, the foundationalist is seeing them as receiving warrant in a way different from the way in which a proposition receives warrant from another when it is (rightly) believed on the basis of that other. It is important to see that a belief is properly basic *in certain circumstances;* typically it will be properly basic in some circumstances but not in others. Consider the belief that I see a tree: this belief is properly basic, for me, in circumstances hard to describe in detail but including my being appeared to in a certain characteristic way; that same belief is not properly basic in circumstances including, say, my knowledge that I am sitting in the living room listening to music with my eyes closed. In the typical case, the proposition in question will receive warrant just by virtue of being accepted in the presence of conditions that do not themselves directly involve other beliefs at all. Often these circumstances will include my having a certain characteristic sort of experience. Thus, what confers warrant upon me when I properly believe that I see a tree is a set of circumstances including experiences of a certain sort—perhaps my being appeared to in that characteristic way. What confers warrant upon my belief that I once visited Oban is the fact that it seems to me that I remember doing so; what confers warrant upon the corresponding conditional of modus ponens, for me, is the fact that it is apparently self-evident for me: it displays that "evident luster."

Of course, a foundationalist is not obliged to hold that the *only* conditions conferring warrant are conditions that do not involve other beliefs. He could hold that, in some cases, what confers warrant on a proposition that is properly basic for me is a set of circumstances that includes beliefs of one sort or another. Perhaps the belief that Sam is in pain is properly basic for me in circumstances that include my being appeared to in a certain characteristic way but also include the belief that I see Sam, or see someone. In such a case, I do not accept the belief in question *on the basis of* the belief that I see Sam (or see someone); that belief is in no way my evidence or part of my evidence for the proposition that Sam is in pain. It is, nonetheless, an element in the set of circumstances that confers warrant, for me, on the belief in question. The foundationalist, accordingly, can sensibly hold that a belief *A* can be part of the warrant-conferring condition for a belief *B*, even if *B* is not accepted on the basis of *A*—even if, indeed, *B* is properly basic.

COHERENTISM CHARACTERIZED

We have noted the fundamental idea of foundationalism and some of its essential features; our discussion thus far will, I think, help us grasp the central thrust of coherentism. As we have seen, the foundationalist rejects circular reasoning. As he sees the matter, a rational noetic structure will not contain a chain that is circular with respect to the basis relation; it will not contain a set $A_0, \ldots, A_n$ of beliefs such that each of the A_i is believed on the basis of A_{i+1}, with A_n being believed on the basis of A_0. Now it is sometimes said that a central difference between foundationalism and coherentism is just that the coherentist does *not* object to circular reasoning, "provided the circle is big enough"; indeed he revels in it, for he sees warrant as arising in just such circular chains. (Again, we restrict ourselves to the special case of *simple* circular reasoning; application to the more general case is easy enough.) He must therefore suppose, if this characterization is correct, that the basis relation in a noetic structure does not simply *transfer* warrant: it somehow *generates* warrant if the chain involved is sufficiently long.

Now this is not at all easy to believe; the intuition relied upon by the foundationalist here is very strong. It seems wholly obvious that even if a person *could* believe a proposition on the evidential basis of itself, this maneuver would not confer any warrant upon the proposition. Suppose I believe, for example, that my dog is an alien from outer space, and suppose I could manage, somehow, to start believing this proposition on the basis—the immediate basis—of itself. Surely I would not thereupon have a greater degree of warrant for this belief than I had before I executed this maneuver. So if the belief in question has no warrant for me apart from what accrues to it by virtue of standing in the believed-on-the-basis-of relationship, then in this case it has no warrant at all. Say that a circular chain of the sort under consideration is *of unit circumference* if the set of beliefs involved is a unit set; and say more generally that it is of circumference n if the set of beliefs involved is n-membered. Then clearly a circle of unit circumference confers no warrant upon its member. But surely the same goes for a circle of circumference 2. If at first I believe both A and B and later manage to believe each on the basis of the other, I am no better off, epistemically speaking, than I was at first. If I accept special relativity solely on the basis of the muon decay phenomena and believe in muon decay solely on the basis of special relativity, then neither has any warrant for me at all. And how could it help to increase the size of the circle? If a circle of circumference n does not produce warrant, surely the same will go for a circle of circumference $n + 1$.[14] Warrant cannot magically arise just by virtue of a large evidential circle. (If I go around the circle twice, will I get twice as much warrant?) If the coherentist really holds that cir-

---

14. In any event, could I not simply interpolate as many items as I need to get a large enough circle?

cular reasoning is a source of warrant, then his views are unlikely indeed.

But why saddle him with anything so implausible? There is a far more charitable way to construe his characteristic claim. He should not be seen as endorsing circular reasoning or making an implausible remark about the properties of the basis relation; he is not claiming that the basis relation is a *source* of warrant. Instead, he makes a suggestion as to the conditions under which a belief is *properly basic* for someone. He is not holding that the basis relation in a rational neotic structure can sometimes be circular; he is instead pointing to a condition under which a belief is properly basic—a condition under which it is rational to hold a belief without accepting it on the evidential basis of other beliefs. On his view, a belief B is properly basic for a person S if and only if B coheres with S's noetic structure—or with the rest of the S's noetic structure, if S already holds B. If B coheres with my noetic structure, then B is warranted for me. Its warrant does not arise, however, by virtue of my believing it *on the basis of* the rest of my noetic structure, so that those other propositions are my evidence—deductive, inductive, or abductive—for B. Indeed, if, for any proposition A I believe, I accept A on the basis of the rest of what I believe, then my noetic structure would contain a host of tight basis circles; for then I would believe A on the basis of $B_1, \ldots, B_n$ and each of the B_i on the basis of A together with the rest of the B_j. (Of course, if we added a dimension and spoke not of *circular* but of *cylindrical* reasoning, then the cylinders in question could be of considerable *height,* even if only of circumference 2.)

So the coherentist does not really tout circular (or cylindrical) reasoning. What he does instead is suggest a different condition for basicality, another source of warrant: he holds that a belief is properly basic for me if and only if it appropriately coheres with the rest of my noetic structure. A *pure* coherentist rejects warrant transmission altogether; for her all propositions that enjoy warrant in a noetic structure are properly basic in that structure. Deduction, induction, and abduction may indeed figure, in one way or another, as elements in the coherence relation, but warrant does not get transmitted by the basis relation from one proposition to another. Of course a coherentist need not be a *pure* coherentist; she can instead embrace an impure or mixed variety. She may hold that the *source* of warrant is coherence but add that warrant is sometimes transferred via the basis relation. Thus I may be warranted in my belief that some horses have quirky personalities by virtue of believing that proposition on the basis of my belief that Clyde is a horse and has a quirky personality; and I may be warranted in that latter belief by virtue of its coherence with the rest of my noetic structure. Global coherentism is compatible with local foundationalism; the view that coherence alone is the source of warrant is compatible with the view that warrant is sometimes transmitted. What is really characteristic of coherentism is not a view about the *transmission* of warrant but a view about its *source*. Seen from the present perspective, therefore, the coherentist reveals her true colors as a foundationalist with unusual views about what is properly basic.

The pure coherentist holds that all warranted propositions in a noetic structure are properly basic in that structure; no warrant gets transmitted. The impure coherentist holds that some propositions may get their warrant by virtue of being believed on the basis of others; but the ultimate source of the warrant in question is coherence. Both accept the view that coherence is the *only* source of warrant; this is the central coherentist claim. According to the ancient or medieval foundationalist, perception and self-evidence or reason are the sources of warrant; according to the modern classical foundationalist, self-evidence and introspection are the sources of warrant. Reid added memory, sympathy, induction, and others. And the coherentist, by contrast, casts her lot with coherence. She holds that coherence alone is a source of warrant. She therefore differs from classical and Reidian foundationalists by holding that coherence is indeed a source of warrant; she differs from them further in holding that nothing *else* is a source of warrant. On the coherentist view, a belief acquires no warrant by virtue of being caused by or in the presence of experience of a certain sort. The fact that I am indeed being appeared to redly confers no warrant, either on my belief that I am perceiving something red or even my belief that I am being appeared to redly; the fact that the corresponding conditional of modus ponens seems to me self-evident confers no warrant, for me, on my belief that that proposition is true. What confers warrant on these beliefs, if indeed they are warranted for me, is just the fact that they appropriately cohere with the rest of what I believe.

COHERENTISM AND THE EVIDENTIALIST OBJECTION

We now come to the ostensible pièce de résistance of this study—an inquiry into the question of whether coherentism offers the resources for a cogent or plausible evidentialist objection to theistic belief. I fear it may be anticlimactic. Of course there is something a bit unnatural or at least ill focused about raising a specifically *evidentialist* objection from a coherentist point of view. The evidentialist objector typically points out, sometimes with sorrow and sometimes with ill-concealed glee, that the traditional theistic arguments do not provide much by way of evidence for the existence of God; and there seems little else that does much better. He then concludes that the evidence for this belief is insufficient; since it is also not properly basic, a noetic structure that contains it displays a defect with respect to warrant, it is warrant defective. According to the coherentist, on the other hand, what makes for warrant nondefectiveness is just coherence with the rest of my noetic structure; and of course there is no reason to see this as connected, in any special way, with the cogency or lack thereof of the theistic arguments. From the coherentist's point of view, the question whether there is a good argument for the existence of God—deductive, inductive, or abductive—recedes into the background. The real question, from this point of view, is whether theistic belief coheres with the rest of the theist's noetic structure. If it does, no further question about warrant defectiveness arises. So presumably the evidentialist objection, thus transmuted, must be the claim that, for all or most theists *T*, theism does not cohere with the rest of *T*'s noetic structure. Of course, even if that were true, it would not follow that the difficulty is to be pinned on belief in God. If all we know is that *T*'s noetic structure is incoherent, then all we know is that a change must be made somewhere; coherentism does not tell us where.

But why should we suppose that many or most theistic noetic structures *are* in fact relevantly incoherent? One answer might be that belief in God is inconsistent in the broadly logical sense: someone might think that it is impossible, for example, for there to be a person who has no body, so that the theistic view of God as a person without a body is incoherent. Theistic belief is impossible in the broadly logical sense; what is thus impossible is incoherent with every noetic structure; theism, therefore, is incoherent with every noetic structure; hence theism is incoherent with the theist's noetic structure.

This argument, however, is deeply problematic from a coherentist perspective. Many propositions are *noncontingent;* they are necessarily true or necessarily false. Propositions of mathematics and logic fall into this category, as do proposed philosophical analyses and, indeed, most philosophical claims and theses. Propositions of this sort, then, on the suggestion in question, have the following characteristic: any such proposition that is coherent with *any* noetic structure is such that its denial is incoherent with *every* noetic structure. But then false philosophical beliefs (along with false noncontingent beliefs generally) will be incoherent with every noetic structure; hence they will be unwarranted for anyone. Either nominalism has no warrant for anyone at all, or realism is thus universally unwarranted. Suppose compatibilism is mistaken: contrary to what the compatibilist says, human freedom is not compatible with universal causal determinism. Then on the suggestion in question, the compatibilist's characteristic claims are incoherent with the rest of his views and hence have no warrant for him—no matter what the rest of his views are and no matter how good the apparent fit between them and his compatibilism. *Falsehood*, for noncontingent propositions and on the suggestion in question, is sufficient for incoherence and hence for absence of warrant.

But surely the coherentist does not (or should not) propose to endorse standards as stringent as all that; surely she will not want to endorse a view according to which truth (in logical, philosophical, theological, and mathematical matters) is a necessary condition of coherence. Further, the suggestion in question is inconsistent with a deep intellectual impulse or motive often underlying coherentism. Coherentism often begins from a sort of pessimism about the human intellectual condition, a pessimism about our powers of attaining the truth. We are "locked into the circle of our own beliefs"; how, then, can we ever have a reason for supposing that what we believe is in fact *true?* The coherentist is then inclined to counsel us to turn from pursuing truth, where our prospects are at best cloudy, to some goal that is more nearly within our reach: coherence. Even if we have little or no reason to suppose our beliefs true, we can at least make sure they are coherent. But on the suggestion in question—the suggestion that possibility is a necessary condition of coherence—this distinction between truth and coherence is rendered nugatory for philosophical and other noncontingent beliefs; on that suggestion falsehood, for such beliefs, is sufficient for incoherence. Presumably, then, the wise coherentist will not adopt that suggestion.

Returning to the claim that it is impossible, in the broadly logical sense, that there be a person without a body, we see from our present vantage point that even if (*per impossibile*) this claim is true, it does not follow that theism is incoherent with the theist's noetic structure. From the coherentist standpoint that will follow only if the *theist*, somehow, accepts views from which it follows that it is impossible that there be a person without a body. And even if he were misguided enough to do that, one way for him to achieve coherence would be for him to give up, not the belief that God is a person without a body, but those views that imply that every person must have a body. So this argument is unsuccessful. (Of course a coherentist might hold on other grounds that no noetic structure containing the belief that there is such a person as God (or the belief there is a person without a body) could possibly be coherent.)

Whatever view he takes on *that* issue, the coherentist objector must at any rate be holding either that most noetic structures that include theistic belief are incoherent, or, more likely, that there is something about theistic belief such that its inclusion in a noetic structure is likely to result in incoherence. But why believe that? To evaluate the prospects for this kind of objection, we must know more about coherence. Now most coherentists are decently reticent about the nature of coherence. We are told that it is more than mere logical consistency but less than mutual entailment; beyond this most coherentists maintain a docorous silence, thus making it difficult indeed to see whether there really is a viable coherentist objection to theistic belief. An outstanding exception is Keith Lehrer's work; his book *Knowledge*[15] is surely as full and articulate a development of coherentist thought as is presently to be found. I shall therefore examine his account of the coherence relation and ask whether, given that account, it can cogently or plausibly be argued that a theistic noetic structure is at least likely to be incoherent.

Now Lehrer speaks throughout about *justification* and *complete justification;* and while coherentists, as I said, are seldom forthcoming about coherence, Lehrer himself says little about justification. It is not wholly clear just what this property is. It is not quite what transforms true belief into knowledge, for Gettier problems stand between complete justification and knowledge. Justification lies in that general neighborhood, however; a person *S* knows *p*, says Lehrer, if and only if he is completely justified in believing *p* in a way that does not depend upon any false belief (p. 21). But while it is not wholly clear just what the relation is between Lehrer's complete justification and what I have called "warrant nondefectiveness," it is at any rate reasonably clear that if a person is completely justified, in Lehrer's sense, in believing *p*, then his noetic structure displays no warrant defect by virtue of his believing *p*. Lehrer's conception of complete justification goes as follows. A person *S*'s *doxastic system* is a set of propositions specifying what *S* believes; it is a set of true propositions of the form *S believes p* such that for any proposition *q*, if *S* believes *q*, then the set contains the proposition *S believes q*. *S*'s *corrected doxastic* system is the subset of his doxastic system that results when we delete from it "every proposition which describes *S* as believing something he would cease to believe as an impartial and disinterested truth seeker" (p. 190); his corrected doxastic system con-

15. Oxford: Oxford University Press, 1974.

tains no statement S believes "because of the comfort it gives him, because of greed, because of hate, and so forth" (p. 189). And a person is completely justified in believing a given proposition if and only if it coheres with his corrected doxastic system.

To explain coherence, Lehrer turns to a notion of *competition:* a statement p competes with a statement q with respect to a doxastic system if and only if that system contains the proposition S *believes that p is negatively relevant to q.* Negative relevance is in turn explained (to a first approximation) as follows: p is negatively relevant to q if and only if q is less likely to be true if p is true than it is otherwise. In order to accommodate certain problems, Lehrer moves on to a more complicated notion, *strong negative relevance* (see proposition 15 below), whose details need not detain us here.

So a competitor of p, with respect to a doxastic system, is a proposition q such that the proposition S *believes that q is strongly negatively relevant to p* is a member of that doxastic system. Then we can say that

(12) S is completely justified in believing p if and only if p coheres with S's corrected doxastic system;

if and only if, that is,

(13) p is believed, in S's corrected doxastic system, to have a better chance of being true than any statement that competes with it (with respect to that doxastic system).

In sum,

(14) S is completely justified in believing p if and only if, for any proposition q such that the proposition S *believes that q is strongly negatively relevant to p* is a member of S's corrected doxastic system, the proposition S *believes that p has a better chance of being true than q has* is also a member of S's corrected doxastic system.

There are problems here. As I have stated (14), it says that S is completely justified in believing p if and only if, roughly, every proposition S *believes* to be strongly negatively relevant to p meets a certain further condition. I am inclined to think this is indeed what Lehrer means; but if it is, then, surely, given Lehrer's difficult and subtle conception of strong negative relevance, few of us will hold any beliefs at all of the form q *is strongly negatively relevant to p.* The official account of strong negative relevance goes as follows:

(15) *q* is strongly negatively relevant to *p* if and only if *q* is negatively relevant to *p* and is such that the disjunction of members
in numerical order of the epistemic partition of *p* for *S* that is
logically equivalent to *q*, is such that no disjunct of those members is irrelevant to *p*. [Pp. 195–96]

If this is what strong negative relevance is, then it will be at best only a
few philosophers who believe, for some pair of propositions *p* and *q*,
that *q* is strongly negatively relevant to *p*. But if I have no beliefs of that
sort, then (14) is much too easily fulfilled for me. For any proposition *p*
you pick, there will be no proposition *q* such that I believe that *q* is
strongly negatively relevant to *p*; but then it immediately follows that I
am completely justified in believing *p*. So, no matter what *p* is, I am
completely justified in believing it.

Presumably Lehrer would be less than wholly enthusiastic about this
outcome; and perhaps we might think to mend matters by speaking (in
proposition 14) not of the propositions that I *believe* to be strongly
negatively relevant to *p* but of the propositions that really *are* thus
relevant (whether or not I believe them to be); and indeed, Lehrer
sometimes writes as if that is what he has in mind. But this suggestion is
out of accord with the general spirit of Lehrer's account; and in any
event it leads to the following difficulty. Suppose I reflect long, hard,
and carefully on the question of whether *q* is strongly negatively relevant to *p* and conclude that it is not. As it turns out, I am mistaken in
this belief; *q* really is strongly negatively relevant to *p*. Furthermore, I
do not believe that *p* has a greater chance than *q* of being true. Then,
on the present suggestion, I could not be completely justified in believing *p*. But surely I could; my making an honest and careful mistake—in
this case about what is strongly negatively relevant to what—is clearly
compatible with my being completely justified in believing *p*.

Another difficulty: a proposition *q* is a competitor of *p*, for me, only
if *q* is negatively relevant to *p*, and "one statement is negatively relevant
to a second if and only if the second statement has a lower chance of
being true on the assumption that the first is true than otherwise" (pp.
192–93). But how shall we understand "than otherwise" here? The
suggestion that immediately leaps to mind is the following. Where *C* is
the conjunction of propositions I believe, *q* is negatively relevant to *p* if
and only if the conditional probability of *p* on *q* & *C* is lower than that of
p on *C* alone. On this way of looking at the matter, *q* is negatively
relevant to *p* *with respect to what I believe;* and *q* is negatively relevant to *p*
if *p* is more likely to be true (has a better chance of being true) on what I
believe *alone* than it does on what I believe augmented by *q*. I say this is

the suggestion that leaps immediately to mind; but it has an unhappy consequence. For if p is a proposition I already believe, then of course p will be entailed by C and hence by q & C, no matter what q is. Hence, no proposition will be negatively relevant to p, if I already believe p. Unless I am confused, then, I will not believe, for any proposition q, that it is negatively relevant to p; hence it will be trivially true that, for any proposition q I believe to be negatively relevant to p, I believe that p has a better chance of being true than q. But then I am automatically completely justified in believing any proposition I do in fact believe. Surely this makes complete justification much too easy to attain.

But how else shall we understand "than otherwise"? Another possibility: We might suppose that p has a certain intrinsic and objective probability (something like its a priori probability on a logical conception of probability); this is the probability it has "otherwise"; and we are to compare with it the conditional probability of p on q, q being negatively relevant to p only if the conditional probability of p on q is less than the intrinsic probability of p. Or we might consider the conditional probability of p not on C (which, as we have seen, has the unfortunate property of entailing p) but on $C \sim p$, subconjunction of C that is maximal with respect to not entailing p. (Of course this will not be unique; if C includes both r and *if r then p*, there will be one such subconjunction containing r and another containing *if r then p*; but let us imagine that we have a way of picking out the most appropriate subconjunction.) Then we could say that q is negatively relevant to p if the conditional probability of p on $C \sim p$ is greater than that of p on ($C \sim p$) & q. (We could also say, perhaps, that q is negatively relevant to p if the probability of p on $C \sim p$ exceeds that of p on q alone.) In these or perhaps other ways we could avoid the unwelcome consequence that a proposition I believe has no competitors.

But then another difficulty rears its ugly head. To be completely justified in believing p, on Lehrer's account, I must believe that p has a better chance of being true than any of its competitors. On the above ways of construing negative relevance, no doubt the proposition "ninety-nine out of a hundred Frisians are Calvinists and Feike is a Frisian" will be negatively relevant to "Feike is not a Calvinist." But can I not be completely justified in believing the latter even if I do not think it has more of a chance of being true than the former? Perhaps I think they *both* have a splendid chance of being true. On any appropriate account of competition each of these would be a competitor of the other; but then I could not be completely justified in believing both and hence could not know them both. But surely I could.

These are some of the difficulties that plague Lehrer's account; they are quasi-technical but nevertheless important. Perhaps with sufficient ingenuity we could circumvent them (and then again, perhaps not). In any event, the important point for our present concern lies in a different direction. Our question is whether the evidentialist objection to theistic belief can be urged plausibly from a coherentist perspective. The question is whether there is reason to think that all, or most, or many noetic structures that include belief in God thereby suffer from warrant defect. Transposed into the coherentist key, that question becomes the question whether the theist's belief that there is such a person as God can plausibly be thought to cohere with the rest of what he believes. Transposed into the specifically Lehrerian key, the question is whether the theist's belief in God can plausibly be thought to cohere with his corrected doxastic system. Could a theist be such that if he were an honest and careful truth seeker, unmoved by greed, fear, anger, lust, desire for comfort, and their like, he would still believe that there is such a person as God, and believe that this proposition has greater chance of being true than any of its competitors? We have only to ask that question to answer it: of course he could. Or, to speak more modestly, there seems in any event not the slightest reason to think that he could not.

I therefore see little hope for a coherentist version of the evidentialist objection to theistic belief. But suppose the objection could be at least partly sustained; suppose many or most theists do in fact have incoherent noetic structures; suppose a given theist has an incoherent noetic structure by virtue of his theism; what would follow? It would not follow that he ought to give up or strive to give up his theism. No doubt his noetic structure is defective by virtue of this incoherence; if apprised of it, no doubt he should strive to correct this defect, should strive to attain coherence. But, of course, striving to give up belief in God is not the only way of pursuing coherence here; he could do so just as well by striving to amend his *other* beliefs in such a way that belief in God no longer fails to cohere with the rest of his noetic structure.

COHERENTISM REJECTED

Coherentism, therefore, offers no aid and comfort to the atheologian intent upon urging the evidentialist objection or something like it. But coherentism, I think, ought in any event to be rejected. Let us recall its essentials. First, there is the crucial claim that coherence is the only source of warrant. The coherentist may concede that warrant can be transferred from one proposition to another by way of the basis relation, but she will hold that the *source* of warrant, in a noetic structure, is coherence and coherence alone. My beliefs get such warrant as they enjoy either by virtue of coherence or by virtue of being believed on the basis of propositions that get *their* warrant that way. She thus takes up a position opposed to that of the standard foundationalist, who endorses as sources of warrant such other processes as perception, memory, introspection, self-evidence, and others. According to the standard foundationalist, certain kinds of beliefs acquire warrant just by virtue of arising in certain circumstances that have nothing to do with coherence; when I am appeared to redly, the belief that I am thus appeared to acquires warrant just because I am then being thus appeared to. When a self-evident proposition displays that evident luster of which Locke speaks, the belief that it is true acquires warrant for me by virtue of that very fact. A common coherentist claim is that all beliefs are on an epistemic par; all stand equally before the bar of coherence; and, in case of failure of coherence, all are equally eligible for revision. The ordinary foundationalist balks at this excess of egalitarian fervor, as he sees it; relative to a given set of circumstances, he says, some beliefs are privileged, acquiring warrant just by virtue of being formed or sustained in those circumstances.

So the coherentist holds two things: that coherence is a source of warrant and that it is the only source of warrant. Thus, she says, coherence is *sufficient* for warrant nondefectiveness, and *necessary* for it in that a proposition is nondefective for me only if it is coherent with my noetic structure or appropriately (deductively, inductively, or abductively) follows from propositions that are coherent with my noetic structure.

I think we can see that she is mistaken on both counts; I shall argue that coherence is neither necessary nor sufficient for warrant nondefectiveness. As to sufficiency: it seems wholly clear that a person's noetic structure might be both thoroughly coherent and thoroughly, indeed, radically, defective with respect to warrant. Consider, first, someone S who, by virtue of some noetic malfunction, believes, whenever he is appeared to redly, that no one is appeared to redly. It is not that he believes that *he* is not appeared to redly; perhaps that is impossible. Let us concede for purposes of argument that necessarily, if S is appeared to redly, then S does not believe that he is not appeared to redly. Let us also concede, for purposes of argument, that, if a person is appeared to redly and pays attention to his phenomenal field (perhaps asking himself whether and how he is being appeared to), then if he is being appeared to redly, he believes that he is. These concessions are consistent with S's being such that whenever he is appeared to redly, he believes that no one is ever thus appeared to; for S, we may add, does not, on these occasions, pay any attention to his phenomenal field. He does not ask himself whether he is being appeared to redly or, indeed, whether he is being appeared to at all. He simply finds himself, under these conditions, believing that no one is ever appeared to redly. This state of affairs is perhaps a bit bizarre and unlikely; nevertheless, it is possible in the broadly logical sense, which is all that is required. (If you find the example too outlandish to consider, modify it to the case where S, when appeared to redly, always believes that no one *else* is being thus appeared to.)

And now, let us add that S's beliefs, on these occasions, are co-herent—for definiteness, coherent in Lehrer's sense. For every com-petitor q of the proposition *no one is ever appeared to redly*, S's doxastic system contains, on the occasions in question, the proposition that he believes that competitor to have less of a chance of being true than does the proposition in question. Furthermore, he is a disinterested (if un-successful) seeker after truth, unmoved by desire for comfort, or by greed or hunger or lust. Thus his corrected doxastic structure coin-cides with his doxastic structure *simpliciter;* this belief is therefore co-herent with his corrected doxastic structure. Let us add that each of the rest of his beliefs also coheres with his corrected doxastic structure. Then S's noetic structure is coherent in the Lehrer sense; and we may suppose still further that it is also coherent in any other reasonable sense a coherentist might propose. Nevertheless his noetic structure is defective; it is not rational in the sense of being nondefective with respect to warrant. S may be *deontologically justified* in this belief; he may be within his rights in accepting it; it may be that it is not within his power to reject it, and it may be that there are no noetic duties he has flouted. Nevertheless his noetic structure is defective; he is not rational in the sense of warrant nondefectiveness.

Take another sort of case. At time t, S (like the rest of us) is such that the proposition *there is no greatest natural number* seems to him self-evident to at least a moderate degree; it has that "evident luster" of which Locke speaks; it exhibits that "clarity and brightness" that ac-cording to Locke a self-evident proposition "displays to the attentive mind." Unlike the rest of us, however, S has been trying to perfect a belief-regulating machine. This machine looks a bit like an early twen-tieth-century electric chair with an IBM personal computer attached; after appropriately positioning the electrodes, you type in a sentence expressing the belief you wish to have and the machine does the rest. To test the machine, S tries it out on himself; he types in the sentence "There is a greatest natural number" and thus acquires the belief that there is a greatest natural number. (He forms no belief as to which number this *is*, except that it is enormously greater than any number we can conceive or standardly represent.) He then adjusts the rest of his beliefs so as to achieve coherence. (Thus he no longer believes that for any positive integers *n* and *m*, *n* + *m* > *n*, although he believes that this law holds for any numbers we can grasp or conceive.) The phenomonology of *S*'s beliefs, however, does not change. *There is no greatest natural number* still displays that evident luster when he considers it, but he nonetheless believes its denial. (Just as, for many of us, the proposition *For every property P there exists a set S such that x is a member of S if and only if x has P* may seem self-evident to at least some degree, despite the fact that we believe its denial.) In this case, as opposed to the preceding one, it may be that *S* is deontologically unjustified in holding the belief he does, for he has himself at *t* knowingly brought it about that he holds at *t'* a belief that he himself at *t* thinks false. However that may be, he is clearly defective with respect to warrant in holding this belief, even though it coheres with the rest of his beliefs. His noetic structure, furthermore, displays warrant defect despite its coherence.

Examples can be multiplied. Timothy is a young artist with an intense, indeed inordinate, admiration of Picasso. Waiting at a supermarket checkout, he idly picks up a copy of the *National Enquirer*, reading therein that Picasso, contrary to what most of us have always thought, was really an alien from outer space. Timothy then forms the belief that he, too, is really an alien from outer space, adjusting the rest of his beliefs so as to achieve coherence. Later he loses this inordinate admiration for Picasso and becomes a disinterested truth seeker. Since his beliefs are coherent, he continues to hold them, in particular continuing to believe that he is an alien from outer space. His noetic structure is then clearly defective, defective with respect to warrant, despite its coherence.

One final example, suggested by Timothy's plight. Suppose at *t* I am in Oxford and know that I am; I am just outside the gates of Balliol College observing a small but noisy flock of gowned undergraduates on their way to the Examination Schools. Each of my beliefs is coherent with my noetic structure, which is itself coherent. Now imagine that I leave Oxford, taking the train to London. My experience then changes in the normal way; my visual, auditory, and kinesthetic experience at *t'*, when I am on the train bound for London, is just what one would expect. Nevertheless I continue to hold exactly the beliefs that I held in Oxford at *t;* I continue to believe that I am in Oxford and that those undergraduates are passing by. My beliefs at *t'* are coherent, for they are the very beliefs I coherently held at *t;* no change has occurred.

Nonetheless my noetic structure at t' is warrant defective; indeed, it is warrant defective *just because* no change occurred in it. Under the conditions in question, my beliefs are not responsive to changes in my experience; they remain fixed despite the extensive changes that occur in my experience. This is a source of warrant defect.

It is therefore clear, I think, that coherence is not a sufficient condition of warrant nondefectiveness. But neither is it necessary. It is entirely possible that one of my beliefs should suffer from no warrant defect, even if it is neither coherent with the rest of my noetic structure nor appropriately follows from ones that are coherent with it. Suppose, for example, that you are an eminent but idiosyncratic epistemologist and I am an unduly impressionable student: you offer me a battery of complex and subtly powerful arguments for the conclusion that no one is ever appeared to redly. I am unable to withstand the force of your argumentation and am convinced. The next day I am reflecting on the significance of what you have proven to me, when suddenly a fire engine roars by, siren screaming. I involuntarily look up to identify the source of the commotion and am appeared to redly; since I have been reflecting about these matters, I notice that I am thus appeared to. Unless my noetic structure undergoes instant metamorphosis (and we can stipulate that it does not), my belief that I am appeared to redly will be incoherent with my noetic structure but nevertheless not warrant defective.

Another example: I am giving a lecture on trees, claiming among other things that no oak trees grow in the state of Washington. Naturally I believe that I have never seen an oak tree in any part of the state. I suddenly notice you in the audience; seeing you jogs my memory; I suddenly seem to remember an occasion on which you and I noticed a particularly luxurient oak on the campus of Western Washington University in Bellingham, Washington. I have the very sort of experience that goes with remembering such a thing; that is to say, I have the sort of experience that goes with remembering that I saw an oak there. At the moment when it seems to me that I do so remember, the proposition that I have seen an oak tree in Washington has warrant for me, despite the fact that at that moment it does not cohere with my noetic structure. I will suddenly find myself believing that I have indeed seen an oak tree in Washington; if for some reason my other beliefs do not alter, the belief in question will not be coherent with my noetic structure. Nevertheless it then has warrant for me, despite the fact that it does not thus cohere. And the change that is called for, of course, is not that of rejecting or trying to reject the belief in question; what is called for is revising the rest of my noetic structure in such a way that it is coherent with the belief in question. Coherence, therefore, is neither necessary nor sufficient for warrant nondefectiveness.

By way of conclusion then: coherentism offers no aid and comfort to the evidentialist objector to theistic belief. The central tenet of coherentism is that coherence and coherence alone is the source of warrant; and while no wholly satisfactory account of the coherence relation seems to be available, insofar as we do have a grasp of that notion there seems to be no reason at all to suppose that all or most noetic structures that include theistic belief are incoherent. Coherentism, however, is in any event mistaken as an account of warrant and warrant defect, so that any help it might have promised the evidentialist objector would be at best of dubious value.

5

Direct Justification, Evidential Dependence, and Theistic Belief

ROBERT AUDI

Philosophers and theologians have held many positions regarding the sorts of grounds that can warrant theistic beliefs. Perhaps the most common philosophical position concerning the proper ground for the belief that God exists, and by implication for belief *in* God as well, is evidentialism: the view that one's belief that God exists is justified only if one has adequate evidence for it.[1] In sharp contrast is fideism, which is roughly the position that faith is the appropriate ground both of belief that God exists and of belief in God. Fideists sometimes leave it unclear whether this is meant to imply that faith justifies the belief that God exists, or simply that, if this belief is based on faith, it needs no

---

An earlier version of part of this essay was delivered at a symposium with Alvin Plantinga (as principal speaker) and Philip Quinn at the Western Division meetings of the American Philosophical Association in 1981. I profited from discussing the issues there, from Plantinga's comments in response, from Quinn's paper, and from informal discussions of the issues at Davidson College, St. Olaf College, and the University of Richmond. A revised version was presented at the Research Conference in the Philosophy of Religion held at the University of Nebraska in April 1984. I benefited from a rigorous commentary by Edward Wierenga and from the general discussion at the conference, as well as from a later discussion at Syracuse University. I am also grateful for comments from William P. Alston, Hardy E. Jones, James A. Keller, David Shatz, and Stephen Wykstra.
    1. In one respect, this is a quite weak version of evidentialism, for it does not require that a justified theistic belief be *based on* the relevant evidence. In what follows I ignore this issue, since what I have to say about evidentialism here applies in either case.

justification.[2] A third major view, which I shall call experientialism, is like evidentialism in affirming that theistic beliefs are rational only if they are justified, and like fideism in denying that their justification requires evidence. On this third view, human experience, including nonmystical experiences, can directly justify belief that God exists. The concern of this paper will be to explore a bold and quite unmystical version of experientialism.

My point of departure is some of the recent work of Alvin Plantinga. In "Is Belief in God Properly Basic?"[3] and "Reason and Belief in God"[4] he subjects evidentialism to intensive criticism. He maintains that one's belief that God exists or, at least, beliefs of propositions self-evidently entailing that God exists, which I shall also call theistic beliefs, may be *properly basic,* that is, such that they may be rationally held other than "on the basis of any other beliefs or propositions at all."[5] Plantinga's defense of this view is well argued and of great epistemological interest. I shall first summarize its main points and then examine some major problems they raise.

A CRITIQUE OF EVIDENTIALISM

There are at least two kinds of theistic responses to evidentialism. One is to accept the evidentialist thesis that one's belief that God exists is justified only if one has adequate evidence for it and to argue that there *is* sufficient evidence for believing that God exists. Another is to attack that thesis and argue that the *rationality* of this belief, which I shall in this paper take to be roughly equivalent to its justifiedness, does not require the believer's having evidence for it. Plantinga's response in the

---

2. I am assuming that epistemic justification is at issue here; but there are also interesting issues concerning whether theistic belief might be thought to need, or normally to have, some other kind of justification (e.g., pragmatic or moral justification). Diogenes Allen applies to theism a conception of justification that seems to differ in some ways from all of these; see his "Motives, Rationales, and Religious Beliefs," *American Philosophical Quarterly* 3 (1966).

3. *Nous* 15 (1981).

4. In *Faith and Rationality,* ed. Alvin Plantinga and Nicholas Wolterstorff (Notre Dame: University of Notre Dame Press, 1983). Wolterstorff's paper in this collection, "Can Belief in God Be Rational If It Has No Foundations?" is also a significant thrust on behalf of what I call experientialism. Its position is quite different from Plantinga's and raises questions I cannot pursue here; but some of what I say here applies to some of Wolterstorff's points. See also Plantinga's "Rationality and Religious Belief," in *Contemporary Philosophy of Religion,* ed. Steven M. Cahn and David Shatz (Oxford: Oxford University Press, 1982). For recent discussion of the kind of view Plantinga defends, see Anthony Kenny, *Faith and Reason* (New York: Columbia University Press, 1983), and Richard Swinburne's detailed review of this and other recent books in *Journal of Philosophy* 82 (January 1985).

5. "Is Belief in God Properly Basic?" p. 42.

papers cited is the latter. But one may, with perfect consistency, hold both that there is sufficient evidence for the existence of God and that rationally believing in God does not require having such evidence.

One of Plantinga's main points is that evidentialism is typically rooted in classical foundationalism, according to which "a proposition (p) is properly basic for S if and only if p is either self-evident or incorrigible (modern foundationalism) or either self-evident or 'evident to the senses' (ancient and medieval foundationalism)."[6] This version of foundationalism, he contends, is self-referentially incoherent.[7] I propose for the sake of argument to assume that this thesis of foundationalism is mistaken and to concentrate instead on his case against evidentialism.

Let us first consider some examples of beliefs that are plausibly considered properly basic yet do not meet the criteria of proper basicality laid down by classical (or at least modern) foundationalism. Plantinga considers three propositions:

(1) I see a tree.
(2) I had breakfast this morning.
(3) That person is angry.

He makes at least three important points about these: first, that one typically believes propositions like these basically, that is, roughly, other than on the basis of some further belief(s) one has; second, that one may be rational in believing such propositions basically, so that the beliefs in question are *properly* basic; and third, that although these beliefs are not based on others, it does not follow that they are groundless. When one sees a tree, one typically has a certain sort of experience, and normally this experience, perhaps together with other factors, both produces and justifies one's noninferential belief that one sees a tree. Similarly, "If I see someone displaying typical pain behavior, I take it that he or she is in pain. Again, I don't take the displayed behavior as *evidence* for the belief; I don't infer that belief from others I hold; I don't accept it on the basis of other beliefs."[8] This belief also appears to be properly basic, though classical foundationalism seems unable to account for its being so. (Other versions of foundationalism can account for this, but they are not Plantinga's concern here.)

---

6. Ibid., p. 44. Plantinga is aware, however, that evidentialism may also arise from coherentism; in his paper in this volume, he assesses coherentism as a basis for evidentialism.
7. See Alvin Plantinga, "Is Belief in God Rational?" *Rationality and Religious Belief*, ed. C. F. Delaney (Notre Dame: University of Notre Dame Press, 1979), esp. pp. 22–77.
8. "Is Belief in God Properly Basic?" p. 45.

One may accept all of these claims of Plantinga's and still wonder how the belief that God exists can be properly basic. Taking off from John Calvin's statement that God "reveals and daily discloses himself in the whole workmanship of the universe," Plantinga suggests: "God has so created us that we have a tendency or disposition to see his hand in the world about us. More precisely, there is in us a disposition to believe propositions of the sort *this flower was created by God* or *this vast and intricate universe was created by God* when we contemplate the flower or behold the starry heavens."[9] On this account, then, it is such beliefs as that God is speaking to me, that God created all this, and that God disapproves of what I have done which are properly basic. But these beliefs self-evidently entail that God exists; hence, if they are properly basic, evidentialism is mistaken. For, Plantinga apparently reasons, some theistic beliefs are properly basic; and even if the belief that God exists is not, we have entailing evidence for God's existence, we rationally believe the propositions expressing it, and we clearly see that they entail his existence.

One might think that if Plantinga is correct, then just about any belief can be properly basic. In rebutting this, he maintains that we presently lack adequate criteria for proper basicality, and he suggests that we should frame criteria in a broadly inductive way. In so proceeding, we must attend to examples. For instance, "Under the right conditions, it is clearly rational to believe you see a human person before you. . . . It is clear, furthermore, that you are under no obligation to reason to this belief from others you hold; under these conditions that belief is properly basic for you."[10] Similarly, "The Christian will of course suppose that belief in God is entirely proper and rational; if he doesn't accept this belief on the basis of other propositions, he will conclude that it is basic for him and quite properly so. . . . Accordingly, the Reformed epistemologist can properly hold that belief in [say] the Great Pumpkin is not properly basic, even though he holds that belief in God is properly basic and even if he has no full-fledged criterion of proper basicality."[11] Granted, a Reformed epistemologist must maintain that there is a relevant difference. But clearly there are candidates for relevant differences. One might, for example, maintain, with Calvin, that God has "implanted in us a natural tendency to see his hand in the world around us; the same cannot be said for the Great Pumpkin, there being no Great Pumpkin and no natural tendency to accept beliefs about the Great Pumpkin."[12]

9. Ibid., p. 46.
10. Ibid., p. 50.
11. Ibid.
12. Ibid., pp. 50–51.

ARE THEISTIC BELIEFS SOMETIMES BASIC?

Let us first try to clarify the key notion of proper basicality. Plantinga uses a number of locutions in characterizing this, but I think he construes a *basic* belief of a person, *S*, as one not *based on* any other belief of *S*'s[13] and a *properly* basic belief of *S*'s as a basic belief which it is rational for *S* to hold other than on the basis of any further belief of his, where presumably 'rational' is used in an epistemic sense implying some degree of epistemic justification. I shall assume this. Let us say, then, that *S*'s belief that *p* is properly basic, in the primary sense of this phrase, if and only if it is both basic and rational.[14] It thus has both a certain psychological status and a certain epistemic status. In different terms, it is *psychologically direct*, since it is not believed on the basis of a further belief of *S*'s (roughly, it is noninferential); and it is *epistemically direct*, that is, directly justified, since its justifiedness (roughly, its epistemic rationality) does not derive from that of a further belief but from something (such as a visual experience) that, though not itself admitting of justification, can render a belief justified.

In a secondary sense, a belief might be called properly basic provided that, other things remaining equal, it *would* be rational for *S* to hold it basically, that is (roughly), to retain it even if he ceased to hold it on the basis of any reason or even to have any reason for it. Thus, one could be experientially so situated that, although one's belief that there is water in a glass before one *does* rest on reasons (for example, on one's belief that one's host is serving only water), it could remain rational even if one ceased to have any reason for holding it and held it simply because of one's experience of drinking from the glass. This secondary sense of a belief's being properly basic is important, and those who think that theistic beliefs can be properly basic in the primary sense are likely to think that they can also be properly basic in the secondary sense; but the latter sense need not directly concern us.

As Plantinga emphasizes, it is hard to characterize basicality, and we also lack an adequate criterion of rationality for basic beliefs. I shall assume both points, and in discussing some possible criteria for the rationality of basic beliefs I hope to clarify the notion of a properly basic belief. My first concern, however, will be whether the theistic

---

13. This terminology is suggested by Plantinga's comments introducing the idea of a basic belief (in "Is Belief in God Properly Basic?" pp. 41–42).

14. This notion must be distinguished from another that Plantinga employs, namely, a proposition's being basic for *S*. For one thing, the latter notion may apply to a proposition not believed by *S*. I imagine Plantinga is thinking of a properly basic belief as not only not based on any other belief expressing evidence for it but such that one's holding it would be rational even if one *had* no belief expressing evidence for it. We need not, however, add this condition to our working characterization.

beliefs Plantinga cites as self-evidently entailing God's existence are plausibly considered basic. In the next section I consider the question of whether, if they are basic, they are rational.

Recall the three examples: (1) I see a tree, (2) I had breakfast this morning, and (3) That person is angry. Consider 1 and 2 first. Imagine that I am looking right at a tree and that I did in fact have breakfast this morning. It is certainly plausible to suppose that neither belief is based on any other belief of mine. Granted, if a skeptic asks me how I know I had breakfast, I may then *form* the beliefs that it seems to me that I remember having it, and that if this is so then I probably did have it. My belief that I had breakfast this morning might then *come* to be based on these beliefs. But that would not entail that the original belief was not basic[15] nor that it was not rational before I came to believe propositions expressing evidence for it.

These negative points are important: Plantinga does not hold that a person who has a properly basic theistic belief cannot come to believe the relevant proposition on the basis of other beliefs. But he denies that the rationality of the former *depends* on the possibility of one's acquiring, by reflection on what one already believes or by other means, beliefs of propositions expressing evidence for the theistic proposition in question.

When we come to example 3, however, it is less plausible to speak of basic belief. Consider a typical case in which S believes, firsthand, that Sam is angry, say on the basis of such indications as Sam's angry behavior or avowal of anger. There is some reason to think that in either case S acquires at least one belief, quite unselfconsciously to be sure, on the basis of which S believes Sam is angry. Perhaps, for example, S sees and thereby believes that Sam is screaming at Tom, and, on the basis of this belief, naturally thinks Sam is angry. The situation *need* not be analyzed along these lines: conceivably the perception of the angry behavior just "directly" produces the belief that Sam is angry. Belief formation processes may, moreover, differ in this respect from one person to another and in a single person over time. But it is arguable that normally one's belief that, say, Sam is angry, is not basic. Let me suggest one reason for holding this.

Suppose S believes that Sue is angry. If we ask why he believes this, we expect him to be able to give a reason, for example that she yelled or that Jane said Sue was angry; and typically a normal adult would not have to cast about for a reason, if his belief that Sue was angry arose in

15. I have argued against this entailment, and have tried to explain why it fails, in "Believing and Affirming," *Mind* 91 (1982).

an ordinary way. It appears that the best explanation, though not the only explanation, of the ease, speed, and spontaneity with which S can give a reason here is that he *already* believed some proposition (such as that Sue screamed) on the basis of which he believed that she is angry. Typically, there would be some fact S observed which he *took* to be an indication of anger, in a way implying that his belief that she is angry is based on his believing that fact. The fact, in turn, would normally be of a kind that can naturally be called evidence, or at least a reason for believing, that she is angry. By contrast, if we ask Jill, a normal adult innocent of philosophy, who sees a tree in front of her, why she believes she sees a tree in front of her, she is likely to be puzzled, and, if she tolerates our query, to say something to the effect that she sees it quite clearly. She is unlikely to cite, and indeed there may well not be, a proposition she believes such that we can plausibly suppose her belief that she sees a tree is based on her believing that proposition. She does not observe facts that she takes to indicate a tree; she observes *the tree*.

This is, to be sure, only a plausibility argument. Without a quite sophisticated theory of the nature of basic belief, we probably cannot fully resolve the question whether, normally, when one observes an angry-looking person and thereby comes to believe that he is angry, this belief is basic. What I hope has emerged, however, is a basis for doubting whether Plantinga's examples of apparently basic theistic beliefs would be basic for a normal adult theist. Let us look closely at several of these beliefs, for there are interesting differences among them.

The first example—believing that God is speaking to one—seems the best. It may be plausibly claimed that one's belief that, say, Jim (a good friend) is speaking to one, can be basic. Why not regard beliefs that God is speaking to one as basic when they arise from what one in some sense hears? But are circumstances in which theists typically believe God is speaking to them epistemically parallel? Or is it more likely that, for example, the theist hears a voice with special characteristics and, on the basis of believing those characteristics to be present, believes God is speaking to him? It might also be pointed out that the belief that Jim is speaking to one is in some way supported by the sight of him, whereas, if it makes sense to speak of seeing God at all, he cannot be seen as a whole in the way a human being can be. This point apparently makes it less likely that one's forming the belief that God is speaking to one is "automatic" in the way one's forming the belief that Jim is speaking to one is. But the point is inconclusive; for *if* God's voice is physically or perhaps just vividly heard, it too might be automatically recognized. There seem to be further relevant differences between the two kinds of hearing, but let us forgo discussing them in order to consider other examples.

In the case of the belief that God disapproves of what I have done, one would think that it might be based on, say, my beliefs that I have done wrong and that God knows what I have done and disapproves of wrongdoing. Consider the belief that God has created all this, said of a beautiful scene in nature. Even when such a belief arises spontaneously, one would think that it might be based on the more general belief that God created the earth, together with the belief that this beautiful scene is not a fortuitous concourse of atoms but a part of the earth God created. Temporally, the experience of the scene may no doubt "immediately" elicit the belief, rather as my seeing a tree elicits the belief that there is a tree before me. But the former is apparently in some epistemic sense mediated by other beliefs in a way the latter normally is not. Granted, on the basis of believing that God disapproves of what one has done, one could form the belief that one has done wrong, but that would show only that beliefs of the former kind can *be* a basis for others, not that they need not themselves *have* a basis in others.

There is an objection to this line of analysis implicit in some of what Plantinga says. Defending the proper basicality of a typical belief that one sees a human person before one, he points out that one is "under no obligation to reason to this belief from others" one holds, and that "under those conditions that belief is properly basic."[16] A related remark is that when I see someone exhibiting typical pain behavior, "I don't take the displayed behavior as *evidence* for that belief; I don't infer that belief from others I hold; I don't accept it on the basis of other beliefs."[17] Let us assume these three points. Even taken together, they do not imply that the belief that the person is in pain is not *based* on any other belief. Surely my belief that Sam is in pain can be (epistemically and psychologically) based on my (perceptually grounded) belief that he cut himself and cried out, even though (a) I do not *take* that as evidence (since I do not conceptualize it as evidence and do not form any belief that it is); (b) I do not *infer* that he is in pain (since I do not go through any mental process of arriving at a proposition from one or more others constituting premises in some sense); and (c) I do not *accept*, but simply form, the belief that Sam is in pain (since I do not consider whether this is so but just "see" that it is). If all this is correct, then we can agree that one is under no obligation to *reason* to the belief that Sam is in pain, yet deny that such beliefs are in general basic.

16. "Is Belief in God Properly Basic?" p. 50.
17. Ibid., p. 45.

It might be replied that if S's belief that p is really based on his belief that q, then he must have inferred p from q, taken q as evidence, and accepted p on the basis of q. I would resist this move both because of my conceptions of inference and of the basis relation between beliefs, and because, if we do resist it, we are better able to make epistemologically useful distinctions, for instance that between temporal and epistemic immediacy. But suppose we accept the move. We shall then be using the locutions 'take as evidence', 'infer from', and 'accept on the basis of' so broadly that it will be at best harder for Plantinga to show that theistic beliefs of the kind he cites are basic. For these phrases will then apply to many beliefs that arise more or less instantly and very spontaneously, including at least many beliefs arising in experiences of a broadly religious kind. On the other hand, suppose that we are careful not to use these locutions too broadly and we *then* construe the basis relation as one which, like inferring, apparently requires a process in consciousness or a conceptualization of some proposition *as* evidence. It may now be less difficult to show that theistic beliefs are often not based on others, but it will be harder to show that they do not *depend* on others for their justification, in the way one's belief that Sam is in pain apparently depends on one's belief that he has cut himself and cried out.

My conclusion in this section, then, is that if we construe the notion of one belief's being based on another in the most plausible way, then Plantinga must do considerably more to establish that beliefs of the sort he wishes to construe as basic really are basic in the typical cases in which people have them. The point is important not only for understanding theistic beliefs but for assessing their justification. For presumably if S's belief that p is essentially based[18] on his belief that q, then his belief that p is rational (in the sense of 'rationally held') only if it is justified by his belief that q; and that, in turn, appears to depend on the latter belief's being justified. Roughly, the idea is that if one's belief of something depends on one's belief of some proposition that functions as one's ground for the first belief, then the first is epistemically dependent on the second and is justified only if the second is. This idea is quite plausible; if it is correct, then if no theistic beliefs are basic, the rationality of such beliefs apparently depends on that of other beliefs, and rational theistic beliefs require evidence after all.

18. I cannot try to define this notion here, but the most important element in it for our purposes is that S's belief that p being based on his belief that q be a necessary condition (other things equal) for his believing p. My point in the text will not hold if his belief that p is also based on his belief that r, in such a way that he would believe p on the basis of r even if he did not believe q.

CAN THEISTIC BELIEFS BE PROPERLY BASIC?

So far, I have focused on the case for construing certain theistic beliefs, in something like a normal Hebraic-Christian setting, as basic. But suppose we grant that they are basic. Surely they *could* be, for some persons at some times. What account can we then give of their rationality?

One might think that propositions entailing the existence of God are *intrinsically* unsuited to be objects of properly basic (human) beliefs. One might appeal, for example, to the nonmaterial nature of God or to the complexity of the concept of God. But such considerations seem indecisive, at least for true propositions. Moreover, they assume the falsity of a standard theistic view. For suppose that God is omnipotent. Then, for any true proposition, he can bring it about that he knows it *directly* (indeed, perhaps his knowing all truths directly is entailed by perfect omniscience). Theists are thus likely to argue that God can also bring it about that the beliefs constituting his direct knowledge are *properly* basic for him (if indeed this does not follow from God's directly knowing them).[19] This reasoning may be controversial, but I shall proceed on the assumption that the propositional objects of theistic beliefs are not intrinsically incapable of being objects of properly basic beliefs.

Supposing they could be, how might they be? In exploring this, I shall not set forth a criterion of properly basic belief (that would be a major undertaking). My procedure will be to examine some good candidates for such beliefs and to explore whether certain theistic beliefs are relevantly similar to them. To simplify matters, let us consider only beliefs with existential import and make the guiding, and presumably uncontroversial, assumption that a properly basic belief has some set of characteristics or relations—other than epistemic dependence relations to beliefs expressing evidence for it—in virtue of which the belief is justified.

Consider my belief that there is paper before me, and assume that it is basic. A number of important points may be plausibly claimed to hold for such a belief: (1) It is experientially grounded, that is, in some way based on concurrent experience. More specifically, it is perceptual (as opposed to, say, introspective), for I believe this in virtue of seeing, or at least apparently seeing, paper before me. (2) This belief is of a kind such that, normally, part of what causes beliefs of that kind to arise and part of what sustains them during the relevant perceptual

19. Presumably the same holds for God's knowledge of the falsity of false propositions. If he can know directly that *p* is true no matter how complicated *p* is, why should we have to know in some other way that not-*p* is false?

experience, is stimulation of the cognitive system by the sort of things the beliefs are about. Here, for instance, a piece of paper reflects light rays to the retina and thereby stimulates the cognitive system. Beliefs like this, then, might be loosely dubbed *veridically caused.* (3) The belief also is of a kind that is in a sense irresistible:[20] in the circumstances just specified, one normally cannot help forming such a belief. (4) The belief exhibits a kind of universality: roughly, any normal person in the relevant circumstances—here, focusing his eyes on the paper in normal light—who has the concepts to form a belief of this kind (for example, the concept of paper), will form the belief. (5) The belief is of a sort such that normally the only plausible explanation of why one has it requires the assumption of its truth. (6) Moreover—and this point is connected with (5)—the truth of the belief is supported by the normally quite readily realizable possibility of the same perceptual object's being perceived in another sensory mode. To be sure, "perceptibility" in another sensory mode is possible even for hallucinatory "objects," but it is not normally either realized or readily realizable.

Much the same sort of thing holds for introspective beliefs about one's present states. Suppose I have been deprived of liquids for thirty-six hours. I will doubtless believe that I am thirsty, and I will believe this in virtue of an experiential state something like a perceptual one. This kind of belief is normally caused by thirst. It is, in these circumstances, irresistible and universal, in appropriate senses; and normally the only plausible explanation of why one has such a belief requires the assumption of its truth. Granted, the belief is only indirectly supportable by experience in other sense modes, but clearly one could have independent grounds for it through those modes. In both examples, the characteristics brought out suffice to make clear why such beliefs are at least likely to be true, which helps to clarify why they should be conceived as justified.[21] Similar points hold for my believing that I had breakfast this morning and for my believing that I see a tree (when I do in fact seem to see one).

I shall not argue that conditions of the sorts just outlined are necessary for the rationality of a basic existential belief. While some of them may be close to expressing necessary conditions, others need clarification before they can even be seriously assessed. The notion of a plausi-

20. I am not suggesting that believing is in general under the control of the will; but in certain cases we apparently can, by a suitable exercise of will, reject or suspend judgment on certain propositions but not others.
21. The relation between justification and truth is a complicated matter, which cannot be pursued here. It may well deserve more attention than it has received, and I address it in detail in "Justification, Truth, and Reliability," in progress.

ble explanation is neither clear nor uncontroversial, for instance; and the status of universality requirements on the rationality of basic beliefs is part of what is at issue between experientialists and evidentialists. But some, at least, of the six conditions have seemed to various philosophers to be necessary for properly basic beliefs, and partly for this reason it is fruitful to explore how they apply to some theistic beliefs of the kind central in Plantinga's attack on evidentialism. Moreover, the comparison between perceptual beliefs and purportedly direct theistic beliefs is in any case considered vitally important by both evidentialists and experientialists; and the latter, who apparently take experiential direct access to God to be typically through the senses, seem to assume the proper basicality of ordinary perceptual beliefs.

Imagine, then, that S believes God is speaking to him. Can this be in virtue of a perceptual or other appropriate justificatory basis? Certainly S can have auditory sensations that give him the impression of a divine voice or, more readily still, can experience in his mind's ear what seems to be a divine voice. Moreover, surely some actual auditory state, possibly one caused by a divine voice, can (given appropriate background factors) produce and sustain the belief. It is far less clear whether the belief is likely to be irresistible in the relevant sense; but presumably it would be for some theists, and we might suppose that it is properly basic only for people for whom it is irresistible.

The application of conditions 4–6 is harder to assess. Concerning condition 4, on the face of it, the belief does not appear appropriately universal, for it would seem that a normal person who has the concept of God and hears the sort of voice imagined might perfectly well suppose he is hallucinating or being duped. This, in turn, bears on condition 5. It indicates some competing explanations of the origin of the theist's basic belief that God is speaking to him, explanations not embodying the assumption of the truth of this belief. Certainly a skeptic would say that the theist might be hallucinating or unknowingly producing the inner voice he takes to be God's. (Note, however, that skeptics tend to say similar things about ordinary perceptual beliefs.) Third, while it makes sense to talk of hearing God speaking to one, it does not clearly make sense to talk of experiencing God, at least with comparable "directness," in any other sensory mode.

It is not clear, however, just how seriously to take these considerations. We could, for example, become so skeptical that we would not form the belief that there was paper before us even when we saw it there. We might believe only that we *seemed* to see paper. If, in addition, our skepticism were abetted by a demon who caused us to believe that there were no physical objects, we might go on to deny that the only plausible explanation of our having the sense impressions we do have (for example, of paper before us) requires us to assume that a piece of paper before us is acting on our senses. Surely, the possibility of some people's becoming skeptical in this way does not undermine the rationality of other people's basic perceptual beliefs, if indeed it undermines the rationality of anyone's basic perceptual beliefs—including the skeptic's—formed under appropriate conditions. Why, then, should the possibility, or even the existence, of a parallel reaction to an apparent divine voice undermine the rationality of the basic theistic beliefs which these voices elicit in theists?

There are, to be sure, potentially significant disanalogies between the two examples. For one thing, there seems to be no standard, reliable way, even for theists, to create conditions under which God will speak to them. For another thing, when God speaks to a person, corroboration by another sense seems, if not inconceivable, then at least generally unavailable. But how significant are these limitations? Suppose some people have a sixth sense but cannot in general seek out the things that they sense through it: they have to wait for circumstances of appropriate stimulation. Would this imply that the relevant basic beliefs are not rational? Undoubtedly, if the occurrence of the claimed sensory experiences could be explained without assuming their truth, and if normal persons could not confirm (or disconfirm) the beliefs formed through the sense, skeptics would scoff and cautious nonskeptics would at least suspend judgment. But would that show that the basic sixth-sensory beliefs of people with a sixth sense are not rational, or that they ought to suspend judgment? I cannot see that either conclusion follows, and perhaps some basic beliefs about God should be considered as arising from a distinctive mode of experience analogous to a sixth sense. If some of them do arise in this way, however, that must be argued; for it is neither clearly true nor confirmed by the sorts of experiences of God reported by most of the theists who say they have experienced God. Those experiences seem perceptually ordinary, at least in being apparently nonhallucinatory and in involving (however vividly) only the five senses.

So far, I have been imaging sixth-sensory perception of ordinary perceptible objects or properties, for example colors. The analogy between such perception and direct acquaintance with God (whether or not such acquaintance is perceptual) is less helpful to the case against evidentialism if what is accessible to the imagined sixth sense is not accessible to any other sense, though socially confirmable in the way theistic beliefs are. It is, arguably, part of our concept of a perceptible external substance that it normally can be perceived in more than one sense mode, if in any. But if minds are substances and can be directly heard, then they are an exception to this which theists are likely to take seriously. Moreover, it is surely not a necessary truth that direct experiential knowledge of external substances is sensory at all. So the theist may simply reject the entire attempt to assimilate the rationality of basic theistic beliefs to that of perceptual beliefs.

Quite apart from the considerations just cited to suggest that, at the very least, properly basic theistic beliefs may have to be regarded as a special case, we have not, of course, canvassed all the plausible candidates for necessary conditions on the proper basicality of existential beliefs. One might certainly argue that a kind of existential belief is not properly basic unless it is at least normally the case that the only (empirically) *possible* explanation of the existence of such a belief requires assuming its truth. One might also hold that the notion of rational belief is universalist in a sense entailing that a belief can be rationally held only if it is in principle confirmable or disconfirmable by any normal person. The first view seems too strong; it would seem to undermine the justification of many amply justified perceptual and memory beliefs. I am less sure about the second, but perhaps in principle theistic beliefs satisfy its requirement.[22] Presumably, it one thinks that there are properly basic theistic beliefs, one would maintain that suitably educated normal persons can confirm them by ascertaining that on appropriate occasions others have formed supporting beliefs.

I am not aware of other plausible requirements on proper basicality which seem to show that theistic beliefs cannot be properly basic, and my conclusion here is that this has not been shown. In saying this I am of course leaving out of account, as Plantinga does in the works that concern us, the coherentist view that there are no properly basic existential beliefs.

PROPER BASICALITY AND EVIDENTIAL DEPENDENCE

There is a danger of misconstruing the importance, for evidentialism, of the conclusion that there can be properly basic theistic beliefs. To see this, consider memorial beliefs. Surely one may properly believe, and even know, without evidence and on the basis of memory, that one has met William Alston and that the Battle of Hastings was fought in 1066. Here, then, we have a kind of properly basic belief. The rationality (and justification) or such beliefs is not dependent on one's having

---

22. An example might be John Hick's case for the possibility of eschatological verification, especially if we put 'confirmation' in place of 'verification'. See, for example, "Theology and Verification," *Theology Today* 27 (1960).

evidence: and one may have none. Let us say that they are not *contemporaneously evidentially dependent*. It does not follow that they are not *justificatorily dependent*, that is, that their justification (and rationality) does not depend on one's having or having had one or more other justified (or rational) beliefs whose justification (or rationality) is or was essential to grounding the current justification (or rationality) of these beliefs. Indeed, it is arguable that such beliefs are *historically evidentially dependent*, in the sense that their justification (and rationality) requires that one once had adequate evidence for the proposition in question, for example had evidence—such as someone's introducing Alston to one *as* William Alston—for the proposition that one has met him.

Now it surely can be argued that, even if a theistic belief is properly basic, it is still not justificatorily independent and indeed is historically evidentially dependent. Suppose that, as a result of testimony and of educative influences early in his life, S came to believe that God exists. S at that time had evidence, even if he did not take it as such, for God's existence; and presumably his belief that God exists was initially based, as were others of his theistic beliefs, on his beliefs to the effect that, say, his parents in some sense knew about God. It is surely arguable that if he had not had such evidence, his present belief would not be properly basic. Perhaps this holds even if his initial theistic beliefs were not (epistemically) *based* on his evidence, even if, for example, they were somehow imitative but not inferential. For if nothing his parents said *consituted* evidence for God's existence, perhaps his resulting beliefs would not have been justified, regardless of whether those beliefs were based on, rather than merely causally grounded in, what they said.

Similarly, S will have once had evidence, for example through testimony, for a voice of a certain sort, heard in certain circumstances, being God's voice. Presumably, he had to learn to recognize the voice. Even if his current belief that God is speaking to him is not based on this evidence, the belief might not be properly basic for him if he had never had the evidence; for, arguably, if it did not have this sort of evidential background, it would not now be rational. If properly basic theistic beliefs are, in this or some other way, historically evidentially dependent, then, while their existence is of great importance, they would not refute evidentialism if the view were formulated (as perhaps it should be) more broadly than at the start of this paper, to take account of the justificatory history of a belief rather than simply S's current evidence. As specified above, evidentialism is the view that one's belief that God exists is justified only if one has evidence for it. This is a *moderate evidentialism*. The more plausible position being explored here—*weak evidentialism*—is that one's belief that God exists is justified only if one has or has had adequate evidence for it. (One might also want to hold that the belief must be somehow memorially connected with the evidence, but we need not address that problem here.)

A useful analogy might be this: while I might have a properly basic belief that this is Alston before me, perhaps it could not be *properly* basic unless I already know (or have a justified belief as to) *who* Alston is; and I could not know that unless I once had evidence, for example from testimony, as to who he is. My properly basic belief, then, might be evidentially dependent on that original evidence. Why should knowing who God is be any less evidentially dependent?

Two points suggest themselves in reply. First, this reasoning apparently makes even knowledge that there is (say) red before me evidentially dependent, since I must already know what redness it in order to know this. Second, it is arguable that knowledge and properly basic (true) belief must not be assimilated: perhaps I must already know who Alston is to know that this is he, but I can have a properly basic belief that this is he simply by virtue of an appropriate confident sense that this is he.

To the first point, one might reply that knowing what redness is, in the relevant sense of the phrase, requires only having experienced (and remembered) redness, and not recognizing it in terms of something else, whereas that is not so for knowing who God is, at least in the limited ways in which human beings can experience him. This rejoinder, though significant, may not be decisive, so let us pass on to the second reply, which concerns me far more. The point of this second reply seems highly plausible: confident memory impressions, by and large, do generate at least prima facie justification; and it may be quite plausibly argued that, if I have a confident impression, based on memory, that this is Alston, then it is proper that I basically believe this is he. Granted, if I have reason to believe that there is an identical twin of his about or if I actually believe that I have never met Alston, then I am unlikely to have the appropriate justification. But such beliefs may well be absent.

Perhaps, however, what applies to the justification (and rationality) of beliefs about human beings does not apply to beliefs about God. It could be argued that a confident impression, based on memory, that God is speaking to me, is not as readily prima facie justified as a corresponding belief about a human being, if only because it takes more to know (of even have a justified belief about) *who* God is. This point is surely controversial, however, and one avenue of reply is to distinguish between elementary and sophisticated knowledge of who God is and to argue that only the former is required to know that he is speaking to one.

Suppose that in this way we do defend the possibility that one can have a properly basic belief that God is speaking to one, without the rationality of the belief's depending on evidence as to who God is. We shall then have paid a certain price. For even if confident memory-based impressions can in this way generate prima facie justification, they certainly do not imply knowledge: the proposition in question need not be true, and even if it is true, S's justification in believing it need not be sufficient to render it knowledge. One would like to think, however, that the sense in which a theistic belief can be properly basic is such that if it is both properly basic and true, then it represents knowledge. (This assumption appears to be presupposed by Plantinga, even if he is not committed to it.)

This point is at least partially balanced by another, however. Suppose that the direct justification of a theistic belief does not entail that if the belief is true then it is knowledge. Knowledge of God may still be possible without the belief in question being justified at all. Some epistemologists have argued that knowledge does not entail justification, and a theist might certainly contend that God could (for example) reveal himself to one in such a way that one knows God is speaking to one even if one fails to be justified in so believing. Such a belief might be argued to be not necessarily unjustified (or irrational) but simply nonjustified, and some would go on to call it a matter of faith. But I take it that Plantinga is arguing not only that (as I would put it) theists may be in the epistemically *successful* position we call knowledge but, nonevidentially, in the epistemically *acceptable* position we call being justified (and rationally believing). In any event, my main emphasis will continue to be on the issue of whether theistic beliefs can be directly justified. But it is important to grasp that theists could shift their emphasis from justification to knowledge, could argue that knowledge does not entail justification, and could stress that God could produce in us knowledge of his existence and nature even if the beliefs in question are not justified.

We have seen so far that there are serious obstacles in the way of showing that theistic beliefs can be directly justified, and that their being so justified does not entail that if they are true they are knowledge. Still, we have found no decisive reason to consider directly justified theistic beliefs impossible. Now, if one can have experiences such as apparently hearing God speaking to one, which nonevidentially render a basic theistic belief justified, then evidentialism is quite mistaken, even if this kind of direct justification does not entail knowledge. As I have stressed, however, a similar thesis might still hold for theistic knowledge: *noetic evidentialism* could be true even if *justificatory evidentialism* is false (and conversely). In any case, our other points about justification remain significant. For instance, it may turn out that if they are correct, then, whatever the *possibility* of directly justified theistic beliefs, there may in fact be no one who has theistic beliefs that are not at least historically evidentially dependent: not, for example, dependent on one's having formed, on the basis of adequate evidence, rational beliefs about what sorts of voices are God's. Further considerations bearing on this possibility will emerge later. We must first explore another way in which theistic beliefs might exhibit justificatory dependence. I have in mind especially the possibility that would-be direct justification may be defeated. This possibility will be examined in the next section.

DEFEASIBILITY

We have already noted that proper basicality is relative to persons. If *S* has lost his hearing and knows this, he will not in general form basic beliefs about what sounds are around him, and if he should form such a belief, it would be unlikely to be rational. The rationality of basic belief may also be relative to circumstances. Suppose that Ann is twelve feet from a bowl of fruit and correctly believes there are apples in it. Before artificial fruit was invented, this basic belief might have been perfectly rational; but after she discovers that many people use artificial fruit, which at that distance she cannot distinguish from real fruit, she is less likely to form the basic belief, at that distance, that there are apples in a fruit bowl she sees, and if she does form this basic belief it may well not be rational. Now, perhaps something similar applies to many mature, reflective theists. Supposing that *S* once did rationally hold some basic theistic beliefs, are they still properly basic when he learns such things as that people sometimes hallucinate voices, that drugs can induce apparently religious experiences, that people have invoked their experience to justify religious beliefs inconsistent with his religious beliefs, that the problem of evil seems to some generally rational people to provide good reason to think God does not exist, and that a number of generally rational people think the best explanation of theistic beliefs is in terms of cultural and psychological factors and does not support the assumption of God's existence?

It is surely arguable that someone in this position can rationally hold theistic beliefs only if he has good reasons for them. If so, natural theology may be required after all to justify such a person's theistic beliefs. A weaker claim would be that such a person need only see how to refute (or to block) arguments against theistic beliefs, and a still weaker view would be that he need only justifiably believe that these arguments *can* be refuted (or blocked).

But even if one of these weaker claims is true, perhaps his theistic beliefs would be rational only if they are in some way sustained by, or at least somehow accountable to, his believing (or perhaps justifiably believing) that the antitheistic arguments (or the relevant ones) are unsound. It is not that he would take this proposition as evidence for God's existence, but his theistic beliefs would in some way be at least accountable to it. To be sure, a theist who believes God is speaking to him would not need to *consider* whether he is hallucinating and rule that out. But perhaps his belief would be rational only if it is in some way accountable to a rational belief (which need not enter his consciousness at the time) that there is no good reason to think experiences of this sort are hallucinatory.

Perhaps these claims can be refuted. In any event, the case against evidentialism will be unsatisfying to defenders of the possibility of properly basic theistic beliefs unless a weaker view, a justificatory dependence thesis, is also shown to be mistaken: the view that, even if rational theistic beliefs need not be *based on* (or sustained by) any other beliefs, their *justification* (and rationality) depend on *S*'s having, or at least having justification for forming, certain other, "self-defensive" beliefs, such as that there is no good reason to think experiences of the relevant kind are hallucinatory. This thesis is not a narrow version of evidentialism, for it does not require *S*'s having evidence for God's existence. What it does require may be interpreted in various ways. Just two will be specified here.

In a strong form, this justificatory dependence thesis says that, in order to have a properly basic theistic belief, one that is both rational and not based on any evidence beliefs, *S* must meet a certain rational standard. He must have, or be able to construct, either an adequate argument against certain putative reasons to believe that God does not exist or at least an adequate argument for the view that there are no sufficient reasons for believing that he does not exist, for example an argument to the effect that Alvin Plantinga has provided such reasonings and has thereby rebutted (say) the argument from evil. We might call this position *argumentalism*. It shares with evidentialism the view that theistic beliefs are justifcatorily dependent, since it takes them to depend for their justification (and rationality) on that of other beliefs; but it seems more plausible. It is, however, also quite inimical to experientialism of the kind that conceives certain theistic beliefs as justificatorily independent.

In a weaker form, the justificatory dependence thesis in question says only that, in order to have properly basic theistic beliefs, S must be such that, given his circumstances and beliefs, he is justified in believing, even if he in fact does not believe, propositions that would at least neutralize any plausible antitheistic considerations of which he is aware or may reasonably be expected to be aware. Perhaps, if he meets this condition, then in principle he also meets the argumentalist standard. But that is not obvious, particularly as applied to people whose capacities to construct arguments are minimal. In any case, if even this weaker thesis is true, then direct theistic beliefs, even if justified, would exhibit a kind of justificatory dependence (and presumably a kind of specifically evidential dependence, since S would at least need to have, or be justified in forming beliefs that express, evidence against the relevant antitheistic considerations).

One might object here that the justification needed to neutralize potential counterarguments is already virtually implicit in S's being justified (or at least fairly strongly justified) in believing that God exists. For if he is justified in this and (as could easily be the case) in believing that if God exists, then there is no sound argument against God's existence, he is ipso facto justified in believing that antitheistic arguments (arguments to the effect that God does not exist) are unsound.[23] (As for skeptical arguments, these at most show that no one knows or justifiably believes that God exists, and one need not have reason to believe these arguments unsound in order to be justified simply in believing the nonepistemic proposition that God exists. One might have to have reason to believe that they are unsound in order to be justified in believing that one *knows or justifiably believes* God exists, but that is another matter.)

Surely this attempt to show a kind of automatic neutralization of potential defeaters is double edged. Suppose that, as theists and nontheists can agree, S is justified in believing that if God exists (*p*), then there is no sound argument having the conclusion that he does not exist (*q*). Why is it more plausible to say that, if he is justified in believing this conditional and *p*, then he is justified in believing *q*, than to say that if he is *not* justified in believing *q*, then he is not justified in believing *p*? Perhaps the objection I am considering is defensible even if the suggested parity is granted. One might argue that the theist is entitled to view the matter from his perspective and to *start* with the supposition

---

23. This objection has been suggested by Edward Wierenga, in correspondence. Peter Klein has defended a similar epistemic principle in *Certainty* (Minneapolis: University of Minnesota Press, 1981), ch. 2.

that his belief that God exists is justified. If skeptics (or atheists) wish to view the matter from their perspective, they may; but the possibility of starting from either position does not show which is right. One might conclude, then, that the mere existence of defeaters which the mature theist should be able to take some account of does not show that properly basic theistic beliefs are justificatorily dependent.

If the epistemic principle under consideration is correct—call it the principle of the transmission of justification across subjectively justified implications (that is, implications one is justified in believing)—then there is indeed a kind of standoff, as just sketched. But the standoff is less favorable to the disagreeing parties than might be thought; for there is surely good reason to think that, if both starting points are legitimate, then neither view is justified and both parties should suspend judgment, unless each has *independent* reasons to think the other mistaken. But rather than compare the starting points, let us consider the epistemic principle.

Are there not cases in which one is justified, even rather strongly justified, in believing something—say *p*, on the basis of testimony one has just heard—and justified in believing that, if it is so, then something else, say *q*, is, yet not justified in believing *q*? Suppose *A* tells us at 11:00 P.M. that *B*, to whom he has just spoken, is calling from Chicago. *A* is credible, and we are justified in believing him. But *B* has given us the message that he will be in class in Lincoln the next morning; B is also credible, and we are justified in believing that he will be in class. Let this proposition be *q*. We are also justified, however, in believing *p*, that the next plane from Chicago to Lincoln (which is in the morning) will not get him to Lincoln in time for the class (which is at 8:00 A.M.); and we are justified, by our knowledge of transportation, in believing that if *p*, then not *q*, that is, that if the next plane will not do so, then *B* will not be in class (he would simply arrange for a substitute, we may suppose). We may even actually believe this conditional, if it does not occur to us when we form the belief that *B* is in Chicago, as it surely need not. Either way, this case certainly looks like a counterexample to the principle. Abbreviating, we are justified at the time in believing that if *p*, then not *q*—that is, if the next plane will not get *B* to class, then *B* will not be there—but we are *also* justified on separate grounds in believing that the plane will not do this (*p*) and that *B* *will* be there (*q*).

The point, in part, is that neither the formation of justified beliefs nor the acquisition of justification for beliefs must wait upon our drawing, or taking account of, all the inferences we are entitled to draw. So we can, on good evidence, become justified in believing *p* even while we are also justified in believing (but do not entertain) the propositions that if *p*, then *q*, and that not-*q*. One could protest that since we were already justified in believing not-*q*, that is, that *B* will not be in class, *and* that if not-*q*, then not-*p*, we were justified in believing not-*p* and should not have formed the belief that *p*, that is, that the next plane from Chicago will not get *B* to Lincoln in time for class. But this objection presupposes the principle and may not be used to defend it. It also suggests that *B*'s avowal that he will be in class has sufficient justification to override our justification (which we may suppose is based on long and wide experience) for believing the airline schedule will not change in the relevant respect. Moreover, at least for defeasible justification—and our concern here is surely not indefeasible justification—it seems possible to be justified, on one basis, in believing *p*, and, on another basis, in believing not-*p*. This point is strongly supported (though not entailed) by the possibility of justification's arising noninferentially from distinct sources, for example perception and memory; and plausible versions of experientialism seem committed to acknowledging this possibility.

It will not help to try to defend experientialism by altering the epistemic principle to read: if *S* justifiably believes that *p*, and that if *p*, then *q*, then *S* is justified in believing *q*. Our example (in its second variant) shows this to be mistaken as well: there the relevant conditional had only been temporarily forgotten and is still believed. In any event, surely not all of those whose theistic beliefs might be plausibly thought to be properly basic should be imagined to believe that, if God exists, then there is no sound argument against his existence.

Suppose, however, that a theist does believe something like this. Just what is believed here? Are *inductively* sound arguments included? If so, then rational theists presumably need not believe, at least prior to extensive philosophical reflection, that there are no sound arguments against God's existence. For inductively sound arguments need only have (suitable) premises that confer a significant probability on their conclusions; their conclusions need not be true. Suppose, then, that a rational theist who knows of such considerations as the inductive argument from evil does believe it sound, and entertains the implication. It seems not unlikely that, far from simply or securely concluding that any antitheistic argument there may be is unsound—in the sense of 'unsound' applicable to inductive arguments—he will have the thought that if he has no independent reason to think such arguments unsound, his own theistic belief may not be rational. This thought would not by itself automatically prevent his believing both directly and justifiably that God exists, but it might lead to his thinking about the purported counterevidence in a *way* that requires his forming some reasons to neutralize it *if* he is to remain justified in his theistic beliefs. It is at least far from obvious that direct justification (or proper basicality) of one's theistic belief would, in the way imagined and unaided by evidential reliance on reasons or reasoning, cancel out all the relevant prima facie defeaters of that justification.

Let me stress that in raising these questions I am not suggesting that none of the basic theistic beliefs of a mature theist who has learned about hallucination and the like can in any sense be *well grounded.* His basic belief that (for example) God is speaking to him can be caused in an appropriate way by God's actually doing so. But one's basic belief that there is fruit on the table can be well grounded in much the same way, yet not be rational. The question here is whether basic theistic beliefs, especially of the kind we have been discussing, can be rational for mature theists who have certain potentially undermining beliefs. I am leaving this open, but I suspect that a positive answer requires more argument than it has so far received.

Argument would be required, I think, even if it is true that "God has so created us that we have a tendency or disposition to see his hand in the world about us." For suppose that he also gave us a disposition to form certain basic perceptual beliefs about our perceived physical environment. Even when these beliefs are true and perceptually well grounded, their rationality may be undermined by various other beliefs we have. I am not sure quite what epistemological significance Plantinga attributes to Calvin's view that God has created us with the disposition just mentioned. Presumably Plantinga does not think that this disposition *grounds* basic theistic beliefs. It might nonetheless be part of what explains their existence and manifestations. But when, for example, God is speaking to *S*, it is presumably God's speaking to him that (at least indirectly) grounds his belief that God is doing so. *S*'s disposition to take the voice to be God's (rather than think it hallucinatory, for instance), has a different status. Thus it will not do to argue that mature theists who have potentially undermining beliefs can have rational basic theistic beliefs simply because those beliefs are grounded in a God-given disposition to see his hand in the world. This disposition might explain in part why they form these beliefs, but its role in making their formation possible (or likely) does not by itself protect their justification from being undermined. Like perceptual justification, it remains defeasible.

If it is true that for people with a certain kind of sophistication, rational basic theistic beliefs, or at least justificatorily independent basic theistic beliefs, are not possible, then, unless the evidentialist objection can be met directly, we reach the rather odd conclusion that as one gains knowledge of the world one may lose knowledge of God, or at least cease to be justified (or rational) in believing he exists. (I say 'at least' to leave open the possibility—which is important for the larger question of evidentialism—that one may directly *know*, without having a justified belief, that God exists.)[24] Perhaps, however, this conclusion should not be altogether unexpected. One might even speculate that a similar thought could have been among those underlying Jesus' words "Truly, I say to you, unless you turn and become like children, you will never enter the kingdom of heaven" (Matt. 18:3). It is difficult to say, of course, under what conditions a basic belief is undermined by other beliefs the theist acquires. If there can be theistic beliefs that are both basic and rational, they may be possible for people of considerable sophistication, provided they do not acquire the sorts of undermining beliefs described above. Someone might protest that if the information is readily available, theists must take account of it, if their theistic beliefs are to remain rational. Perhaps. But if this line is to be reasonably pressed, one would like to know why it would not undermine the rationality of the basic perceptual beliefs of people with no knowledge of hallucinations and illusions. There are possible explanations, no doubt, but I cannot pursue them now.

PERMISSIVENESS

We have so far been largely concerned with whether experientialism can justify enough. We should now ask whether experientialism (as represented in Plantinga's work) justifies too much and must count as properly basic many irrational beliefs, such as that the Great Pumpkin returns every Halloween. As I have sketched the case for the rationality of basic theistic beliefs, one factor is whether the only plausible explanation of someone's holding them requires assuming their truth. Clearly, not just any belief meets this condition. If anyone believes that the Great Pumpkin returns every Halloween, plausibly explaining this belief surely does not require assuming its truth. But Plantinga rejects the rationality of belief in the Great Pumpkin mainly on a quite different

24. A number of epistemologists have conceived of knowledge in such a way that it apparently does not entail justified belief; I am here leaving this possibility open. A good example of this view is Frederick I. Dretske's conception of knowledge as information-produced belief. See, for example, *Knowledge and the Flow of Information* (Cambridge, Mass.: MIT Press, 1981). If knowledge does not imply justification, the possibility of direct knowledge of God, suitably produced by him, may well be less difficult to show than the possibility of directly justified (roughly, properly basic) belief about him. For a more recent discussion arguing against the entailment, see William P. Alston's "Justification and Knowledge," read at the Seventh World Congress of Philosophy in 1983.

ground: that there is "no Great Pumpkin and no natural tendency to accept beliefs about the Great Pumpkin."[25] The reasoning apparently used here needs examination.

Is the idea here that a natural tendency to accept beliefs is necessary, or sufficient, for their being properly basic, at least when they arise under certain conditions? Plantinga seems to suggest that such a tendency is necessary under certain conditions; but it is not clear what conditions he might impose. We can imagine certain unnatural beliefs, which one must learn to form, turning out to be properly basic. Consider certain beliefs about others' thoughts, say beliefs formed through strange but reliable telepathic signals. As for the possibility that, under certain conditions, our having a natural tendency to form certain basic beliefs is sufficient for their rationality, I am again unable to assess this without further specification. On certain plausible assumptions, it might be argued that by virtue of evolutionary considerations, if there is such a tendency, it must be toward true beliefs. But exploring this hypothesis and its relation to rational belief is not possible here. It may be, in any event, that Plantinga is interested only in the the special case of a tendency created in us by God. If so, it would seem that the relevant beliefs are properly basic if formed under the conditions that naturally evoke the tendency. But this would not be because the tendency by itself is an adequate ground for them; it would presumably be because God would not cause us to tend to form irrational basic beliefs.

This last point is important in understanding Plantinga. I take his case for the rationality of basic theistic beliefs to be in part a case for their possible well-groundedness. If we have a natural tendency, created by God, to form such basic beliefs, one would expect that they are well grounded. But for all that, the God-given tendency seems epistemologically secondary. It does help to explain why we form basic theistic beliefs and why God in some sense reveals himself to us in the situations in which his so doing is the ground of our theistic beliefs formed in response to those revelations. For it would be strange if, having created the relevant tendency in us, he never provided the natural occasions for its realization. But what renders the basic theistic beliefs rational, I take it, is their grounds, for example, God's actually speaking to one or evoking in one a sense of his presence in a beautiful scene.

I have so far talked as if it were plausible to suppose we have the natural tendency Plantinga describes. But do we? Why, then, have so many people of so many sorts been nontheists? One could point out

---

25. "Is Belief in God Properly Basic?" p. 51.

that some have been ignorant, others corrupted by skepticism, and still others not brought by God into circumstances that activate the tendency to form beliefs about him. But is this a better explanation than that some people have not been taught or have not learned religious beliefs, where that explanation is so understood that it does not presuppose God's existence? And imagine a cult, say of the Great Oz, who is so conceived that he cannot be God under another name. Suppose its votaries made similar claims about the existence of a natural tendency to form basic Ozistic beliefs and they argued that Hebraic-Christian (and other) influences have prevented widespread realization of this tendency. They might also maintain that they have Ozian experiences in which they are directly aware of Oz. How might the kind of experientialism we are considering undermine the rationality of their religous beliefs?

Perhaps Plantinga is not obligated to tell us. He has not, after all, argued that the *only* properly basic theistic beliefs are Hebraic-Christian. But suppose that some cultists, deeply impressed by the world's evil, make claims, of the sorts we are considering, for beliefs about Diablo, whom they conceive as an omnipotent demon. Their truth might be incompatible with some major Hebraic-Christian beliefs. Would he countenance Diablistic beliefs as properly basic? I think not, since he presumably wants to suggest that properly basic true beliefs, or at least our properly basic theistic beliefs, are knowledge, and such a suggestion is far less plausible on the assumption that there are incompatible properly basic beliefs (perhaps *as* properly basic). But I am not sure by what reasoning he would rule this out. We are, he suggests, to use a broadly inductive procedure in framing criteria of proper basicality.[26] Yet if beliefs with the immense ontological content and great conceptual complexity of theistic beliefs may be plausibly taken by theists as intuitively acceptable candidates for properly basic beliefs, it becomes an important question why Ozists and all manner of cultists cannot find an epistemologically comparable route to a host of prima facie unjustified existential beliefs. I am not suggesting that Plantinga's position must after all allow just any belief to be properly basic, but as stated it does seem to allow too much.

CONCLUSION

I have suggested that on one construal of the notion of basic belief, the theistic beliefs most likely to seem basic are apparently not basic in the

---

26. For a critical discussion of Plantinga's use of this procedure see Philip L. Quinn's "In Search of the Foundations of Theism," read in part, in an earlier version, at the Western Division meetings of the American Philosophical Association in 1981.

circumstances in which they naturally occur. Assuming, however, that they are basic, it becomes at least difficult to show how they can be directly (roughly, nonderivatively) justified (or rational). We considered various candidates for requirements on the rationality of basic beliefs; while we found no reason to think that theistic beliefs could not be directly justified, we also saw no good reason to conclude that any in fact are. They apparently can be, in Plantinga's terms, properly basic. I have argued, however, that proper basicality does not entail justificatory independence and that even if evidentialism in a strong form is false, weaker, kindred theses, such as that theistic beliefs are justificatorily dependent, may be true. So far, they have not been refuted.

If my reasons for these conclusions are sound, then contrary to the impression one might get in reading Plantinga, the proper basicality of theistic beliefs is consistent with foundationalism as such. Foundationalist views may or may not employ criteria of basicality that exclude properly basic theistic beliefs or even justificatorily independent theistic beliefs. Supposing that properly basic theistic beliefs are possible, however, it is not clear that they can be maintained by mature theists who have acquired other beliefs in the light of which it seems that they can rationally accept theism only if they either have evidence for it or, at the very least, have adequate reason to think that certain antitheistic arguments are unsound.

A related problem left unsolved here is whether the proper basicality for which Plantinga argues is consistent with a like status for alternative or even incompatible religious beliefs. A victory against evidentialism may seem pyrrhic for the Hebraic-Christian philosophical tradition if incompatible religious views can equally claim proper basicality. How conforting should it be to know that one's basic religious beliefs have a favorable epistemic status if incompatible, even outlandish, religious beliefs, can also have it? This is a difficult question. In any case, there are many ways to distinguish the Hebraic-Christian tradition from others. Some of these approaches would use reason to support it, for example through natural theology. But defense of the tradition need not be direct; it might consist partly in rebutting competing views or apparently undermining evidence. It does appear, however, that for at least a large proportion of theists, their theistic beliefs are rational only if they are at least indirectly supported by one or more beliefs expressing evidence or reasons.

Supposing that theistic beliefs are justificatorily dependent, we must remember that there are many ways in which their justification may depend on other beliefs. It may turn out that the only kind of evidentialism that can be cogently defended is so highly qualified as to be far less objectionable to the fideistic tradition than one might initially think possible. On this broad issue a great deal more remains to be said. All I shall add now is that our conclusions do not imply, nor, indeed, does foundationalism imply, that evidentialists must put "reason above faith," if this means either that rational persons will not believe in God unless they think they have good evidence for his existence, or that they will not believe in him unless they think there are better grounds for believing he exists than for thinking that he does not, or even that a rational person must suppose that theists ought to have evidence for theistic beliefs. There are certainly many other possible views one might associate with the idea of putting reason above faith. But, however many of them are attributable to one or another evidentialist, a great many are not implied by evidentialism as conceived in this paper, or indeed by foundationalism, which, properly understood, implies that there can be nonevidentially justified beliefs, and can allow its proponents a great deal of latitude regarding what sorts of beliefs these are.

PART TWO

Religious Commitment, Moral Obligation, and the Problem of Evil

6

The Problem of Total Devotion

ROBERT MERRIHEW ADAMS

THE PROBLEM

"Hear, O Israel: The Lord our God, the Lord is one; and you shall love the Lord your God with all your heart, and with all your soul, and with all your might" (Deut. 6:4). This text, which holds a place of honor both in Judaism and in Christianity, expresses a demand for devotion—for total devotion—which is central to theistic religion quite generally. The problem that I mean to discuss can be seen as arising when this demand is paired, as it is by Jesus, with another familiar commandment of religious ethics: "You shall love your neighbor as yourself" (Lev. 19:18; Matt. 22:39). If love to God is to occupy all our heart and soul and strength, what will be left to love or care about our neighbor? This problem has troubled many religious thinkers, notably including St. Augustine, who states it by saying that when God commanded us to love him "with the whole heart, the whole soul, the whole mind, he left

I am indebted to several groups with whom I have discussed versions of this material. Laura L. Garcia, Philip L. Quinn, and Edward Sankowski provided full written comments, which have been most helpful. Others whose comments have led to identifiable changes in the chapter are William P. Alston, José Benardete, Christopher Hughes, John Ladd, and Peter van Inwagen. The support of a fellowship at the Center of Theological Inquiry in Princeton during the writing of the paper is gratefully acknowledged.

no part of our life that should be free and (as it were) leave room to want to enjoy something else."[1] There may be something misleading about this formulation of the problem, although Augustine is not the only thinker to have posed it in these terms.[2] The heart, after all, is not like a dwindling reserve of petroleum, and love cannot be conserved by hoarding it. We might be tempted to think the whole problem merely verbal, a sophistical trick, because in some contexts 'with all your heart' can be a synonym of 'wholeheartedly', signifying only an unconflicted enthusiasm, which does not imply that one has no emotional force left to sustain any distinct and independent motive.

Nevertheless, I believe there is a real problem here. Religious devotion is more than wholeheartedness or unconflicted enthusiasm. It is supposed to occupy a person's life so fully that nothing is left outside the realm in which it reigns. The history of spirituality affords many testimonies to the sweeping character of the claims of devotion to God—not least in the frequency with which independent interests in finite things have been seen as rivals and threats to religious devotion and, figuratively speaking, as a form of "idolatry," offering to the creature what properly belongs to God alone. The problem, then, is not essentially one of the distribution of scarce emotional resources. The problem is rather how a genuine and serious interest in something finite (such as love for one's neighbor) can be a part of one's life that at the same time expresses love for God—as it must, if one's whole life is to be devoted to God.

When I say that the problem of total devotion is a real problem, I do not mean that it is an open question whether devotion to God is compatible with love for one's neighbor. Many (perhaps all) theistic traditions can point to saints who have manifested both qualities in exemplary fashion. St. Francis and Gandhi and Mother Teresa come quickly to mind. Typically the saints themselves would deny that they have arrived at the point of loving God with absolutely all their heart and soul and strength or at the point of loving their neighbor perfectly as themselves. But it would be quite implausible to suppose that their love of neighbor only slips through the gaps left by the imperfection of their love for God. On the contrary, their love of neighbor seems to be

1. Aurelius Augustinus, *De doctrina Christiana* I, xxii, 21. I translate from the text in *Corpus scriptorum ecclesiasticorum latinorum*, vol. 80, ed. William M. Green (Vienna: Hoelder-Pichler-Tempsky, 1963). A widely available English translation is by D. W. Robertson, Jr., *On Christian Doctrine* (New York: Liberal Arts Press, 1958).
    2. Cf. Charles Hartshorne, *The Logic of Perfection and Other Essays in Neoclassical Metaphysics* (Lasalle, Ill.: Open Court, 1962), p. 40.

highly integrated with, and supported by, their love of God and not in conflict with it. Our problem, then, is not one of establishing the possibility of the union of these loves but of understanding how it is possible.

Maybe the best way of reaching this understanding would be to study the lives of the saints, but I shall follow a more abstract approach here. First I will present and criticize an influential solution offered by St. Augustine. Then other possible contributions to a solution will be considered, culminating in those that seem to me most satisfying.

AUGUSTINE'S TELEOLOGICAL SOLUTION

"Whoever rightly loves a neighbor," according to St. Augustine, ". . . loving him as himself, pours back all the love of himself and of the neighbor into that love of God which suffers no stream to be led away from it by whose diversion it might be diminished."[3] The problem, of course, is how this is to be done. Augustine's clearest answer is in terms of the subordination of means to end. He distinguishes between *enjoying* something and *using* it. "For to enjoy is to cling with love to some thing for its own sake [*propter se ipsam*]; whereas to use is to apply what is used to the obtaining of that which you love (provided it ought to be loved)."[4] What is used, in other words, is treated as a means to the end of enjoyment. Augustine introduces this distinction in order to make the point that God is to be enjoyed but other things, his finite creatures, ought only to be used. He likens us, in a memorable image, to exiles returning to their native land, in which alone they can find happiness. In such a case we would have to use various means of transport and other provisions in order to complete our trip. But "the pleasures of the journey" present a temptation: if we were "converted to enjoying those things that we ought to use," we would wish to prolong our travels instead of hastening home. In this way we would be alienated from our true country. "Thus, away from the Lord as wanderers in this mortal life, if we want to return to our own country where we can be blessed, we ought to use this world and not enjoy it."[5] St. Augustine explicitly applies this schema to the love of one's neighbor: "For it is commanded us to love each other; but it is a question whether man is to be loved by man for his own sake or for the sake of something else. For if for his own sake, we enjoy him; if for the sake of something else, we

3. *De doctrina Christiana* I, xxii, 21.
4. Ibid., I, iv, 4.
5. Ibid., I, iv, 4.

use him. But it seems to me that he is to be loved for the sake of something else. For as for what should be loved for its own sake, the blessed life consists in that. . . . But cursed is he who puts his hope in man."[6]

What does it mean, in this context, to speak of "using" one's neighbor and loving him "for the sake of" God? The most natural interpretation is in terms of a desire-plus-belief pattern of teleological reasons for desires. You desire a state of affairs S for the sake of an end E if you desire S because you desire E and believe that S would be conducive to E. If you desire S for its own sake, on the other hand, your motivation is not entirely of this sort; you desire S at least partly as an end in itself and not only because you desire E and believe that S would be conducive to E. Augustine clearly conceives of love as at least largely a matter of desire. If we love our neighbor, we will desire his well-being and will desire some relationship with him. If we love our neighbor for his own sake, we will desire these states of affairs for their own sake; whereas we will desire them only because we desire some divine end to which we believe them conducive if we love our neighbor only for God's sake, as St. Augustine thinks we ought. Thus we are to use our neighbor, desiring nothing regarding him except as a means or way of realizing the divine end. What is the divine end? Most of what Augustine says suggests that it is one's own enjoyment of God, and I shall assume that here. Other possibilities will be canvassed later.

This solution to the problem of total devotion, with St. Augustine's sponsorship, has had a powerful—and I think a baneful—influence on Western religious thought and practice. It has molded a great deal of asceticism, both Catholic and Protestant. A brief—and vivid—example is Jonathan Edwards's youthful resolution "that no other end but religion shall have any influence at all on any of my actions."[7] It would be unfair to suppose that these views are fully representative of Augustine. Much that he says about love, for instance, in his beautiful homilies on 1 John, seems to proceed from a more attractive conception of the relation between neighbor love and devotion to God. Nonetheless, he does endorse the doctrine that God is to be enjoyed and all other beings are to be used only as means to the enjoyment of God; to the best of my knowledge, he gives us no other solution to the problem of total devotion that is so clearly articulated as this one. I shall refer to it as "Augustine's teleological solution."

6. Ibid., I, xxii, 20.
7. *The Works of President Edwards: With a Memoir of His Life,* vol. 1, ed. Sereno Dwight (New York: S. Converse, 1829), p. 71.

Its clarity is doubtless one reason for the influence it has enjoyed, as is the centrality of means-end relationships to so much thinking about motivation. But there is also a profounder reason. Augustine's teleological solution of the problem of total devotion is rooted in his vision of human life as a quest for infinite satisfaction, fueled by a torrent of desire that cannot rest in anything less. This vision, which animates Augustine's famous narrative of his own life, is the very center of his apologetics, his case for theistic religion. Countless readers have found in it a persuasive picture of their own need and aspiration. And the great danger that attends the quest for infinite satisfaction, as Augustine sees it, is idolatry; it is the danger that we shall seek our infinite satisfaction, not in our invisible Creator, but in his visible creatures, who are by no means equipped to provide it. Experience testifies of this danger. How often do we seek from career or marriage, parents or children, a satisfaction that, if not infinite, is at least far more than they could ever give. We demand of them what only God could give and the results are unhappy. Augustine links this with the problem of total devotion in his statement that "as for what should be loved for its own sake, the blessed life consists in that." The implication is that, if we loved another human being for his or her own sake and not merely as a means to the enjoyment of God, we would be seeking our infinite satisfaction (idolatrously) in that fellow human. I do not think that is true, but if it were, Augustine's teleological solution of the problem of total devotion would be virtually forced on the theist.

The solution has unacceptable consequences, however. In the first place, if taken seriously, it imposes absurd restrictions on the enjoyment of the simple pleasures of life. Suppose I am offered the choice of eating either strawberries or apples, at equal cost and with a trusted physician's assurance of equal benefit to my health. Could Augustine approve of my choosing the strawberries just because I like their flavor better? Not in accordance with his theory of enjoying and using. For if I do choose the strawberries just because I prefer their flavor, I will be enjoying them, adhering to them for their own sake (or to their flavor for its own sake) and not just using them as means to the enjoyment of God.

Far more important for Christian ethics than sensory pleasures is the love of one's neighbor. The gravest disadvantage of Augustine's teleological solution of the problem of total devotion is that it does not allow for anything that really deserves the name of *love* of one's neighbor. For it implies that the neighbor is not to be loved for his own sake. His well-being and our fellowship with him are to be desired only as a means to our enjoyment of God. But what is really loved must be loved for its own sake. Where something is regarded only as a means or instrument, we can say that we "value" it but not that we "love" it. I do not *love* my car, for example, unless it means something to me that transcends its resale value and its usefulness for transportation. Similarly, if I do not desire the neighbor's well-being, or any relationship with him, except because I believe it will help me to enjoy God as I desire, I do not love my neighbor. This is reason enough to reject Augustine's teleological solution to the problem of total devotion.

It is also reason to reject other solutions that differ from it only in the specification of the religious end to which all other ends are to be subordinate as mere instruments or means. Whether the end that dominates in this way be the vision of God or Christian perfection or the coming of God's Kingdom, there will in any case be no room for the neighbor really to be loved. If I desire your well-being or my relationship with you only because I believe it will be conducive to one of these divine ends, then I do not really love you. That is at least partly due to the fact that these ends do not essentially involve you. I could in principle see God or attain Christian perfection without you, and the Kingdom of God could come without you. If I am seeking nothing, at bottom, except in order to realize one of these ends, then it does not matter, except incidentally, that *you* are involved.

LOVE'S RELIGIOUS DESIRES

What about divine ends that do essentially involve particular neighbors? Might they afford a more satisfactory solution to the problem of total devotion? Two such ends come to mind. The first, a version of the neighbor's well-being, is that the neighbor enjoy God. The second, a relationship that I might desire with the neighbor, is that we enjoy God together. The second of these, at least, is a divine end for the sake of which St. Augustine seems in some passages to think the neighbor might be loved.[8] Desiring these ends for their own sake, we could love God *in* loving the neighbor. On the one hand, the neighbor could truly be loved in this way, because he is not incidental to these ends but essentially involved in them. We would be desiring his well-being and a good relationship with him for their own sake. On the other hand, God also would be loved in these desires; for a desire that those I love should enjoy God and that it should be God that we enjoy together expresses love for God no less than would a desire that I myself should enjoy God. Moreover, these are desires that we would in any event

---

8. *De doctrina Christiana* I, xxix, 30.

expect to find in one who loves both God and her neighbor, and they do commonly characterize the love that serious theists have for other people. Love for God will naturally give a certain shape to what we envisage and desire as good for people that we love and for our relationship with them.

The desire that the neighbor enjoy God with us illustrates a point about the sharing of love that deserves comment here. When we think of love's desire for relationships, we often think only of two-membered, one-to-one relationships. This is romantically appealing but unrealistic. To love another person is not necessarily to want to be alone in the universe with her. The relationships that we desire and prize with other people are not only two-person relationships but also three-person, four-person, and in general many-person relationships. We may arrange a dinner party because we want to relate to all of a specific group of people at the same time and to participate in their relation to each other. And when a person leaves a family or working unit or circle of friends, by divorce or taking a different job or going away to college, one feels sad, not just for the loss of a two-membered relationship, but for the loss of a many-membered relationship involving that person. Even where the one-to-one relationship can be maintained outside the group and the n-membered relationship in the group can be restructured as an n-minus-one-membered relationship, one is still apt to miss the specific n-membered relationship of which that person was an essential member. In such a case one does prize the individual person for her own sake, but the relationship one desires, while involving some one-to-one interaction, is a relationship of which other people are members, too.

To be unable to prize many-person relationships in this way, to insist exclusively on one-to-one relationships, would typically be evidence of possessiveness or jealousy. The possessive lover wants to limit the life of the beloved to their two-membered relationship with each other. A nonpossessive lover wants the beloved to live a larger life and wants to share it with him. Hence the nonpossessive lover will want to be part of many-membered relationships with the beloved and will prize them when they arise. As possessiveness is no virtue in love, there is no reason to suppose that either God or the neighbor is less perfectly loved if we desire to enjoy God with the neighbor than if we desired to enjoy either to the exclusion of the other.

This approach to the problem of total devotion, in terms of desires for religious ends that essentially involve the particular neighbor, differs in its structure, and not only in the religious ends proposed, from Augustine's teleological solution. For it does not subordinate the neighbor or the neighbor's good or our relationship with the neighbor as a means to a higher end. It does not provide a desire-plus-belief reason for loving the neighbor or desiring the neighbor's good, and it makes no use of the contrast between enjoying and using.

I think this approach to the problem is correct, as far as it goes, and provides the main point at which an understanding of love for God in terms of *desire* for a divine *end* can enter into an acceptable solution. But I hesitate for two reasons to call it a complete solution of the problem of total devotion. (1) This approach does not explain how I could be loving God in desiring for myself or my neighbor anything other than an explicitly divine end, such as the enjoyment of God, and therefore it does not show how total devotion could be compatible with prizing more mundane enjoyments (such as the taste of strawberries) for their own sake, either for oneself or for one's neighbor. (2) It provides no way of tracing love for the neighbor to a root in love for God. It does show how love for God and love for the neighbor can unite in desire for the same state of affairs. Given that one loves God and the neighbor, one will naturally want the neighbor to enjoy God. But why love the neighbor at all? No answer to that question is provided here, although the ideal of total devotion suggests that love for the neighbor should spring from love for God. The desire that the neighbor enjoy God (and enjoy God with us) can be part of love for the neighbor, but it is not a reason for loving the neighbor.

RELIGIOUS REASONS FOR LOVE

There certainly can be religious reasons, rooted in devotion to God, for loving the neighbor, but I think they are not to be understood in terms of desire for a divine end. One can love someone for her devotion to God or as a child of God or for the sake of the image of God in her, just as one can love a person for her beauty or her courage or her human vulnerability. These reasons indicate characteristics that one finds attractive in the person. To say that you love a person for such a characteristic is not to say that you have a general desire or liking for it that you think she is a way of satisfying. You need not like or desire vulnerability to find it appealing, and your interest in the beauty or the religious devotion of a person you love is quite different from your interest in the beauty or religious devotion of a stranger. Loving someone for the sake of the image of God in her does not imply a desire for one more image of God than you would have without her. Perhaps you know enough images of God not to care about one more or less as such, but you prize her for the sake of the image of God in her. To love a person for reasons like these is not to regard her as a means or way to the satisfaction of an ulterior end. Yet such reasons for loving someone can be an expression of love for God.

To show that loving someone for religious reasons is not necessarily regarding her as a means or way to an ulterior end is to show that having religious reasons is compatible with loving someone as an end in herself and to that extent for her own sake. When we say that we want to be loved for our own sake, however, we may have something more in mind. The objection to being loved for one's money rather than for one's own sake is indeed very apt to be an objection to being regarded as a mere means to the enjoyment of one's possessions. But being loved for one's own sake (or "for oneself," as we might rather say in this context) can also be contrasted with being loved for one's looks or one's cheerfulness, without any implication that the latter entails being regarded as a means to an ulterior end. The complaint is rather that what is valued in one is too small or peripheral or accidental a part of oneself. It is not obvious what reasons for love would be exempt from this complaint. Even moral character is sufficiently accidental and changeable that being loved only for one's moral virtues might be contrasted with being loved for oneself. By the same token, loving someone solely for her religious devotion might not amount to loving her for herself, in one sense that concerns us. Loving someone for the sake of the image of God in her is an interesting case. It may seem comparatively safe from this criticism, in view of the central, important, and essential place that the image of God is thought to occupy in the constitution of human selfhood. On the other hand, it could seem too much like "loving" someone for her similarity to her mother, which hardly counts as loving her for herself. Probably you are loved for yourself if you are loved for the intrinsic glories of the image of God in you and not just for the relation of similarity to God—but how much does loving you for the first of this pair of reasons express a love for God?[9]

For these and other reasons it is not clear how much religious reasons for love can help with the problem of total devotion. Perhaps a complete solution based on such reasons would require us to take it as an ideal to have religious reasons for *all* our loves. That is not obviously unacceptable. But would we have to go further and take it as an ideal to have *only* religious reasons for our loves? And would that be accept-

---

9. I have had to deal very briefly here with issues about the meaning of 'for the sake of', 'for one's own sake', and 'for oneself', and about what it is to have a reason for loving someone. I hope to publish a fuller discussion of these issues elsewhere.

able? Surely it would be "too pious" to make it an ideal never to have it
as a reason for loving someone that he is cute or that he is your son. In
at least some cases one might have religious versions of such reasons.
Instead of loving your son simply because he is your son, for instance,
you might love him because God has given him to you as a son. Maybe a
sense of having received a gift and a trust (and from whom, if not from
God?) is in fact often implicit in loving a child because it is one's own.
Probably, however, it would be objectionably artificial to divinize *all*
reasons for love in this way.

I conclude that religious reasons for love are likely to provide at best
a partial solution to our problem. Fortunately, other approaches remain to be explored. In this exploration the next two sections will be
devoted to making sure that we do not overlook the obvious.

PUTTING GOD FIRST

One thing certainly demanded in devotion to God is that one put God
first in one's life. This is often characterized as loving God more than
anything else. As a popular hymn puts it,

> Jesus calls us from the worship
> Of the vain world's golden store,
> From each idol that would keep us,
> Saying, "Christian, love me more."[10]

Putting God first can also be understood more narrowly, and perhaps
more clearly, as the most stringent of loyalties—a loyalty that one will
not go against for the sake of any desire or other loyalty. If one is
prepared to abandon, disobey, or slight God in order to please or obey
or pamper a parent, spouse, child, teacher, boss, or friend, then one
has made an idol of that person. Whenever any other interest conflicts
with loyalty to God, one must decide for God.

Of course, other interests do not always conflict with loyalty to God.
They may incline us to the same action that is demanded by loyalty to
God or at least to actions not forbidden by God. This suggests a simple
solution to the problem of total devotion. Why not say that love for
one's neighbor and for other creatures is compatible with perfect devotion to God, provided that one loves God more and thus is fully prepared and disposed to set aside any desire arising from one's love of
creatures if it should conflict with loyalty to God?

10. "Jesus Calls Us," by Cecil Frances Alexander (1852), quoted from *The Hymnal*
(Philadelphia: Presbyterian Board of Christian Education, 1939), no. 223.

There is something right about this suggestion. Putting God first, in this sense, is a part—the most obvious and maybe the most important part—of the ideal of total devotion. But it is not the whole of it, and therefore this solution to the problem is not completely satisfying. Devotion to God is not conceived of simply as the absolutely first among a number of independent interests. It is supposed to be more encompassing, so that other good motives must find their place within it and all of life can be a worship of God. The idea that one should be loving God in loving the neighbor is very deeply rooted.

How this idea can be understood, I will continue to explore in the remaining sections of this paper. In the present section I will dwell on a more specific difficulty with the suggested simple solution to the problem of total devotion. The difficulty is that putting God first does not suffice to exclude idolatry. 'Idolatry' signifies here not just worshiping an image of a deity but, more broadly, giving to a creature what belongs only to God.

What belongs only to God? Not love, desire, or enjoyment as such. I am arguing that it is compatible with theistic devotion to have these affections for creatures. Theists likewise generally suppose that it is right to admire, trust, and even obey creatures in various ways on various occasions. What belongs only to God is indeed a sort of love, praise, trust, and obedience; but it is a very special sort. It is called "worship"; but that may not clarify very much, because what is meant is not a particular sort of easily recognized religious behavior, such as attending church or synagogue, but something more comprehensive and life encompassing.

One thing that clearly is meant is indeed the most stringent of loyalties. But what belongs to God alone is more than just a kind of loyalty. It is more broadly a type of importance in the believer's life. One is to "center one's life in God," to find one's principal identity in being a child of God and one's principal security in being loved by God. This is quite different from any desirable sort of love for one's neighbor. By contrast with this, idolatry would be found, not in loving another human being very much, but in feeling that life would be meaningless without him; not in the most intense enjoyment of philosophy, but in feeling that one would not be oneself if one could not do philosophy; not in liking other people and wanting to be their friend, but in feeling that one would be worthless if rejected by them.

In these examples we can see two reasons why putting God first does not suffice to exclude idolatry. First, loving God more is not enough, because the love that belongs to God differs more than quantitatively from the love that may properly be directed toward creatures. It occupies a different place in the organization of life. One does not arrive at idolatry simply by intensifying a proper love for creatures but by depending on them as one should depend on God. Because idolatry is not a merely quantitative matter, it can subsist even where one loves God still more than the idol. Indeed, one does not necessarily love the idol at all. The danger of idolatry lurks at least as much in authority and envy as in beauty and desire. To organize one's life around pleasing a boss or winning the respect of a professional rival is idolatrous, even if one neither likes nor loves that person.

Second, the most stringent loyalty to God is not enough, for one could still organize the meaning of one's life idolatrously around a finite object even if one were fully resolved and disposed to sacrifice it if loyalty to God should require—indeed, even if one actually had sacrificed it. It can be argued, for example, that that is exactly what the "knight of infinite resignation" is doing in Kierkegaard's *Fear and Trembling*. He has "concentrate[d] the whole substance of his life and the meaning of actuality into one single desire,"[11] for a particular beloved person, and then has renounced her for the sake of God. But he keeps the concentrated passion for the human beloved ever "young"[12] in his heart, for that is what makes his resignation "infinite" and thus constitutes it a relation to God. This outward renunciation of the beloved does not abolish but shelters the "knight's" idolatry of her—shelters it from the vicissitudes and banalities of marriage, for instance—so that he can still define in relation to her the meaning of his life and even of his devotion to God. His passion for her still crowds out interests in other finite things and defines the possibility (or rather, impossibility) of happiness for him.[13] This is an idolatry that can remain in the organization of the heart even when God is voluntarily preferred to the idol.

OBEDIENCE

Another solution to the problem of total devotion is suggested by the following argument:

> God commands love for the neighbor.
> Obedience to God's commands is an expression of love for God.
> Therefore love for the neighbor is an expression of love for God.

11. Søren Kierkegaard, *Fear and Trembling* and *Repetition*, ed. and trans. Howard V. Hong and Edna H. Hong (Princeton: Princeton University Press, 1983), p. 43.
12. Ibid., p. 44.
13. Ibid., p. 50.

There is something right about this, as we shall see, but there are also serious objections to it.

The argument presupposes that, since God commands love for the neighbor, love for the neighbor can be a form of obedience to God. But that seems wrong. In loving our neighbor we are to desire her well-being. To say that this desire is a form of obedience to God is to say that it is motivated by a certain reason of a desire-plus-belief or resolution-plus-belief pattern. It is to say that we desire our neighbor's well-being because we want (or are resolved) to do what God commands and we believe that he commands us to desire her well-being. But this is not a reason for the desire for the neighbor's well-being: it is only a reason for wanting or trying to have this desire. For this reason commends, not the neighbor's well-being, but the desire for it; whereas a reason for a desire must commend the object of the desire, rather than the desire itself. In a desire-plus-belief reason for desiring S, it is S that must be believed conducive to E, or a way of realizing E. But what is here believed to be a way of doing what God commands is not the neighbor's well-being but the desire for it. Commending a desire could provide a reason for the desire only if the desire had itself as part of its aim or object. But the desire in this case is no part of its own aim or object; its whole object is the neighbor's well-being. Therefore this desire cannot be a form of obedience.[14]

Still, it might be replied, the desire for the neighbor's well-being could be motivated in another way by reverence for the will of God. For God wills the neighbor's well-being as well as our desire for it. This suggests another reason that could be a reason for the desire, because it commends the object of the desire. We could desire the neighbor's well-being because we desire that God's will be done and believe that

14. If the desire for our neighbor's well-being cannot be a form of obedience, it might be thought to follow that it cannot be commanded; but I do not mean to draw that conclusion. The fact that it cannot be fulfilled with the motivational pattern characteristic of obedience certainly implies that the command to love one's neighbor as oneself is not a *typical* command and cannot function exactly as commands typically do. Nevertheless it is demanded of us by society—and, most theists would say, by God—that we desire our neighbor's well-being for its own sake. This demand is backed by the informal authority of society—and by the divine authority, as theists believe. And if it becomes clear that we have no desire for our neighbor's well-being for its own sake, persons concerned may rightly react with disapproval, reproach, and a sense of grievance. (In "Involuntary Sins," *Philosophical Review* 94 [1985], pp. 3–31, I have discussed much more fully our liability to blame for states, such as desire, that are not directly voluntary.) For that reason, I think it makes sense to regard ourselves as *commanded* to desire our neighbor's well-being for its own sake. In the same way I think we are rightly said to *promise* to love our spouses, even though one cannot exactly love *out of* a desire to keep one's promise.

God wills the neighbor's well-being. Similarly, we could desire a good relationship with the neighbor because we believe that God wills that, and we desire that God's will be done. But this suggestion falls prey to substantially the same difficulty as Augustine's teleological solution of the problem of total devotion. If we desired the neighbor's well-being and a good relationship with her *only* out of a desire that God's will be done, we would not desire them for their own sake. It would not matter to us whether God's will be fulfilled by those states of affairs rather than by any others that he might have willed instead. And in this case we would not love the neighbor. Of course we may desire these states of affairs *partly* out of a desire that God's will be done and partly for their own sake, out of love for the neighbor. But then the love for the neighbor is not a form or expression of reverence for God's will but a separate motive for desiring some of the same states of affairs.

There are certain desires from which, of their very nature, there is no direct path to their fulfillment. Consider the desire to be unconcerned about one's motivational state. The keener it is, the farther it is from fulfillment. Likewise, if I want, for all the self-interested reasons in the world, to love another person unselfishly, a great gulf may still separate me from the love that I desire, for it is not the sort of thing that I can do for any of those reasons. The desire to live according to God's will is at least partly of this nature too, if God wills that we should love our neighbor. Its fulfillment involves caring, for their own sake, about things (such as the neighbor's well-being) that are quite distinct from one's own living according to whatever God's will may be. If one's desire to live according to God's will is so all-consuming as to prevent one from caring about anything else for its own sake, it will get in the way of its own fulfillment. The ideal of total devotion ought not to be an all-consuming desire of this sort. It should be something less self-concerned, and, as I shall explain below, I think it should not be entirely a matter of desire.

Nonetheless, realism will assign to self-conscious ethical choice an important role in the love of our neighbor. Without spontaneous desires and affections that are not forms of obedience, as I have argued, there is no love of the neighbor. But in practice we are not likely to love very well if we rely only on such spontaneity. We need to make voluntary efforts to pay attention to other people, to be helpful to them even when we do not feel like it, to study our own motives and actions self-critically, and so forth. These voluntary efforts can be obedience to God. They cultivate the soil in which less voluntary aspects of love can flourish. Thus love for the neighbor can be seen as growing out of devoted obedience to God—though that is still not quite the same as an explanation of how loving the neighbor can be a way of loving God.

TRUST

My understanding of the problem of total devotion seems to resist any tidy reduction to one answer, but if I have a single chief constructive proposal to make, it is the following. Both the quest for God and enjoyment of God play a prominent part in St. Augustine's account of love for God, and rightly so. One loves God both in seeking fellowship with him and in actually having and enjoying fellowship with him. Of these two phases of love for God, Augustine's teleological solution to the problem of total devotion locates love for the neighbor and any other legitimate interest in creatures within the quest for God. This leads to the objectionable consequences of that solution. A more acceptable solution would find a rightful place for love of the neighbor and for other interests in creatures primarily in the other phase of love for God—in the realization and enjoyment of fellowship with him, rather than in the quest for it. That is my proposal, and the remainder of this paper will be devoted to it. In the present section I will discuss a relatively indirect way in which a trusting love for God, secure in the actuality of fellowship with him, can be reflected in love for creatures. Then, in the two following sections, I will go on to more direct connections between love for creatures and two aspects of the fulfillment of love for God—namely, the enjoyment of God and the inspiration that consummates the surrender of the heart to God.

A mundane model may help us to see how love for creatures can be a reflection of trusting love for God. We find that, among small children of the same age and in the same circumstances, some are much more inclined than others to cling closely to their mothers, to keep them always in sight, and to pester them for attention. The knowledgeable observer will not conclude that the more "clinging" children love their mothers more than the more independent ones. On the contrary, the more dependent children probably have a relationship with their mothers that, if not less loving, is at any rate weaker in certain respects. The more independent children are apt to be those that feel more secure in their mother's love and care, and they are therefore able to turn their attention with less anxiety to other things. This sense of security is, in part, a manifestation of their love for their mothers.

More precisely, the sense of security is a function of love for their mothers (and/or other persons on whom the child depends) plus trust or confidence that they are available when and if the child desires to turn to them. We might be tempted to say that the sense of security is a function not of the love but only of the trust. But that would be a mistake, for belief in the availability and beneficence of someone to whom the child was not attached would not have the same effect.

In this example the most important point for our present purpose is that the strength of a loving personal relationship can be reflected in attention to things other than the loved person. Paradoxical as this may sound in the abstract, it is plausible enough when we say that a child's sense of security in its mother's love frees it to pay attention to things other than the mother, whereas without this assurance its energies would be absorbed in seeking and clinging to maternal care or in coping with the lack of it. In empirical corroboration of this point, it has been observed that children of from one to three years of age are more apt to be absorbed in playing with toys and exploring their environment in their mother's presence than in her absence[15]—a finding that would not be expected on the assumption that interest in mother and independent interests in other objects simply compete for the child's attention and are not otherwise related.

The same point can be illustrated from adult life. Most of us would be able to concentrate more fully on the task of writing a paper on some impersonal subject, such as formal logic, if we felt secure in one or more love relationships than we would if we were experiencing disruption in a love relationship or felt that no one loved us. Of course this is not the only possible pattern of relationship between these types of interest. For both adults and children, it is possible to steel oneself to invest one's interest in other things, in the conviction that love is impossible. The point I want to make is just that there is a pattern—and obviously the happiest pattern—in which a lively and independent interest in other things reflects one's love for, and trust in, some person.

This point can be applied to the relation between love for God and love for creatures. If one both loves God and trusts in God's love, this will issue in an inner peace or sense of security. And this, as many religious thinkers have argued, will free one to take a lively interest in God's creatures for their own sake—to enjoy his gifts with un-self-conscious gratitude and to love one's neighbor. Here a love for God, combined with faith in him, provides an atmosphere of gladness and security in which a love for the creature can be encompassed.

ENJOYMENT

We have just explored a way in which trust in the fulfillment of one's love for God may permeate one's other interests, but rather indi-

---

15. See John Bowlby, *Separation*, vol. 2 of *Attachment and Loss* (New York: Basic Books, 1973), ch. 3. Much in Bowlby's three-volume work is relevant to my argument in this section.

rectly—not as coinciding with them or providing a positive impulse toward them but as a source of freedom to have them or pursue them and as a frame of mind, a confidence, in which they can be pursued. I want now to focus on an idea that establishes a more direct connection between the two loves, by arguing that God can be enjoyed, with love, in enjoying creatures.

I mean to use the word 'enjoy' in its ordinary sense and not necessarily according to Augustine's definition. It is important to the argument, and I think also obviously true, that enjoying the beloved is one of the forms that love characteristically takes. This is not to say that love is always pleasant. Enjoyment is present in widely varying degrees in different loves and at different times. Nevertheless, enjoyment is an important aspect of love. And it is a familiar phenomenon that we can enjoy a person we love in enjoying something else.

We seek shared pleasures for the enhancement of our loves—a delicious meal, a great concert, a beautiful day at the beach or in the woods; or more personally, the joys of conversation or the physical pleasures of sex. Why are these seen as enhancing love? Perhaps at least partly because there is not a sharp line between enjoying something *with* another person and enjoying the other person. How do we enjoy other people? Most broadly, I suppose, by enjoying our experience of them. In particular, that includes enjoying our relationships with them, which includes enjoying what we do together.

Besides enjoying what we do together, we enjoy other people in our experience of their personal characteristics and what they do individually. We enjoy the sound of their voices, the look or the touch of their bodies. We enjoy their ideas and their feelings, whether explicitly expressed or read by us between the lines. We enjoy the grace of their gestures or the cuteness of their expressions, the wit and style or the candor and intensity of their conversation and letters. In all of this we enjoy the other people themselves: this is the sort of thing we mean when we speak of enjoying another person.

In many of these cases, however, we do not enjoy *only* the other person. This is most obviously true of the shared pleasures. We enjoy the caviar and the music for their own sake, too, and would very likely still enjoy them if eaten or heard alone. But even the other person's ideas and performances are apt to be enjoyed for themselves at the same time that we enjoy the person in enjoying them. The joke I heard her tell would still amuse me if it came to me impersonally in the pages of a magazine.

The usual word for the relationship between these enjoyments is that we enjoy the other person "in" enjoying something else—for instance, "in" enjoying the music. Several characteristics of this relationship may be noted: (1) If we enjoy another person in enjoying the music, we enjoy both the person and the music. If I say, "I enjoyed listening to the music with him," it makes sense to ask me, "What did you like about the experience?" For normally, if we enjoy an experience, we can give reasons for that by picking out features of the experience that we like. If I enjoyed the music, I can answer truly, "I liked the music." If I enjoyed the other person, I can answer truly, "I liked sharing it with him." If I enjoyed the other person in enjoying the music, I must have liked both of these distinguishable features of the experience. (2) Although the enjoyment of the music and of the other person are distinguishable in this way, they are so fused into a single experience that in some sense they are not separate. And (3) each enjoyment enhances the other. We would normally say, not that we like the music better, but that we enjoy it more, because we enjoy sharing the experience with someone else; and we would say that we enjoy the other person more because we enjoy the music that we hear together. (4) If we enjoy the other person in enjoying the music, we like the music and the sharing with the other person, each for its own sake, or at any rate not merely as a way or means to the other. The claim that I liked the music merely as a way or means to the sharing could be understood according to a liking-plus-belief pattern of reasons for liking (analogous to the desire-plus-belief pattern of reasons for desire discussed above) as meaning that I liked the music only because I liked sharing an experience with the other person and regarded listening to the music as a way of doing that (much as one might enjoy selling something only because one liked making money and saw the transaction as a way of making money). If I liked the music only for this reason, it would be misleading to list the music in addition to the sharing as something that I liked about the experience or to say that I enjoyed the other person "in enjoying the music."

Are there cases in which one enjoys another person alone and not in enjoying something else? I suppose so. One might enjoy an experience about which one did not particularly like anything except that it was an experience of seeing *her*. But such experiences can claim no preeminence. The enjoyment of conversation and of sexual intercourse, for instance, is not in general of this type, in view of the intellectual and sensory pleasures typically involved in them. It would be bizarre to take it as an ideal of love to enjoy the other person only alone and never in enjoying something else.

Similar things can be said about *enjoying God*. When people speak of it, they normally have in mind cases in which an experience of God is enjoyed. This should not be understood too subjectivistically, as if it were not God himself that is enjoyed but only a state of one's own mind. (A similar antisubjectivistic caution applies to what I said about enjoying other people in general by enjoying our experience of them.) But if someone said, "I have never experienced God, but I have often enjoyed him," one would wonder what was meant.

How does one experience God? Believers often say they experience the Creator in his works. Suppose one enjoys the sunlight on the autumn leaves and is the more excited because one catches there (as one believes) a glimpse of the beauty of the Creator at work. If this is indeed an experience of God, it seems right to say that it is one in which one enjoys God, enjoys what he does, *in* enjoying the light and the leaves. Likewise, if one experiences and enjoys God through a piece of religious literature or a religious liturgy, one would (at least in typical cases) be enjoying God *in* enjoying the literature or the liturgy. And most important here, if I experience the love of my friends as a manifestation of the love of God, that would normally be a case in which I am enjoying both God and my friends in enjoying this social experience and am enjoying God *in* enjoying my friends. The creature is enjoyed, in these cases, as something more than a means to the enjoyment of God. It is because one enjoys the light, the leaves, the friend, and the friend's love for their own sake that one sees and appreciates in them the glory of God, so as to praise him for them and enjoy him in enjoying them.

It has been pointed out to me that in some cases it would be odd to say that we enjoy a creator himself in enjoying his works. Do we enjoy Rembrandt himself in enjoying his paintings? Perhaps not. Rembrandt is gone and has left his works behind for us to enjoy. But God is not like that. On theistic as opposed to deistic conceptions of creation, he has not gone away and left his works behind; he remains unceasingly active in them. To the example of the painter may be contrasted that of a dancer, who cannot go away and leave his performance behind. (Or if he leaves a motion picture of his work, there is nothing odd about saying we enjoy him in enjoying the film.) Now, in a theistic as opposed to a pantheistic view, God's creatures are more distinct from him than the dance is from the dancer. But they are not as separable from him as paintings are from the painter. God is neither as wholly immanent in his works as the dancer in the dance nor as purely transcendent over them as the painter in relation to his paintings. These reflections suggest that the immanent aspect of God's relation to his creation is important to the possibility of loving God in loving his creatures.[16]

16. To this extent I agree with Hartshorne's treatment of the problem of total devotion in *The Logic of Perfection*, pp. 40–41. But I am not prepared to carry the affirmation of divine immanence as far as he does or to rely on it so completely for the solution of the problem.

It is not only in enjoying his creatures that God is enjoyed. There are experiences in which God alone is enjoyed. I take that to be true of some experiences of communion with God or of the presence of God, where the experience is of nothing else. This is certainly an important and valuable form of experience of God and enjoyment of God. But I think it would be a mistake to take it as an ideal to enjoy God only in this way, to the exclusion of enjoying him in enjoying his creatures. With some trepidation, I am inclined to say that that would be to make a sort of idol out of this type of experience, substituting too private a deity for the Lord of all who shows his glory in many works and gifts. Another way in which one may enjoy God alone is in his presence in suffering, in which he is enjoyed but the suffering is not. But clearly it would be perverse to seek to enjoy God only in that way.

To the extent, therefore, that enjoyment can be a form of love, love for God and love for creatures can coincide in enjoying God in enjoying his creatures.[17] Perhaps one should aspire to such a religious consciousness that God would be enjoyed in *all* one's enjoyment of creatures. Before this suggestion can be accepted, however, we must confront a possible protest against such an all-encompassing ideal of religious devotion. It would be objectionably possessive, as was noted above in the section "Love's Religious Desires," to want your beloved's life to be limited to a two-person relationship with you. You should be able to enjoy many-person relationships with each other. But you might think it perfectly appropriate to want your beloved *also* to concentrate, some of the time, on *you alone,* and not to enjoy you *only in* enjoying your children or your friends. "Two's company, but three's a crowd," we say, meaning that we want time to be alone in twosomes. A religious ideal that would have us always conscious of God's involvement in every situation—or even a belief in God's omnipresence and omniscience—might therefore seem to threaten a desirable intimacy with the intrusion of a third party.

It must be acknowledged, I think, that there is a sense of being absolutely alone with another human being (or indeed of being absolutely alone with oneself) that may, not unreasonably, be welcomed by nontheists but that is hardly compatible with theistic faith. But theists need not regret the loss of this particular solitude. We do not (or should not) want to take our parents along on our honeymoon—but God is different. Theists must say that we should want to "take him along" even (or perhaps especially) on our honeymoon. God's imma-

17. And perhaps in enjoying the creatures *in* enjoying God, as Philip Quinn has suggested that I should say.

nence helps in understanding the relevant difference here between him and our human parents. A continuing relation to him is built into the structure of our selfhood and of any relationship between human persons. I do not have to look away from my human partner to see God, and you do not grasp my true selfhood better by abstracting from my relation to God. For this reason I am inclined to say that God could appropriately be enjoyed in all legitimate enjoyment of creatures.

INSPIRATION

It is a truism that shared interests make a frienship more perfect. When we speak of sharing interests, we mean being interested in the same things for their own sake; we do not mean just being interested in the friend's interests for the sake of the friendship. Thus, if my wife loves tennis and I have never cared about it, I might play tennis with her and even "cultivate an interest" in tennis, for the sake of our relationship; but as long as that is my sole motive in the matter, we do not yet share an interest in tennis. That occurs only when I too am interested in tennis for its own sake.

Similarly, it is plausible to suppose that fellowship with God would be perfected by sharing God's interests, loving and hating what he loves and hates. One will be more fully in tune with God if one loves fidelity and hates lying as he does and if one loves one's neighbor as he does. "God is love, and he who abides in love abides in God, and God abides in him" (1 John 4:16).

God loves the neighbor for the neighbor's own sake. So if my only interest in the neighbor is that I would like to have a better relationship with God and think that loving the neighbor would contribute to that, I do not yet share God's interest in the matter, as I do not yet love the neighbor. That occurs only if I love the neighbor for his own sake.

If this line of thought is right, then those who desire fellowship with God have reason to want to love their neighbor for their neighbor's own sake. But this is one of those desires that I discussed above, whose nature permits no direct path from the desire to its fulfillment because the fulfillment involves having a motivation that is not based on the desire. Such desires have in some measure to let go if they are to enjoy full satisfaction. That is generally true of the desire for friendship, and much in the history of humankind's wrestling with grace suggests that it is also true of the desire for friendship with God.

If sharing God's love for the neighbor enhances fellowship with God, that constitutes an important connection between love for God and love for the neighbor. Can we go further and say that, if in fellowship with God one shares God's love for the neighbor, the love for the neighbor is a form or part or expression of one's love for God? We do seem to think that shared love for a third object can be manifestation of love for a friend. Perhaps "Love me, love my dog" is rarely meant as a serious statement about love, but it is surely no accident that people do not say only "Love me, put up with my dog." We test people's love for us by their appreciation and concern, not only for us, but also for what they see us love and care about. A lack of love for the children of one's marriage not only is a sin against them but also is rightly apt to be seen as a deficiency in one's love for one's spouse. Conversely, we think that the shared love of parents for their children ought to be in some way an expression of their love for each other. (Of course, one might have strong and good reasons for not sharing some interests of the beloved. Perhaps he has some interests that are bad, base, or even wicked. I do not say it would be a test of love to share such interests.)

Why do we take the actual sharing of acceptable interests as a test of love? Why is it not enough that the lover *wants* to share the beloved's interests? The main reason, I suspect, is that the failure to enter into the desires and affections of the other person suggests that one's heart is closed against her in a way that seems to us unloving. I will develop this point in connection with a solution to the problem of total devotion gleaned from Anders Nygren's great book *Agape and Eros*.

Rejecting Augustine's teleological solution, Nygren holds that the relation between love for God and love for the neighbor should be conceived nonteleologically. "God is not the end, the ultimate object, but the starting-point and permanent basis of neighborly love. He is not its *causa finalis* but its *causa efficiens*. . . . It is not as being loved, but as loving, that God sets love in motion."[18]

This fits nicely with Nygren's conception of love for God as surrender rather than quest. I think Nygren goes, indeed, to an indefensible extreme in excluding the theme of quest from the Christian type of love for God, but my interest here is in what he does include in that love. "Man's love for God signifies that man, moved by [the] Divine love, gratefully wills to belong wholly to God."[19] According to Nygren's interpretation of Jesus, "To have love for God means . . . exactly the same as to be possessed by God, to belong absolutely to Him. . . . Love towards God . . . is the *free*—and in that sense spontaneous—surrender of the heart to God."[20]

18. Andres Nygren, *Agape and Eros*, trans. Philip S. Watson (New York: Harper & Row, 1969), p. 216.
19. Ibid., p. 213.
20. Ibid., p. 94.

To be possessed by God is to have God acting in us and through us. If we are possessed by God, then "our" love for the neighbor can be God's love for the neighbor, for the neighbor's own sake, at work in us. And that is how Nygren thinks it is with Christian neighbor-love: "In the life that is governed by Agape, the acting subject is not man himself; it is—as Paul expresses it—God, the Spirit of God, the Spirit of Christ, the Agape of Christ. . . . The Christian has nothing of his own to give; the love which he shows to his neighbor is the love which God has infused into him."[21] Nygren could have added (though I have not found that he did) that this love for the neighbor is a part of one's love for God. For letting God do this in one is part of one's willingly being possessed by God, which Nygren identifies with love for God.

Nygren's position bristles with problems, but I will try to show that the approach it exemplifies is plausible. One problem is that, like many other theologians, Nygren often seems to have a straightforwardly causal understanding of what it is to be possessed by God. On this understanding, God inspires us or infuses his love for our neighbor into us simply by causing us to love the neighbor. But it is hard to see how God's causing that neighbor-love in me could constitute a part or form or expression of my loving God—any more than it would constitute my loving a brain surgeon if the surgeon caused me to share her feelings for a third person by stimulating my brain with an electrode.

There is another way of thinking about being inspired or possessed by God, however, which makes it easier to see that state as a form of love for God. Although divine inspiration undoubtedly has unique characteristics, we can find a model for this way of thinking in very mundane cases in which we say that one person's feeling, desire, or other state of mind is "inspired" by another person's. In such inspiration there is certainly an influencing that is broadly speaking causal. But if an emotion is inspired in me in this way, I am engaged in the process in a way in which I would not be if the other person were simply operating on me. I know, or at some level sense, his emotion and respond to it, and it is in my apprehending and responding that he influences me. In this my heart is not closed against him but open to him; and because we expect this of love, sharing the beloved's interests can be a test of love—though I am not denying that inspiration can also take place without love.

Because the one who is inspired participates in the process in this way, there is a place in this model for Nygren's description of love toward God as free and spontaneous surrender of the heart to God and

21. Ibid., p. 129.

as *willing* to belong to God—though 'willing' is not quite the right word for it, because this is not a straightforwardly voluntary process. Desires and emotions inspired in us by those of another person are not in general voluntarily adopted. Opening one's heart to a friend in the sense that now concerns us is not a voluntary action; it is not something one does by consicously trying. It does not even come about primarily as a result of wanting to do it. The heart may remain closed, though one wants very much to open it, if one is too distrustful. This opening of the heart is therefore an aspect of love that does not fit very well in a conception of love that focuses too exclusively on the passionate quest. It is a matter of letting the other person in, so to speak, rather than going out and grabbing him. It is a trusting rather than a controlling aspect of love—but it is nonetheless love. If our love for the neighbor is inspired by God's in this way—that we believe in God's love for the neighbor, or sense it, and respond to it by loving the neighbor ourselves, for the neighbor's own sake—then our love for the neighbor is a response to God as well as to the neighbor, and it can be an expression of love for God.

This position invites an objection that will be worth thinking about. Let us imagine a friendship between Tom and Joe such that Tom's likes, dislikes, desires, affections, and so on vary with Joe's and are "carbon copies" of Joe's. In that case we want to say that Tom's affections are not *genuine;* Tom does not genuinely love what Joe loves. Why should we not conclude that our love for our neighbor is not genuine if it is inspired by God's love for the neighbor—and more generally, that desires, emotions, and attitudes inspired by someone else's are not genuine?

The key to a response to this objection is the difference between *imitation* and *inspiration.* The way Tom's affections are described in the proposed counterexample, we take them to be imitative, and imitative feelings are not genuine. But affections and desires do not have to be original or unconventional in order not to be imitative. People can be at once very conventional and very genuine in their love for their family, for example. There are also many cases in which genuine feelings and interests that are not particularly conventional are inspired by those of other people. One can quite genuinely "imbibe a deep love of Mozart" from one's father or "catch" one's roommate's "infectious" enthusiasm for political action.

What makes the difference, then, between imitative phoniness and inspired genuineness? The most crucial difference is that in imitation one is responding only to what one imitates and not (except very superficially) to the ostensible object of the supposed affection or feeling;

whereas in inspiration there is a much deeper interplay of response to the object and to the other person by whom one is inspired. In imitation, in other words, one copies the other person; whereas in inspiration one enters into the other person's response to the object.

A connected point is that inspired affections and interests are not as dependent as imitative ones on a continued sense of the affections and interests of the person from whom we got them. They are not fickle, as imitative responses are. Inspiration, in the present sense, changes the person who receives it. If my "love" for Mozart disappeared as soon as I thought my father's did, that would be a strong reason for saying that it was imitative and not a genuine love. If I had really imbibed a love of Mozart, I would now be responding to the music for its own sake and not solely to my father, and my love for it would not be so dependent on my perception of my father.

This point might be thought to conflict with claims that we ought to be so possessed by God as to be instantly responsive to his inspiration and totally plastic under the impressions of his Spirit. But I believe this objection involves a theological misconception. In the ideal of surrendering the heart to God there is a place for a response to God that is immediate and variable, but also a place for permanent transformation (which often takes a long time). God is not fickle in his loves and has no desire for a devotion that readies itself to join him in fickleness. The love for one's neighbor that is a fruit of God's Spirit is precisely one that will retain much of its vigor when one is gripped by doubts about God or angry at him or feeling religiously dry.

I do not want to leave the impression that I think the inspiration of human love by divine love is as ordinary and unmysterious as the mundane models I have been using might suggest. In this connection I will make the following observations. We do not love our neighbor as ourselves. Reflecting on the pervasiveness of self-centered motivation, perhaps all of us have sometimes wondered whether we really loved anyone at all. I know how needy and how grasping, when it comes to love, I and others close to me are. And yet it is my experience that from time to time (fairly often, thank God!) we give each other a love that is purer and better than anything we have to give.[22] I cannot prove that this is not an illusion, but I am sure it is not. I take it to be an experience of God—of God loving us, in us and through us—and that is not the least of the reasons for prizing the experience.

In this context I can begin to give an acceptable sense to Nygren's

---

22. Cf. Karl Barth, *Church Dogmatics*, vol. I/2, trans. G. T. Thomson and Harold Knight (Edinburgh: T. & T. Clark, 1956), pp. 450–54.

claim that "in the life that is governed by Agape, the acting subject is not man himself" but "the Spirit of God." Yet this is only half the truth. God's love would not be experienced as it is in such a case if the human subject were not loving too—much less perfectly, but nonetheless really. Here the human love participates in the divine, not just causally as its product, but sacramentally as its vehicle.

7

Moral Obligation, Religious Demand, and Practical Conflcit

PHILIP L. QUINN

Almost all philosophers would concede that conflict among what are often described as prima facie moral obligations is possible and sometimes occurs. The question of whether there can be conflict among what are described, by contrast, as actual moral obligations is vexed. Some philosophers argue that such conflicts do occur, or at least are easily imaginable, and hence are possible.[1] Others argue that such conflicts cannot occur, or at least could not occur from the perspective of an ideally complete and adequate moral theory.[2] The arguments on both sides of the question are impressive. In my opinion, the philosophical contest so far has resulted in a standoff. Be that as it may, it is

Earlier versions of this paper were read at the University of Miami in January 1984, in Lincoln, Nebraska, at the NEH Research Conference in the Philosophy of Religion in April 1984, and at the University of Notre Dame in November 1984. All three audiences engaged me in lively discussion, for which I am grateful. Keith Yandell's formal comments at the NEH conference were extensive and illuminating. I also received helpful criticism from Robert Audi, David Burrell, Clement Dore, C. Stephen Evans, William K. Frankena, Jorge Garcia, Ramon Lemos, Gary Rosenkrantz, Edward Wierenga, and others.

1. On this side of the controversy, I find especially helpful Ruth Marcus, "Moral Dilemmas and Consistency," *Journal of Philosophy* 77 (1980): 121–36, and Bas van Fraassen, "Values and the Heart's Command," *Journal of Philosophy* 70 (1973): 5–19.

2. On this side of the controversy, I find particularly illuminating Earl Conee, "Against Moral Dilemmas," *Philosophical Review* 91 (1982): 87–97, and R. M. Hare, *Moral Thinking* (Oxford: Clarendon Press, 1981).

worth noting that, if such conflicts were to occur, they would be, as usually conceived, internal to the moral realm.

In this paper I discuss the possibility that there are conflicts between moral obligations and other practical requirements rooted outside the moral realm. In particular, I intend to take seriously the possibility of conflict between actual moral obligations and the demands of religious living imposed by divine fiat. Many philosophers, myself included, have been tempted to assimilate all such religious demands to moral requirements and for that reason to suppose that a divine command theory might be needed to account for at least part of the moral realm.[3] But I now think that giving in to this temptation is likely to misrepresent, if not mask completely, an important philosophical issue by portraying all possible conflicts between moral obligations and religious demands as internal to the moral realm. And so I shall be exploring the possibility that some such conflicts are better depicted as pitting against one another claims stemming from the moral realm and claims whose source is external to the moral realm.

The paper has three parts. In the first section, I develop the technical apparatus I need to formulate several distinct theses about general conflicts of practical requirements. In the second section, I defend the claim that one of the stronger theses, when it is interpreted as a claim about possible conflicts of moral and religious requirements is possibly true. And in the third section, I argue that, given a certain plausible epistemological view, one might be justified in believing that one was subject to such conflicting moral and religious demands. I confess at the outset to a painful awareness that the arguments of the second and third sections are far from conclusive. The best I can hope from them is that they will serve to render some claims—which otherwise would probably seem eccentric, if not obviously false—plausible enough to merit further consideration by those philosophers antecedently disposed to take religious demands seriously.

AN ANATOMY OF CONFLICTS OF REQUIREMENTS

I will employ the concept of requirement generically and somewhat technically to express the characteristic 'binding force' or 'compellingness' shared by moral obligations and religious demands. Since for me 'requirement' is a term of art, I do not claim my usage will correspond exactly with the use of the term 'obligation' in ordinary moral

    3. Philip L. Quinn, *Divine Commands and Moral Requirements* (Oxford: Clarendon Press, 1978).

discourse. The letter p, primed when necessary, will serve as a variable ranging over states of affairs; the letter x, primed if necessary, will function as a variable ranging over individual human agents; and the letter a, primed when necessary, will play the role of a variable ranging over particular actions (which may or may not be performed). The symbol '+' will represent an operator that turns pairs of nouns or noun phrases into conjunctive nouns or noun phrases. Following in most respects a procedure used previously by Roderick M. Chisholm, I take three schematic locutions as primitive and use them to formulate five schematic definitions.[4] The first primitive schema is $pRxa$; it may be read informally in English as 'p would require that x do a' or 'p, when it obtains, requires that x do a'. The second is Op; it may be read informally in English as 'p obtains'. And the third is MOp; it may be read informally in English as 'It is logically possible that p obtains'. The definition schemata are these:

(D1) p requires that x do a = Df Op & $pRxa$.

(D2) The requirement that x do a, which would be imposed by p, would be overriden by p' = Df $pRxa$ & $\sim(p + p'Rxa)$.

(D3) The requirement that x do a, which is imposed by p, is overridden by p' = Df $pRxa$ & $\sim(p + p'\ Rxa)$ & Op + p'.

(D4) p would indefeasibly require that x do a = Df $pRxa$ & $(\forall p')$ $(MOp + p' \supset p + p'Rxa)$.

(D5) p indefeasibly requires that x do a = Df $pRxa$ & $(\forall p')$ $(MOp + p' \supset p + p'Rxa)$ & Op.

Although, as Chisholm has shown, other important practical concepts can be defined in terms of our three primitive locutions, I will need only those defined above to formulate the theses about conflicts of requirements I propose to discuss.

In order to formulate these theses, I need to add one primitive schematic locution to the stock I have adapted from Chisholm's discussion of requirement. It is xIa, and it may be read informally in English as 'x and a are such that it is physically impossible that she or he does it'.[5]

The weakest thesis about conflicts of requirements I am going to consider may be formally stated as follows:

4. See Roderick Chisholm, "Practical Reason and the Logic of Requirement," *Practical Reason*, ed. Stephan Körner (Oxford: Basil Blackwell, 1974).

5. One could formulate stronger but parallel theses by using the notion of logical impossibility in place of the notion of physical impossibility.

(T1) $(\exists x)\,(\exists a)\,(\exists a')\,(\exists p)\,(\exists p')\,((Op\ \&\ pRxa)\ \&\ (Op'\ \&\ p'Rxa')\ \&\ xIa + a').$

Paraphrased into English, this thesis asserts that there are an agent, a pair of actions, and a pair of states of affairs which are such that (a) one of the states of affairs requires that the agent do one of the actions, (b) the other state of affairs requires that the agent do the other action, and (c) it is physically impossible for the agent to do both actions. So no matter what an agent of whom (T1) is true does, there will be at least one thing the agent is required to do and does not do. Still, it should be noted that (T1) only asserts the existence of conflict of requirements of a rather innocuous sort. It is consistent with (T1) to claim that, in every case in which an agent is subject to two such conflicting requirements, at least one of the requirements imposed on the agent by a certain state of affairs is overridden by another state of affairs. If we were to define the notion of there being a prima facie requirement that an agent perform an action as there existing some state of affairs such that it requires that the agent perform the action, then we could say that (T1) asserts no more than that there are cases of prima facie requirements that conflict in the sense that it is physically impossible for the agent on whom they are imposed to satisfy them both. Since most philosophers would allow that there are or can be conflicts of prima facie obligations internal to the moral realm, I take it that most philosophers would grant that something like (T1) is true or, at least, possible within the moral realm.

A stronger and, therefore, more interesting and controversial thesis about conflicts of requirements may be stated formally in this way:

(T2) $(\exists x)\,(\exists a)\,(\exists a')\,(\exists p)\,(\exists p')\,((Op\ \&\ pRxa)\ \&\ (Op'\ \&\ p'Rxa')\ \&\ xIa + a'\ \&\ \sim(\exists p'')\,(Op''\ \&\ \sim(p'' + pRxa))\ \&\ \sim(\exists p''')\,(Op'''\ \&\ \sim(p''' + p'Rxa'))).$

Paraphrased into English, this thesis says that there are an agent, a pair of actions, and a pair of states of affairs which are such that (a) one of the states of affairs requires that the agent do one of the actions, (b) the other state of affairs requires that the agent do the other action, (c) it is physically impossible for the agent to do both actions, and (d) neither of the aforementioned requirements is overridden by any state of affairs. In other words, (T2) asserts the existence of cases of conflicting prima facie requirements in which neither of the conflicting requirements is in fact overridden. If, by contrast to the notion of a prima facie require-ment, we were to define the notion of there being an actual requirement that an agent perform an action as there being a prima facie requirement that the agent perform the action and there being no state of affairs that in fact overrides that prima facie requirement, then we could say that (T2) asserts that there are cases of conflicting actual requirements. I take it that those philosophers who assert that there are or can be conflicts of actual moral obligations would grant that something like (T2) is true or possible within the moral realm, and presumably philosophers who deny this would hold that, internal to the moral realm at least, nothing like (T2) is true or possible. It is worth noting that (T2) does not entail that there is no state of affairs such that, were it to obtain, one or the other of the conflicting actual requirements would be overridden; it entails only that no such state of affairs does obtain. Hence, it could be that (T2) is true but only contingently so. If one thinks of conflicts of requirements of the sort whose existence is asserted by (T2) as the stuff some tragedies are made of, the world could be only contingently endowed with such tragedies. Other possible worlds might be without conflicts of actual requirements of this sort and thus luckier than ours in virtue of being without tragedy of this kind.

As I see it, all the appearances that must be saved by an explanation of moral conflict can be saved, though perhaps in a somewhat Procrustean manner, by asserting that something like (T1) is true within the moral realm and without postulating that something like (T2) is true internal to the moral realm. After all, even if one of two conflicting prima facie moral requirements is overridden, it is not thereby rendered illusory or made to disappear. According to (D3) and (D1), if the requirement that an agent perform an action that is imposed by one state of affairs is overridden by another, it remains true that the former state of affairs does require that the agent perform the action. And so, for instance, if the agent fails to satisfy the overridden requirement, regret or even remorse may be an appropriate moral attitude or emotion.[6] But I also think there is real intuitive plausibility to the complaint, which would be made by those philosophers who hold that something like (T2) is true internal to the moral realm, that such an explanation, though it saves the appearances, is not the best explanation of the appearances, because to a certain extent it trivializes moral conflict by failing to face up to its tragic depths. However, since this paper is not about the possibility of conflict internal to the moral realm,

---

6. In *Foundations of Ethics* (Oxford: Oxford University Press, 1939), p. 85, W. D. Ross says: "It remains hard fact that an act of promise-breaking is morally unsuitable, even when we decide that in spite of this, it is the act that we ought to do."

I shall assume, for the sake of argument, that if we confine our attention to the moral realm, only conflicts of the sort whose existence is asserted by (T1) and not those of the kind whose existence is asserted by (T2) are to be discovered.

Many theists hold that divine commands impose requirements but not merely contingently. Requirements imposed by divine command are supposd to be indefeasible. And so, if I am to depict accurately the kind of conflict between religious requirements imposed by divine command and moral requirements I shall later on argue is possible, I believe I must first formulate some additional theses about conflict of indefeasibly imposed requirements with others.

The first of these theses may be formally stated in the following way:

(T3) $(\exists x)\,(\exists a)\,(\exists a')\,(\exists p)\,(\exists p')\,((Op\ \&\ pRxa)\ \&\ (Op'\ \&\ p'Rxa'\ \&$
$(\forall p'')\,(MOp' + p'' \supset p' + p''Rxa'))\ \&\ xIa + a').$

This thesis asserts that there are an agent, a pair of actions, and a pair of states of affairs which are such that (a) one of the states of affairs requires that the agent do one of the actions, (b) the other state of affairs indefeasibly requires that the agent do the other action, and (c) it is physically impossible for the agent to do both actions. Clearly (T3), like (T1), is fairly innocuous. Though the indefeasible requirement whose existence it asserts cannot be overridden, the requirement said to be in conflict with the indefeasible requirement is only asserted to be a prima facie requirement. (T3) does not entail that the requirement which is not said to be indefeasible is in any case an actual requirement; for all (T3) says, that requirement is overridden in every case where (T3) holds.

There would be ineluctable conflict of the strongest sort if the following thesis were true:

(T4) $(\exists x)\,(\exists a)\,(\exists a')\,(\exists p)\,(\exists p')\,((Op\ \&\ pRxa$
$\&\ (\forall p'')\,(MOp + p'' \supset p + p''Rxa))$
$\&\ (Op'\ \&\ p'Rxa'\ \&\ (\forall p''')\,(MOp' + p''' \supset p' + p'''Rxa'))\ \&\ xIa$
$+ a').$

What this thesis says is that there are an agent, a pair of actions, and a pair of states of affairs which are such that (a) one of the states of affairs indefeasibly requires that the agent do one of the actions, (b) the other state of affairs indefeasibly requires that the agent do the other action, and (c) it is physically impossible for the agent to do both actions. Since both of the conflicting requirements said to exist by (T4) are indefeasible, neither can be overridden, and so conflict of this sort can have no happy resolution.

I believe many of the classical discussions of alleged conflicts between moral and religious requirements can be consistently interpreted as involving the assertion of nothing stronger than (T3). Thus, for example, when considering the persecution of heretics, Kant has this to say:

> That it is wrong to deprive a man of his life because of his religious faith is certain, unless (to allow for the most remote possibility) a Divine Will, made known in extraordinary fashion, has ordered it otherwise. But that God has ever uttered this terrible injunction can be asserted only on the basis of historical documents and is never apodictically certain. After all, the revelation has reached the inquisitor only through men and has been interpreted by men, and even did it appear to have come from God Himself (like the command delivered to Abraham to slaughter his own son like a sheep) it is at least possible that in this instance a mistake has prevailed.[7]

Ignoring for the time being the epistemological questions raised by this passage, we might read Kant as presupposing the following analysis of the situation. Some states of affairs morally require that the inquisitor refrain from each particular act of killing his victim. This is always at least a prima facie requirement, but one thing could override it. If God were to command the inquisitor to perform a particular act of killing his victim, such a divine command would indefeasibly require that the inquisitor perform that particular act of killing, but in that case the prima facie requirement to refrain from that act of killing would be overridden. Similarly, when Kierkegaard talks about the teleological suspension of the ethical in his discussion of the story of Abraham and Isaac, we might, by placing a lot of weight on the notion of suspension, interpret him as holding that God's command to Abraham imposes on Abraham an indefeasible requirement to perform a particular act of killing Isaac, that this requirement conflicts with the prima facie moral requirement that Abraham refrain from performing that action, and that the moral requirement in question is suspended in the technical sense of being overridden. So we could save the appearances, I think, without assenting to any thesis about conflicts of requirements stronger than (T3).

7. Immanuel Kant, *Religion within the Limits of Reason Alone*, trans. T. M. Greene and H. H. Hudson (New York: Harper & Row, 1960), p. 175.

But reflection on Kierkegaard's *Fear and Trembling* suggests to me an alternative that is both troublesome and philosophically interesting, namely, that what I shall call 'Kierkegaardian conflict' is possible.[8] Abstractly and formally stated, the thesis of Kierkegaardian conflict is this:

$$(T_5) \quad (\exists x)\,(\exists a)\,(\exists a')\,(\exists p)\,(\exists p')\,((Op \;\&\; pRxa$$
$$\&\; (\forall p'')\,(MOp + p'' \supset p + p''Rxa))$$
$$\&\; (Op' \;\&\; p'Rxa'$$
$$\&\; \sim(\exists p''')\,(Op''' \;\&\; \sim(p' + p'''Rxa')))\; \&\; xIa + a').$$

What (T_5) asserts is that there are an agent, a pair of actions, and a pair of states of affairs which are such that (a) one of the states of affairs indefeasibly requires that the agent do one of the actions, (b) the other state of affairs requires that the agent do the other action, (c) this second requirement is in fact not overridden by any state of affairs and so is an actual requirement, and (d) it is physically impossible for the agent to do both actions. In the next section, I propose to offer a defense of the possibility of an instance of (T_5) in which the indefeasible requirement is a religious requirement imposed by divine command and the conflicting requirement that is not overridden is a moral requirement.

THE CASE FOR KIERKEGAARDIAN CONFLICT

In a Kierkegaardian spirit, the particular instance of (T_5) whose possibility I intend to defend is this:

(K) (i) God's commanding that Abraham perform a particular act of killing Isaac indefeasibly requires that Abraham perform that act of killing Isaac.

(ii) Isaac's being an innocent child requires that Abraham refrain from performing that act of killing Isaac.

(iii) The requirement that Abraham refrain from performing that act of killing Isaac, which is imposed by Isaac's being an innocent child, is overridden by no state of affairs.

8. Though I think Kierkegaard may be read as having some such possibility in mind, I adopt this epithet mainly for its suggestive value. I make no claim to have done the detailed exegetical work that would be needed to justify conclusively attributing (T_5) to Kierkegaard. It has been suggested to me that Kierkegaard does not claim that Kierkegaardian conflicts can or do occur but does hold that one can be prima facie justified in believing oneself to be in a situation of Kierkegaardian conflict. I argue in support of this claim about justification in the third section of this chapter.

(iv) Abraham and that act of killing Isaac are such that it is physically impossible that he both perform and refrain from performing it.

What is there to be said in support of the view that (K)(i)–(iv) are compossible? I shall endeavor to explain.[9]

One crucial assumption for my argument is that the moral realm is not the only source of ultimate values whose realization might be promoted by human actions. The tendency to moralize the whole of our lives is to be resisted. Of course, not all philosophers who accept this general way of looking at things would agree on how precisely the moral realm is to be circumscribed. Some would say it extends no farther than the regulation of interpersonal relations; others would push its limits to the welfare of all sentient beings. I will not here try to settle the question of how to fix the outer boundaries of the realm of moral value. I shall, however, make two plausible assumptions about the internal structure of the moral realm. First, whenever an agent confronts a set of actions that are alternatives, there is at least one that is best from the point of view of promoting the values internal to the moral realm, even if a best action is only indifferent. I say that in each set of alternative actions there is *at least* one best because I wish to allow that in some such sets there are several tied for first place. The second assumption is that, in at least some cases where an agent confronts a set of alternative actions that contains a unique best from the point of view of promoting the values internal to the moral realm, the state of affairs in virtue of which that action is uniquely best imposes on the agent a moral requirement to do that action which is not overridden by any state of affairs. I do not say this is so for *all* such cases, in order to allow that the best may sometimes be supererogatory rather than required, because there are limits to what morality can demand by way of saintly or heroic behavior.[10]

Applying these assumptions to the case of Abraham and Isaac, I think we can see that (K)(ii)–(iv) are compossible. Of the two options

9. Perhaps it is worth emphasizing at this point that I am arguing only for the possibility of Kierkegaardian conflict and that I use the case of Abraham and Isaac merely for illustrative purposes. I suppose most devout theists would hope, and perhaps even trust, that such a possibility, if it is a possibility, will never be actual. If such theists also believe that the story in Genesis 22 contains literal truth, they will need an interpretation of that story which reads it as something other than a case of Kierkegaardian conflict. But such interpretations abound, and some of them are independently plausible.

10. A view supported in different ways by recent arguments in James S. Fishkin, *The Limits of Obligation* (New Haven: Yale University Press, 1982), and Samuel Scheffler, *The Rejection of Consequentialism* (Oxford: Clarendon Press, 1982).

available to Abraham, performing or refraining from performing a particular act of killing Isaac, refraining clearly can be morally better than killing. Refraining would not require any especially heroic or saintly behavior on Abraham's part. Isaac's being an innocent child is precisely the kind of consideration that is suitable for imposing moral requirements. And though there might be some states of affairs that would, if they obtained, override this requirement, it is surely possible that none of them do obtain and, hence, that the requirement is not overridden.

Since it is not an aim of this paper to argue for the coherence of theism, I shall take it for granted that (K)(i) is possible. What does need to be argued is that (K)(i), on the one hand, and (K)(ii)–(iv), on the other, are compossible. Even many theists will hold that the reason God's commanding Abraham to perform a particular act of killing Isaac indefeasibly requires that Abraham perform that act is that God is essentially perfectly good. They will then be tempted to suppose that God's commanding Abraham to perform that act of killing Isaac is a state of affairs that overrides the requirement imposed by Isaac's being an innocent child that Abraham refrain from performing the act. If this were correct, then (K)(i) and (K)(iii) would not be compossible.

I grant that God's being perfectly good explains why his commanding Abraham to perform a particular act of killing Isaac indefeasibly requires that Abraham perform that act. I deny, however, that God's goodness is exclusively moral goodness, and for that reason I deny that God's command that Abraham perform a particular act of killing Isaac overrides the moral requirement that Abraham refrain from performing that act. In short, because the requirements imposed by divine command spring from a realm of value not wholly coincident with the moral realm, they are not necessarily moral requirements at all. Hence, they are not necessarily moral requirements so stringent that they would override all other moral requirements, and so they do not necessarily override conflicting moral requirements.[11] Of course I do not claim that God is utterly careless of the welfare of his human creatures and altogether indifferent to the values of the moral realm. Sometimes

11. An interesting question is whether, apart from nonmoral requirements indefeasibly imposed by divine commands, moral requirements always override nonmoral requirements if there is conflict. In the absence of a detailed characterization of how the moral realm is to be circumscribed, it is clearly not possible to answer this question. But if one does not trivialize the question by defining moral requirements as those that would be overriding if there were conflict, then it seems to me that a negative answer is quite plausible. In support of such an answer, I would cite considerations of the kind presented by Bernard Williams, in "Ethical Consistency," collected in his *Problems of the Self* (Cambridge: Cambridge University Press, 1973).

divine commands do impose moral requirements indefeasibly, and sometimes moral requirements imposed by divine command do override other requirements, moral and nonmoral. But I think that this is not necessarily always the case, and so I hold that (K)(i) and (K)(iii) are compossible. Because the requirement indefeasibly imposed by God's command to Abraham is a religious requirement rooted outside the moral realm and not just a particularly stringent moral requirement, it does not override the supremely urgent moral requirement that Abraham refrain from killing Isaac imposed by the fact that Isaac is an innocent child. And so, I think, genuine Kierkegaardian conflict based on conflicting and incommensurable moral and religious values and requirements is possible.

Perhaps it will be allowed that my argument so far suffices to cast some doubt on the view that Kierkegaardian conflict is known to be impossible. But, it will be said, the defense of my view would be stronger if I could present a positive account of divine goodness that would serve as a basis for a positive insight into the possibility of requirements arising from divine commands coming into Kierkegaardian conflict with moral requirements. This I cannot do. Indeed, I think there are good religious reasons for believing that it is something no human is capable of doing. It would be presumptuous to suppose that any of us understands God well enough to give a complete account of his perfections; respectable traditions of religious thought hold that no human grasp of the divine nature can be adequate to exhaust any of its ingredient perfections. But I can do something less ambitious, namely, remind the reader that within orthodox theistic thought there are models of divine goodness that are supposed to enable us to get a partial insight into what divine goodness is but that do not identify divine goodness with moral goodness. One such model is the plenitude of being model. When God's perfections are summed up by saying that he is the *ens realissimum*, what is being asserted, I think, is at least this: God's goodness consists at least in part in his being metaphysically perfect in the sense of being metaphysically complete and self-sufficient and in his being the source of all existence and lesser metaphysical perfection in the creaturely domain.[12] Some such notion of metaphysical goodness seems to underlie the characteristic Leibnizian claim that, when God chooses to create the best of all possible worlds, it is the world that ranks highest on a scale combining considerations of sim-

---

12. The plenitude of being model obviously also has implications for how the problem of evil can be treated, some of which are being worked out in unpublished research by Thomas V. Morris.

plicity of natural laws and variety of creaturely denizens. It is not at all obvious that a world that is best in this sense is also best in the sense of maximally realizing the values of the moral realm. For this reason it seems to me possible that some of the values God cares about having his human creatures pursue—enough that by command he imposes on them indefeasible requirements for certain actions—should be nonmoral values and that on this account those indefeasible requirements should possibly sometimes be in Kierkegaardian conflict with moral requirements.

Of course, the plenitude of being model is not the only alternative to thinking of divine goodness as exclusively moral goodness. Perhaps divine goodness has a dimension that is more akin to aesthetic goodness than to any other realm of goodness with which we humans are familiar. And maybe divine goodness has aspects that are and will always remain completely inscrutable to us. I do not intend to rule out such possibilities. Rather I wish to assert these two theses: (1) it is God's goodness that explains why his commands indefeasibly impose requirements, and (2) it is the fact that divine goodness has nonmoral components that explains why those indefeasibly imposed religious requirements can sometimes be in Kierkegaardian conflict with moral requirements.

The argument of this section will be complete when I have done what I can to fend off what I consider the most powerful objection to the defense I have been mounting of the possibility of Kierkegaardian conflict. Succinctly stated, the objection may be put this way. For the sake of argument, let it be granted that divine commands would indefeasibly impose requirements and that some of these requirements would be nonmoral, religious requirements. Let it also be granted that there are possible conflicts between such indefeasibly imposed religious requirements and moral requirements. It does not follow from these assumptions that any such cases are possible cases of Kierkegaardian conflict. It may yet be that in every such case the very state of affairs—namely, a certain divine command having been issued—which indefeasibly imposes a certain religious requirement also overrides any conflicting moral requirement. Hence, it may be conceded that there are distinctively religious values that impose nonmoral requirements indefeasibly and also denied that there are any cases, actual or possible, of Kierkegaardian conflict. Strictly speaking, all that must be granted if we accept the assumptions in question is that, in possible cases of conflict between indefeasible religious requirements and moral requirements, the religious requirements have priority and are the actual requirements to which one is subject. It need not also be granted that the conflicting moral requirements are not overridden.

Obviously, the objection has the logic of the situation right. The possibility of Kierkegaardian conflict does not follow from the assumptions so far made about diverse realms of value as sources for conflicting requirements. In effect, this is why I earlier acknowledged that one could save the appearances without asserting anything stronger than (T3). Moreover, the additional assumption that would be needed to complete a deductive argument for the possibility of Kierkegaardian conflicts, namely, that there are possible cases where indefeasible requirements rooted in the realm of religious values conflict with requirements that spring from the realm of moral values and yet are not overridden, seems to beg the question against the objector.

But, though I think the appearances can be saved without acknowledging the possibility of Kierkegaardian conflicts, I do not believe they are best saved in that fashion. As I see it, the best explanation of the appearances appeals to the possibility of Kierkegaardian conflict. In order to make a case for this claim, I can only ask the reader to reflect carefully on what the appearances are, as they manifest themselves in Kierkegaard's treatment of the story of Abraham and Isaac in *Fear and Trembling* or in similar vividly and imaginatively portrayed cases.[13] When I engage in such reflections, I am convinced that the moral requirement, imposed by Isaac's being an innocent child, that Abraham refrain from killing Isaac, is not overridden by God's command to Abraham, even though the command indefeasibly imposes a conflicting religious requirement. To suppose that the moral requirement is overridden in this case seems to me to involve a failure to acknowledge the ultimacy of certain moral values and our commitments to them. But to suppose that God's command to Abraham does not indefeasibly impose a religious requirement seems to me to involve a similar failure to acknowledge the ultimacy of certain religious values and our commitments to them. Either supposition strikes me as a response to the story that misses what is deepest and most poignant about it. And so I think the tables should be turned, so to speak, and the burden of proof placed squarely on the shoulders of the objector. Assuming that religious and moral values can conflict, what justifies the supposition that

13. But not everyone will agree with me about what the appearances are. A useful presentation of a contrasting view is G. Outka, "Religious and Moral Duty: Notes on *Fear and Trembling*," *Religion and Morality*, ed. G. Outka and J. P. Reeder (Garden City: Doubleday, 1973).

in each possible case of conflict of this sort pursuit of one of the two conflicting values must be better on some common scale of value than pursuit of the other? Why not allow that in certain possible cases of conflict the values of diverse realms are simply incommensurable? When requirements rooted in the realm of moral value and not overridden by anything internal to that realm conflict with requirements that spring from the realm of religious value and are not overridden by anything internal to that realm in certain possible cases, what justifies the assumption that there must be some more inclusive and more ultimate realm of value within which one or the other of the two conflicting requirements is overridden? My reflections on such questions convince me that there is no argument that would justify such assumptions without begging the question against the proponent of the thesis that Kierkegaardian conflicts are possible.

This concludes the case for Kierkegaardian conflict. It is, of course, not a proof that Kierkegaardian conflicts are possible. I think it likely that there is no proof of the claim that does not sooner or later beg the question against its opponents by appeal to some theoretical principle as open to doubt as the claim. But I consider it equally likely that there is no disproof of the claim that does not also beg the question against its proponents sooner or later by appeal to some theoretical assumption every bit as questionable as the negation of the claim is. As in the case of alleged conflicts of actual obligations within the moral realm, the direct philosophical arguments lead to a standoff, if I am right. However, the appearances of conflicts between moral and religious requirements, as I see them, are better explained on the hypothesis that Kierkegaardian conflicts are possible than on the hypothesis that they are not, and so I conclude that it is rational to believe that Kierkegaardian conflicts are possible. It is in this sense that I defend the claim that Kierkegaardian conflicts are possible. Because I have refrained from endorsing the parallel claim about the best explanation of the appearances of conflicts of obligations internal to the moral realm in this paper, I have not in this sense defended that possibility.

ON JUSTIFYING KIERKEGAARDIAN CLAIMS

In this section, I argue that it is possible in a certain sense to be justified in believing that one is in a situation of Kierkegaardian conflict. Though there are several ways to explain the concepts from normative epistemology I shall be using, the simplest procedure in the present context is to note their close analogy with the concepts involving requirement that I developed in the first section of this paper. One begins with the notion of a state of affairs being such that it would justify a belief for a person. A state of affairs justifies a belief for a person just in case it obtains and would justify that belief for that person. The justification of a belief for a person, which would be provided by one state of affairs, would be overridden by another just in case the first state of affairs but not the conjunctive state of affairs would justify the belief for the person. And the justification of a belief for a person, which is provided by one state of affairs, is overridden by another just in case (1) the first state of affairs would justify the belief for the person, (2) it is not the case that the conjunctive state of affairs would justify the belief for the person, and (3) the conjunctive state of affairs obtains. Since the formal definitions would exactly parallel those given in the first section, I do not bother to state them here. Because justification understood in this way may be overridden, it is a kind of prima facie justification. Though it may not in fact be overridden in a particular case, it is not indefeasible.

For the sake of vividness, I will conduct my argument for the possibility of being justified in believing one is in a situation of Kierkegaardian conflict in terms of the particular instance of (T5) formulated as (K)(i)–(iv) in the preceding section. One is to suppose that the believer in question is Abraham or a counterpart of Abraham.

My first step is to argue that Abraham could be justified in believing (K)(iv). Abraham could grasp and accept the perfectly obvious truth that the particular act of killing Isaac referred to in (K)(iv) is such that it is physically impossible that he both perform and refrain from performing it. This for him would justify belief in (K)(iv). Hence, it is possible that Abraham is justified in believing (K)(iv).

My next step is to argue that Abraham could be justified in believing (K)(ii). Abraham could be justified in believing that Isaac is an innocent child, that killing Isaac would have a major negative impact on Isaac's welfare and, perhaps, the welfare of others as well, and that killing Isaac would have no positive impact on the welfare of sentient beings large enough to outweigh its negative impact on Isaac and others. Moreover, Abraham could be justified in believing that refraining from killing Isaac would involve no saintly or heroic behavior on his part. Taken together, these things would justify for Abraham belief in (K)(ii). Therefore, it is also possible that Abraham is justified in believing (K)(ii).

My third step is to argue that Abraham could be justified in believing (K)(i). Abraham could grasp and accept the conceptual truth that God, if he exists, is essentially perfectly good. This would justify for him the belief that God's commanding him to perform a particular act of killing Isaac would indefeasibly require that he perform that act. Moreover,

Abraham could have an experience in optimal conditions that seemed to him to be an experience of God's commanding him to perform that particular act of killing Isaac. Appealing to recent arguments by Alston and Plantinga, whose general import is to show that sometimes beliefs about the contents made manifest in such experiences and based directly on such experiences are at least prima facie justified, I claim that the occurrence of such an experience in optimal conditions would justify for Abraham the belief that God commands him to perform that act of killing Isaac.[14] Taken together, these two beliefs, if justified, would in turn justify for Abraham belief in (K)(i). Hence, it is possible that Abraham is justified in believing (K)(i).

The next and, I suspect, most controversial step is to argue that Abraham could be justified in believing (K)(iii). Abraham could be justified in believing that no state of affairs bearing on the promotion of the values internal to the moral realm overrides the requirement that he refrain from performing the particular act of killing Isaac referred to in (K)(iii). Abraham could also, I claim, be justified (for instance, on the basis of considerations that went into the argument of the preceding section of this paper) in believing that no state of affairs pertinent to the promotion of the values internal to the religious realm, including the state of affairs of God's commanding that he perform that act of killing Isaac, overrides the moral requirement that he refrain from performing that act. And Abraham could be justified in believing that no state of affairs bearing on the promotion of values in any realm diverse from the moral and the religious, such as the aesthetic, overrides the requirement that he refrain from that particular act of killing Isaac. Taken together, these three beliefs, if justified, would further justify for Abraham belief in (K)(iii). Therefore, if my argument in the preceding section has enough force to provide prima facie justification for a belief by Abraham that God's command that he perform a particular act of killing Isaac would not override the moral requirement that he refrain from killing Isaac, as I think it does, it is also possible that Abraham is justified in believing (K)(iii).

14. See William P. Alston, "Religious Experience and Religious Belief," *Nous* 16 (1982): 3–12, and Alvin Plantinga, "Is Belief in God Properly Basic?" *Nous* 15 (1981): 41–51. One might construe the Genesis story as saying that Abraham's epistemic blessings also included prima facie justified beliefs about the past history of his interactions with God that would serve as independent inductive backing for his belief that he had been divinely commanded. Thus, for example, Abraham had reason to believe that, when he was niney-nine years old, God had promised him a son (Genesis 17) and knew that, when he was one hundred years old, he had astonishingly been given a son (Genesis 21). Such evidence would serve to strengthen the prima facie justification of his belief that he had been divinely commanded.

The final step is to argue that Abraham could be justified in believing (K)(i)–(iv). By the arguments of the preceding four paragraphs, Abraham could be justified in believing each of (K)(i) through (K)(iv). By the argument of the preceding section, Abraham could be justified in believing that the hypothesis that (K)(i) through (K)(iv) are compossible is rational.[15] Taken together, these two beliefs, if justified, would in turn justify for Abraham belief in (K)(i)–(iv). Hence, it is possible that Abraham is justified in believing (K)(i)–(iv).

This concludes the argument for the claim that it is possible to be justified in believing one is in a situation of Kierkegaardian conflict. It is worth repeating that this is not a terribly strong claim, since the kind of justification in question is only prima facie justification. Though there are, I have argued, states of affairs that would justify for someone belief in (K)(i)–(iv), there are also states of affairs that would override such justification. For example, there are states of affairs that would for Abraham override the justification of the belief that God commands that he perform a particular act of killing Isaac provided by his religious experience. An interesting question is whether in every possible case in which Abraham is prima facie justified in believing (K)(i)–(iv) something does override his justification. Is it possible both that Abraham is prima facie justified in believing (K)(i)–(iv) and that Abraham's justification for believing (K)(i)–(iv) is not overridden? For all I know it is possible, since I can think of no argument that shows it to be impossible. So perhaps it is possible that Abraham has actual and not merely prima facie justification for believing (K)(i)–(iv). Hence, maybe it is even possible to have actual justification for believing oneself to be in a situation of Kierkegaardian conflict. I shall conclude with the bold conjecture that this is indeed possible. And then I am prompted to ask: Is there an argument that shows that this conjecture is false?

EPILOGUE

One way in which philosophy can be edifying is to bring us to see new possibilities. When philosophy succeeds in performing this function, it teaches us that the world might be stranger by far than pedestrian common sense would allow. This paper has been an attempt to edify by broadening our horizon of possibilities.

15. And, assuming the argument of the preceding section is sound, Abraham will have no grounds for supposing he will, and some grounds for supposing he will not, confront at this point in his reasoning an analogue of the lottery paradox, according to which the belief that no ticket in a large lottery will win is justified because each ticket probably will not win.

In reading this paper to various groups, I have been struck by the fact that many in my audiences are preoccupied with actualities. They ask, But do situations of Kierkegaardian conflict actually occur? In response to this question, I have nothing helpful to say. Of course I hope they do not occur, but I cannot prove they do not. Or they ask, Do you think you will ever actually be justified in believing you are in a situation of Kierkegaardian conflict? Curiously enough, I do not think so.

When I try to imagine myself playing the role of Abraham, I cannot imagine I would ever regard myself as justified in believing that God had commanded me to kill Isaac. Were I to hear a voice issuing such an order, I am very sure I would conclude that the order was not a divine command. But when I ask myself why I would come to that conclusion, something interesting emerges. The conclusion would not rest on a confident belief that a perfectly good God could not issue such a command; it would be based on a deep skepticism about my ever being justified in believing that a divine command had been addressed directly to me.

Would the fact that such skepticism is bone-deep in me be of any special significance? Perhaps. Of course, maybe it would only betoken a properly humble appreciation of my own unworthiness to be the recipient of a direct divine command. But maybe it would show that, being situated as I am in a predominantly secular culture, I can conceive of certain possibilities for justified belief that I cannot quite imagine being actual for me. If it showed this, I would be under pressure to admit that my culture has the power to shut me off from understanding imaginatively and firsthand the kind of faith needed to play the role of Abraham. And I would be reluctant to concede so much influence in determining what I can imagine to the contingencies of my culture. Like many intellectuals, I am inclined to fancy I can transcend, if only in imagination, most of the limits of my culture. But perhaps the range of my imagination is severely constricted just because I am to a large extent the product of an incredulous culture. If so, then the fact that I can conceive possibilities I cannot quite imagine being actual for me may give me a hint about how grace might be needed to work certain kinds of religious transformations in my life.

8

Religion and the
Queerness of Mortality

GEORGE I. MAVRODES

Many arguments for the existence of God may be construed as claiming that there is some feature of the world that would somehow make
no sense unless there was something else that had a stronger version of
that feature or some analogue of it. So, for example, the cosmological
line of argument may be thought of as centering upon the claim that
the way in which the world exists (called "contingent" existence) would
be incomprehensible unless there were something else—that is, God—
that had a stronger grip upon existence (that is, "necessary" existence).

Now, a number of thinkers have held a view something like this with
respect to morality. They have claimed that in some important way
morality is dependent upon religion—dependent, that is, in such a way
that if religion were to fail, morality would fail also. And they have held
that the dependence was more than psychological, that is, if religion
were to fail, it would somehow be *proper* (perhaps logically or perhaps
in some other way) for morality to fail also. One way of expressing this
theme is by Dostoevsky's "If there is no God, then everything is permitted," a sentiment that in this century has been prominently echoed by
Sartre. But perhaps the most substantial philosophical thinker of the
modern period to espouse this view, though in a rather idiosyncratic
way, was Immanual Kant, who held that the existence of God was a
necessary postulate of 'practical' (that is, moral) reason.[1]

1. Perhaps, however, Kant was not entirely clear on this point, for in some places he
talks as though it is only the *possibility* of God's existence that is a necessary postulate of

On the other hand, it has recently been popular for moral philosophers to deny this theme and to maintain that the dependence of morality on religion is, at best, merely psychological. Were religion to fail, so they apparently hold, this would grant no sanction for the failure of morality. For morality stands on its own feet, whatever those feet may turn out to be.

Now, the suggestion that morality somehow depends on religion is rather attractive to me. It is this suggestion that I wish to explore in this paper, even though it seems unusually difficult to formulate clearly the features of this suggestion that make it attractive. I will begin by mentioning briefly some aspects that I will not discuss.

First, beyond this paragraph I will not discuss the claim that morality cannot survive psychologically without the support of religious belief. At least in the short run, this proposal seems to me false. For there certainly seem to be people who reject religious belief, at least in the ordinary sense, but who apparently have a concern with morality and who try to live a moral life. Whether the proposal may have more force if it is understood in a broader way, as applying to whole cultures, epochs, and so forth, I do not know.

Second, I will not discuss the attempt to define some or all moral terms by the use of religious terms, or vice versa. But this should not be taken as implying any judgment about this project.

Third, beyond this paragraph I shall not discuss the suggestion that moral statements may be entailed by religious statements and so may be "justified" by religious doctrines or beliefs. It is popular now to hold that no such alleged entailment can be valid. But the reason usually cited for this view is the more general doctrine that moral statements cannot be validly deduced from nonmoral statements, a doctrine usually traced to Hume. Now, to my mind the most important problem raised by this general doctrine is that of finding some interpretation of it that is both significant and not plainly false. If it is taken to mean merely that there is *some* set of statements that entails no moral statement, then it strikes me as probably true, but trivial. At any rate, we should then need another reason to suppose that religious statements fall in this category. If, on the other hand, it is taken to mean that one can divide the domain of statements into two classes, the moral and the nonmoral, and that none of the latter entail any of the former, then it is false. I, at any rate, do not know a version of this doctrine that seems relevant to the religious case and that has any reasonable likelihood of

morality. For a discussion of this point see M. Jamie Ferreira, "Kant's Postulate: The Possibility or the Existence of God?" *Kant-Studien* 17, no. 1 (1983): 75–80.

being true. But I am not concerned on this occasion with the possibly useful project of deducing morality from religion, and so I will not pursue it further. My interest is closer to a move in the other direction, that of deducing religion from morality. (I am not quite satisfied with this way of putting it and will try to explain this dissatisfaction later on.)

For the remainder of this discussion, then, my project is as follows. I will outline one rather common nonreligious view of the world, calling attention to what I take to be its most relevant features. Then I shall try to portray some sense of the odd status that morality would have in a world of that sort. I shall be hoping, of course, that you will notice that this odd status is not the one that you recognize morality to have in the actual world. But it will perhaps be obvious that the "world-view" amendments required would move substantially toward a religious position.

First, then, the nonreligious view. I take a short and powerful statement of it from a 1903 essay by Bertrand Russell, "A Free Man's Worship."

> That man is the product of causes which had no prevision of the end they were achieving; that his origin, his growth, his hopes and fears, his loves and his beliefs are but the outcome of accidental collocations of atoms; that no fire, no heroism, no intensity of thought and feeling, can preserve an individual life beyond the grave; that all the labors of the ages, all the devotion, all the inspiration, all the noonday brightness of human genius, are destined to extinction in the vast death of the solar system, and that the whole temple of man's achievement must inevitably be buried beneath the debris of a universe in ruins—all these things, if not quite beyond dispute, are yet so nearly certain that no philosophy which rejects them can hope to stand. Only within the scaffolding of these truths, only on the firm foundation of unyielding despair, can the soul's habitation henceforth be safely built.[2]

For convenience, I will call a world that satisfies the description given here a "Russellian world." But we are primarily interested in what the status of morality would be in the actual world if that world should turn out to be Russellian. I shall therefore sometimes augment the description of a Russellian world with obvious features of the actual world.

What are the most relevant features of a Russellian world? The following strike me as especially important: (1) Such phenomena as minds, mental activities, consciousness, and so forth are the products of entities and causes that give no indication of being mental themselves.

2. In Bertrand Russell, *Mysticism and Logic* (New York: Barnes & Noble, 1917), pp. 47–48.

In Russell's words, the causes are "accidental collocations of atoms" with "no prevision of the end they were achieving." Though not stated explicitly by Russell, we might add the doctrine, a commonplace in modern science, that mental phenomena—and indeed life itself—are comparative latecomers in the long history of the earth. (2) Human life is bounded by physical death and each individual comes to a permanent end at his physical death. We might add to this the observation that the span of human life is comparatively short, enough so that in some cases we can, with fair confidence, predict the major consequences of certain actions insofar as they will affect a given individual throughout his whole remaining life. (3) Not only each individual but also the human race as a species is doomed to extinction "beneath the debris of a universe in ruins."

So much, then, for the main features of a Russellian world. Because the notion of benefits and goods plays an important part in the remainder of my discussion, I want to introduce one further technical expression—"Russellian benefit." A Russellian benefit is one that could accrue to a person in a Russellian world. A contented old age would be, I suppose, a Russellian benefit, as would a thrill of sexual pleasure or a good reputation. Going to heaven when one dies, though a benefit, is not a Russellian benefit. Russellian benefits are only the benefits possible in a Russellian world. But one can have Russellian benefits even if the world is not Russellian. In such a case there might, however, also be other benefits, such as going to heaven.

Could the actual world be Russellian? Well, I take it to be an important feature of the actual world that human beings exist in it and that in it their actions fall, at least sometimes, within the sphere of morality—that is, they have moral obligations to act (or to refrain from acting) in certain ways. And if they do not act in those ways, then they are properly subject to a special and peculiar sort of adverse judgment (unless it happens that there are special circumstances that serve to excuse their failure to fulfill the obligations). People who do not fulfill their obligations are not merely stupid or weak or unlucky; they are morally reprehensible.

Now, I do not have much to say in an illuminating manner about the notion of moral obligation, but I could perhaps make a few preliminary observations about how I understand this notion. First, I take it that morality includes, or results in, judgments of the form "N ought to do (or to avoid doing)_____" or "It is N's duty to do (or to avoid doing)_____." That is, morality ascribes to particular people an obligation to do a certain thing on a certain occasion. No doubt morality includes other things as well—general moral rules, for example. I shall, however, focus on judgments of the sort just mentioned, and when I speak without further qualification of someone's having an obligation I intend it to be understood in terms of such a judgment.

Second, many authors distinguish prima facie obligations from obligations "all things considered." Probably this is a useful distinction. For the most part, however, I intend to ignore prima facie obligations and to focus upon our obligations all things considered, what we might call our "final obligations." These are the obligations that a particular person has in some concrete circumstance at a particular place and time, when all the aspects of the situation have been taken into account. It identifies the action that, if not done, will proerly subject the person to the special adverse judgment.

Finally, it is, I think, a striking feature of moral obligations that a person's being unwilling to fulfill the obligation is irrelevant to having the obligation and is also irrelevant to the adverse judgment in case the obligation is not fulfilled. Perhaps even more important is the fact that, at least for some obligations, it is also irrelevant in both these ways for one to point out that he does not see how fulfilling the obligations can do him any good. In fact, unless we are greatly mistaken about our obligations, it seems clear that in a Russellian world there are an appreciable number of cases in which fulfilling an obligation would result in a loss of good to ourselves. On the most prosaic level, this must be true of some cases of repaying a debt, keeping a promise, refraining from stealing, and so on. And it must also be true of those rarer but more striking cases of obligation to risk death or serious injury in the performance of a duty. People have, of course, differed as to what is good for humans. But so far as I can see, the point I have been making will hold for any candidate that is plausible in a Russellian world. Pleasure, happiness, esteem, contentment, self-realization, knowledge—all of these can suffer from the fulfillment of a moral obligation.

It is not, however, a *necessary* truth that some of our obligations are such that their fulfillment will yield no net benefit, within Russellian limits, to their fulfiller. It is not contradictory to maintain that, for every obligation that I have, a corresponding benefit awaits me within the confines of this world and this life. While such a contention would not be contradictory, however, it would nevertheless be false. I discuss below one version of this contention. At present it must suffice to say that a person who accepts this claim will probably find the remainder of what I have to say correspondingly less plausible.

Well, where are we now? I claim that in the actual world we have some obligations that, when we fulfill them, will confer on us no net Russellian benefit—in fact, they will result in a Russellian loss. If the world is Russellian, then Russellian benefits and losses are the only benefits and losses, and also then we have moral obligations whose fulfillment will result in a net loss of good to the one who fulfills them. I suggest, however, that it would be very strange to have such obligations—strange not simply in the sense of being unexpected or surprising but in some deeper way. I do not suggest that it is strange in the sense of having a straightforward logical defect, of being self-contradictory to claim that we have such obligations. Perhaps the best thing to say is that were it a fact that we had such obligations, then the world that included such a fact would be absurd—we would be living in a crazy world.

Now, whatever success I may have in this paper will in large part be a function of my success (or lack thereof) in getting across a sense of that absurdity, that queerness. On some accounts of morality, in a Russellian world there would not be the strangeness that I allege. Perhaps, then, I can convey some of that strangeness by mentioning those views of morality that would eliminate it. In fact, I believe that a good bit of their appeal is just the fact that they do get rid of this queerness.

First, I suspect that morality will not be queer in the way I suggest, even in a Russellian world, if judgments about obligations are properly to be analyzed in terms of the speaker rather than in terms of the subject of the judgment. And I more than suspect that this will be the case if such judgments are analyzed in terms of the speaker's attitude or feeling toward some action, and/or his attempt or inclination to incite a similar attitude in someone else. It may be, of course, that there is something odd about the supposition that human beings, consciousness, and so forth, could arise at all in a Russellian world. A person who was impressed by that oddity might be attracted toward some "teleological" line of reasoning in the direction of a more religious view. But I think that this oddity is not the one I am touching on here. Once given the existence of human beings with capacities for feelings and attitudes, there does not seem to be anything further that is queer in the supposition that a speaker might have an attitude toward some action, might express that attitude, and might attempt (or succeed) in inciting someone else to have a similar attitude. Anyone, therefore, who can be satisfied with such an analysis will probably not be troubled by the queerness that I allege.

Second, for similar reasons, this queerness will also be dissipated by any account that understands judgments about obligations purely in terms of the feelings, attitudes, and so forth of the subject of the judgment. For, given again that there are human beings with consciousness, it does not seem to be any additional oddity that the subject of a moral judgment might have feelings or attitudes about an actual or propsective action of his own. The assumption that morality is to be understood in this way takes many forms. In a closely related area, for example, it appears as the assumption—so common now that it can pass almost unnoticed—that guilt could not be anything other than guilt *feelings,* and that the "problem" of guilt is just the problem generated by such feelings.

In connection with our topic here, however, we might look at the way in which this sort of analysis enters into one plausible-sounding explanation of morality in a Russellian world, an explanation that has a scientific flavor. The existence of morality in a Russellian world, it may be said, is not at all absurd because its existence there can be given a perfectly straightforward explanation: morality has a survival value for a species such as ours because it makes possible continued cooperation and things of that sort. So it is no more absurd that people have moral obligations than it is absurd that they have opposable thumbs.

I think that this line of explanation will work only if one analyzes obligations into feelings, or beliefs. I think it is plausible (though I am not sure it is correct) to suppose that everyone's having feelings of moral obligation might have a survival value for a species such as Man, given of course that these feelings were attached to patterns of action that contributed to such survival. And if that is so, then it is not implausible to suppose that there may be a survival value for the species even in a moral feeling that leads to the death of the individual who has it. So far so good. But this observation, even if true, is not relevant to the queerness with which I am here concerned. For I have not suggested that the existence of moral feelings would be absurd in a Russellian world; it is rather the existence of moral *obligations* that is absurd, and I think it important to make the distinction. It is quite possible, it seems to me, for one to feel (or to believe) that he has a certain obligation without actually having it, and also vice versa. Now, beliefs and feelings will presumably have some effect upon actions, and this effect may possibly contribute to the survival of the species. But, so far as I can see, the addition of actual moral obligations to these moral beliefs and feelings will make no further contribution to action nor will the actual obligations have an effect upon action in the absence of the corresponding feelings and beliefs. So it seems that neither with nor without the appropriate feelings will moral obligations contribute to the survival of the species. Consequently, an "evolutionary" approach such as this cannot serve to explain the existence of moral obligations, unless one rejects my distinction and equates the obligations with the feelings.

And finally, I think that morality will not be queer in the way I allege, or at least it will not be as queer as I think, if it should be the case that every obligation yields a Russellian benefit to the one who fulfills it. Given the caveat expressed earlier, one can perhaps make some sense out of the notion of a Russellian good or benefit for a sentient organism in a Russellian world. And one could, I suppose, without further queerness imagine that such an organism might aim toward achieving such goods. And we could further suppose that there were certain actions—those that were "obligations"—that would, in contrast with other actions, actually yield such benefits to the organism that performed them. And finally, it might not be too implausible to claim that an organism that failed to perform such an action was defective in some way and that some adverse judgment was appropriate.

Morality, however, seems to require us to hold that certain organisms (namely, human beings) have in addition to their ordinary properties and relations another special relation to certain actions. This relation is that of being "obligated" to perform those actions. And some of those actions are pretty clearly such that they will yield only Russellian losses to the one who performs them. Nevertheless, we are supposed to hold that a person who does not perform an action to which he is thus related is defective in some serious and important way and an adverse judgment is appropriate against him. And that certainly does seem odd.

The recognition of this oddity—or perhaps better, this absurdity—is not simply a resolution to concern ourselves only with what "pays." Here the position of Kant is especially suggestive. He held that a truly moral action is undertaken purely out of respect for the moral law and with no concern at all for reward. There seems to be no room at all here for any worry about what will "pay." But he also held that the moral enterprise needs, in a deep and radical way, the postulate of a God who can, and will, make happiness correspond to virtue. This postulate is "necessary" for practical reason. Perhaps we could put this Kantian demand in the language I have been using here, saying that the moral enterprise would make no sense in a world in which that correspondence ultimately failed.

I suspect that what we have in Kant is the recognition that there cannot be, in any "reasonable" way, a moral demand upon me, unless reality itself is committed to morality in some deep way. It makes sense only if there is a moral demand on the world too and only if reality will in the end satisfy that demand. This theme of the deep grounding of morality is one to which I return briefly near the end of this paper.

The oddity we have been considering is, I suspect, the most important root of the celebrated and somewhat confused question, "Why should I be moral?" Characteristically, I think, the person who asks that question is asking to have the queerness of that situation illuminated. From time to time there are philosophers who make an attempt to argue—perhaps only a halfhearted attempt—that being moral really is in one's interest after all. Kurt Baier, it seems to me, proposes a reply of this sort. He says:

> Moralities are systems of principles whose acceptance by everyone as overruling the dictates of self-interest is in the interest of everyone alike though following the rules of a morality is not of course identical with following self-interest. . . .
> The answer to our question 'Why should we be moral?' is therefore as follows. We should be moral because being moral is following rules designed to overrule self-interest whenever it is in the interest of everyone alike that everyone should set aside his interest.[3]

As I say, this seems to be an argument to the effect that it really is in everyone's interest to be moral. I suppose that Baier is here probably talking about Russellian interests. At least, we must interpret him in that way if his argument is to be applicable in this context, and I will proceed on that assumption. But how exactly is the argument to be made out?

It appears here to begin with a premise something like

(A) It is in everyone's best interest (including mine, presumably) for everyone (including me) to be moral.

This premise itself appears to be supported earlier by reference to Hobbes. As I understand it, the idea is that without morality people will live in a "state of nature," and life will be nasty, brutish, and short. Well, perhaps so. At any rate, let us accept (A) for the moment. From (A) we can derive

(B) It is in my best interest for everyone (including me) to be moral.

And from (B) perhaps one derives

(C) It is in my best interest for me to be moral.

3. Kurt Baier, *The Moral Point of View* (Ithaca: Cornell University Press, 1958), p. 314.

And (C) may be taken to answer the question, "Why should I be moral?" Furthermore, if (C) is true, then moral obligation will at least not have the sort of queerness that I have been alleging.

Unfortunately, however, the argument outlined above is invalid. The derivation of (B) from (A) *may* be all right, but the derivation of (C) from (B) is invalid. What does follow from (B) is

(C′) It is in my best interest for me to be moral *if everyone else is moral.*

The argument thus serves to show that it is in a given person's interest to be moral only on the assumption that everyone else in the world is moral. It might, of course, be difficult to find someone ready to make that assumption.

There is, however, something more of interest in this argument. I said that the derivation of (B) from (A) may be all right. But in fact is it? If it is not all right, then this argument would fail even if everyone else in the world were moral. Now (A) can be interpreted as referring to "everyone's best interest" ("the interest of everyone alike," in Baier's own words) either collectively or distributively; that is, it may be taken as referring to the best interest of the whole group considered as a single unit, or as referring to the best interest of each individual in the group. But if (A) is interpreted in the collective sense, then (B) does not follow from it. It may not be in *my* best interest for everyone to act morally, even if it is in the best interest of the group as a whole, for the interest of the group as a whole may be advanced by the sacrificing of my interest. On this interpretation of (A), then, the argument will not answer the question "Why should I be moral?" even on the supposition that everyone else is moral.

If (A) is interpreted in the distributive sense, on the other hand, then (B) does follow from it, and the foregoing objection is not applicable. But another objection arises. Though (A) in the collective sense has some plausibility, it is hard to imagine that it is true in the distributive sense. Hobbes may have been right in supposing that life in the state of nature would be short, etc. But some lives are short anyway. In fact, some lives are short just because the demands of morality are observed. Such a life is not bound to have been shorter in the state of nature. Nor is it bound to have been less happy, less pleasurable, and so forth. In fact, does it not seem obvious that *my* best Russellian interest will be further advanced in a situation in which everyone else acts morally but I act immorally (in selected cases) than it will be in case everyone, including me, acts morally? It certainly seems so. It can, of course, be observed that if I act immorally then so will other people, perhaps reducing my benefits. In the present state of the world that is certainly true. But in the present state of the world it is also true, as I observed earlier, that many other people will act immorally *anyway*, regardless of what I do.

A more realistic approach is taken by Richard Brandt.[4] He asks, "Is it *reasonable* for me to do my duty if it conflicts seriously with my personal welfare?" After distinguishing several possible senses of this question, he chooses a single one to discuss further, presumably a sense that he thinks important. As reformulated, the question is now: "Given that doing x is my duty and that doing some conflicting act y will maximize my personal welfare, will the performance of x instead of y satisfy my reflective preferences better?" And the conclusion to which he comes is that "the correct answer may vary from one person to another. It depends on what kind of person one is, what one cares about." And within Russellian limits Brandt must surely be right in this. But he goes on to say, "It is, of course, no defense of one's failure to do one's duty, before others or society, to say that doing so is not 'reasonable' for one in this sense." And this is just to bring the queer element back in. It is to suppose that besides "the kind of person" I am and my particular pattern of "cares" and interests there is something else, my duty, which may go against these and in any case properly overrides them. And one feels that there must be some sense of "reasonable" in which one can ask whether a world in which that is true is a reasonable world, whether such a world makes any sense.

This completes my survey of some ethical or metaethical views that would eliminate or minimize this sort of queerness of morality. I turn now to another sort of view, stronger I think than any of these others, which accepts that queerness but goes no further. And one who holds this view will also hold, I think, that the question "Why should I be moral?" must be rejected in one way or another. A person who holds this view will say that it is simply a fact that we have the moral obligations that we do have, and that is all there is to it. If they sometimes result in a loss of good, then that too is just a fact. These may be puzzling or surprising facts, but there are lots of puzzling and surprising things about the world. In a Russellian world, morality will be, I suppose, an "emergent" phenomenon; it will be a feature of certain effects though it is not a feature of their causes. But the wetness of water is an emergent feature, too. It is not a property of either hydro-

4. Richard Brandt, *Ethical Theory* (Englewood Cliffs, N.J.: Prentice-Hall, 1959), pp. 375–78.

gen or oxygen. And there is really nothing more to be said; somewhere we must come to an end of reasons and explanations. We have our duties. We can fulfill them and be moral, or we can ignore them and be immoral. If all that is crazy and absurd—well, so be it. Who are we to say that the world is not crazy and absurd?

Such a view was once suggested by William Alston in a criticism of Hasting Rashdall's moral argument for God's existence.[5] Alston attributed to Rashdall the view that "God is required as a locus for the moral law." But Alston then went on to ask, "Why could it not just be an ultimate fact about the universe that kindness is good and cruelty bad? This seems to have been Plato's view." And if we rephrase Alston's query slightly to refer to obligations, we might be tempted to say, "Why not indeed?"

I say that this is perhaps the strongest reply against me. Since it involves no argument, there is no argument to be refuted. And I have already said that, so far as I can see, its central contention is not self-contradictory. Nor do I think of any other useful argument to the effect that the world is not absurd and crazy in this way. The reference to Plato, however, might be worth following for a moment. Perhaps Plato did think that goodness, or some such thing related to morality, was an ultimate fact about the world. But a Platonic world is not very close to a Russellian world. Plato was not a Christian, of course, but his world view has very often been taken to be congenial (especially congenial compared to some other philosophical views) to a religious understanding of the world. He would not have been satisfied, I think, with Russell's "accidental collocations of atoms," nor would he have taken the force of the grave to be "so nearly certain." The idea of the Good seems to play a metaphysical role in his thought. It is somehow fundamental to what *is* as well as to what ought to be, much more fundamental to reality than are the atoms. A Platonic man, therefore, who sets himself to live in accordance with the Good aligns himself with what is deepest and most basic in existence. Or to put it another way, we might say that whatever values a Platonic world imposes on a man are values to which the Platonic world itself is committed, through and through.

Not so, of course, for a Russellian world. Values and obligations cannot be deep in such a world. They have a grip only upon surface phenomena, probably only upon man. What is deep in a Russellian world must be such things as matter and energy, or perhaps natural

5. William P. Alston, ed., *Religious Belief and Philosophical Thought* (New York: Harcourt, Brace & World, 1963), p. 25.

law, chance, or chaos. If it really were a fact that one had obligations in a Russellian world, then something would be laid upon man that might cost a man everything but that went no further than man. And that difference from a Platonic world seems to make all the difference.

This discussion suggests, I think, that there are two related ways in which morality is queer in a Russellian world. Or maybe they are better construed as two aspects of the queerness we have been exploring. In most of the preceding discussion I have been focusing on the strangeness of an overriding demand that does not seem to conduce to the *good* of the person on whom it is laid. (In fact, it does not even promise his good.) Here, however, we focus on the fact that this demand— radical enough in the human life on which it is laid—is *superficial* in a Russellian world. Something that reaches close to the heart of my own life, perhaps even demanding the sacrifice of that life, is not deep at all in the world in which (on a Russellian view) that life is lived. And that, too, seems absurd.

This brings to an end the major part of my discussion. If I have been successful at all you will have shared with me to some extent in the sense of the queerness of morality, its absurdity in a Russellian world. If you also share the conviction that it cannot in the end be absurd in that way, then perhaps you will also be attracted to some religious view of the world. Perhaps you also will say that morality must have some deeper grip upon the world than a Russellian view allows. And, consequently, things like mind and purpose must also be deeper in the real world than they would be in a Russellian world. They must be more original, more controlling. The accidental collocation of atoms cannot be either primeval or final, nor can the grave be an end. But of course that would be only a beginning, a sketch waiting to be filled in.

We cannot here do much to fill it in further. But I should like to close with a final, and rather tentative suggestion, as to a direction in which one might move in thinking about the place of morality in the world. It is suggested to me by certain elements in my own religion, Christianity.

I come more and more to think that morality, while a fact, is a twisted and distorted fact. Or perhaps better, that it is a barely recognizable version of another fact, a version adapted to a twisted and distorted world. It is something like, I suppose, the way in which the pine that grows at timberline, wind blasted and twisted low against the rock, is a version of the tall and symmetrical tree that grows lower on the slopes. I think it may be that the related notions of sacrifice and gift represent (or come close to representing) the fact, that is, the pattern of life, whose distorted version we know here as morality. Imagine a situation, an "economy" if you will, in which no one ever buys or trades for or seizes any good thing. But whatever good he enjoys it is either one which he himself has created or else one which he recieves as a free and unconditional gift. And as soon as he has tasted it and seen that it is good he stands ready to give it away in his turn as soon as the opportunity arises. In such a place, if one were to speak either of his rights or his duties, his remark might be met with puzzled laughter as his hearers struggled to recall an ancient world in which those terms referred to something important.

We have, of course, even now some occasions that tend in this direction. Within some families perhaps, or even in a regiment in desperate battle, people may for a time pass largely beyond morality and live lives of gift and sacrifice. On those occasions nothing would be lost if the moral concepts and the moral language were to disappear. But it is probably not possible that such situations and occasions should be more than rare exceptions in tbe daily life of the present world. Christianity, however, which tells us that the present world is "fallen" and hence leads us to expect a distortion in its important features, also tells us that one day the redemption of the world will be complete and that then all things shall be made new. And it seems to me to suggest an "economy" more akin to that of gift and sacrifice than to that of rights and duties. If something like that should be true, then perhaps morality, like the Marxist state, is destined to wither away (unless perchance it should happen to survive in hell).

Christianity, then, I think is related to the queerness or morality in one way and perhaps in two. In the first instance, it provides a view of the world in which morality is not an absurdity. It gives morality a deeper place in the world than does a Russellian view and thus permits it to "make sense." But in the second instance, it perhaps suggests that morality is not the deepest thing, that it is provisional and transitory, that it is due to serve its use and then to pass away in favor of something richer and deeper. Perhaps we can say that it begins by inverting the quotation with which I began and by telling us that, since God exists, not everything is permitted; but it may also go on to tell us that, since God exists, in the end there shall be no occasion for any prohibition.

9

The Empirical Argument
from Evil

WILLIAM L. ROWE

It is one thing to argue that the existence of evil is logically inconsistent with the existence of the theistic God and quite another thing to argue that the world contains evils that render the existence of the theistic God unlikely. The former is the logical argument from evil; the latter is the empirical argument from evil.[1] Of these two, I believe the empirical argument is the more serious threat to classical theism. Like the former, however, it too has come under vigorous attack. In what follows I will try to set forth a strong version of the empirical argument, examine two important objections that have been advanced against it, determine whether the argument can survive these objections, and assess the epistemological status of theism in the light of the argument.

I

Those who believe that the world contains evils that render theism improbable need not hold that just any evil renders theism unlikely.[2]

An earlier version of this paper was presented at a conference in Philosophy of Religion in Lincoln, Nebraska, April 12–14, 1984. I am grateful to Eleanore Stump, my commentator at the conference, for helpful criticisms and comments.

1. This argument has been called 'evidential', 'probabilistic', and 'inductive'. Although I previously referred to it as the 'evidential' argument, it seems less misleading to call it the 'empirical' argument. The argument reaches the conclusion that the existence of God is unlikely given certain *empirical* facts about the world.

2. A parallel may be drawn here between the logical argument from evil and the empirical argument. Someone who holds that the existence of evil is logically inconsistent

But intense human and animal suffering on a rather large scale—for example, the suffering occasioned by the Lisbon earthquake—may be thought to do so. For our purpose it will be sufficient to consider intense human and animal suffering occasioned by natural forces. I shall take it as an obvious truth that such suffering is intrinsically evil. It is also obvious that such suffering occurs daily and in considerable abundance in our world.

In setting forth the empirical argument, I will use 'O' to abbreviate the phrase 'an omnipotent, omniscient, wholly good being'. Standard (classical) theism is here understood as any view that holds that O exists. (I will later distinguish restricted and expanded versions of standard theism.)

Two claims are essential to the strong version of the empirical argument from evil. The first is that there are things we know or have good reason to believe that make it likely that the following proposition is true:

(A)   There exist evils that O could have prevented, and had O prevented them the world as a whole would have been better.

Second, the empirical argument holds that the following proposition is true, if not a conceptual truth.

(B)   O would have prevented the occurrence of any evil it could prevent, such that had O prevented it the world as a whole would have been better.[3]

Since (A) and (B) entail

(C)   O does not exist,

---

with the existence of God may hold that *any evil whatever* is inconsistent with standard theism. Another position that can be held, however, is that it is only certain kinds (or a certain kind) that logically cannot exist if the theistic God exists. Similarly, the proponent of the empirical argument might hold that standard theism is rendered improbable by the existence of any evil whatever. On the other hand, he may hold that it is the existence of certain kinds, amounts, and degrees of evil that renders theism unlikely.

3. Most theists subscribe to something like (B). But although it has the appearance of truth, (B) has been brought into question by some, and rejected by others. See, for example, Alvin Plantinga, "The Probabilistic Argument from Evil," *Philosophical Studies* 35 (1979); George Schlesinger, *Religion and Scientific Method* (Dordrecht: D. Reidel, 1977), chs. 9 and 10; and Michael Peterson, *Evil and The Christian God* (Grand Rapids: Baker, 1982), chs. 4 and 5. These questions and objections do cast some doubt on (B). A full defense of the empirical argument would need to take account of them. For purposes of this paper, however, I will suppose that (B), or something quite like it, is true.

if (A) is probable and (B) is true, then it is probable that theism is false. The empirical argument, however, is not to be identified with the argument: (A), (B), therefore (C). Rather, the empirical argument is an argument that seeks to provide a good reason for thinking that (A) is more probable than not, that (B) is true, and, therefore, that (C) is probably true. Our ultimate judgment of the worth of the empirical argument depends, therefore, on our estimate of its success in showing that (B) is true and that (A) is probable in relation to certain things we know or have good reason to believe.

Before we examine these issues it will be helpful to see why the empirical argument is so modest with respect to (A). Why does the argument seek to establish only that (A) is probable? Why does the argument not endeavor to show that (A) is something we know with certainty, following perhaps from our knowledge of the existence of evil and certain truths concerning omnipotence? It will help us to answer this question if we consider three ways in which evil may be related to O. The first way is being *needful* for O.

> An evil E is needful for O just in case E is preventable by O, some good state of affairs G can be obtained by O only by permitting E, and the world as a whole would be better with G and E than it would without G and E.

The second way is being *recalcitrant* for O.

> An evil E is recalcitrant for O in case E is preventable by O, some evil state of affairs E' is preventable by O only by permitting E, and the world as a whole would be better with E and not E' than it would with E' and not E.

The third way is being *permissible* for O.

> An evil E is permissible for O just in case E is preventable by O and *either* some good state of affairs G can be obtained by O only by permitting E (or some evil just as bad), and the world as a whole would be at least as good with G and E as it would be without G and E, *or* some evil state of affairs E' is preventable by O only by permitting E (or some evil just as bad), and the world as a whole would be at least as good with E and not E' as it would be with E' and not E.[4]

---

4. An evil may be permissible for O without being either needful or recalcitrant for O. If E and E' are equally bad and O must permit one or the other for the greater good of the world, then each is permissible for O but neither is needful for O. Nor, of course, would either E or E' be recalcitrant for O. However, any evil that is needful or recalcitrant for O is permissible for O.

The idea of an evil being needful for O is intended to capture what some philosophers have had in mind when they have spoken of an evil being related to a greater or outweighing good in such a manner that O can obtain the greater or outweighing good only by permitting the evil. The idea of an evil being recalcitrant for O is intended to capture what philosophers have had in mind when they have spoken of an evil being related to some greater evil in such a manner that O can prevent the latter only by permitting the former. But it is worth noting that these notions are not the same. Consider, for example, the idea of an evil being necessary for some outweighing good. According to Plantinga, "a good state of affairs G *outweighs* an evil state of affairs E if and only if the conjunctive state of affairs G *and* E is a good state of affairs."[5] This account of 'outweighing', as plausible as it is, has two consequences we should note. The first, a somewhat peculiar consequence, is that a good whose value is, say, $+2$ may outweigh an evil E whose disvalue is -5. For suppose we have a good G whose value is $+7$. The conjunctive state of affairs G_1 (G and E) has a value of $+2$. But G_1, as well as G, will outweigh E. For the conjunctive state of affairs G_2 (G_1 and E) is equivalent to G_1, and thus is a good state of affairs. "But if a good state of affairs G includes an evil state of affairs E, then the conjunctive state of affairs G *and* E is equivalent to G (just as a proposition A is equivalent to A & B if A entails B)."[6] The second consequence is that if there is some good state of affairs G that outweighs an evil state of affairs E, then— no matter how unrelated the two may be—there will be a good state of affairs G_1 (that is, G and E) that outweighs E and is such that O can obtain it (G_1) only by permitting E.

We can avoid these two consequences by slightly altering Plantinga's account.

(1) An evil is *outweighed* if and only if there is a good state of affairs G such that the conjunctive state of affairs G and E is a good state of affairs.

Given that G has a value of $+7$, E a value of -5, and the conjunctive state of affairs G_1 (G and E) a value of $+2$, it follows that E is *outweighed*. But we need not say that G_1, whose value is $+2$, itself outweighs E, whose value is -5. Nor need we say that there is some good state of affairs that outweighs E such that O can obtain it only by permitting E.

5. "The Probabilistic Argument from Evil," p. 7.
6. Ibid.

There is a good state of affairs that O cannot obtain without permitting E, namely G_1, but we need not say that G_1 itself outweighs E.

The important point, however, is that on neither account of *outweighing* do we have anything quite like an evil being *needful* for O. On Plantinga's account, a good G may outweigh an evil E and be such that O cannot obtain it without permitting E and yet not be such that in relation to it E is needful for O. Suppose G outweighs E but is obtainable without permitting E. G_1 (G and E) will then outweigh E and will be obtainable only by permitting E. Is E then *needful* for O? No. For E is needful in relation to G_1 only if the world would be better as a whole with G_1 than it would without E. But since O can obtain G without permitting E, the world as a whole may well be better without G_1. For O can obtain the good part of G_1 (i.e., G) and prevent the bad part of G_1 (i.e., E).

Suppose that G does not include E but cannot be obtained by O without permitting E. Suppose, furthermore, that the conjunctive state of affairs G_1 (G and E) is a good state of affairs. On Plantinga's account of outweighing, G will outweigh E, and on the slightly altered account E will be outweighed. But on neither account must it be true that E is *needful* for O. For there may be some good state of affairs G' that is better than G but obtainable only if E is prevented. E then will be outweighed by a good G that O cannot obtain without permitting E, but E will not be needful for O, since the world, we may suppose, will be better if O prevents E, thus forsaking G, but obtains G', which is better than G.

Returning now to proposition (A), we can perhaps begin to see why the empirical argument does not endeavor to *prove* (A), to establish (A) as something known with certainty. If (A) is true, then there exist evils that are *not permissible* for O. And I think if we consider some particular evil and ask ourselves how we might know of it that it is not permissible for O, we shall be able to see how very difficult it would be for us to be in the position of knowing such a thing. (Of course, we might know that *some* of the evil that exists is not permissible for O, without being able to know of any *particular* evil that it is not permissible. But prospects for this *general* knowledge seem no more promising than are the prospects for *particular* knowledge.) Consider, for example, the enormous amount of suffering occasioned by the Lisbon earthquake. If that evil is not permissible for O, then *no* possible good G is such that it is obtainable by O only if O permits that evil, and the world as a whole would be at least as good with G as without that evil. Can we know with certainty that this is so? To know that no possible good stands in this relation to the suffering occasioned by the Lisbon earthquake it seems that we would have to know all the possible goods there are and be sure of each that in relation to it the evil in question is not permissible by O. We just do not have such knowledge.

For all we know, there are qualities we have never thought of, qualities that, if present in a state of affairs, would render that state of affairs a great intrinsic good. Since these great intrinsic goods would be unknown to us, we would not be able to know that O could obtain them without permitting certain evils. At best we know some of the things that are intrinsically good. We know, for example, that happiness, knowledge, love, and the admiring contemplation of beauty are intrinsically good. With respect to such goods we might reasonably judge that they would be obtainable by O without O's having to permit the suffering of the Lisbon earthquake or something just as bad. But we do not know that there will not occur states of affairs hitherto unimaginable by us, states of affairs that are great intrinsic goods and in relation to which certain evils are needful to O. To have such knowledge we should require omniscience.

It is tempting to object that, even if there are possible goods of which we presently have no knowledge whatever, nevertheless such goods would be obtainable by O without O's having to permit the evils that occur in our world. It is tempting to so object because it is evident that evils that are needful for us in relation to certain goods are not needful for O in relation to those goods. Certainly, most of the good states of affairs that are obtainable by us only if we permit some evil would be obtainable by O without O's having to permit that evil. This is true. Evils that are needful for us would not be needful *in the same way* for O. Leibniz's general may have to permit the suffering and death of some of his troops in order to achieve the good of the safety of the women and children from the attacking forces. But it would be child's play for O to achieve the latter without permitting the former. It is also true, however, that an evil *may* be needful for O and yet not needful for us at all. For if an evil is needful for X, then some intrinsic good is obtainable by X, but only if X permits that evil. Clearly there are ever so many possible goods obtainable by O that are not obtainable by us at all, no matter what we permit. If such goods are obtainable by O only if O permits some evil E, E may be needful for O but not needful for us. Furthermore, we must remember that by virtue of his omnipotence O may be able to bring good out of evil in such a way that the balance of good over evil in the universe is increased. Not only do we not know all possible goods, we also do not know what lies within the power of omnipotence to bring about. Specifically, we do not know that omnipotence cannot achieve great intrinsic goods by virtue of the evils he permits. As Augustine reminds us, "Nor would a Good Being permit evil to be done except that in His Omnipotence He can turn evil into good."[7]

Augustine's idea that evil may be *turned into* good can be given two distinct, coherent interpretations. The first way of turning evil into good is by producing a good whole consisting of two parts, the evil part and a good part that is obtainable only by permitting the evil part. Since the whole, composed of the evil part and the good part, is itself good, the good part *outweighs* the evil part, thus making the whole itself good. Here the evil part is justified, if it is justified, by the good part that cannot otherwise be obtained. When evil is thus outweighed, the other part of the whole will be good and *better than* the whole that is composed of it and the evil part. A second and perhaps more interesting way in which evil may be "turned into" good is by being *defeated* rather than outweighed by some good.[8] When evil is defeated it is a part of a whole that is good but whose goodness is *not* exceeded by the other part of the whole. Although plausible examples of the defeat of evil are much more difficult to construct than are examples of evil being outweighed, the following example, drawn from Chisholm, may illustrate the nature of the relation involved in the defeat of evil. The contemplation of some wrongful act on my part may be itself, as opposed to the wrongful act, neutral in value. If I then am filled with remorse and displeasure in contemplating my wrongful act, the remorse and displeasure considered in itself is bad, an evil, but the whole of which it is a part may be something that is good, something that is better than the other part of the whole (the contemplation of my wrong act), a part that has less value than the whole (my being filled with remorse and displeasure in contemplating my wrongful act). Here we may say that the whole is made *better* by the presence of its bad part, the remorse and displeasure. The crucial difference between outweighing evil and defeating it is that in the former case the other part is better than the whole that consists of it and the evil part; whereas, in the latter case, the defeat of evil, the whole is better than the other part. When evil is thus defeated we may be grateful for its presence, for if the other part of the whole existed alone, the world might well contain less value.

---

7. *Enchiridion*, ch. 100.
8. The notion of evil being *defeated* is analyzed by Roderick Chisholm in "The Defeat of Good and Evil," *Proceedings and Addresses of the American Philosophical Association* 42 (1968–69): 21–38. The account of defeat I present is due to Chisholm. Also see A. C. Ewing's discussion of the same idea, as applied to the problem of evil, in *Value and Reality* (London: Allen & Unwin, 1973), pp. 215–25.

The relevance of these two ways of turning evil into good for our problem is as follows. If O is justified in permitting evil by virtue of the evil being outweighed by some other part of a good whole, we must believe that O could not obtain the good part without permitting the evil. But if O is justified in permitting evil by virtue of the evil being defeated, we need not hold that O could not have obtained the other part of the good whole without permitting the evil part. When evil is outweighed, it plays a negative role in the production of the good whole and is tolerated only because the other part of the whole could not otherwise be obtained. When evil is defeated, it plays a positive role in the production of the good whole and is accepted even though the other part might be obtained without it.

We noted earlier that even though an evil E is outweighed, it will not follow that E is permissible for O. For, in the first place, the other part of the good whole that includes E will be better than the whole and may be obtainable by O without permitting E (or something just as bad). And in the second place, if the other part of the good whole is not obtainable by O without permitting E, it may still be true that some good greater than it could have been obtained by O if, but only if, O had prevented E. In similar fashion, if an evil E is defeated, it may still be that, had O prevented E, he could have achieved a greater good than the good whole that includes the evil E that is defeated.

With these thoughts in mind, we can now return to the original premise A, the proposition that there exist evils which are such that O could have prevented them, and had O prevented them the world as a whole would have been better. Conceding, for the reasons given, that we cannot demonstrate (A) or know with certainty that it is true, we must now consider the weaker claim that (A) is a proposition that we have good reasons to think true. This claim is the crucial point in the version of the empirical argument from evil here being considered.

As we have seen, if an evil E is such that had O prevented it the world as a whole would not have been better, then either (a) there is some good G that O could obtain only by permitting E (or some evil just as bad) and the world as a whole would not have been better had it lacked G and E or (b) there is some evil state of affairs E' such that O could prevent E' only by permitting E (or some evil just as bad) and the world as a whole would not have been any better had it contained E' and lacked E. Let us concentrate our attention on the first of these: the question of whether the evils that exist are such that had an omnipotent being prevented any of them, without permitting others equally bad or worse, some good would have been lost with the result that the world as a whole would have been no better. In an earlier paper,[9] I argued that we have rational grounds for thinking that this is not so, for thinking that some instances of suffering, for example, could have been prevented by omnipotence and that their prevention would have resulted in a better world. What grounds? I there claimed that (A) is a rational belief given three things: first, our knowledge of the vast amount of intense human and animal suffering that occurs daily in our world; second, our understanding of the goods that do exist and that we can imagine coming into existence; and third, our reasonable judgments as to what an omnipotent being can do. To these three I now would add a fourth: our reasonable judgments of what an omniscient, wholly good being would endeavor to accomplish with respect to human and animal good and evil in the universe. To illustrate this claim, I set forth an example of intense suffering (the intense suffering of a fawn badly burned in a forest fire occasioned by lightning) and observed that as far as we can determine it serves no greater good at all, let alone one that is otherwise unobtainable by an omnipotent being. Recognizing, however, that, appearances to the contrary, it might nevertheless serve such an outweighing or defeating good, I then claimed that it seems quite incredible that all the instances of suffering that serve no greater good we know or can think of should nevertheless be such that none could have been prevented by an omnipotent being without loss of a greater good.

II

These claims about what rationally justifies us in accepting (A) have been challenged by several philosophers. My reasoning, it has been suggested, amounts to nothing more than an argument from ignorance: we do not know of any good that would justify O in permitting the fawn's suffering; therefore, there is none.[10] It has been suggested that my reasoning is correct only if we assume that, if there were such goods justifying O in permitting the daily sufferings in our world, we would know what they are—an assumption that at worst is false and at best begs the question against traditional theism.[11] It has been sug-

9. "The Problem of Evil and Some Varieties of Atheism," *American Philosophical Quarterly* 16, no. 4 (October 1979): 335–41 (hereafter PEVA).

10. Bruce A. Reichenbach, *Evil and A Good God* (New York: Fordham University Press, 1982), pp. 25–42.

11. The general point that the assumption in question begs the question is developed by M. B. Ahern in *The Problem of Evil* (New York: Schocken, 1971). This point is ex-

gested that what I cite as evidence for (A) cannot possibly be evidence, since if O existed the things I point to are just what one would expect to be the case.[12] I cannot here deal with all the criticisms that have been advanced. But all of these objections are philosophically important and merit serious discussion. I propose to discuss here two of the important criticisms that have been advanced.

The first objection I shall discuss has been set forth at some length and with great care by Stephen Wykstra. We can best appreciate his objection if we begin with a major point in my reasoning; namely, that we are unable to think of any good that exists or might come into existence that both outweighs the fawn's suffering and could not be obtained by an omnipotent, omniscient being without permitting that suffering.[13] If we agree with this point, we might then claim that

(2) It appears that the fawn's suffering is pointless—that is, it appears that the fawn's suffering does not serve an outweighing good otherwise unobtainable by an omnipotent, omniscient being.

We can now see Wykstra's basic objection. Put in its simplest terms it comes to this: if someone claims that it appears that S is not P, that person is entitled to that claim only if he has no reason to think that, if S were P, things would strike us pretty much the same. Thus, on detecting no sour odor, the person with a cold is not entitled to the claim that it appears that the milk is not sour, because he presumably has a reason (the cold) to think that if the milk were sour things would appear pretty much the same—he would still detect no odor of sourness. Now let us return to (2). Wykstra believes that we are not entitled to affirm (2) because, in his judgment, we have good reason to think that were the fawn's suffering actually to serve an outweighing good, otherwise unobtainable by O, things would strike us pretty much the same way—we

panded and defended by F. J. Fitzpatrick, "The Onus of Proof in Arguments about the Problem of Evil," *Religious Studies* 17 (March 1981): 19–38. Also see Delmas Lewis, "The Problem with the Problem of Evil," *Sophia* 22, no. 1 (April 1983): 26–35.

12. Stephen Wykstra, "Difficulties in Rowe's Case for Atheism" (paper presented at the Pacific Division Meeting of the APA, March 1984). Also see Wykstra's "The Humean Obstacle to Evidential Arguments from Suffering: On Avoiding the Evils of 'Appearance'" and my reply, "Evil and the Theistic Hypothesis: A Response to Wykstra," both in *International Journal for Philosophy of Religion* 16, no. 2 (1984).

13. In exposition of Wykstra's views I will sometimes omit the possibility of good *defeating* evil. This is done only for convenience and simplicity. A full account would recognize that evil may be either outweighed or defeated.

would still be in the position of not being able to think of any good that exists or might come into existence that both outweighs the fawn's suffering and could not be otherwise obtained by an omnipotent, omniscient being. The reason he gives is that were O to exist, it would be very likely that the outweighing good in relation to which O must permit the fawn's suffering would be a good quite beyond our ken. And if such a good were beyond our ken, then we would still be in the position of not being able to see what good is served by the fawn's suffering. Thus Wykstra concludes that were O to exist, the fawn's suffering would very likely have just the feature I claim it to have—of serving no outweighing good we know to exist or can think of that is otherwise unobtainable by an omnipotent, omniscient being.

It is helpful, I think, to view Wykstra's objection as having two steps. The first step is the claim that in the situation described we are entitled to affirm proposition 2 only if the following proposition is true:

(3) We have no reason to think that were O to exist things would strike us in pretty much the same way concerning the fawn's suffering.[14]

The second step in Wykstra's objection is the claim that (3) is false. For were O to exist, Wykstra thinks it likely that the outweighing good in relation to which O must permit the fawn's suffering would be a good beyond our ken.

My response to Wykstra will focus entirely on the second step in his objection: the step that claims that were O to exist things would strike us in pretty much the way they do as far as instances of human and animal suffering are concerned.

Given the history of humans and animals and the sorry tale of their sufferings through the ages and given our inability to discover, among the goods we know or can imagine, goods that both outweigh these sufferings and are unobtainable by omnipotence unless these suffer-

---

14. It is important to note that Wykstra might also be holding that in the situation described we are entitled to affirm proposition 2 only if (3′) is true.

(3′) We have reason to think that were O to exist things would strike us differently concerning the fawn's suffering.

He might then argue that (3′) is false and that, therefore, it is *not* reasonable to believe that were the fawn's suffering actually to serve an outweighing good, otherwise unobtainable by an omnipotent being, things would likely strike us differently concerning the fawn's suffering. In the discussion that follows I have taken Wykstra to be arguing that (3) is false. It would be another matter to determine whether, in the situation described, (3′) is also necessary for being entitled to claim (2), and another matter yet to determine whether (3′) is true or false.

ings are permitted, why should we think, as Wykstra does, that this is just how things would likely be, if O exists? It is true, as Wykstra observes, that O's mind can grasp goods that are beyond our ken. The idea, then, is that since O grasps goods beyond our ken, we have reason to think it likely that the goods in relation to which O permits many sufferings would be *unknown* to us. Let us look at Wykstra's reasoning here. He starts with

(4) O can grasp goods beyond our ken.

moves to

(5) It is likely that the goods in relation to which O permits many sufferings are beyond our ken.

and concludes with

(6) It is likely that many of the sufferings in our world do not appear to have a point; we cannot see what goods justify O in permitting them.

The difficulty with this reasoning is that the move from (4) to (5) presupposes that the goods in question *have not occurred*, or, at the very least, that if they have occurred they, nevertheless, remain quite unknown to us (in themselves or in their connections with the sufferings in our world). And, so far as I can see, the mere assumption that O exists gives us no reason to think that either of these is true. If O exists, it is indeed likely, if not certain, that O's mind grasps many good states of affairs that do not obtain and that *prior to their obtaining* we are simply unable to think of or imagine. That much is reasonably clear. But the mere assumption that O exists gives us no reason whatever to suppose *either* that the greater goods in virtue of which he permits most sufferings are goods that come into existence far in the future of the sufferings we are aware of *or* that, once they do obtain, we continue to be ignorant of them and their relation to the sufferings.

The fact that O's mind can apprehend nonactual good states of affairs that we are not able to think of gives us reason to assent to the following proposition:

(7) If O exists, then the outweighing goods in relation to which some sufferings are permitted by O are, *antecedent to their obtaining*, beyond our ken.

But this proposition is insufficient to justify the claim that, if O were to exist, the sufferings in our world would appear to us as they in fact do.

I conclude, therefore, that Wykstra has not provided adequate justification for the second step in his objection. And without that step, the objection fails.

Earlier, I characterized standard theism as any view that asserts that O exists. Within standard theism, we can distinguish *restricted* theism and *expanded* theism. Expanded theism is the view that O exists, conjoined with certain other significant religious claims, claims about sin, redemption, a future life, a last judgment, and the like. (Orthodox Christian theism is a version of expanded theism.) Restricted theism is the view that O exists, unaccompanied by other, independent religious claims. Standard theism implies that the sufferings that occur are permitted by O by virtue of outweighing or defeating goods otherwise unobtainable by O. Restricted standard theism gives us no reason to think that these goods, once they occur, remain beyond our ken. Nor does restricted standard theism give us any reason to think that the occurrence of the goods in question lies in the distant future of the occurrence of the sufferings that O must permit to obtain them. So I conclude, contrary to Wykstra, that the mere hypothesis of O's existence gives us no good reason to think that things would appear to us just as they do so far as the sufferings of animals and humans in our world are concerned. I conclude, therefore, that we have been given no adequate reason to reject my view that the items mentioned at the outset give us reason to believe that (A) is true and, therefore, that O does not exist.

But what about expanded theism? Suppose, for example, that we add to the hypothesis that O exists the claim made by Saint Paul in his letter to the church at Rome: "For I reckon that the sufferings we now endure bear no comparison with the splendor, as yet unrevealed, which is in store for us." Playing fast and loose with biblical hermeneutics, suppose we set forth the Pauline doctrine as follows:

(8) The goods for the sake of which O must permit vast amounts of human and animal suffering will be realized only at the end of the world.[15]

---

15. In criticism of Ahern, Fitzpatrick argues in "The Onus of Proof" that the theist *needs* to give a reason why the evils should appear to be unrelated to greater goods otherwise unobtainable by omnipotence. He argues that such a reason exists in the traditional doctrine that the justifying good is God himself and that God's nature is inscrutable in this life. Since this good is unknowable it should not be surprising that we are unable to understand what necessary connections hold between it and present evils. Although there are several points to be made in response to his view, it is worth noting that this, too, is a version of expanded theism.

We now have a version of expanded standard theism, a version we may call EST, consisting of the conjunction of the proposition that O exists and proposition 8. EST is not rendered unlikely by the items that render restricted standard theism (RST) unlikely, for precisely the reason Wykstra so clearly and carefully sets forth. Given EST we have some reason to think that the fawn's suffering might well appear to us just the way it does appear. So the fact that it appears to us as it does in no way renders EST more unlikely than it otherwise is.

We have, then, two versions of standard theism, RST and EST. EST entails RST but is not entailed by it. RST is rendered unlikely by the facts about suffering we have alluded to; EST is not rendered unlikely by those facts. Where does this leave us? Does it mean that the theist who is worried about the empirical argument from evil need worry no more, just do a little expanding and the evidence will no longer render his cherished belief unlikely? Strictly speaking, he can do exactly that and be satisfied that the facts of suffering will not render his expanded theism more unlikely than it otherwise is. But in the world of the intellect, as well as in the world of commerce, it seems that everything has its price. If e disconfirms h (in the sense of making h more unlikely than it otherwise is), we can conjoin h with a proposition that clearly entails or makes e likely (call this conjunction h') and no longer worry about e, for e will not disconfirm h'. But the price is that h' will then be of itself as unlikely as h was, given e. So if the facts about suffering do render RST unlikely, there is not much to be gained by retreating to EST.[16]

16. Robert M. Adams has suggested an interesting response to this conclusion. Basic to his response, I believe, is the contention that the probability of RST, given the facts about evil I have alluded to, is not something that we can, as it were, *read from* the propositions in question. It is a matter of *judgment* on our part. Beginning with this point, Adams suggests the following response. I have claimed that RST is significantly disconfirmed by E (the facts about evil), that the probability of RST, given E, is a good deal lower than the probability of RST alone. (I have also claimed that the probability of RST, given E, is low. But this second claim is not as relevant to the point Adams is making.) EST, since it implies E (or makes E likely), is not disconfirmed by E. But since EST entails RST, EST is just as improbable, given E, as is RST. The reason this can be so, even though EST's probability is not lowered by E, is that the probability of EST, given E, is a function not only of any tendency of E to disconfirm it, but also of the prior probability of EST, the probability of EST alone. Thus, even though E does not disconfirm EST, since EST commits us to much more than does RST, the probability of EST alone may be *much lower* than the probability of RST alone. In fact, given that EST accounts for E and entails RST, its prior probability *must be* much lower than RST's, *if* the probability of RST on E is a good deal lower than the probability of RST alone.

The point just made can be turned around and expressed as follows. Given that EST implies E and is thus not disconfirmed by E, and noting that EST entails RST, if the probability of EST alone is not much less than the probability of RST alone, then it

III

Having seen the flaw in Wykstra's important objection to the empirical argument from evil, let us look at another criticism. In an interesting article "The Problem with the Problem of Evil," Delmas Lewis proposes two objections to the argument I put forth in PEVA. His first objection concerns what he described as "a logical gap between the acknowledged fact that *apparently* pointless evils exist and the assertion that *genuinely* pointless evils exist" (p. 29). Lewis agrees that there are many instances of evil that are *apparently* pointless. That is, he agrees that we are unable to think of goods that either do exist or might come into existence that both outweigh the instances of suffering (evil) and are such that omnipotence could not have obtained them without permitting the instances of suffering. But the question he asks is how we can get from this fact (*apparently* pointless suffering) to instances of suffering (evil) which are such that no goods have existed, do exist, or will exist which are such that they both outweigh the suffering and are such that omnipotence could not have obtained them without permitting the

---

cannot be true, as I have claimed, that the probability of RST, given E, is much less than the probability of RST alone, that RST is significantly disconfirmed by E. We now have two possible judgments before us: (1) the judgment as to how much less probable RST is, given E, than it is apart from E; (2) the judgment as to how much less probable EST is than RST. If we are confident about one of these judgments, we can conclude what our other judgment should be. Adams sees me as starting with a particular judgment of (1) and arriving at the appropriate judgment concerning (2). And his perception is exactly right. But he notes, given that these are matters of judgment, that one might start with a particular judgment of (2) and then arrive at the appropriate judgment concerning (1). And here Adams sees the theist as perhaps supplementing RST with an hypothesis such that the result accounts for E and is not significantly less probable than RST. And if the theist can be confident that the result—EST or some other supplementation of RST that would account for E—is not significantly less probable than RST alone, then the theist can rationally conclude that E does not significantly disconfirm RST.

Adams's response, so far as its general strategy is concerned, strikes me as exactly right. A theist who is initially troubled by the empirical argument from evil has four different ways of responding. First, the theist may claim that his own judgment of the probability of RST, given E, is far different from mine, that the facts about evil I have alluded to are perhaps just as likely, given the existence of O, as they are given the nonexistence of O. Second, the theist can agree with me that RST is indeed disconfirmed by E but note that other facts F make RST so likely that given E and F it is reasonable to accept RST. Third, the theist may agree that RST is disconfirmed by E but hold some other proposition which, although not itself evidence for RST, is such that the conjunction of it with E does not disconfirm RST. Finally, following Adams's lead, the theist may *argue* that E does not significantly disconfirm RST by showing that there are not implausible hypotheses that, when added to RST, produce a result that both accounts for E and is not significantly less probable than is RST itself. To pursue this last way would be to endeavor to give some not implausible suggestions concerning O's reasons for permitting E. Whether the theist can succeed in this task remains to be seen.

instances of suffering in question (*genuinely* pointless suffering). "If Rowe's project is to succeed, he must *show* how the former fact provides a good reason to believe that the latter assertion is true" (p. 29, italics added). Here I think Lewis may be demanding too much. If my project is to succeed, then the former fact must *be* a good reason for the latter assertion. And if the former fact is a good reason for the latter assertion, then my project succeeds. *Showing* that the former fact is a good reason for the latter assertion is another project, an important and interesting project, but it is not something that must be undertaken, let alone accomplished, in order for the initial project to succeed—the initial project being simply that of *giving* what is a good reason for thinking that there exist instances of suffering (evil) that are genuinely pointless.

It is important to see the difference between Wykstra's objection and the objection advanced by Lewis. Although he would not put it in this way, we can say that Wykstra endeavors to give a reason why *apparently* pointless suffering is *not* a good reason for thinking that *genuinely* pointless suffering exists. In response, I have tried to show that his reason is inadequate. Lewis, however, says in effect that since my reason for thinking that genuinely pointless suffering exists does not *entail* that genuinely pointless suffering exists (the logical gap), it cannot be a good reason unless I prove that it is a good reason. But this is surely incorrect. I may have succeeded in giving a good reason for P without either proving or being able to prove that my reason for P is a good reason, and this, even though my reason does not entail P.

To be fair to Lewis, perhaps we should distinguish two projects: giving a good reason for (A) and showing that the reason given for (A) is a good reason. Although I may accomplish the first project without accomplishing the second, I may utterly fail to convince others that I have accomplished the first unless I do accomplish the second. We may then understand Lewis to be drawing our attention to the importance of this second project.

Continuing with his objection, Lewis notes that instances of apparently pointless suffering would entitle us to infer that they are genuinely pointless if we knew the following principle to be true.

> (E) If there are goods for the sake of which O must permit instances of intense human and animal suffering then we would know or be able to imagine these goods and understand why O must permit the sufferings in order to obtain them.[17]

---

17. This is not Lewis's formulation of principle E. It does, however, express the same general idea, and it fits more closely the structure of my argument. Lewis's principle E is:

Now, of course, if we could establish the truth of this principle, we could establish the truth of (A) and, given (B), establish the nonexistence of O. But I think it should be clear that our prospects for *establishing* this principle are not very bright. We could imagine a version of expanded theism that entails this principle. Such a *gnostic* version of standard theism might hold that O would wish to enlighten us concerning evil, not leaving it as a dark mystery for us to puzzle over. On this view, O would have revealed to us just *what* the goods are in virtue of which he permits intense human and animal sufferings, and he would have enlightened us as to *why* he can obtain them only by permitting that suffering. Of course, this gnostic version of standard theism would be in serious trouble, and we would have good grounds for rejecting it.

Lewis agrees that there is much suffering that is apparently pointless. But because of the logical gap between apparently pointless suffering and genuinely pointless suffering, he thinks we are rationally justified in believing the latter on the basis of the former only if we accept this principle and have good reasons for accepting it (or have recourse to some other way of bridging the gap). He thinks we have no good reasons to accept it. He also thinks that to accept the principle is to beg the question against traditional theism. He remarks: "The insistence on the limitations of human knowledge in regard to God's providence is a characteristic tenet of orthodox Christianity (and, it may be added, of orthodox Judaism and Islam as well). It follows that any attempt to argue from evil to the non-existence of God by assuming (E), or some equivalent proposition, amounts to begging the question in favor of the critic's view" (p. 30).

About the charge of begging the question, I have two comments. First, appeal to this principle does not beg the question against restricted standard theism, since it is no part of restricted standard theism to hold views about God's providence that render evil a dark mystery. And if we have good reason to reject restricted standard theism, those reasons will be grounds for rejecting any expanded version of standard theism, including orthodox Christianity, Judaism, and Islam. Second, any person who has grounds for accepting the principle will have grounds for rejecting orthodox Christianity, Judaism, and Islam, and this will be so even if, according to these expanded versions of theism, the principle in question is false. It is a small defect of our principle that these expanded versions of theism imply its falsity. Such question begging shows only that the critic would be ill-advised to try to

---

"If there is a morally sufficient reason which explains why an omniscient, omnipotent being could not prevent some instance of evil without thereby losing some greater good or permitting some evil equally bad or worse, then we would know it" (p. 30).

convince an adherent of one of these expanded theisms to give up her view by appealing to this principle; it will not show that the critic does not have good and solid grounds for holding these expanded theisms to be false.

What of Lewis's implicit claim that the logical gap between apparently pointless suffering and genuinely pointless suffering can be rationally bridged only if we have good reasons to accept this principle or some other principle that bridges the gap? In general, I do not think this is correct. That things appear to us to be a certain way is itself justification for thinking things are this way. Of course, this justification may be defeated. But apart from such defeat, the fact that things appear to us to be a certain way renders us rationally justified in believing that they are that way. If in order to be justified in moving from appearances to reality we had always first to justify a principle linking the two, we would be hard put to avoid skepticism.[18]

But what of the principle itself? Are there really no considerations that speak in its favor? I am inclined to think that there are. In the first place, unless we are excessively utilitarian, it is reasonable to believe that the goods for the sake of which O permits much intense human suffering are goods that either are or include good experiences of the humans that endure the suffering. I say this because we normally would not regard someone as morally justified in permitting intense, involuntary suffering on the part of another, if that other were not to figure significantly in the good for which that suffering was necessary. We have reason to believe, then, that the goods for the sake of which much human suffering is permitted will include conscious experiences of these humans, conscious experiences that are themselves good. Now the conscious experiences of others are among the sorts of things we do know. And we do know the beings who undergo the suffering. So if such goods do occur we are likely to know them.

Perhaps the good for which *some* intense suffering is permitted cannot be realized until the end of the world, but it certainly seems likely that much of this good could be realized in the lifetime of the sufferer. Indeed, when religion was young, expectations of the good to come tended to be imminent. Theodicies that emphasize a heavenly afterlife at the end of the world are forged in the grim recognition that we have no heaven on earth. But the issue here is what is reasonable to believe concerning the good experiences of those who suffer, experiences ob-

---

18. For a related view see Richard Swinburne, *The Existence of God* (Oxford: Oxford University Press, 1979), pp. 254–71. Swinburne, however, would not agree with my use of the "appears-so, is-so" principle. For some critical comments on Swinburne's view see Wykstra's paper "The Humean Obstacle to Evidential Arguments from Suffering."

tainable by omnipotence only by permitting that suffering. In the absence of any reason to think that O would need to postpone these good experiences, we have reason to expect that many of these goods would occur in the world we know.

By some such line of reasoning as the above, the principle in question can be shown to be plausible, a reasonable candidate for belief. So my answer to Lewis concerning appealing to Principle E in order to bridge the gap from apparently pointless suffering to genuinely pointless suffering is twofold. First, we do not need to establish the principle. And, second, the principle is plausible, a good candidate for rational belief.

When we consider the vast amount of intense human and animal suffering occasioned by natural forces and find ourselves utterly unable to think of outweighing or defeating goods that omnipotence can obtain only by permitting such suffering, we are, I think, rationally justified in concluding that there are instances of suffering that omnipotence could have prevented with the result that the world would have been better. Surely, if O were to exist, the world would likely contain much less human and animal suffering than it does. Against this judgment, the defenders of restricted standard theism can point to two things. First, given his omniscience, O will know of nonactual goods that are not known to us. Second, given his omnipotence, O will be able to realize some of these goods in the future. These two points show us that the incredible amounts of seemingly pointless human and animal suffering that form the history of our world *might be* related to future outweighing or defeating goods in such a manner that O can obtain these goods only by permitting those amounts of suffering. But when we take into account the likelihood that the goods in question would involve good experiences of those who suffered and consider how such goods would have to be connected to the sufferings in question so as to be obtainable by omnipotence only at the cost of the sufferings, our judgment must be that this possibility is very unlikely. Surely it is reasonable to believe otherwise, to believe that at least some of this suffering could have been prevented by omnipotence with the result that the world would have been better. And to believe this is to believe the crucial premise of the empirical argument: that there exist evils that O could have prevented and had O prevented them the world would have been better.

IV

There are two ways of developing the empirical argument from evil. The first way, followed in this paper, is to start with the fact that there exist vast amounts of human and animal suffering that seem to us to serve no good whatever, let alone one that is otherwise unobtainable by omnipotence. The second way is to start from the somewhat less complex fact that the world contains vast amounts of intense human and animal suffering. With either of these as the starting point, one then must claim that it gives us grounds for thinking that an omnipotent, omniscient, wholly good being does not exist. In this final section, I propose to discuss briefly the second way, relate it to the first, and use the results to illuminate the epistemological status of theism in the light of the empirical argument from evil.

The basic point of the second way is that the existence of vast amounts of human and animal suffering tends to disconfirm the existence of O. Intense human and animal suffering in a world supposedly under the control of O is like the presence of dirt in a room supposedly under the control of a powerful being who aims at making the room clean and attractive—its occurrence tends to disconfirm the existence of such a being. If the only information we possessed relevant to the existence of O were that the world contains humans and animals that suffer enormously, we would have good reason to think it more likely than not that O does not exist.

The tendency of the existence of vast amounts of intense human and animal suffering to disconfirm the existence of O can be defeated. Two kinds of defeat are possible. The first kind occurs when we add to the proposition concerning evil a proposition that tends to confirm the existence of O to a greater degree than the evil tends to disconfirm it. Thus the theist who possesses strong rational grounds for believing that O exists may *accept* the tendency of the existence of vast amounts of human and animal suffering to disconfirm the existence of O, holding that this tendency is defeated when his rational grounds for assent are taken into account. The second kind of defeat consists in appealing to a proposition that, if true, would explain why it is that O would permit the existence of vast amounts of human and animal suffering. Unlike the first sort of defeat, the added proposition need provide no confirmation of the existence of O. Instead, the added proposition will be such that its conjunction with the proposition that O exists will make the existence of vast amounts of human and animal suffering likely. Consider, for example, the following proposition.

(9) Were O to exist, O would have to permit much human and animal suffering so as to secure goods that render the world as a whole better than it otherwise would be.

Proposition 9 does not confirm the existence of O, but its *conjunction* with the proposition that there exists a vast amount of human and animal suffering *does not disconfirm* the existence of *O*. Thus, if the theist has rational grounds for (9), he may accept the tendency of vast amounts of human and animal suffering to disconfirm the existence of *O*, holding that this tendency is defeated when (9) is taken into account.

The first of the two ways of developing the empirical argument is somewhat stronger than the second. (Of course, like the second, it too can be defeated.) Its starting point is not merely the existence of vast amounts of human and animal suffering. To this it adds that much of this suffering is such that we are quite unable to think of goods that would justify *O* in permitting it. By thus strengthening the starting point we increase the likelihood that there exist instances of suffering that are genuinely pointless (proposition A). And, as we saw at the outset, the justification of the existence of genuinely pointless suffering is the fundamental issue in the empirical argument from evil.

Some theists hold that the facts about suffering in our world have no tendency at all to disconfirm the existence of *O*. They hold that the existence of vast amounts of apparently pointless suffering provides no reason whatever to think that there are any instances of genuinely pointless suffering. In addition, they hold that the kind of knowledge we would have to possess to be in a position to rationally believe that some suffering is genuinely pointless is a knowledge that theism itself says we do not and cannot possess in this life. In short, they hold with F. J. Fitzpatrick that "the problem of evil cannot legitimately function as an argument for atheism."[19] For the argument will work only if we can determine that suffering is indeed pointless, but such determination would "deny a fundamental point of theistic belief and therefore . . . beg the question against the theist."[20]

In this paper I have been arguing that such a view is mistaken. I have argued that the existence of apparently pointless suffering does tend to disconfirm the existence of *O*, for it provides rational support for the view that some suffering is in fact pointless. Although the argument may involve claims that beg the question against certain versions of *expanded* standard theism, it does not involve claims that beg the question against *restricted* standard theism. Furthermore, I have pointed out that begging the question against some forms of expanded theism does not render an argument for atheism useless. The argument may be a perfectly good argument and one for whose premises its proponents have good reasons. So I would say that the problem of evil can legitimately function as an argument for atheism.

19. "The Onus of Proof," p. 28.
20. Ibid.

10

Redemptive Suffering: A Christian Solution to the Problem of Evil

MARILYN MCCORD ADAMS

> For the word of the cross is folly to those who are perishing, but to us who are being saved it is the power of God.
>
> 1 Cor. 1:18

Christians believe that God is effectively dealing with the problem of evil through the cross—primarily the cross of Christ and secondarily their own. In the Gospel of Luke, Jesus follows the prediction of his own martyrdom (Luke 9:22) with a charge to his disciples: "If any man would come after me, let him deny himself and take up his cross daily and follow me. For whoever would save his life will lose it; and whoever loses his life for my sake, he will save it. For what does it profit a man if

I owe whatever is right in this paper to those who, at various times in my life, have tried to teach me how to follow Christ—most recently, A. Orley Swartzentruber, rector of All Saints' Episcopal Church, Princeton, New Jersey; Allan Wolter, OFM, of Catholic University of America; James Loder of Princeton Theological Seminary; Jon Olson of Bloy House and Christ Church, Ontario, California; and many friends at the Community of Jesus in Orleans, Massachusetts. The sharp objections and subtle reflections of my colleague Rogers Albritton and of my critics, especially David A. Conway of the University of Missouri, St. Louis, have—at least at times—restrained me from claiming too much. Finally, I am indebted to my husband, Robert Adams, who, by living with me, practices what I preach! The errors are due to my own sinful confusion.

he gains the whole world and loses or forfeits himself?" (Luke 9:23–
25). Yet these points are rarely mentioned in discussions of the problem of evil among analytic philosophers, no doubt because of their
paradoxical nature, noted by St. Paul himself. How can the suffering of
the innocent and loyal at the hands of the guilty and hard-hearted solve
the problem of evil? Why is it not simply another witness against the
goodness of God who commends it?

My purpose in this paper is to reintroduce reflection on the meaning
of the cross into discussion (at least among Christian philosophers) of
the problem of evil, in the hope that, as faith seeks understanding, our
deepest contributions will become more articulate for us and less scan-
dalous to others. My bold contention will be that the Christian approach to evil through redemptive suffering affords a distinctive solution to the problem of evil, for believers and unbelievers as well.

SOME METHODOLOGICAL REFLECTIONS

Discussions of the problem of evil among analytic philosophers of religion have focused on *God's* responsibility for evils and have concentrated on the theoretical, or so-called logical, problem of evil. It is asked
how the propositions

(T1) There is an omnipotent, omniscient, and perfectly good God

and

(T2) There is evil in the world

can be logically consistent in view of the assumption that

(T3) A perfectly good being would want to eliminate all of the evil
      that he could.

Proposed solutions involve arguing that even secular ethics admits exceptions to (T3), where the evils in question are prerequisite to or
necessary consequences of greater goods. Nevertheless, it is conceded
that

(T4) The fact that an evil was necessary for a greater good would
      provide an omniscient and omnipotent being with an excuse,
      only if the evil were a logically necessary prerequisite to or
      consequence of the good.

Defenses are then fleshed out by citing purported logically possible, morally legitimate excuses—either that the evils are logically necessary to the best of all possible worlds, or that each evil is logically connected with some great enough good, or that the risk of evil is logically implied by the good of free creatures. Philosophers usually dismiss the "factual" problem—that of whether (T1) and (T2) are both true—as philosophically intractable. After all, how could one establish that this *is* the best of all possible worlds or prove that each piece of evil was logically connected with some great enough good? Again, is it not overwhelmingly plausible—pace Plantinga[1]—that

> (T5) God could do more than he does to prevent or eliminate evils,

even on the assumption that rational creatures have free will? When all is said and done, most Christians settle for "incomplete" as the most benign possible verdict on any attempted philosophical solution, and the rest is left to "pastoral care."[2]

I believe that Christianity does provide a distinctive resolution of the "logical" problem of evil and for believers an answer to the "factual" problem as well. To extract these results, however, it is necessary to approach the matter indirectly and to keep the following observations in mind.

First, it is necessary to remember that Christianity is primarily a religion, concerned to teach people how to live and serve God in the here and now. The problem of evil for Christians is posed by the question,

> (Q1) How can I trust (or continue to trust) God in a world like this (in distressing circumstances such as these)?

A Christian is committed to obey Christ in everything and to count on him to see to his good and preserve his life in any and every circumstance. Sometimes things happen in his life or in those of others close to him or in the world at large that radically shake his convictions. The Christian believer will not be reassured by the observation that it is *logically possible* for an omnipotent and omniscient being to prove trustworthy in and through these circumstances. For it is his *actual* commitments that are at issue; he needs to restore his confidence that God is

---

1. Alvin Plantinga, *God, Freedom, and Evil* (New York: Harper & Row, 1974), pp. 49–64.
2. Ibid., p. 64.

actually trustworthy in the present situation. This problem is indeed a pastoral one, but it has a philosophical dimension in that it might be partially alleviated by some sort of explanation of how God is being good to created persons, even when he permits and/or causes evils such as these.

Second, evil is a problem for the Christian only insofar as it challenges his faith in God's goodness; yet, for the Christian, God's goodness remains at bottom a mystery. (*a*) For one thing, the typical Christian does not arrive at the conclusion that God is good by taking a Cliffordian survey of all of the available data, tallying the evidence on both sides, and finding that the "scientific" case for God's goodness is stronger. Usually he is moved by personal and/or corporate experiences of deliverance from some concrete difficulty—"They cried to the Lord in their trouble; and He delivered them from their distress" (Ps. 107:6, 13, 19, 28)—or big or little theophanies in which the believer is permitted to "taste and see that the Lord is good" (Ps. 34:8). The Christian may come away deeply convinced of God's goodness and saving power without being able to articulate any clear recipe for predicting his behavior in future situations. (*b*) Further, it is fundamental to biblical religion that God's goodness cannot be comprehended by us in terms of a simple formula in this life. This is in part because the divine nature is eternally beyond the creature's conceptual grasp. But it is also part of God's deliberate design, since it is necessary to make possible the relationships He wants with us and for which we were created. For what God wants most from us is wholehearted trust and obedience. Yet it is conceptually impossible to trust someone if you know in advance every move that he will make. Again, even if such knowledge were possible, it would be a source of great temptation. For example, if God were known to have a fixed policy of rendering temporal goods for well-doing and temporal evils for wickedness, then the observant might even try to manipulate the equation to use God as a means to their ends.

These latter points are well illustrated by the story of Job, who apparently thought that divine goodness could be captured in the simple act–consequence principle. Job paid his social and religious dues, and God blessed him. When Satan was allowed to take away the temporal benefits and to afflict Job with a loss of material goods, family, health, and moral approval, however, Job was pressed to his limits and eventually demanded a hearing. Job had kept his side of the contract, but God was reneging on his; Job wanted a day in court. God answers Job with a theophany: Job is reprimanded for his insolence in presuming to grasp divine goodness in such a simplistic way; he is allowed to see and experience God's goodness but told that he will have to trust God to save him in his own way, without advance billing of his plans. Job had loved God too much for his effects and benefits; now he has seen God and must love him for himself.

Third, while we cannot get a simple, clear analysis of divine goodness that will enable us to trace the hand of God in every situation the way the simple act–consequence principle promised to do, we can get a general idea of God's character, purposes, and policies from the collective experience of God's people over the centuries. The principal sourcebook for this general description is the Bible; a secondary source is the history of the Church. Nevertheless, the Christian story does not bridge the above-mentioned "incompleteness" gap by providing answers to such questions as

(Q2) Why does God not do more than he does to prevent or eliminate evils?

(Q3) Why did God make a world in which there are evils of the amounts and kinds found in this world, instead of one with fewer or less severe kinds?

(Q4) Why did God make a world such as this instead of one entirely free from evils?

To the extent that Christians do not know the answers to these questions, evil must remain a mystery from the Christian point of view. The Bible and church history do shed light on this question,

(Q5) How does God fit evils, of the amounts and kinds we find in this world, into his redemptive purposes?

and thereby suggest an answer to

(Q1) How can I trust (or continue to trust) God in a world like this (in distressing circumstances such as these)?

as well as a resolution of the philosopher's (logical and factual) problem of evil.

Finally, although the Christian religion does not hold that evil is an illusion or deny the grim fact that many have to struggle for survival and meaning in a world plagued by pain, disease, death, and wickedness, it teaches that the place to begin in grappling with the problem of evil is not the *evils without* but the *evils within*, not the evils that just happen or that are charged to others but one's own contributions to the problem. Christians believe that unless a person is willing to confront God's way of dealing with his own sin, he may not be able to appreciate God's approach to other evils or to discover the most fruitful way of living with them. To see how this works and how from this starting point it is possible to arrive at a Christian approach to the problem of evil through redemptive suffering, it is necessary to review briefly the doctrinal presuppositions of such a conclusion.

SIN AS THE PRIMARY EVIL FOR CHRISTIANS

Freedom and the actuality of sin. According to biblical religion,

> (T6) God's primary interest in creation is the rational creatures, particularly the human beings, whom he has made.

Further, as Psalm 8 eloquently reflects, God did not make us because human beings were just the touch he needed to make this the best of all possible worlds; rather

> (T7) God made human beings to enter into nonmanipulative relationships of self-surrendering love with himself and relationships of self-giving love with others.

So far from altering the characters to improve the plot, God is represented in the Old Testament as directing the course of history with the end of bringing his people into the relationship with himself that he desires. Nevertheless,

> (T8) God cannot get the relationships he wants with human beings unless he makes them with incompatibilist free wills.

For if human beings are free in the compatibilist sense only, then their free and voluntary actions are the sorts of things that either have causes outside the agent himself or occur in part by chance. Surely, if God's primary purpose in creation is to enter into such loving relationships with human beings, he would not leave it simply to chance whether they cooperate with or reject him. On the other hand, if each free human choice or action is completely determined by a causal chain or chains whose first member is God, then God's relationships with human beings will be manipulative in the highest degree, like those of a computer expert with the robot he designs, builds, and completely programs. Again, how could God hold human beings accountable for their responses to his offers of friendship, if it were at his discretion whether they occurred by chance or were completely determined by him? Yet, these relationships are bought with a price, for

(T9)   Not even an omnipotent God can introduce incompatibilist free creatures into the world without accepting the possibility, which he is powerless to exclude, that they will sin.

Although human beings are thus free to cooperate with God or not, it was his purpose in creation that we should, and

(T10)   As creator, God has the right that we should submit to him in complete and voluntary obedience and offer ourselves in service to others.

We sin when we show contempt for God by willfully refusing to render what we owe. And as Christ taught in the Sermon on the Mount, sin is not only, or even primarily, a matter of misdeeds but of inner attitudes and emotions.

Second, God's response to the problem of human sin begins with divine judgment. Biblical religion conceives of divine goodness as righteous love. God's righteousness expresses itself in the desire for honest and open relationships with created persons, ones in which role expectations are clear and conflicts explicit and dealt with rather than glossed over or suppressed. Thus, God's judgment of sin is an expression of his righteousness, because

(T11)   As righteous, God has a right to make us face the truth about who we are, who he is, who Christ is, and his rightful claims over us,

and

(T12)   God will not forgo this right of judgment.

He would not be wrong to judge us, even if no benefit accrued to us therefrom. Nevertheless, divine judgment is also an expression of his love, because

(T13)   God's interest in judgment is not condemnation and punishment but forgiveness and reconciliation.

As our creator, he knows that

> (T14) A human being's deepest longing is to be known and loved just as he is;

and he also realizes that

> (T15) Human beings, whether by nature or as a consequence of the fall, cannot really forget sin, whether their own or someone else's.

God therefore shows his love when in judgment he brings everything out on the table between him and the sinner, so that everyone knows that the love that follows is not based on false pretenses. We see this clearly in Jesus' encounter with the woman at the well: he tells her everything that she ever did, not to join the citizenry in condemning her scandal but to show that his offer to exchange drinks of water with her was made with full knowledge of what sort of sinner she was (John 4:7–30, 39–42).

The Christian's experience of divine judgment and the forgiveness of sins, his continued experience of the restored and ever-deepening relationship, convinces him of God's love at such a level that he is able to affirm in times of trial that

> (T16) God would not allow us to suffer evils that could not have, with our cooperation, a redemptive aspect,

and to keep trusting, his lack of answers for (Q2)–(Q4) notwithstanding.

GOD'S STRATEGY IN JUDGMENT

The direct approach. From a biblical point of view, God's right of judgment is in no way conditioned on any therapeutic effects it may have for us. And the book of Revelation implies that he has the means and will eventually force the unwilling to face the facts: "Behold, he is coming with the clouds, and every eye will see him, every one who pierced him; and all the tribes of the earth will wail on account of him" (Rev. 1:7). There is the picture of Judgment Day on which all the secrets of our hearts will be made known, not only to us but in front of everyone else.

Yet God knows that this sort of judgment would not usually be redemptive for fallen human beings. And the author of Revelation represents it as a method of last resort, to be used by God when time has run out on his offer of salvation. When someone judges us, looking down from a position of superior power or righteousness (the way the Pharisee regarded the tax collector in the temple, Luke 18:11–12), our reaction is apt to be hostile. We search wildly for countercharges and slander our accuser; we blame someone else and/or rationalize our behavior as no worse than others in our inferior position. No matter how much our judge insists that he is telling us for our own good, we are apt not to believe him but to hate him for adding guilt and shame to the burden of our implicitly recognized sin.

Indirect pedagogy. Since—by (T13)—God is interested in judgment as an occasion for repentance and reconciliation, he confronts a pedagogical problem; how to face us with our sin in such a way that we will accept the verdict and repent. The best way is an indirect approach that does not ram the truth down our throats but entices us to participate in arriving at the verdict.

In the Old Testament, the prophets sometimes resort to stories or speak in figures. Consider God's judgment of David for his affair with Bathsheba and contrivance of Uriah's death. Nathan tells David the story of a rich man who eats a poor man's pet lamb instead of taking an animal from his own large flocks, and he elicits from David a verdict of guilty and a sentence of death. Then Nathan proclaims, "You are the man," and because David really loves God, he repents and God forgives him. The first child dies, but another son, Solomon, becomes a great king and builds the temple of the Lord (2 Sam. 11–12).

Jesus tells parables for a similar reason. For example, the Good Samaritan story is told to a self-righteous man who wants a definition of 'neighbor' so that he will not have to waste his efforts at being good on people who do not fall into that category. Jesus does not use the confrontational approach: "You do not really love God or care about other people, or else you would not be asking that question" or "You think you have your 'religious act' together, but in God's eyes you are further from the kingdom than the people you despise and exclude." Rather than provoke hostility in his questioner, Jesus tells him a story about how to be neighborly and commends the Good Samaritan's help of the needy man. The young man can go away and ponder Jesus' answer and reflect on the difference between Jesus' starting point and his own. Dealt with in this gentler way, he may perhaps have a change of heart.

Sometimes such indirect approaches do not work, however. If the person is especially reluctant to see and if the sins in question are inner attitudes that are apparently easier to hide, he may successfully resist the conclusion that Jesus wants him to draw. The Pharisees and Sadducees were like this. Their outward acts were correct and legal, so that it was easy for them to defend themselves and to argue that they were better than most people. They repeatedly refused the insight that they were self-righteous and contemptuous of others and that they had lost faith in the redemptive power of God. In cases of this sort, God is left with a more expensive, noncoercive strategy: redemptive suffering as epitomized in martyrdom and the cross.

GOD'S COSTLY APPROACH TO THE PROBLEM OF EVIL: MARTYRDOM AND THE CROSS

What is a martyr? A martyr is simply a witness, in the sense relevant here, someone who gives testimony about a person, some events, or an ideal and who is made to pay a price for doing it. Usually the cost involves the loss of some temporal goods. for example, the experience of social disapproval or exclusion, the deprivation of educational and professional opportunities, economic losses, moral disapproval, imprisonment, exile, and death. The price a martyr is willing to pay is a measure of his love for and loyalty to what he believes to be the truth and/or that to which he bears witness. Martyrdom in the good sense is not a subtle manipulative maneuver to get one's way in the long run by making people feel guilty about one's short-term sufferings. On the contrary, the martyr usually does not actively seek martyrdom, both because he is diffident about his being able to pay the price and because he does not wish to provoke others to evil. Given this characterization, I want to suggest that martyrdom is an expression of God's righteous love toward the onlooker, the persecutor, and even the martyr himself.

Martyrdom as a vehicle of God's goodness to the onlooker. For onlookers, the event of martyrdom may function as a prophetic story, the more powerful for being brought to life. The martyr who perseveres to the end presents an inspiring example. Onlookers are invited to see in the martyr the person they ought to be and to be brought to a deeper level of commitment. Alternatively, onlookers may see themselves in the persecutor and be moved to repentance. If the onlooker has ears to hear the martyr's testimony, he may receive God's redemption through it.

Martyrdom as potentially redemptive for the persecutor. In martyrdom, God shows his goodness—both his righteous judgment and his redemptive mercy—not only in relation to the onlooker but also in relation to the persecutors. First of all, the martyr's sacrifice can be used as an instrument of divine judgment, because it draws the persecutor an external picture of what he is really like—the more innocent the victim, the clearer the focus. Consider the case of a businessman who commutes to New York City from the suburbs every day; he loves his family and works hard to provide them with a nice home, his children with an Ivy League education, his wife with an attractive social circle, and so on. As the pressures of his business increase, he falls increasingly silent and follows his 8:30 P.M. dinner with more and more drinks. His patient and loving wife tries to get him to talk, but he insists that nothing is wrong. One night after he has drunk even more than usual, his wife says quietly but firmly, "I think you've had enough." He protests that everything is fine, but she repeats, "I think you've had enough," whereupon he hits her and knocks her out. At first he thinks he has killed her, but she recovers and no charges are pressed. In this incident, the man's anger and hostility, which he had been so carefully hiding (more from himself than from everyone else) by drowning in drink, is externalized on a comparatively innocent victim. He cannot rationalize away his behavior in terms of any commensurate attack from her. It is an occasion of judgment, in which the man is brought face to face with who he really is and with the choice of seeking help or pursuing ruin.[3]

In attempting to bring reconciliation out of judgment (T13), God may find no more promising vehicle than martyrdom for dealing with the hard-hearted. What Pharisee would give the "holier than thou" posture a hearing? When indirect approaches fail, Jesus repeatedly confronts the Pharisees in the Gospels, but they will not listen. Finally, he bears the cost of divine judgment upon them by accepting martyrdom at their hands. In allowing himself to be crucified, he permits their sinful attitudes to be carried into action and externalized in his own flesh. Because he is a truly innocent victim, his body is the canvas on which the portrait of their sins can be most clearly drawn. In their great jealousy and mistrustfulness toward God, they had subjected his Messiah to a ritually accursed death. Unable to hear divine judgment through other media, there was at least a chance that they would be moved by the love of such a martyr and accept the painful revelation.

Nevertheless, the strategy is noncoercive, as it must be to accord with divine purposes (T7 and T8), and it does not always work. Our commuter chose to admit his need, seek help, and change his life-style; by contrast, the Pharisees and Sadducees who handed Jesus over to be crucified used their superior knowledge of the law and the prophets to

3. I owe this example to James Loder's lectures.

assure themselves against the ambiguous evidence that Jesus could not be the Messiah: he was born at the wrong address and was following the wrong script, associating himself too closely with God on the one hand and with sinners on the other. They rationalized their action—"it was expedient that one man should die for the people" (John 18:14)—and then took his death by crucifixion as clinching evidence that Jesus was not the one. Surely it would be some kind of pragmatic contradiction for God's Messiah to be ritually unclean and hence unfit to enter God's presence!

The cross of Christ is the primary expression of God's goodness in a fallen world. First, it is the principal means of divine judgment, because Christ is the only truly innocent victim, the clearest picture of who his persecutors are. The Christian disciple is called to share his Master's redemptive work by taking up his cross daily (Luke 9:23–25). But the disciple's sins give his persecutors many handles for explaining away their behavior. Christians can be martyrs and fill up the sufferings of Christ (Col. 1:24) only to the extent that he cleanses them first. That is why continual repentance is not only necessary for the Christian's own reconciliation with Christ but also the best contribution he can make toward solving the problem of evil.

Second, the cross of Christ is the chief expression of God's love for the persecutor. If the persecutor is moved to repentance by the love of the martyr, it is the martyr whom he will thank and love. According to Christian belief, God was so eager to win our love that he became incarnate and volunteered for martyrdom himself (John 3:16–18).

Martyrdom as a vehicle of God's goodness to the martyr. For the potential religious martyr, the threat of martyrdom is a time of testing and judgment. It makes urgent the previously abstract dilemma of whether he loves God more than the temporal goods that are being extracted as a price. Especially if the price is high (but surprisingly even when the price is low), he will have to struggle with his own divided loyalties. Whatever the outcome, the martyr will have had to face a deeper truth about himself and his relations to God and temporal goods than ever he could in fair weather.

Nevertheless, the time of trial is also an opportunity for building a relationship of trust between the martyr and that to which he testifies. Whether because we are fallen or by the nature of the case, trusting relationships have to be built up by a history of interactions. If the martyr's loyalty to God is tested, but after a struggle he holds onto his allegiance to God and God delivers him (in his own time and way), the relationship is strengthened and deepened. The Bible is full of such stories. God calls Abraham and makes him a promise to multiply his descendents. But accepting the promise involves trials: "Do you trust me enough to leave your homeland?" (Gen. 12). Abraham grows old: "Do you trust me enough to do this in your old age?" (Gen. 15, 18). When God provides Isaac, Abraham feels called by God to sacrifice him: "Do you trust me to keep my promise to you even though I am asking you to do something that would seem to make that impossible?" (Gen. 22). Abraham trusted God, and their relationship is celebrated as a hallmark by Jews and Christians to this day. Again, with the children of Israel God repeatedly asks: "Do you trust me enough to get you out of Egypt? . . . to give you food and water in the desert? . . . to bring you victorious into the land I have promised you?" The story records the tests they failed (see Ps. 106). Nevertheless, they looked back on the exodus experience as central to building their relationship with God. Despite their disobedience and his punishment of them, they were his and he was theirs in a way that would have been impossible had they stayed in Egypt with its fleshpots, leeks, and cucumbers.

Further, through his pioneering redemptive act (Heb. 2:10), God in Christ turns martyrdom into an opportunity for intimacy and identification with him. If one person loves another, he not only wants to know what it is like *for* that person, he wants to know what it is like to *be* that person. If the cross of Christ does not unveil the mystery of why God permits so much suffering in the first place (that is, the mystery of why [T5] is true), it does reveal his love in becoming incarnate to suffer with us. He is not content to be immutable and impassible, to watch his writhing creation with the eye of cool reason. He unites himself to a human consciousness and takes the suffering to himself. Thus, he knows from experience what it is like for pain to drive everything else from a finite consciousness and to press it to the limits of its endurance. When the martyr regains his wits enough to notice, he can recognize Christ crucified as providing the company that misery loves. Beyond that, the more the believer loves his Lord, the more he wants to know what it was like for him, what it is like to be him. The cross of Christ permits the martyr to find in his deepest agonies and future death a sure access to Christ's experience. No doubt it was this perspective that made the early church rejoice in being counted worthy to suffer for the Name (Acts 5:41). Moreover, as the believer enters into the love of Christ and shares his love for the world, he will also be able to appreciate his own suffering as a welcome key into the lives of others.

Thus God uses the harassments of his people by sinners both as instruments of divine judgment and as opportunities for relationship building, intimacy, and identification. The religious martyr who perseveres at the cost of his life wins his highest good. For in loving God more than any temporal good and trusting God to see to his good in the face of death, he is rightly related to God. He is also freed from the power of evil, because evil controls us only by bribing us with temporal goods we want more than we want to obey God. There is no remaining capital with which to "buy off" the martyr who is willing to pay the highest price for his loyalty. Finally, such a martyr has become heir to Christ's promise that "the pure in heart . . . shall see God" (Matt. 5:8).

THE MARTYRDOM MODEL AND ITS LIMITATIONS

I have proposed martyrdom as a paradigm of redemptive suffering. And the redemptive potential of many other cases that, strictly speaking, are not martyrdoms can be seen by extrapolation from the considerations of the preceding section. (*a*) For instance, there is suffering in which the victim not only will not but cannot obtain the benefits of relationship development. Some are too witless to have relationships that can profit and mature through such tests of loyalty. Some people are killed or severely harmed too quickly for such moral struggles to take place. At other times the victim is an unbeliever who has no explicit relationship with God to wrestle with. Even so, this type of suffering may provide the persecutor and onlooker with opportunities for reconciliation. (*b*) Alternatively, much suffering comes through natural causes—disease, natural disaster, or death—and so apparently involves no personal persecutor (other than God) who can be moved to repentance by the victim's plight. Here, nevertheless, the victim's faith in God may be tried and emerge stronger.

When all is said and done, however, not all suffering can be seen to have a redemptive value via this model. For example, what about cases at the intersection of types (*a*) and (*b*), where no one observes suffering naturally inflicted on the young or mentally deficient?

Further, some would argue that the cost/benefit ratio for such a "redemptive" strategy renders it morally unconscionable: the price for the victim is too high and the success rate is too low, both in relation to God's goals with the persecutor and in relation to his purposes with the martyr. Martyrdom often deepens the cruelty of the tormenter and tempts the victim beyond what he can bear (for example, in modern brainwashing). The possible conversion of the persecutor and onlooker and the possible enriching of the victim's faith are not, it is claimed, goods great enough or (often) probable enough to justify such losses on the victim's side. In short, it seems there would have to be more in it for those who suffer in order for such divine license to sinners and noninterference with nature to be morally justifiable. Yet, what further goods could there be?

THE VISION OF GOD AND THE PROBLEM OF EVIL

In my opinion, suffering cannot seem a wise, justifiable, or loving redemptive strategy except when embedded in the larger context of a Christian world view.

Intimacy with God as the incommensurate good. Christians believe that

> (T17) The best good is intimacy with God and the worst evil is his absence.

Human beings were made to be happy enjoying a "face-to-face" intimacy with God. Genesis implies that Adam and Eve experienced it in the garden (Gen. 2–3) and it is that to which the saints look forward in heaven. By contrast, hell will be some sort of existence entirely bereft of God's presence. Unbelievers may find this latter point difficult to credit, since they deny the existence of God and yet find in the world as it is many goods to be enjoyed and satisfactions to be taken. A Christian will not be surprised at human pleasure in things here below, because he insists that the whole earth is full of the glory of God. When we appreciate a beautiful mountain scene or immerse ourselves in Mozart or are lost in a Cezanne painting, we are experiencing God shining through the mask of his creatures. When humans share deep, satisfying intimacy, part of the joy they taste is God in the middle of it. And this is so whether or not he is recognized there. Since ordinary human experience is thus "God-infested," we are in no position to imagine the horror of a creation in which he was entirely hidden from view. St. Paul speaks for Christians when he acknowledges that "now we see in a mirror dimly, but then face to face. Now I know in part; then I shall understand fully, even as I have been understood" (1 Cor. 13:12). Nevertheless, for a few saints and perhaps on rare moments in the lives of most Christians, it seems as if God drops his mask to give the believer a more direct if still unclear view. Maybe it was out of such a rapturous experience that St. Paul wrote with confidence that "the sufferings of this present time are not worth comparing with the glory that is to be revealed to us" (Rom. 8:18) and counted "everything as loss because of the surpassing worth of knowing Christ Jesus as my Lord" (Phil. 3:8). In other words,

(T18) The good of "face-to-face" intimacy with God (the evil of his total absence) is simply incommensurate with any merely temporal evils (goods).

St. Stephen cannot help forgiving his murderers when he sees Jesus (Acts 7:56–8:1); the martyrs "have forgot their bitter story in the light of Jesus' glory."

Morally sufficient reasons and the incommensurate good. If a face-to-face vision of God is an incommensurate good for human beings, that will surely guarantee, for any cooperative person who has it, that the balance of goods over evils will be overwhelmingly favorable. Indeed, strictly speaking, there will be no *balance* to be struck. And no one who received such benefits would have any claim against God's justice or complaint against his love. God will have bestowed on those who see him "up close" as great a good as such a finite container can take. If so, it seems that God's justice and love toward creatures can be vindicated apart from any logically necessary connection between the evils suffered here below and some great enough good. In short, where 'excuse' is taken to mean 'morally sufficient reason',

(T4) The fact that an evil was necessary for a greater good would provide an omniscient and omnipotent being with an excuse, only if the evil were a logically necessary prerequisite to or consequence of the good,

is false. This is not to say that, subjectively speaking, a person in the middle of terrible suffering might not complain, doubt, or rail against God. Nevertheless, retrospectively, from the viewpoint of the beatific vision, no one would be disposed to blame God for not eliminating or preventing various evils or to regard God's love as limited or insufficient. And St. Paul is able to adopt this position even in prospect (Rom. 8:18).

Divine wisdom, temporal evils, and the meaning of life. What about the interpretation of (T4) on which 'excuse' means 'prudential justification'? After all, if God wants the saints to enjoy the beatific vision (which ex hypothesi has no logically necessary connection with temporal evils), is not their sojourn through this vale of tears a waste (foolish management) for him as well as "a pain" for them? Could God really be serious about this life if his principal response to its ills were simply to obliterate it in a final cloud of glory? Would not such a scenario rob our earthly suffering of any meaning? Once again, does not the conjunction of (T4) and (T5) combine to show that God is foolish?

This objection assumes that the only way that an omnipotent, omniscient God's permission of evils could be rationalized is by a logically necessary connection between the actual evils and great enough goods. Traditionally, Christians have disagreed. After all, the rationality of a person's behavior is in part a function of his purposes and his consistency and efficiency in pursuing them. No doubt God could have "brought many sons to glory" (Heb. 2:10) without a detour through the temporal world. His not doing so is explained by his wider and over-arching purpose in creation, which is to raise the finite and temporal above itself into relationship with the infinite and eternal. His persistent commitment to relationships with created persons (T6 and T7) reaches a radical focus in the Incarnation. The evils of sin, sickness, and death were not part of God's original intentions but a by-product of his creation of free persons and/or a plurality of mutually interfering natures (for example, humans, birds, and mosquitoes), and the Christian does not know (T5) why he permits so many of them. (For Christians, the answers to Q2–Q4 remain a mystery.) Nevertheless, the Christian revelation does say that God incarnate faces evils in deadly earnest, ultimately on the cross. It would not be consistent for the God who is so committed to the temporal order as to enter it and suffer in it himself to snatch his people out of it in some gnostic ascent. Thus enduring temporal suffering, God's people share in the divine commitment to the temporal order.

Suffering as a vision of the inner life of God. For all that, I believe Christian mysticism would not hesitate to admit a logically necessary connection between temporal suffering and a very great good, on the ground that temporal suffering itself is a vision into the inner life of God. The relation is thus not one of logically necessary means or consequence but rather that of identity. Perhaps—pace impassibility theorists—the inner life of God itself includes deep agony as well as ecstatic joy. Alternatively, the divine consciousness may be something beyond both joy and sorrow. Just as for Otto human beings can only experience the divine presence now as *tremendum* (a deep dread and anxiety), now as *mysterium* (an attraction beyond words), so perhaps our experiences of deepest pain as much as those of boundless joy are themselves direct (if still imperfect) views into the inner life of God. Further, just as lesser joys and pleasures (for example, the beauty of nature, music, or painting) may be more obscure visions of the glory of God, so also lesser degrees of suffering.

Instructed by Christian mysticism, I suggest that a Christian might endorse not only

(T18) The good of face-to-face intimacy with God (the evil of his total absence) is simply incommensurate with any merely temporal evils (goods)

but also

(T19) Any vision into the inner life of God has a good aspect, this goodness at least partly a function of the clarity of the vision.

He need not go so far as to maintain that *any* vision of God, however obscure or painful, has an *incommensurately* good aspect. Nor need he deny that

(T20) Experiences of suffering have an evil aspect proportionate to the degree of suffering involved.

Nevertheless, he might be led to reason that the good aspect of an experience of deep suffering is great enough that, from the standpoint of the beatific vision, the victim would not wish the experience away from his life history, but would, on the contrary, count it as an extremely valuable part of his life.

Note that, unless the Christian maintains that any experience of suffering whatever has an incommensurately good aspect, he will not claim to rest his whole defense on this putative logically necessary connection of identity alone. Rather, his vindication of divine goodness might still rely heavily on the incommensurate goodness of the beatific vision itself. Nevertheless, Christians believe that God intends to be *good* to his people in calling them to share his dogged pursuit of relationships within the temporal order. The fact of (T19) might be seen to lend credibility to the wisdom in this divine purpose, by giving a depth of meaning to their temporal suffering independently of its *external* relations to *other* logically independent goods, whether eternal or temporal.

Objections. The danger in this Christian-mystical suggestion (as Ivan Karamazoff and J. S. Mill contended about other attempts to draw a logically necessary connection between temporal evils and great enough goods) is that it runs the risk of making suffering seem too good. To begin with, someone might object that if suffering were a vision of the inner life of God, there would be nothing wrong with our hurting people, and especially with our causing them great suffering. For such experiences are alleged in (T19) to have a good aspect in some direct proportion to their intensity. A Christian could reply, "Non sequitur." God is the one who is responsible for ensuring that each person's life is, with that person's cooperation, a great good to him on the whole. Christians believe that God calls his people to share in his work. But God is the one who defines the finite person's responsibility for another's good. Christians could agree with secular moralists that sometimes one person has an obligation or at least a right to cause another person to suffer for his own good—for example, by spanking the two-year-old that runs out into the street or by speaking a painful word of correction. But Christian mysticism would neither compel nor countenance the suggestion that any created person has a vocation to sadism (or to masochism, either).

Again, someone might charge, on this view it would be fully compatible with divine goodness if human beings suffered eternally in hell forever. Indeed, insofar as suffering lasted forever, it would constitute for the damned soul an infinite good.

A twofold reply is possible: First of all, given (T11) and (T12), Christians do not believe that God would be wrong to consign sinners to eternal punishment. Second, it is arguable whether, given (T18), it is accurate to conceive of hell as the continuance of temporal evils, however sinister, rather than as the absence of God. As noted above, I doubt that we have any notion of how devastating that would be, although we might speculate with C. S. Lewis that the absence of God would bring a total disintegration of created personality.[4] In any event, hell considered as everlasting temporal punishment is not the "good" Christians believe God to have in mind for his people. For one thing, not every good is fitting for every sort of creature. As Aristotle observed in rejecting Platonic forms long ago, the putative metaphysical good of immutability is logically (metaphysically) ruinous to plant and animal natures. Similarly, some adult freedoms and pleasures are harmful for children. Perhaps omnipotence would be inappropriate for created persons of limited wisdom and good will. And even if the everlasting temporal suffering of a created person would have a good aspect, and indeed accumulate toward an infinite sum, it is a good that would break down and destroy the creature (in something of the way the tortures of brainwashing do). A loving God would not, any more than a loving parent, want to give his children goods that would naturally tend to destroy them.

4. C. S. Lewis, *The Problem of Pain* (New York: Macmillan, 1962), pp. 125–26.

A more profound answer to this second objection reverts to (T7) and the nature of the relationships for which God created us, namely, relationships of intimate sharing and loving self-giving. He wants us to share not merely his agony (or the aspect we experience in this life as agony) but also his joy. He wants us to enjoy our relationship with him and wants to make us happy in it. Needless to say, the experience of everlasting temporal torment does not "fill the bill"; for that we need a more balanced view of God.

CONCLUSION

Christians will not want to depreciate the awfulness (awefulness) of suffering in this life, by the innocent and the guilty, by the intelligent and the witless alike. They will not appear beside racks of torture to proclaim that it does not really matter or to exhort the victim to gratitude. Nevertheless, they see in the cross of Christ a revelation of God's righteous love and a paradigm of his redemptive use of suffering. Christian mysticism invites the believer to hold that a perfectly good God further sanctifies our moments of deepest distress so that retrospectively, from the vantage point of the beatific vision, the one who suffered will not wish them away from his life history—and this, not because he sees them as the source of some other resultant good, but inasmuch as he will recognize them as times of sure identification with and vision into the inner life of his creator.

For Christians as for others in this life, the fact of evil is a mystery. The answer is a more wonderful mystery—God himself.

PART THREE

The Divine Nature

11

Analogy and Foundationalism in Thomas Aquinas

RALPH MCINERNY

In this paper, inspired by some recent criticisms and defenses of Thomism, I propose to do three things. First, I will recall what St. Thomas Aquinas has to say about the characteristics of those shared terms he calls analogical names. Second, I will add a few things about the application of this doctrine of analogous terms to talk about God. Third, I will relate Thomas's thought to recent discussions in epistemology and make some tentative suggestions as to its relation to foundationalism and evidentialism. What Thomas has to say about the way we come to know and talk about God certainly sounds like a species of foundationalism, but it can be argued that believers who object to foundationalism need find no foe in Thomas.

I

The account of analogy that follows remains controversial, though not so much as it was when I first developed it in *The Logic of Analogy* (The Hague: Martinus Nijhoff, 1961). Students of St. Thomas, even while reluctantly acknowledging a logical dimension to his teaching on analogy, persist in speaking of it as chiefly a metaphysical doctrine. That is, the dominant interpretation remains that 'analogy' directly names a real relation between God and creature, despite the fact that the key passages in the text of Aquinas will not bear this reading. Nevertheless,

I shall now speak of Thomas's teaching on analogy as if such misunderstandings did not exist, particularly since I do not intend to deal with them here.

The Nature of Logic

It is then still necessary to emphasize that when St. Thomas Aquinas uses the term 'analogy' and related terms (*analogia, analogice, secundum analogiam*), he is more often than not speaking about speaking and not directly about the way of the world. The doctrine of analogy is, in short, a logical doctrine and not a metaphysical one. Thomas rarely seems to use the word to refer to real relations among things but usually has in mind relations among the several meanings of a single term. Such a reminder should be wholly unnecessary when it is a question of texts that speak of the *nomen analogicum*, but Thomists have been for so long in the grips of the idea that analogy is a metaphysical doctrine, bearing on real relations and preeminently on the real dependence of everything other than God on God as its cause, that insistence on the logical character of Thomas's doctrine has been rejected as nominalist or—perhaps just as bad—the sort of thing one under the influence of analytic philosophy might say.

The force of the reminder depends, of course, on a grasp of what Thomas means by calling a doctrine logical. How better refresh our minds on this than by observing Thomas's way of dealing with the hoary problems of universals?[1] He asks us to notice the difference between

(1) Man is rational.
(2) Man is a species.
(3) Man is seated.

While the subject terms of the three sentences are the same, their predicates differ. The difference between the predicates of (1) and (2) can be brought out by comparing:

A

Man is rational.
Socrates is a man.
Therefore, Socrates is rational.

---

1. This discussion of universals relies principally on Thomas's *On Being and Essence*.

And:

B

> Man is a species.
> Socrates is a man.
> Therefore, Socrates is a species.

Why is argument *B* faulty and *A* not? Argument *B* may be thought to be like, though not identical in type to, a third argument:

C

> Man is a three-letter word.
> Socrates is a man.
> Therefore, Socrates is a three-letter word.

The conclusion of *C* is manifestly false, and we avoid making this sort of inference by, when writing, giving such sentences as the first premise of *C* the form:

(4) 'Man' is a three-letter word.

The quotation marks make it clear that it is the word *man*, that orthographic symbol, we are talking about and not anything it may be taken to stand for. Similar examples are:

(5) 'Man' is a noun.
(6) 'Man' is the subject of sentence 5.

Needless to say, there are important differences among (4), (5), and (6) and their ilk, but their similarity both among themselves and with (2) seems clear. Nonetheless, we would not render (2) as

(2') 'Man' is a species.

If we did, we would very likely be giving an account of what I meant earlier when I said that (1), (2), and (3) have the same subject. 'Man' as the type of which the subjects of (1), (2), and (3) are tokens has been called a linguistic universal. But this does and does not accord with Porphyry's definition of 'species' as that which is predicated of numerically different things. The way 'man' is common to the subjects of (1), (2), and (3) differs from the way in which 'man' is common to Socrates, Xanthippe, and the Duke of Paducah:

(7) Socrates is a man.

(8) Xanthippe is a man.

(9) The Duke of Paducah is a man.

These are noticeably different from:

(10) 'Man' in (1) is a token of 'Man'.

But enough. Sentence 2 may be like sentences in which 'man' occurs precisely as an orthographic symbol or a part of speech, but it is clearly not in every way the same.

How does (2) differ from (1)? Thomas puts it this way: in (1) the predicate is said per se of the subject, whereas in (2) the predicate is said of the subject only per accidens. That is, "rational" is part of what 'man' means but "species" is not. Example (3) is added to give us another way in which something is predicated per accidens of man.

If (3) is true, it is not true because of what 'man' means, as if whatever is human is seated. The sentence happens to be true in case something that is human is seated. Admittedly (3) is an odd way of expressing the random fact that at the University Mall an arthritic shopper has collapsed on one of the plastic pews available there. Still, contrasting it with (1) brings out the difference between remarks that are true because of the nature of the subject as such and those that are true, if they are, because of what befalls something in which that nature is found.

Very well. Accidents of individuals versus properties or components of natures—that is the way the difference between (1) and (3) would be developed by Thomas. Is this of any help in understanding (2)? We do not want to say that this sentence is true because some individual human person is a species any more than we want to say that being a species is part and parcel of being a person. If (2) is true per accidens, where is the accident in virtue of which it is true?

Thomas's answer is that, just as (3) is true because of an accident of some individual in which human nature is found, so (2) is true because of an accident the nature has as a result of being known by such a mind as ours. To be a species is to be predicated of many numerically different things (or to be in many numerically different things). Something one is found in many. Human nature is not numerically identical in persons; in reality, it is simply multiple. It is thanks to the abstractive character of the human mind, which perceives the similarity between the individuals and formulates in a concept their common nature, that there is something one that relates to the many.

Logical relations—like being a species or, generally, being a universal, being a premise or a conclusion, being a middle term, and so on—accrue or happen to things as they are known by human beings. If concepts of natures are first intentions, these mental relations are second intentions. A word that is common to many because what it means is found in them all is a universal. Prophyry in his *Isagoge* distinguished five such universals: genus, species, difference, property, and accident.[2] His work was meant as an introduction to the *Categories,* which Thomas takes to be the first of Aristotle's logical writings. Does this entail that substance, quantity, quality, relation, and the other categories are logical relations?

(11) Man is a substance.

Sentence 11 is clearly like (1), yet substance is a category, a category is a universal and precisely a genus. We are bothered because we imagine this argument in the offing:

D

Man is a substance.
Substance is a genus.
Therefore, man is a genus.

But the first premise of *D* is like (1) and the second is like (2). What 'substance' means is predicated of human persons, but to be a genus is not true per se of the nature meant by 'substance'. *What is categorized* are real natures, but the *categorizing* is an activity of the human mind and generates relations among the natures *as known.* It will scarcely surprise that second intentions can only be discussed with reference to first intentions.[3]

2. See *Porphyry's Introduction to the Predicaments of Aristotle,* trans. Charles Glenn Wallis in The Classics of the St. John's Program (Annapolis: St. John's Press, 1938). It is at the outset of this little work that Porphyry wrote: "I shall keep away from the deeper questions but shall aim rightly at the simpler, i.e., I shall refuse to say whether genus and species are subsistent, or are located only in naked understanding, and if subsistent, whether they are corporeal or incorporeal, and whether separate from sensibles or subsisting in them." Those three questions constitute the "problem of universals," and commentators from Boethius on eagerly discussed them.

3. "What is first known [*prima intellecta*] are things outside the soul, the things which first draw the intellect to knowledge. But the intentions which follow on our mode of knowing are said to be secondly known [*secunda intellecta*]; for the intellect comes to know them by reflecting on itself, by knowing that it knows and the mode of its knowing" (*On the Power of God,* q. 7, art. 9).

Analogy as Logical

We now proceed to recall the Thomistic doctrine of analogy. Consider a list made up of:

(7) Socrates is a man.

(8) Xanthippe is a man.

(9) The Duke of Paducah is a man.

When we say that (7), (8), and (9) have the same predicate, we refer to more than the orthographic symbols *m-a-n*; it is what that term means, the concept for which it stands, that is said of the individuals referred to by the subjects of those sentences. That meaning of the predicate is the account we would give if someone asked us what we meant by asserting Socrates, Xanthippe, and the Duke of Paducah to be human. What I mean, we should reply, is that each is a rational animal. The common or shared predicate gets the same account in each of its occurrences.

"Things are said to be named univocally which have both the name and the definition answering to the name in common."[4] That is how Aristotle defines the situation we have just discussed. But it is not always like this. "Things are said to be named equivocally when, though they have a common name, the definition corresponding with the name differs for each."[5] We might imagine that Aristotle has in mind the fun we have with words like 'pain'/'pane', 'been'/'bin' (or 'been'/'bean'), 'bough'/'bow', and the like, but he seems to have in mind the more restricted case when it is the same orthographic symbol that receives differing accounts. The mind floods with examples of words with multiple meanings—'deck', 'charge', 'pen', 'trunk', 'nail', 'page', 'peg', on and on—and we, being simple souls, begin to chuckle as we ponder the difference between 'Peg o' my heart' and 'peg of my leg', 'French leaves' and the 'leaves' of a table, 'tell' as in tale and 'tell' as in archaeology. Suddenly our language seems a veritable hotbed of ambiguity—only potential ambiguity, of course. It is because we are so seldom misled by this sort of thing that it can be so much fun.

Even when there seems to be no connection whatsoever between one account of a word and another, knowing the language ordinarily suffices to avoid confusion. The sole of your shoe and the sole of my fish may be historically related for all I know, but my being able to understand English sentences in which they occur is not dependent on any

4. Aristotle, *Categories*, 1a6–7.
5. Ibid., 1a1–2.

arcane etymological (or ichthyological) knowledge. No one is likely to be misled by:

(12) They pick shoots in the garden.

And:

(13) They shoot picks in the garden.

Presumably Aristotle invites us to think of these garden variety instances of equivocation in order that we might become alert to more subtle occurrences that not only mislead but vitiate arguments.

St. Thomas calls an analogous term a kind of equivocal term.[6] A term that receives several accounts that are wholly unrelated may be called purely equivocal. Sometimes, however, the accounts are related; there is not pure diversity in the several accounts a common term receives. Call this controlled ambiguity or equivocation. Or, with Thomas, call it analogy.

(14) Science is a virtue.

(15) Temperance is a virtue.

(16) Faith is a virtue.

Lists like (14)–(16) at once invite assent and make us wary. There seems to be something right about calling such diverse things virtues, but there are dangers too. When our sense of danger predominates, we may say either that science is not a virtue or that it is not one in the same sense temperance is.

We need an account of 'virtue'. Thomas works with this Latin rendering of Aristotle: *virtus est quod bonum facit habentem et opus eius bonum reddit* (virtue is what makes the one having it good and renders his act good). This account, he feels, fits the occurrence of the term better in (15) than in (14). His reason is that the double occurrence of "good" in the account indicates that virtue more properly connects with appetite: *bonum est quod omnia appetunt* (the good is what all seek). The object of seeking, wanting, willing is what is first called good. Temperance is a habit regulating our pursuit of sense pleasure such that the compre-

---

6. "Now this mode of community [analogy] is a mean between pure equivocation and simple univocation. For in analogies the idea is not, as it is in univocals, one and the same; yet it is not totally diverse as in equivocals; but the name which is thus used in a multiple sense signifies various proportions to some one thing: e.g., 'healthy,' applied to urine, signifies the sign of animal health; but applied to medicine, it signifies the cause of the same health" (*Summa theologica* I, q. 13, art. 5).

hensive good we desire is safeguarded; furthermore, it is not merely a capacity to behave in a certain way in the presence of pleasurable objects, it is the disposition to do so. When science is called a virtue, we mean that the mind has the capacity to achieve its end or good (that is, truth), but science does not give the disposition, only the capacity. This is why Thomas thinks science is a virtue only in a secondary sense and requires for its fitting use virtues in the primary sense. Applied to science, the "good" figuring in the account of 'virtue' is an extended sense—the good of the mind, not the good of the person as such—and a fixed appetitive disposition is not had. This leads Thomas to say that the definition of 'virtue' is unequally exhibited by temperance and science, being primarily (*per prius*) saved in temperance and only secondarily (*per posterius*) in science.[7]

Faith, taken to be a determination of the mind to the truth revealed by God, is like science a habit of mind rather than of appetite. Nonetheless, because here the mind accepts the truth, not because it understands it, but as a means to the good of salvation, the notion of virtue is said to be more perfectly saved in faith than in science.

An analogous term, then, is one that is said of a number of things, with the meaning or account it receives varying as said of each of them. But more than diversity of account is involved. The ordering of the meanings—*per prius et posterius*—reveals that later accounts are parasitic on an earlier one, that the first and obvious meaning of the term acts as a control over extended meanings of the same term. Just as I mention Rover's intrinsic disposition when I say his coat or food is healthy—the one being a sign of it and the other its cause—so the sense that 'virtue' has when said of such habits as temperance is the measure of what we mean by it in calling faith and science virtues. The idea is that we lay hold of the extended meaning by considering the primary meaning. The ordered set of meanings of the analogous term are thus thought of as instructive, as leading the mind from what it already knows to what it knows only imperfectly. Just as a metaphor leads the mind from one thing to another by a kind of inference, so the analogical extension of a term is meant to be an instrument of illumination.

7. In *Summa theologica*, I, q. 16, art. 6, Thomas gives as a rule for analogous names that *ratio propria non invenitur nisi in uno*. He there uses the familiar Aristotelian example of 'healthy' (though his purpose is to discuss how 'truth' is analogously common to God and creatures). Your dog is more properly called healthy than is his sleek coat or his cereal, since he has health, whereas his coat is a sign of it and his cereal is a cause of it. Whether he says that an account is saved *per prius et posterius* in many or that there are several accounts one of which is primary, his meaning is the same. This is an exegetical point perhaps too recherché to pursue here.

II

The notion that the many meanings of an analogously common term lead us from what is more easily knowable to what is known only with difficulty is emphasized when Thomas applies his doctrine of analogy to those names common to God and creature. He begins with the reminder that, since we name things as we know them, our words will first of all be of things most easily known by us. This reminder is taken to mean that, since our concepts are formed against the background of our sense experience, the connatural object of the human mind is to know the nature or quiddity of sensed things. Obviously, this interpretation presents difficulties for any human claim to know God, on the assumption that God is not a material substance.

The doctrine of analogy is thus crucial in St. Thomas's account of how our talk about God—or his talk to us about himself in our language—can be meaningful. We name things as we know them; we first know sensible things; we come to know God as the cause and origin of sensible things; so we name him from sensible things, and one way we do this is by analogically extending names from creature to God.[8] What we know of creatures functions as a means of understanding something about God.

Thomas's use of the doctrine of analogy to explain certain names common to God and creatures is misleadingly uncomplicated. Consider such a list as this:

(17) Socrates is wise.

(18) God is wise.

As in our first reaction to (14), (15), and (16), we want to agree and disagree. If both a human person and God are called wise, the term cannot mean the same thing in the two cases. Can the meanings even be related? Mindful of the infinite distance between creature and God, we may wish to say that there can be no comparison, that human wisdom is as folly compared with God's, that God's wisdom is so transcendent that we equivocate in calling both God and creature wise.

However reverent this reaction might be, it could end by undercut-

---

8. I say "one way" because, while all talk about God is, for Thomas, dependent for its intelligibility on talk about creatures, not all talk about God consists in the analogical extension to God of terms appropriate to creatures. Negative and relative names (e.g., immaterial, cause) denominate God by denying some creaturely limitation of him or designating him as cause of the creature. The analogous term is only one instance of the way talk of creatures controls talk of God.

ting the very point of Scripture. God speaks to us in our language and by various stories and accounts leads our minds from the familiar human world to a world beyond. If the referents in this world could not play the pedagogical role assigned them, Scripture would be otiose, fit only for the obfuscations of those scholars who seem to regard it as revelatory only of the tribal mores of our primitive predecessors. But we know better. The parable of the Prodigal Son has the force it does in giving us an intimation of God's mercy because we know what sons and fathers are, we have at least a second-hand acquaintance with profligacy, and perhaps we have from time to time been the recipient of a forgiveness we did not deserve. To be able to think of our relation to God by means of this story is to be led from the more easily known to what is more difficult to know.

It thus appears that any name analogically common to God and creature will in its usual, obvious, and primary meaning apply first to creature and secondarily to God. Nonetheless, we may reverse that order in noting that the wisdom we get some intimation of in God is infinitely superior to any created wisdom. Here Thomas makes use of a progression he learned from Pseudo-Dionysius.

(18) God is wise.

(19) God is not wise.

(20) God is superlatively wise.

In order to show that (18) and (19) are not contradictories, Thomas must hold that (18) stresses one component of the account of 'wise' and (19) another. The *via affirmationis* asserts that the divine knowledge sees everything in the light of what is absolutely first; the *via negationis* makes clear that in God, unlike the case of a human person, this is not a quality distinct from himself, something he acquired and could lose. The *via eminentiae* thus stresses that, if the quality of wisdom we find in persons like Socrates seems fittingly attributed to God, it is not in him an accident, and we must thus say that God's wisdom is unlike and above in mode and manner the created wisdom with which we began.

III

Now, how might one characterize the theory of knowing and naming incorporated in what St. Thomas teaches about analogous terms and our ability to know and talk about God? Here is the way it has been characterized by Nicholas Wolterstorff.

Aquinas offers one classic version of foundationalism. There is, he said, a body of propositions which can be known by the natural light of reason—that is, propositions which can become self-evident to us in our earthly state. Properly conducted scientific inquiry consists in arriving at other propositions by way of reliable inference (demonstration) from these. In addition, there are propositions that God reveals to us and which we ought to accept. A few of these (for example, that God exists) can be inferred from propositions knowable by the natural light of reason. But most of them are not of this sort. Nor can they become self-evident to us. In short, they cannot be known, and we must simply believe them on the ground of the credibility of the revealer.[9]

This is a reasonably good summary of Thomas's position. He thinks some things are more readily knowable to us than others. He thinks there are nongainsayable things we know right off. He thinks we extend our knowledge by connecting it to what we already know, the latter being the foundation of the former. And he does think that, although some of the things that have been revealed by God about himself can be known from our knowledge of the world, the vast majority of revealed truths are accepted as true because God has revealed them.

Wolterstorff finds this doctrine to be fraught with dangers. This way of looking at things—he calls it foundationalist—is pretty well dead and Wolterstorff thinks it would take a feat of prodigious imagination to revive it.[10] What exactly has brought foundationalism into so parlous a condition that a belief in epistemological resurrection is required in order to be sanguine about its future?

One reason for his pessimism is that the foundationalism he summarizes in three propositions[11] has to do with theories. This is in some ways unfortunate, as it suggests that the foundationalist (and thus St. Thomas, if he is one) holds that whenever you hold something to be true on the basis of some foundation, you are in the realm of theory and science and the like. If I am asked why I think Austin Clifford McInerny is my father and David Joseph McInerny is my son, I can give reasons and I might even agree, though reluctantly, that I am building up a theory, but I would certainly draw the line at the suggestion that I am engaged in science. Unless 'science' is understood in its primary and unpretentious sense as knowledge of whatever kind. Understood as *scientia*, the kind of knowledge that is gained as a

9. Nicholas Wolterstorff, *Reason within the Bounds of Religion* (Grand Rapids: Eerdmans, 1976), pp. 26–27.
10. Ibid., p. 29.
11. Ibid., pp. 24–25.

result of a demonstrative or apodictic syllogism, when from necessarily true premises a necessarily true conclusion necessarily follows, science is knowledge in the strongest sense of the term. But, far from characterizing human knowledge by and large, scientia is something difficult to come by. Nonetheless, Thomas, like Aristotle, thought there were three great kinds of it: natural science, mathematics, and divine science or metaphysics or natural theology. These distinct sciences have distinct subject matters following on formally different ways of defining.[12] The *propter quid* demonstration analyzed in the *Posterior Analytics* is realized unequivocally in geometry, less obviously in natural science, and scarcely at all in metaphysics. Nor should we think of the procedure of the nonmathematical sciences as deductive. In his commentary on Aristotle's *Physics*,[13] Thomas distinguishes the *ordo determinandi* of the science from its *ordo demonstrandi,* the former reflecting the fact that we move from general to specific knowledge of a subject matter, but the specific is not deduced from the generic.

I mention these matters to illustrate that, even where the concept of strict science is applicable, we should not imagine the lockstep, deductive procedure some uses of 'foundationalism' suggest. A fortiori, in speaking of human knowledge in all its amplitude, the concept of strict science is not going to provide a fitting model. Nonetheless, if foundationalism is taken to mean that some things are more knowable and thus more basic than others, then St. Thomas is indeed a foundationalist.[14] Furthermore, St. Thomas is a foundationalist with respect to our knowledge of God, and it is this, I suspect, rather than the pure epistemological issue, that explains why philosophers like Wolterstorff have set their faces so resolutely against foundationalism.

It should be noted, however, that something has happened since the days when Wolterstorff wrote the little book from which I have been quoting. We find him now *defending* Aquinas, if not foundationalism, by seeking to separate Thomas from those who, like Locke, are evidentialists. Presumably, Wolterstorff earlier thought that Thomas's foundationalism and his natural theology entailed things about religious belief, but he no longer thinks so. Now he finds his target in the views

12. This familiar doctrine is found most succinctly expressed in St. Thomas's exposition of Boethius's *De trinitate*, q. 5. Cf. Paul Wyser, *Thomas von Aquin in librum Boethii de Trinitate* (Fribourg, 1948).

13. *In I Physicorum*, lect. 1.

14. I do not mean to deny that he is a foundationalist in the strict sense provided by Wolterstorff's presentation, only that such strict foundationalism has a very restricted role to play and is not the model of the full range of human knowledge. Nonetheless, foundationalism in a looser sense characterizes Thomas's view of human knowledge in all its amplitude.

of Locke. Perhaps it would not be too simplistic to say that evidentialism, Lockean or otherwise, holds that each and every religious believer has an obligation to seek evidence for his beliefs. It seems right to say that Thomas lays no such universal obligation on believers. Nonetheless, Wolterstorff's irenism is a bit surprising. It seems to derive from three sources; first, a suggested but undeveloped sociology of knowledge that distinguishes between the social and cultural milieu in which Locke wrote and that in which Thomas and other medievals wrote; second, the suspicion that John Calvin is saying things very much like what Thomas said; and, third, a much more profound and sympathetic reading of Thomas. I hope it will not seem churlish if I express some misgivings about his account of Aquinas. Wolterstorff seems to me overly anxious to save Thomas from a pitfall that Thomas himself would not acknowledge.

How does Wolterstorff know that Thomas is not an evidententialist, that is, one who thinks the believer has an obligation to provide evidence for his beliefs? There seem to be three reasons. One is that natural theology is not an ad hoc activity, fashioned in response to a worry about the reasonableness of theism. Rather, it is part of a great enterprise with overlapping parts—in short, a part of philosophy in Thomas's commodious sense of the term. A second reason is that Thomas thinks knowledge of God is natural to man—indigenous, as Wolterstorff says—and thus not an object of worry. (Unless such indigenous knowledge can be the result of inference, this is misleading, since Thomas sketches the arguments he thinks implicit in the widespread conviction that there is a God, for example, from the order around us. Is it the argument one does not worry about or the simple claim that God exists?) Third, the evidentialist presupposes that one can justifiably believe only on the basis of good arguments. Wolterstorff takes it to be obvious that Thomas is not an evidentialist because Thomas nowhere suggests that every believer must be interested in natural theology.

Wolterstorff's interesting and nuanced discussion seems to me to suffer from an inadequate understanding of the distinction (which he cites) between preambles and articles of faith, between theism and religious faith. He does not make sufficiently clear that natural theology, even if developed to a fare-thee-well, could never ground, prove, or be evidence for the articles of faith as such. Thomas's foundationalism and optimistic attitude toward theism never obscure the line between the natural and supernatural orders.

Rather than go on about Wolterstorff's work and run the risk of seeming to regard it as anything other than a remarkable achievement,

I will take it that the main concern of believers is the suggestion that foundationalism and/or evidentialism require us to say things about faith that are reductionist, demeaning, or both. Is the believer to accept the notion that his faith is founded on evidence in such a way that he can, upon demand (usually hostile), produce that evidence *and* the way in which his faith in God and Jesus Christ follow on that evidence? *Absit.* Faith is a gift and grace that has no compelling natural antecedents; it is not the product of proof, the ineluctable conclusion of some argument whose premises are truths in the common domain. If foundationalism is taken to call the nature of faith as a gift into question, then foundationalism must be rejected. Does the foundationalism of Thomas Aquinas lead him into heterodoxy regarding the nature of faith? Can Thomas hold the things surveyed in the first two parts of this paper without saying things about the gift of faith that believers must reject?

It is clear that Thomas himself considered his theory of knowledge and language to be quite compatible with his Christian fatih. On another occasion, I characterized some antifoundationalist accounts of faith as fideism. By fideism I mean the claim that nothing we know counts for or against the truths of faith. Thomas is a foundationalist who rejects fideism and holds that faith is a gift. We want to know if Thomas can consistently hold:

(21) Faith is a gift and not the result of proof.

(22) Nothing we know entails the falsity of Christian beliefs and some things we know count in favor of their truth.

(23) The truths of faith are not counted among those self-evident or foundational for all.

Proposition 23 follows on Thomas's epistemology, according to which the proper and commensurate object of the human intellect is the quiddity of sensible reality; thus, if none of the truths of Christian faith is a truth about sensible reality, none of them is going to be among the first truths we know.[15] It will be objected that, even if truths about God cannot be foundational on this assumption (God not being the essence or quiddity of sensible reality), nonetheless many believed truths encompass sensible reality, notably, the truth that it has been created by God.

Proposition 22 addresses that objection. It must be remembered that Thomas holds that theism can be philosophically established. He holds

---

15. I have in mind the doctrine to be found in *Summa theologica*, I, q. 12.

that, although truths about God are not among the first we can know, given the nature of human knowledge, there are some truths about God that can be known on the basis or foundation of what we easily and naturally first know. It is well known that Thomas regards some proofs formulated by pagan philosophers to be sound and to establish the truth of propositions equivalent to 'God exists'. He holds further that there are other truths as to what God is and is not that pagans have or could come to know. Needless to say, this creates a problem for him.

If faith is a gift, thanks to which, among other things, we hold certain things to be true of God, such truths being accepted because God revealed them, *and* if the truths Thomas says philosophers have come to know are found among the truths about God the Christian believes, then some of the truths about God I believed from my mother's knee are knowable truths and I can in principle produce convincing arguments on their behalf. One way out of this would be to say that faith is the gift whereby we accept truths that we have not proved but that we could prove. But this makes faith a temporary expedient, not the one thing needful. That may be what Hegel held, but it is not Thomas's view.

Thomas does not equate revealed truths about God and truths of faith. Truths of faith are truths about God that cannot be known in this life and thus are and must be accepted as true solely on the authority of God who reveals them. Not all truths about God that show up in revelation are like this; that there is a God, for example, a truth without which nothing else in Scripture would make sense. If it has thus been revealed that God exists and if human beings came to know that God exists independently of Scripture and faith, then God's existence is not a truth of faith in the sense stated above. Truths about God that are not truths of faith in the narrow sense but that have been revealed are what Thomas means by *praeambula fidei*. Is this doctrine incompatible with what motivates the antifoundationalism of some Christians, namely, that faith is a gift, not learned, not acquired by natural effort, and so forth?

Thomas is not suggesting that by establishing those truths about God that he numbers among the praeambula fidei, any believer has or could deduce, come to know the truth of, or say he has evidence for truths of faith in the proper sense, namely, the Christian mysteries: that Christ is human and divine, that he has redeemed us from our sins, that thanks to his resurrection we can if faithful look forward to eternal union with him and the Father in heaven, that there is a trinity of persons in God, and so on. The preambles of faith are not premises on the basis of which the truth of the mysteries can be established. The believer accepts all the truths God has revealed immediately—as a package, so to say—precisely because God reveals them, and his faith did not follow necessarily from any cognitive prelude and does not require that he engage in some research project of a philosophical or theological sort. So why does Thomas bother to develop this doctrine? Who needs it if nobody needs it?

The answer is that he is guided by revelation, specifically the opening chapter of the Epistle to the Romans. Paul enumerates the misdeeds of the pagan Romans and calls them inexcusable. Why? Because from the things that are made they could come to knowledge of the invisible things of God. The traditional understanding of this is that pagans qua pagans can from knowledge of the world come to some knowledge of God and that such knowledge entails moral principles that ought to guide their lives. We know that Paul elsewhere appeals to the Unknown God of the Athenians as a point of reference for the good news he brings. This suggests that one who already accepts the truth that there is a God has fewer impediments to the news that God has become incarnate in Christ than someone who is an atheist. This does not mean that the natural knowledge of God entails the Christian good news about God incarnate in Christ, nor does it mean that such knowledge is a necessary prerequisite for hearing the good news. What, then, is the significance of Paul's remarks?

Thomas uses what he takes to be the Pauline conception of praeambula fidei in an argument on behalf of the reasonableness of faith. If some of the things that have been revealed can be known to be true, it is reasonable to say that the rest are in themselves intelligible. This is what is meant by (22), the denial of fideism. Some things we know count on behalf of the truth of what we believe; nothing we or anyone else knows could establish the falsity of what we believe.

To whom are these arguments addressed, the believer or the non-believer? The believer does not need them. He accepts Christ as the way, the truth, and the life. The nonbeliever? But such an argument is not conclusive or would invite derision if it were presented as conclusive. Thomas regards such considerations as ones some believers are bound to engage in because of their walk of life—believers like ourselves, believers who write for and against foundationalism. We want to be as clear as possible as to what we do and do not believe, what is and is not entailed by faith, and so on. It seems pragmatically inconsistent for us to question the appropriateness for some believers to engage in such discussions.

The fact that God's revelation includes things known independently of and with at least logical priority to truths of faith may be seen more clearly if we consider the fact that God uses human language to communicate with us. When we speak of biblical languages we do not mean that there are languages only believers understand. The contemporaries of Jesus knew Aramaic and he was counting on that when he spoke to them. They also knew about fishing and farming and fathers and sons and other things to which Jesus appeals as the vehicles of truths hitherto unknown and that can be known to be true only with the help of grace. Thomas takes this to be an appeal to what is more obvious and knowable by us. Of course this does not mean that if you know about prodigal sons and forgiving fathers you thereby know the truth of our relation to God. As a teacher, Jesus appeals to what his listeners already know in order to draw them on to what they do not know. But again, this teaching is not simply drawing out the implications of what the listeners already know. As Kierkegaard reminds us in *Philosophical Fragments.* Jesus is not a teacher like all others; he is sui generis.

What, then, can we conclude about Thomas as a foundationalist? His teaching on analogy and his application of it to talk about God seem clearly to put him among those who deny that truths about God can be basic for human knowers and that they must consequently be shown to be true by being grounded in what *can* be basic for humans, truths about sensible objects. "God exists" could be basic only if 'God' were the name of some physical object, such as a tree or a flash of lightning. To this we object that the truths about God that we accept as believers cannot be grounded in the appropriate way on truths about sensible things. And Thomas agrees. His doctrine of analogy would have it that we can understand the meaning of the mysteries of faith—to the degree we do—on an analogy with sensible things, but that their truth is not so grounded. Thus, so far as philosophical theism is concerned, Thomas would seem to be foundationalist. With respect to the truths peculiar to Christian faith, however, Thomas is not a foundationalist, save in the weaker sense that the meanings of the terms used to express these truths require a grasp of their meanings as they are used to speak of things less than God. What Thomas calls the *mysteria fidei* count as basic propositions. They are precisely the principles or starting points of the theology based on Sacred Scripture.[16] Indeed, in an effort to show how basic the truths held by religious faith are, Thomas suggests that if *per impossibile* the believer had to choose between truths nongain-

---

16. Look at *Summa theologica*, I, q. 1, where Thomas draws a parallel between self-evident truths as the principles of philosophical science and revealed truths (in the sense of mysteria fidei) as the principles of theology as he is writing of it.

sayable by all and the mysteries of faith, he would give up the former before he would the latter.[17] If Thomas is a foundationalist and/or evidentialist, he is not of the sort who rightly draw the fire of believers. And this, I think, is why such patient and sympathetic readers as Wolterstorff end by counting him an ally rather than a foe.

17. This is to be found in *Disputed Questions on Truth,* q. 14.

12

Monotheism

WILLIAM J. WAINWRIGHT

The purpose of this paper is to explore the relation between the divine attributes and monotheism, to show that monotheism is a necessary consequence of other things theists want to say about God. It is to be hoped that our inquiry will thus both increase our understanding of the nature of these attributes and illuminate monotheism itself.

I

One of the most popular arguments for monotheism is the argument from the world's unity. If there were several designers who acted independently or at cross-purposes, we would expect to find evidence of this in their handiwork—for example, one set of laws obtaining at one time or place and a different set of laws obtaining at a different time or place. We observe nothing of the sort. On the contrary, as far as we can determine, the same laws hold at all places and at all times in the universe. Indeed, the unity of the world, the fact that it exhibits a uniform structure, that it is a single cosmos, strongly suggests some sort of unity in its cause—that there is either a single designer or several designers acting cooperatively—perhaps under the direction of one of their number.

The evidence does not compel us to conclude that there is only one designer, and the ablest proponents of the argument from design have been aware of this. Thus Paley asserts that the argument proves only "a unity of counsel" or (if there are subordinate agents) "a presiding" or "controlling will."[1] Nevertheless, considerations of simplicity suggest that we ought to posit only one designer. For it is a vague but generally accepted dictum that entities ought not to be multiplied beyond necessity, and there are no compelling reasons for postulating the existence of two or more cooperating designers. While some human artifacts are produced by several artifacers, others are produced by only one artifacer. Furthermore, the most persuasive reason for postulating several designers is the existence of evil and (apparent) disorder, for it is tempting to explain evil and disorder by postulating conflicts between two or more opposed powers. But this consideration provides no reason for preferring the hypothesis of several cooperating designers to the hypothesis of a single designer, for both hyoptheses presuppose a "a unity of counsel"; that is, once we have decided that (natural) good and (natural) evil are consequences of the operation of a single system of laws and that their cause must therefore be unitary, the existence of evil and disorder is no longer relevant to the question of monotheism (though it may be relevant to the question of the goodness of the cause).

In spite of its plausibility and historical importance, the argument from the world's order suffers from at least one limitation. A posteriori arguments of this type cannot be used to show that there can only be one God—that monotheism is *conceptually* required by the theist's understanding of divinity.[2] The remainder of this paper will be devoted to attempts to establish such a connection.

II

It is sometimes argued that there could not be two gods, because nothing would distinguish them. For example, two gods could not be dis-

1. William Paley, *Natural Theology: Selections* (Indianapolis: Bobbs-Merrill, 1963), p. 52. Cf. J. S. Mill, *Theism* (New York: Liberal Arts Press, 1957), p. 7, and F. R. Tennant, *Philosophical Theology*, II (Cambridge: Cambridge University Press, 1968), pp. 121–22.

2. Thomas Morris has pointed out to me that the argument from the world's order does not preclude the possibility that other designers are responsible for the order of other cosmoi that are neither spatially nor temporally related to our own. While this is true, I do not think that it affects the argument's soundness. In the absence of any reason to believe that there actually *are* other cosmoi, there appears to be no reason to postulate the existence of other designers. On the other hand, Morris's point does underscore the a posteriori and probable character of the argument. I would like to take this opportunity to express my gratitude for Morris's very helpful comments on an earlier version of this paper.

tinguished on the basis of their spatiotemporal position, for either God has no spatiotemporal position (he is spaceless and timeless) or his spatiotemporal position is the whole of space and time (he is omnipresent and everlasting).[3]

There are traditions in which the divine is said to possess no properties or (alternatively) to possess all properties. Thus the Brahman is sometimes said to be *neti, neti* (not this, not that), and it is sometimes said to be all things. In either case, it would be impossible to distinguish two Brahmans. But this view is incoherent. In the first place, if the Brahman is real, the two characterizations are equivalent,[4] and therefore if one is true the other is true. But in that case the view in question either ascribes (all) properties to something that has no properties or (alternatively) denies (all) properties of something that has all properties. In the second place, nothing can be real that either lacks all properties or has inconsistent properties.[5]

The most sympathetic interpretation of the claim that the divine is neti, neti is that nothing is an (adequate) image or icon of the divine and, similarly, the most sympathetic interpretation of the claim that the divine is all things is that everything is a (more or less adequate) image or icon of the divine. Understood in this fashion, there are certain rough parallels between Hindu claims about Brahman and the claims that have been made about God by some Christian mystics. It is important to realize, however, that some icons or images are believed to be better or more adequate than others. Thus, in Vedānta, Brahman is characterized as "being-consciousness-bliss," and this is thought to be a better or more apt characterization than "matter" (*prakriti*). Similarly, Pseudo-Dionysius takes it for granted that those qualities that can be legitimately ascribed to divinity and also (from another point of view) denied of it range from those that are "most akin to It" to those "which differ most from the ultimate goal."[6] The view that we are examining thus implies that the divine is more like some things than others; that,

---

3. God might, of course, be aspatial and everlasting, but the point would be unaffected.

4. If a thing must exist in order to have properties, then from the fact that it is false that Brahman has P, it does not follow that Brahman has $\bar{P}$ (the complement of P). But *if* the Brahman exists, then, if it lacks P, it has $\bar{P}$ and vice versa. Hence, if the Brahman is neither extended nor unextended, it is both unextended and extended, etc. Alternatively, if it has both the property of being extended and the property of being unextended, then it is neither unextended nor extended, etc.

5. Anything that has all properties has inconsistent properties—for example, the properties of being colored and noncolored.

6. *Dionysius the Areopagite on the Divine Names and the Mystical Theology*, trans. C. E. Rolf (London: SPCK; New York: Macmillan, 1957), p. 198.

for example, the divine is more like consciousness or being than their complements. It is therefore misleading to say either that the divine possesses no properties or that it possesses all properties, for it possesses such properties as the property of being more like consciousness than nonconsciousness and lacks such properties as the property of being more like nonconsciousness than consciousness.

But granted that the divine has some properties and lacks others, is it possible to distinguish two divine beings by their properties? The remainder of this section will examine attempts to show that it is not possible to do this. The first argument proceeds from God's necessity, the second from God's simplicity, and the third from his perfection. As we shall see, each argument founders on the fact that God possesses some of his properties contingently.

A

In *Summa contra gentiles* (*SCG* I, 42, 8), Aquinas argues that two necessary beings could only "be distinguished by something added either to one of them only, or to both." But in that case "one or both of them must be composite," and since "no composite being is through itself a necessary being," at least one of the two beings would not be unconditionally necessary and so would not be God.

Aquinas's argument depends upon the assumption that "every composition . . . needs some composer," and that, therefore, if God were composite, he would "have an efficient cause" and so would not be (unconditionally) necessary (*SCG* I, 18, 5). The assumption's plausibility depends at least partly upon thinking of a composite entity's attributes as a "plurality" of detachable parts brought together or composed into a unity by an external cause. This makes a certain amount of sense when some of an entity's properties are accidental, for, it might be argued, where P is an accidental property of A, that A has P must have a cause (explanation), and since P is an *accidental* property of A, that A has P cannot be explained by its own nature. The argument would then be that two or more necessary beings could only be distinguished on the basis of their accidental properties but that any being with accidental properties is a composite entity that requires an external cause and is therefore *not* necessary.

I do not find this convincing. In the first place, it is not clear why two necessary beings could not be distinguished by a difference in their essential properties, that is, it is not clear why two necessary beings must have the *same* essential properties. Indeed, if the doctrine of the Trinity is coherent, the thesis is false. The Son does not possess the attribute "being unbegotten," although this attribute is essential to the Father;

and the Father does not possess the attribute "being begotten," although this attribute is essential to the Son; and yet both Father and Son are necessarily existing divine beings.[7] In the second place, it is not clear that the possession of accidental properties can only be explained by appealing to external causes. That God knows that this world is actual is not essential to him, but his possession of this property is explained by his (contingent and accidental)[8] decision to create it, and this decision is not external to him. Nor is it clear that it requires any explanation other than his own infinite goodness and the goodness of the world he brings into being.[9] It is thus not clear that aseity is incompatible with the possession of accidental properties and it is therefore not clear that it is impossible to distinguish two necessary beings by a difference in those properties.

B

Let us assume that God is simple in the sense that, for any two of his properties P and Q, either P is identical with Q or P is logically equivalent to Q (that is, it is impossible for him to possess P without possessing Q and vice versa). Let us further suppose that there are two gods. If both are God, then both possess the properties that are essential to divinity. Call these D. If the two differ, each possesses some property that the other lacks. Suppose, for example, that the first possesses a property H and the second possesses its complement $\bar{H}$. Since each is God, each is simple. Hence either H is identical with D and $\bar{H}$ is identical with D, or H is logically equivalent to D and $\bar{H}$ is logically equivalent to D. Therefore, either H is identical with $\bar{H}$ or H is logically equivalent to $\bar{H}$. But this is incoherent, and even if it were not, the possession of H and $\bar{H}$ could not be used to distinguish between them, since either H and $\bar{H}$ are the same property or H and $\bar{H}$ are logically equivalent properties. It would therefore seem that, if God is simple, there cannot be two gods.

One might argue, however, that the most that is required by the

7. Although one could perhaps argue that while the Father and Son are distinct hypostases, they are not, in the requisite sense, distinct necessary beings.

8. Contingent because it is not necessarily instantiated, accidental because it is not essential to him. Since God is a necessary being, any property that is not essential to him is contingent and vice versa.

9. The latter implies, of course, that it is possible for an explanation of a free decision to be sufficient (i.e., fully adequate) even though the explicans does not entail its explicandum. Although I shall not argue the point, this appears to me to be (necessarily) true of (contra-causally) free decisions. My argument also presupposes that the goodness of the created world (i.e., the fact that any world of that sort would be a good one) is not an external cause—perhaps because value facts are not causes, or because these facts are an aspect of God's intellect or are constituted by his knowing them or something of the sort, or both.

doctrine of simplicity is that God's essential properties are either identical with each other or equivalent to one another. Furthermore, God's contingent properties cannot be identical with or equivalent to his essential properties, since the latter are necessarily instantiated[10] while the former are not. It follows that if H and $\bar{H}$ are contingent properties of the two divine beings, they are neither identical with nor equivalent to D. The plausibility of the argument from simplicity would thus appear to depend upon the assumption that God cannot have contingent properties.

C

John of Damascus argues that because God is perfect, he is necessarily unique.[11] The only way in which one god could be distinguished from another would be by coming "short of perfection in goodness, or power, or wisdom, or time, or place," but in that case "he would not be God." Aquinas offers a similar argument. According to Aquinas, if there were several gods, there would be several perfect beings, but "if none of these perfect beings lacks some perfection," and if none of them has "any admixture of imperfection . . . nothing will be given in which to distinguish the perfect beings from one another."[12]

Arguments of this type appear to make two assumptions. The first is that properties can be exhaustively divided into three classes. The first class is the class of imperfections, that is, limitations (for example, my inability to lift anything weighing more than 200 pounds) or privations (for example, blindness or sin—properties that imply some defect, some deviation from the standard appropriate for evaluating beings of the kind in question). The second class is the class of mixed perfections, that is, good-making properties that entail some limitation (for example, being human, or being corporeal) or privation (for example, repentence). The third class is the class of pure perfections, that is, perfections that entail no limitation or privation (for example, being, goodness, love, knowledge, power, unity, or independence). The second assumption is that God possesses all and only pure perfections.

Both assumptions are false, for God possesses some properties that are not imperfections, mixed perfections, or pure perfections. Consider, for example, artificial properties such as the property of "either being in this room or not being divisible by 4," negative properties such

10. Or, at least, they are necessarily instantiated if God necessarily exists.
11. John of Damascus, *Writings*, trans. Frederic H. Chase, Jr. (Washington, D.C.: Catholic University of America Press, 1958), p. 173.
12. *SCG* I, 42, 3.

as "not being a frog," intentional properties like "being thought of by Anselm," and relational properties like "is simultaneous with." God has these properties. But while they entail no limitation or imperfection (and so are neither imperfections nor mixed perfections), they are not perfections and are therefore not pure perfections.

One could, of course, argue that properties of this sort are not "real" properties (that is, do not genuinely characterize the beings that have them) and that the first assumption would be more accurately expressed as "All *real* properties can be exhaustively divided into the appropriate subclasses." But even this appears to be false. For consider the property "is the ultimate cause of my existence." This property appears to be a real property, but while God has it, it appears to be not a perfection but rather a contingent *expression* of a (pure) perfection, namely, the exercise of creative power. (God is perhaps better for exercising creative power, but he is not better for having created *me*.) But neither is it a limitation or privation (though it is not, of course, a *full* or *complete* expression of the relevant divine perfection). Nor does it appear to be a mixed perfection. (God's creating a world containing William Wainwright precludes his creating worlds that lack this feature, but it entails no inherent limitation in his creative abilities.) It would appear to follow that (*a*) some real properties are not imperfections, mixed perfections, or pure perfections; and (*b*) many of God's real properties are not pure perfections. God possesses not only artificial, negative, intentional, and relational properties but also a number of real though contingent properties[13] that are expressions of his perfections.[14] Although these properties entail no imperfection, they cannot be pure perfections because they are not perfections. Both of the assumptions on which the argument appears to rest would thus seem to be false.

13. The tradition argues that properties like "knows that I am the author of this paper" or "is the cause of my existence" are not real properties of God (though God really has them, i.e., it is true that God stands in these relations to me). This position appears to me to be not only implausible but incoherent. Knowing and acting are (as Hartshorne has pointed out) paradigm cases of "real" properties.

14. Are the former expressions of perfections? For example, couldn't God's not being a frog be regarded as an expression of his transcendence of space, time, and matter? Perhaps it could but (*a*) it is not clear that this maneuver will work with respect to such properties as "is thought of by Anselm," or even "is simultaneous with" (although the latter could perhaps be regarded as an expression of his eternity or omnipresence). Furthermore, (*b*) "not being a frog" (as distinguished from *God's* not being a frog) is not *itself* an expression of a perfection. (To suppose that it was would be to suppose that everything *other* than frogs had a common goodmaking property of which "not being a frog" was the expression.) By contrast, it is plausible to suppose that "is the ultimate cause of my existence" is itself an expression of a perfection, namely, creative power.

D

The arguments that have been examined in this section are subject to a common difficulty—that God appears to possess some of his properties contingently. The question to be asked at this point is whether two gods could be distinguished on the basis of a difference in their contingent properties. It is clear that some contingent properties will not serve our purpose. "Knows that Jones exists" would (in a world containing Jones) be a property of any omniscient being. "Creates Smith" would (in a world containing Smith) be a property of any creator. Perhaps all of God's real but contingent properties are expressions of his knowledge, goodness, and creative power. And perhaps it is not possible for two gods to exhibit different expressions of these attributes: two omniscient beings would know the same things; being supremely good, their appreciations and valuations (for example, loving Peter) would presumably be identical, and each would be the creative ground of everything that exists. Perhaps, then, two perfect beings could not be distinguished on the basis of a difference in their contingent properties.

The fact remains that the arguments that we have examined in this section are unsound because they fail to recognize that God does appear to have (real) contingent properties. Furthermore, there seems to be no general principle that would preclude the possibility that the type of contingent properties that God can have could be used to distinguish two gods. I conclude that the sort of argument examined in this section is unpromising.

III

Are there sound arguments for God's essential unicity? It seems to me that there are.

A

If it is necessarily true that God's causal activity is the necessary and sufficient condition of the existence of everything else, then there are at least three reasons why God might be thought to be unique. For if there were two gods, it would seem that (a) neither would be the ground of the world, (b) God would be self-caused, and (c) God would not be self-existent.

Consider, first, the following argument.

(1) Necessarily, if anything is God, its creative volition is the necessary and sufficient causal condition of the existence of every other concrete object. Suppose that

(2) Contingent beings exist and there are two gods. It follows that

(3) Each is a necessary and sufficient causal condition of the existence of the set of contingent beings. (From 1 and 2.) Therefore,

(4) The first is a sufficient causal condition of the existence of the set of contingent beings. (From 3.) Hence

(5) The second is not a necessary causal condition of the existence of the set of contingent beings. (From 4.) Again,

(6) The first is a necessary causal condition of the existence of the set of contingent beings. (From 3.) Hence

(7) The second is not a sufficient causal condition of the existence of the set of contingent beings. (From 6.) Therefore,

(8) The second is neither a necessary nor a sufficient causal condition of the existence of the set of contingent beings. (From 5 and 7.)

A similar argument will show that

(9) The first is neither a necessary nor a sufficient causal condition of the existence of the set of contingent beings. It follows that

(10) Neither god is either a necessary or a sufficient causal condition of the existence of the set of contingent beings. (From 8 and 9.) Hence

(11) If contingent beings existed and there were two gods, each would be a necessary and sufficient causal condition of the existence of the set of contingent beings and neither would be a necessary and sufficient causal condition of the existence of the set of contingent beings. (From 2–10.)

But since

(12) The consequent is absurd,

(13) It is impossible that contingent beings exist and there are two gods. (From 11 and 12.) Thus

(14) If contingent beings exist, there cannot be two gods. (From 13.)[15]

Furthermore, if Hartshorne and others are correct in thinking that some contingent being or other must exist, no possible world contains two gods, that is, God is necessarily unique.

15. For an argument of this sort, see Scotus, *Philosophical Writings*, trans. Allan Wolter (Edinburgh: Thomas Nelson, 1962), p. 87.

Consider, next, the following argument.

(1) Necessarily, if anything is God, its creative volition is the necessary and sufficient causal condition of the existence of every other concrete object. Hence

(15) If there were two gods, the will of each would be the necessary and sufficient causal condition of the existence of the other. (From 1.)

(16) The type of causality in question is transitive. (If x is a necessary and sufficient causal condition of y, and y is a necessary and sufficient causal condition of z, then x is a necessary and sufficient causal condition of z.) Therefore,

(17) If there were two gods, the will of each would be the necessary and sufficient causal condition of its own existence. (From 15 and 16.)

(18) Nothing can be a cause of itself in the sense in question, that is, nothing can be such that its creative volition is a necessary and sufficient causal condition of its own existence. Therefore,

(19) There cannot be two gods. (From 17 and 18.)

Finally, consider this argument.

(1) Necessarily, if anything is God, its creative volition is the necessary and sufficient causal condition of the existence of every other concrete object.

(15) If there were two gods, the will of each would be the necessary and sufficient causal condition of the existence of the other. (From 1.)

(20) Necessarily, anything that is self-existent is such that its existence is not caused by another being. Hence

(21) If there were two gods, then neither would be self-existent. (From 15 and 20.)

(22) Necessarily, if anything is God, it is self-existent. Therefore,

(23) If there were two gods, then neither would be God. (From 21 and 22.)

(24) It is impossible for there to be two gods, neither of which is God. Therefore,

(19) It is impossible for there to be two gods. (From 23 and 24.)

Each argument hinges on the truth of proposition 1, which asserts that God's creative volition is both a necessary and a sufficient causal condition of the existence of every other concrete object. But if "sufficient condition" is taken in a strong sense, namely, that x is a sufficient condition of y if and only if *given x alone, y* exists or occurs, there are reasons for thinking that (1) is false. Suppose, for example, that Abel will exist if and only if Adam and Eve freely copulate, and that Adam and Eve would freely copulate if they were created. By creating Adam and Eve, God brings about Abel's existence. Furthermore, given the truth of the relevant subjunctive conditional, there is a clear sense in which God's doing so is not only a necessary but a sufficient causal condition of Abel's existence. For it is true that if God creates Adam and Eve, Adam and Eve will beget Abel. It is not, however, sufficient in the strong sense, namely, that God's intention alone is sufficient to ensure Abel's existence. For the latter also depends upon what Adam and Eve will freely decide to do. Theistic intuitions clearly support the claim that it is necessarily true that God's creative volitions are a causally sufficient condition of the existence of every other concrete object in at least a weak sense. It is less clear that they support the claim that it is necessarily true that God's creative volitions are a sufficient causal condition of the existence of every other concrete object in the *strong* sense.

But if the first argument is to be valid, "sufficient condition" must be construed in the strong sense. The inferences from (4) to (5) and from (6) to (7) are legitimate only upon the assumption that if a cause is sufficient to produce an effect, no other cause is a necessary condition of that effect. This is true only if a causally sufficient condition is a condition that is such that it alone is sufficient to produce its effect. (Ingesting a large quantity of arsenic is, in a standard sense, causally sufficient to produce death, since it is true that, if one ingests a large quantity of arsenic, he will die. But many other conditions are causally necessary if this event is to take place—that one's constitution is normal, that one is not given an antidote, and so forth.) The other two arguments are valid even if "sufficient condition" is used in a weaker sense, for there appears to be no sense in which God's existence can be said to be causally dependent upon anything else or upon his own creative volition.[16]

16. If each god's existence depends upon the volition of the other and those volitions are free, then each god's volition is a sufficient condition of its own existence only in the weak sense. But even this is impossible, for (to use Alvin Plantinga's terminology) nothing can strongly *or weakly* actualize its own existence. It is perhaps worth noting that this distinction will not relevantly affect the truth of (16); (16) is true if "sufficient condition" is read throughout in either the strong or weak sense. "X is a sufficient condition of y (in the strong sense)" and "y is a sufficient condition of z (in the weak sense)" does not entail "x is a sufficient condition of z (in the strong sense)" but it does entail "x is a sufficient condition of z (in the weak sense)."

The first argument is therefore weaker than the others. It is valid only if "sufficient condition" is construed in a strong sense, but if "sufficient condition" is construed in a strong sense, there are reasons for thinking its first premise is false. Furthermore, the first argument does not show that God is necessarily unique but shows only that if contingent beings exist, only one god exists. The other two arguments are valid regardless of whether "sufficient condition" is used in a strong or weak sense, and, since they show that God's uniqueness is entailed both by the (logical) fact that nothing is self-caused and by one of God's essential attributes (namely, his aseity), they show that God is necessarily unique.

But it would be a mistake to dismiss even the first argument too quickly. Traditional theists have often supposed that God's decrees are, in the strong sense, causally sufficient and not merely necessary conditions of the existence of every other concrete object. If some creatures are free, then it is by no means clear that this is true. But even theists who are indeterminists would presumably endorse

(1′) Necessarily, if any x is God, then for every concrete object distinct from x, the activity of x is causally necessary for its existence, and if there are in fact one or more contingent beings distinct from x, then the activity of x is causally sufficient (in the strong sense) for the existence of at least one of them.

Proposition 1′ is sufficient to yield our conclusion.[17] For if the first god is a causally necessary condition of the existence of every other concrete object, then the second god is not the causally sufficient condition (in the strong sense) of the existence of *any* contingent being, and vice versa. And similarly, if the first god is the causally sufficient condition (in the strong sense) of the existence of at least one contingent being, then the second god is not a causally necessary condition of the existence of at least one concrete object that is distinct from himself, and vice versa.[18]

Furthermore,[19] if God is a necessary being (that is, if God exists and is God in every possible world), then the logical possibility of contingent

17. This was pointed out to me by Morris.
18. Proposition 1′ is also sufficient to generate the conclusions of the other two arguments, for "causally necessary condition" is transitive. The proposition entails that the creative volition of each god is a causally necessary condition of the existence of the other and is thus a causally necessary condition of its own existence.
19. As Morris also pointed out to me.

beings is sufficient to generate the conclusion that there can be only one god. For consider:

(1') Necessarily, if any *x* is God, then for every concrete object distinct from *x,* the activity of *x* is causally necessary for its existence, and if there are in fact one or more contingent beings distinct from *x,* then the activity of *x* is causally sufficient (in the strong sense) for the existence of at least one of them. Suppose that

(25) Contingent beings are possible and there are two gods. It follows that

(26) There is a possible world *w* in which contingent beings exist (from 25), and that, because each god is necessary,

(27) Both gods exist in *w.* (From 25.) Hence

(28) Each god is a necessary causal condition of the existence of each contingent being in *w,* and each god is the sufficient causal condition (in the strong sense) of at least one contingent being in *w.* (From 1', 26, and 27.) But, as we have seen,

(29) It is impossible that each god is a necessary causal condition of the existence of each contingent being in *w* and each god is the sufficient causal condition (in the strong sense) of at least one contingent being in *w.* (For if one god is a necessary causal condition of the existence of each contingent being in *w,* the other is not the sufficient causal condition—in the strong sense—of any of them.) Hence

(30) It is impossible that contingent beings are possible and there are two gods, that is, it is necessarily true that if contingent beings are possible, it is false that there are two gods. (From 1' through 29. If *p* together with one or more necessary truths entails *q* and *q* is impossible, *p* is impossible.) But

(31) It is logically possible that contingent beings exist. (For they do exist.) Hence

(32) It is necessarily true that it is logically possible that contingent beings exist. (From 31. What is possible is necessarily possible.) Therefore,

(33) It is necessarily false that there are two gods. (From 30 and 32.)

B

Al-Ghāzali argues that there cannot be two gods, for "were there two gods and one of them resolved on a course of action, the second would be either obliged to aid him and [*sic*] thereby demonstrating that he was a subordinate being and not an all-powerful god, or would be able to oppose and resist thereby demonstrating that he was the all-powerful and the first weak and deficient, not an all-powerful god."[20] The argument from omnipotence can be formulated as follows.

(1) Necessarily, it is possible for the wills of distinct persons to conflict. (This appears to be included in the notion of being a distinct person.) Therefore,

(2) Necessarily, if there are two distinct, essentially omnipotent persons, their wills can conflict. (From 1.)

(3) It is necessarily false that the wills of two omnipotent persons conflict. Therefore,

(4) It is necessarily false that the wills of two essentially omnipotent persons can conflict. (From 3. If there is a possible world in which their wills can conflict, then there must be a possible world in which they are both omnipotent and their wills do conflict.) Therefore,

(5) It is impossible for there to be two distinct, essentially omnipotent persons. (From 2 and 4.) It follows that if

(6) It is necessarily true that omnipotence is an essential attribute of God, then

(7) It is impossible for there to be two gods. (From 5 and 6.)

Premise 3 is proved in this way.

(8) Necessarily, if the will of an omnipotent person conflicts with another person's will, the latter's will is thwarted by the former's will. (If it was not, the omnipotent person would not be omnipotent.)

(9) Necessarily, if a person's will is thwarted by another's will, then that person is not omnipotent. Therefore,

(10) Necessarily, if there were two omnipotent persons and their wills conflicted, then (since each of their wills would be thwarted) neither would be omnipotent. (From 8 and 9.)[21]

20. *Al-Ghāzali's Tract on Dogmatic Theology*, trans. A. L. Tibawi (London: Luzac, 1965), p. 40. For a more carefully formulated version of the argument, see Scotus, *Philosophical Writings*, pp. 89–91.

21. There is a possible confusion that ought to be avoided. Louis Werner argues ("Some Omnipotent Beings," *Crítica* 5 [May 1971]: 55–72) that if one omnipotent being wills that everything be green all over while another omnipotent being wills that everything be red all over, then, even though both wills are frustrated (since if each is omnipotent, neither gets its way), it does not follow that either being is not omnipotent. This does not follow, according to Werner, because willing that everything be green (or red) when

(11) It is impossible for there to be two omnipotent persons neither of which is omnipotent. Therefore,

(3) It is impossible for the wills of two omnipotent persons to conflict. (From 10 and 11.)

I have three comments to make about this argument. (*a*) The fourth step is frequently omitted in formulations of the argument. Because (3) entails (4), its inclusion is not strictly necessary. Nevertheless, the failure to clearly distinguish between (3) and (4), or to state (4), seems to me to have sometimes obscured the force of the argument. Persons might be distinct even though their wills never conflicted. But if (1) is true, they cannot be distinct if it is *impossible* for their wills to conflict. What must be shown therefore is not just that the wills of two (essentially) omnipotent persons do not conflict but that they *cannot* do so.

(*b*) Since we are trying to show that the wills of two gods *cannot* conflict, it is crucial that the argument address itself to the implications of the concept of *essential* omnipotence. If two omnipotent persons are essentially omnipotent, then the possibility of conflict is excluded. But if at least one of them is not essentially omnipotent, it is not. For in that case, there could be a possible world in which their wills do conflict though (since it is impossible for both of their wills to be effectual) at least one of them will not be omnipotent in that world. While (3) entails (4), (3) does not entail

(4′) It is necessarily false that the wills of two omnipotent persons can conflict.

If there is a possible world in which the wills of two omnipotent persons *x* and *y* can conflict, then there must be a possible world in which the wills of *x* and *y* do conflict. But if at least one of them is not essentially omnipotent, it does not follow that both *x* and *y* are omnipotent in that world. Hence, the fact that there are no possible worlds in which there are two omnipotent persons with conflicting wills is not sufficient to show that there is no possible world in which there are two omnipotent beings whose wills can conflict.

---

an omnipotent being has willed that everything be red (or green) involves willing what is logically impossible, and it is generally agreed that the fact that a being cannot effectually will what is logically impossible does not count against that being's omnipotence. But this will not do, for what the omnipotent being wills is not that "everything is green (or red) when an omnipotent being has willed that everything be red (or green)" but that "everything is green (or red)," and the latter is neither intrinsically impossible nor impossible for an omnipotent being.

(*c*) The first premise is often unstated, but it, too, is essential to the argument. Thomas Morris has suggested, however, that all that is required for persons to be distinct is that it be possible that their wills differ.

What would it be like for two persons *x* and *y* to be such that, while it is possible for their wills to differ, it is not possible for them to conflict? Suppose that *x* can only do *A, B,* and *C* and *y* can only do three quite different tasks *D, E,* and *F.* Assuming that one can only will to do what one has the power to do,[22] it is possible for the wills of *x* and *y* to differ even though it is not possible for their wills to conflict, and yet we would not, I think, hesitate to speak of them as different persons. It follows that, strictly speaking, (1) is true only where the wills of distinct persons at least partly range over the same set of contingencies. However, in the case that is of interest to us, this condition is met, for if the powers of *x* and *y* are limited to different and restricted ranges of contingencies, then neither is a plausible candidate for an omnipotent being.

The significant question is whether it is possible for there to be two persons whose wills range over the same set of contingencies but who are such that, while their wills can differ, they cannot conflict. Morris thinks that this is possible and envisages a case in which it is impossible for *x* to will *A* and *y* to will not-*A* (or vice-versa) but in which it is possible for *x* to will *A* and for *y* neither to will *A* nor to will not-*A* (or vice versa). Their wills could thus differ even though they could not conflict.

Is this possibility sufficient to ensure distinctness of persons? It seems to me that it is not. My intuition is that, if I somehow *cannot* will anything that is opposed to what some other person wills, my selfhood or identity as a separate person is endangered. If, then, this impossibility is logical or metaphysical and not merely contingent, the threat to my independent identity is more severe. The necessity in question (namely, that *x* and *y* cannot will opposed things) *may* be compatible with the existence of two distinct consciousnesses and two distinct wills, but it is not clear to me that the latter are sufficient for the existence of two distinct *persons.* (Consider in this connection cases of multiple personality, split brains, and so forth, where we have something like the latter but hesitate to say that we are *literally* dealing with two different persons.)

Furthermore, even if the possibility of difference were sufficient to ensure independent identity (which I doubt), it is by no means clear

---

22. One can will to do something that one cannot do if one mistakenly thinks that one can do it, but mistakes cannot be ascribed to potential gods.

that the wills of two essentially omnipotent beings could differ in the way Morris suggests. For suppose they can. Then, where s is some contingent state of affairs that is within the range of omnipotence, x can make y impotent with respect to s (and vice versa). For even though it is intrinsically possible for y to determine whether or not s will occur, x, merely by willing s, makes it impossible for y to will not-s. That is, x, as it were, takes power over s out of y's hands. And yet one would think that if y is essentially omnipotent and s is within the range of its power, no (contingent) circumstance of this sort[23] could make it impotent with respect to s.[24]

C

According to Ockham,[25] "God" can be understood in at least two ways. By "God" one may mean "something more noble and more perfect than anything else besides Him," or one may mean "that than which nothing is more noble and more perfect."[26] If "God" is construed in the first sense, there can only be one god, for consider the following argument.

(1) Necessarily, if any being is God, it is more perfect than any other being. Therefore,

(2) Necessarily, if there were two distinct beings and each were god, the first would be more perfect than the second and the second would be more perfect than the first. (From 1.) But

(3) It is impossible for there to be two beings, each of which is more perfect than the other. Therefore,

(4) It is impossible for there to be two gods. (From 2 and 3.)[27]

23. Contingent circumstances can make God impotent. For example, that e occurs at t makes God impotent with respect to e's occurrence or nonoccurrence at any time after t—but this seems to involve a rather different sort of consideration.

24. This line of thought was suggested to me by Scotus's third argument from omnipotence (*Philosophical Writings*, pp. 90–91).

25. *Philosophical Writings*, trans. Philotheus Boehner (Indianapolis: Bobbs-Merrill, 1964), pp. 139–40.

26. The range of comparison could be either all actual beings or all possible beings. I will assume that it is all possible beings, for it appears to be a conceptual truth that nothing *could* be "more noble and more perfect" than God.

27. Cf. Aquinas: "It is not possible that there be two highest goods since that which is said by superabundance is found in only one being" (*SCG* I, 42, 2). The argument is very ancient. According to R. M. Grant, it was attributed to Xenophanes in a "Graeco-Roman treatise ascribed to Aristotle" (*The Early Christian Doctrine of God* [Charlottesville: University Press of Virginia, 1966], p. 107).

But if "God" is construed in the second sense, Ockham thinks that it cannot be shown that there can only be one god, for it is not clear why there could not be two equally perfect beings each of which was such that no actual or possible being surpassed it.

It might be thought that Ockham is mistaken. If there were two unsurpassable beings, A and B, then it seems that there would be something that would surpass either one of them, namely, both of them (A + B surpasses A and A + B surpasses B), for, as Scotus says, "any perfection that can exist in numerically different things is more perfect if it exists in several than if it exists merely in one."[28] Since nothing can surpass an unsurpassable being, it follows that there cannot be two unsurpassable beings.

But this is unconvincing. In saying that God is unsurpassable, we are surely saying no more than that it is impossible for there to be a *being* that is greater than God: we are not saying that it is impossible for there to be a *state of affairs* (such as the existence of God together with the existence of something else) that would be more valuable than the state of affairs consisting solely in God's existence. (In spite of what has sometimes been said, it would seem that the existence of God together with the existence of the world he has created is a more valuable state of affairs than the state of affairs consisting in God's existence alone.) Since two unsurpassable things are not a being, the argument fails.

But whether it is or is not possible for there to be two unsurpassable beings, it does appear to be impossible for there to be two gods. For it would seem to be a conceptual truth that God is unsurpassable. It follows that if there were two gods, each would be unsurpassable. But there cannot be two unsurpassable beings each of which *is God*. For part of what is meant in speaking of something as God is that its nature is such that it is an appropriate object of total devotion and unconditional commitment.[29] If, however, there were two unsurpassable beings, our devotion and commitment should be divided between them. (As Scotus says, if there were two infinite goods, "an orderly will . . . could not be perfectly satisfied with but one infinite good.")[30] Since they are equally perfect, it would be inappropriate to be totally devoted and unconditionally committed to either one of them. It follows that neither would

28. Scotus, *Philosophical Writings*, p. 88.

29. Unconditional commitment and total devotion is not exclusive commitment and devotion. Faithful Christians, for example, are committed to their neighbors. But this commitment is incorporated in their commitment to God, while their commitment to God is not incorporated in any other commitment. (Cf. Robert Adams's chapter in this volume.)

30. Scotus, *Philosophical Writings*, p. 87.

be God. Therefore, if it is a conceptual truth that God is an unsurpassable being, he must be unique.

There is really no need to introduce the concept of unsurpassability in the first place, for God's uniqueness follows directly from the fact that he is an appropriate object of total devotion and unconditional commitment.[31]

Consider the following argument.

(5) God is by definition a being who is worthy of total devotion and unconditional commitment. Therefore,

(6) Necessarily, if there were two gods, there would be two beings each of which was worthy of total devotion and unconditional commitment. (From 5.) Therefore,

(7) Necessarily, if there were two gods, then each of them ought to be an object of these attitudes. (From 6.) But

(8) Necessarily, if we ought to adopt these attitudes, then we can do so. Hence,

(9) Necessarily, if there were two gods, we could be totally devoted and unconditionally committed to each of them. (From 7 and 8.) However,

(10) It is impossible to be totally devoted and unconditionally committed to two distinct beings. Therefore,

(11) It is impossible for there to be two gods. (From 9 and 10.)

I have two comments to make about this argument.

(*a*) It rests upon two assumptions—first, that if a being is worthy of worship (total devotion and unconditioned commitment), then it ought to be worshiped; second, that the obligation to worship it is indefeasible.

A proposition of the form "*x* deserves *y*" does not always entail a proposition of the form "one ought to contribute to *x*'s having *y*." While it may be true that the Detroit Tigers deserve to win the pennant, it does not follow that I have an obligation to promote, encourage, aid, or abet their doing so. Nevertheless, the entailment does hold in some cases. For example, "*s* is admirable (deserves to be admired)" entails

---

31. While no explicit appeal to the concept of unsurpassability is necessary, being an appropriate object of theistic attitudes and being unsurpassable are conceptually connected, for a being must be unsurpassable if it is to be an appropriate object of these attitudes. Furthermore, since a being would not be an appropriate object of theistic attitudes if another unsurpassable being existed, it follows that, if an appropriate object of these attitudes exists, no other unsurpassable being exists and that God is therefore necessarily *greater* than any other actual being.

"one (that is, anyone) ought to admire it." Furthermore, being worthy of worship appears to be analogous to being admirable in at least one relevant respect. The obligation to promote, encourage, aid, or abet Detroit's winning the pennant depends upon one's relation to the Tigers (whether one is a Detroit player, for example, or a Tiger fan). One's obligation to admire something that is genuinely admirable does not essentially depend upon its relation to the person who has that obligation. I ought, for example, to admire a deed of heroism whether or not I am its beneficiary. Now it seems to me that being worthy of worship imposes similar obligations—that whether or not a being should be worshiped depends not only on its relation to me (that it is my creator or redeemer, for example) but on its intrinsic qualities (its "excellency," to use a term of Jonathan Edwards) and that the latter is sufficient to impose the obligation. Furthermore, if I have such an obligation, it would appear to be indefeasible. The nature of the obligation appears to be such that it cannot be defeated by any other obligation. Nor can one excuse one's lack of devotion or commitment to God by pleading inability.

If this reasoning is correct, then (6) entails (7). Furthermore, because the obligations referred to in (7) are actual obligations, (7) entails (8). "I ought to return John's gun" (since I promised to do so) and "I ought not to return John's gun" (since he is not in his right mind) do not entail "I can both return the gun and not return it." But in this case neither obligation is indefeasible and, in the circumstances envisaged, the only actual obligation I have is the obligation not to return the gun. Because "I ought to return the gun and I ought not to return the gun" does not entail "I have an actual obligation to both return and not return the gun," there is no reason to infer that I can do both. By contrast, both of the obligations referred to in (7) are indefeasible and are therefore actual and not merely prima facie obligations. Now while one can have a prima facie obligation to do something that one is unable to do, it is by no means clear that one can have an actual obligation to do something that one is unable to do. Step 7 appears, then, to entail that I can worship both deities.[32]

32. I am assuming that (a) if an obligation is indefeasible, it is an actual obligation; (b) if O is an actual obligation and O' is an actual obligation, then (O and O') is an actual obligation; and (c) if O is an actual obligation, then I can do O. One might object that (d) "one has an actual obligation to do x and y" does not entail "one can do x and y" precisely *because* (e) one can have incompatible actual obligations. (Cf. Quinn's paper in this volume.) But (e) appears to me to be far less obvious than principle (c), to which it is an objection. For a recent attempt to show that "ought" does not entail "can," see Walter Sinnott-Armstrong, "'Ought' Conversationally Implies 'can,'" *Philosophical Review* 93

(*b*) Proposition 10 could be challenged in two ways. Morris has objected that it would be possible to be unconditionally committed to each of two distinct beings provided that their wills were necessarily harmonious, for, if their wills were necessarily harmonious, they could not require of us conflicting acts. It seems to me, however, that this objection should be discounted for, as I have already argued (section 3B), the wills of distinct person are necessarily opposable.

It is perhaps less clear why devotion cannot be divided between two beings. The answer, I think, is that the sort of devotion appropriate to God involves (among other things) centering one's life in God (cf. Robert Adams's chapter in this volume), and while one can center one's life in *x*-and-*y*, one cannot center one's life in *x* and *also* center one's life in *y*. The devotion that God requires would thus appear to be inherently indivisible.

D

While the unicity proofs that have been examined in this section were designed to show that there can be no more than one god in any particular possible world, they can be employed to show that there can be no more than one god in all possible worlds, that is, that it is true not only that only one actual being can be God but also that only one possible being can be God. In order to show this we need only add that God is a necessary being, that is, that God exists and is God in all possible worlds. Given this assumption, it follows that if there were two distinct beings each of whom was God in some possible world, each would be God in all possible worlds. But, as our arguments have shown, it is impossible for there to be two gods in the same possible world. It is therefore impossible for there to be two distinct beings each of whom is God in some possible world; that is, only one possible being can be God.

E

The uniqueness proofs that were examined in section 1 and in this section do not preclude the existence of the Trinity.

(*a*) Since the unity of the cosmos is compatible with the existence of several cooperating causal agents, it is a fortiori compatible with the existence of the Trinity.

(1984): 249–61. If, however, an actual obligation is not merely an obligation to which no other prima facie obligations are opposed but an obligation that arises from the "*whole nature*" of the act—that is, depends on "*all* the morally significant kinds it is an instance of" (W. D. Ross, *The Right and the Good* [Oxford: Oxford University Press, 1930], p. 20)—and if, as it seems to be, "being an act which one cannot perform" is a morally significant kind, it is not clear that his arguments and counterexamples are persuasive.

(*b*) The first set of arguments considered in this section depends upon a common assumption, namely, that God is (necessarily) the cause of every other concrete object. The second and third arguments in the set can only be deployed against the Trinity if we assume that the hypostases are distinct concrete objects in the relevant sense. The repudiation of this assumption appears to be implied by the Church's rejection of tritheism. The first argument in the set can only be deployed against the Trinity if we assume that the relevant attribute, namely, being the causally necessary and sufficient condition of the existence of contingent beings,[33] is an attribute of each person rather than of the Trinity as a whole (that is, of the Trinity considered as a single concrete entity). While some Christian theologians seem to have endorsed this assumption,[34] the more common view has been that the divine intellect and will are aspects of a (single) divine essence that subsists in three hypostases; it is false that there are three distinct creative wills and therefore false that there are three distinct creative wills each of which is a necessary and sufficient causal condition of the existence of contingent beings. Since the three arguments in the first set cannot be deployed against at least some orthodox conceptions of the Trinity, it is reasonable to conclude that the argument from God's causal activity does not preclude the existence of the Trinity.

(*c*) The omnipotence proof does not rule out the existence of the Trinity, for the hypostases are not distinct persons in the nontechnical sense of "person" employed in the argument. They are not distinct persons in the ordinary sense of "person" since their wills cannot conflict. Either there is only one will (which is part of the one *ousia*) or the (distinct) wills of the three hypostases necessarily concur.

(*d*) Our last argument precludes the existence of the Trinity only if each person is, in abstraction from the others, an appropriate object of total devotion and unconditional commitment. In spite of the aberrations of some Christians, it is reasonably clear that the object of the Christian's ultimate concern is the triad and not one or more of the persons considered in isolation. Christian attitudes towards the Father, for example, are inseparable from Christian attitudes towards the Son. Christ is worshiped *as* the son of the Father, and the Father is worshiped *as* the one who fully reveals himself in Christ. It follows that Christians are only committed to regarding the *triad* as the appropriate object of theistic attitudes and that the argument from the appropri-

33. Or a causally necessary condition of every contingent being and the causally sufficient condition (in the strong sense) of at least one of them.

34. The nineteenth-century social trinitarians explicitly held a position of this sort. It is perhaps implicit in the positions of many second- and third-century church fathers.

ateness of these attitudes cannot therefore be used to show that a trinity of persons is impossible.

F

Most Old Testament scholars think that the religion of the early Israelites was neither monotheistic nor polytheistic but "monolatrous." While the existence of other gods was not denied, Israel was to worship no god but Yahweh. In virtue of the Mosaic covenant, Yahweh became the "confederate god" of Israel, and they became his people. This was monolatry and not monotheism. It was the selection of one god out of many for exclusive worship by a particular group as a group."[35] In part, "this is the characteristic position taken by a national religion: in practice, only the gods of one's own nation are significant." Nevertheless, it was unique, for "one of the distinguishing characteristics of the Israelite religion is the belief that there are not several gods of Israel, but only one, Yahweh, who claims exclusive devotion."[36]

There are no unambiguous assertions of monotheism from the pre-exilic period. On the contrary, when Naaman (2 Kings 5) takes some of the soil of Canaan back to Damascus, he is assuming that the "deity could be worshipped only in the area where his power held sway."[37] "1 Samuel 26:19 says that outside Israel David would have to serve other gods." "Judges 11:24 presupposes . . . that Chemosh is the god of the Moabites just as Yahweh is the god of Israel."[38] On the other hand, Elijah asserts the powerlessness of Baal, Amos insists upon Yahweh's power over the surrounding nations, and many preexilic psalms exhalt the incomparability of Yahweh's power and majesty. "There is no god to compare with you, no achievement to compare with yours" (86:8). "Yahweh, God of Sabaoth, who is like you?" (89:8). "For Yahweh is a great God, a greater king than all other gods" (95:3). "For you are Yahweh most high over the world, far transcending all other gods" (97:9). "I have learnt for myself that Yahweh is great, that our Lord

35. T. J. Meek, *Hebrew Origins* (New York: Harper Torchbooks, 1960), p. 215, quoted in Frank E. Eakin, *The Religion and Culture of Israel* (Boston: Allyn & Bacon, 1971), p. 108.
36. Helmer Ringgren, *Israelite Religion* (Philadelphia: Fortress Press, 1966), p. 67. The shema (Deut. 6:4) literally reads "Hear, O Israel, Yahweh our god Yahweh alone [one]," which permits several readings. Exod. 20:3, which is sometimes translated "You shall have no other gods besides me," is equally ambiguous. (The word translated as "besides" can also be translated as "before," "in addition to," "together with," "beyond," or "above.") As Eakin says, the thrust of the demand made in the decalogue is that "Yahweh makes exclusive claim upon Israel . . . he will tolerate no divided allegiance" (*Religion and Culture of Israel*, pp. 70 and 108).
37. Eakin, *Religion and Culture of Israel*, pp. 108–9.
38. Ringgren, *Israelite Religion*, p. 66.

surpasses all other gods" (135:5). Notice that while the incomparability of Yahweh's power and greatness are stressed in these passages, it is presupposed that other gods exist. Even texts which *could* be interpreted monotheistically are ambiguous, for example, Ps. 96:4–5a: "Yahweh is great . . . he is to be feared beyond all gods. Nothingness, all the gods of the nations." The first explicit affirmations of monotheism are found in Deutero-Isaiah: "Thus says Israel's King . . . 'I am the first and the last; there is no other god besides me'" (Isa. 44:6; cf. 45:5).

But even though monotheism is not *explicitly* formulated until after the Exile, biblical scholars agree that the religion of Israel was "incipiently" monotheistic from its (Mosaic) beginning. But why is this the case? Three things appear to me to be decisive. In the first place, "we encounter very early the idea that Yahweh is the creator of heaven and earth (Gen. 14:22; cf. also Gen. 2:4 [J])."[39] Now, it is true that polytheistic religions frequently include a creator in their pantheons. Furthermore, these creators are often relatively unimportant. Nevertheless, there does appear to be a natural transition from the claim that a god has created heaven and earth to the claim that he is lord of heaven and earth, and from there to monotheism. In the second place, there are, as we have seen, "repeated affirmations . . . that Yahweh is the greatest and mightiest of the gods."[40] Finally, the religion of Israel is, from its beginning, unique in demanding exclusive worship; only Yahweh is to be worshiped by Israel. The extension of this idea to the idea that Yahweh alone is to be worshiped by everyone, while perhaps not inevitable, is certainly natural. If these considerations are correct, then the characteristics of Yahweh that eventually led to the assertion that Yahweh is the only god were his creation of heaven and earth, his power and greatness, and his right to exclusive worship. Now, if the contentions of this paper are sound, the most successful arguments for monotheism are those that proceed from God's causal activity, from his omnipotence, and from the claim that he alone is worthy of worship, total devotion, and unconditional commitment. It would appear to follow that the most powerful arguments for God's unicity correspond to those features of Israel's religion that historically led to monotheism. This suggests that the arguments in question can be appropriately regarded as philosophical explications or "approximations" (Ricoeur) of a faith that from its inception was implicitly monotheistic. The argu-

39. Ibid., p. 67.
40. Ibid., p. 99.

ments, if sound, stand on their own merits, but they are rooted in the texture of biblical faith.

IV

The arguments that were considered in section 3 rest upon certain intuitions about God's nature—that he is the necessary and sufficient causal condition of the existence of every other concrete object, that he is essentially omnipotent, and that he is worthy of total devotion and unconditioned commitment. In commenting on an earlier version of this paper, Morris granted that monotheism follows from my premises but argued that the premises are question begging. Circularity could only be avoided by basing the arguments on more general theistic intuitions, that is, on theistic intuitions that are neither explicitly monotheistic nor explicitly polytheistic. For example, arguments of the sort found in section 3A would not be question begging if they were based on the intuition that nondivine things are dependent on divine things—an intuition shared by both polytheists and monotheists. But unfortunately this intuition is not sufficient to establish my conclusion, for (*a*) it does not entail that each god is a necessary and sufficient causal condition of the existence of each contingent thing and (*b*) it does not entail that each god is a cause of the others. Similarly, the sort of argument found in section 3C would not be circular if it were based on the more general intuition that any divine being is worthy of a devotion that is not divided and shared with any devotion to a nondivine being. But, of course, this too is insufficient to yield a monotheistic conclusion. Morris concluded that the prospects for devising noncircular arguments that would establish the truth of monotheism are unpromising.

Are my arguments question begging? Given that the other premises are necessarily true, the suspect premises (A1, B6, and C5) entail my conclusion. In this sense, a monotheistic conclusion is contained in those premises. They are, in other words, implicitly monotheistic. But this is precisely what I have been trying to show. My project was not to convince polytheists that monotheism is true or to help theists who have not yet decided between polytheism or monotheism to resolve their doubts but, more modestly, to show how attributes that are regarded as essential to God and that are not *explictly* monotheistic entail monotheism and, by doing so, to contribute to our understanding of its nature.

But the project that Morris has in mind is undoubtedly more exciting. Could we construct proofs of monotheism that are based on more widely shared intuitions, intuitions shared by polytheists as well as theists? I am not sure, but it appears to me that the most promising route to explore is to pursue the suggestion that monotheism is implicit in the attitudes involved in any sort (polytheistic or monotheistic) of theistic worship.

It is relevant in this connection to call attention to a phenomenon that sometimes occurs in polytheism, namely, that *during* worship the god is treated as if he or she was unlimited and supreme and is given epithets that properly belong to other members of the pantheon.[41] (And it should be noted that "polytheistic" systems that elevate one god or principle to the supreme position and reinterpret the others as its agents or expressions—for example, late Paganism and Hinduism—are, as Ralph Cudworth pointed out, essentially monotheistic.)

My suggestion, however tentative, is this. The religious attitudes that are bound up with theism (whether polytheistic or monotheistic) have a certain inner logic. They tend to lead the devotee to magnify the object of his devotion by denying limitations and adding perfections. The logical limit of this tendency is the ascription of such properties as universal sovereignty and unlimited power, and it is upon these notions that the crucial premises of the arguments found in sections 3A and 3B depend. The same attitudes have a tendency to lead the devotee to unreservedly commit himself to and center his life on the god to whom he is devoted. I suggest, then, that these more general theistic attitudes can be appealed to in support of the intuitions that underly the key premises of the arguments considered in the last section. Whether these more general intuitions are sufficiently clear to yield a proof is, however, a moot question.

41. This occurred, for example, at a certain stage of Vedic polytheism.

13

God, Creator of Kinds and Possibilities: *Requiescant universalia ante res*

JAMES F. ROSS

Problem: Does God create from a universal domain the divine exemplars? That's so familiar that it seems unimaginable for a theist to disagree.[1] Yet it is inconsistent to say that God works from a domain of kinds and individuals (or exemplars, such as natures, haecceities, individual essences, or complete concepts) lying outside his will, determined by his nature.

For Neoplatonists, God's prismatic self-knowledge "refracts" a universal domain, the divine ideas of all the kinds of things there might be and of all the things of those kinds there might be. These divine ideas provide suitable ranges for a two-name account of predication and a three-tiered extension for quantified modal logic and a treasury of propositions or states of affairs to settle truth values about how things

---

1. Descartes, Ockham, Bradwardine, and Wycliffe all said, from time to time, that possibility and necessity *ad extra* fall within God's will. Some denied divine exemplarism. Descartes did not think there were natural kinds—though I am not sure he did not think there are exemplars of res extensa and res cognitans. We know Ockham, despite his nominalism, was explicit that there are divine exemplars. Bradwardine is said to claim that God created the essences of creatures. I do not know whether he followed that to its natural consequence. And Wycliffe, in *De actibus animae*, says such outlandish things about God's power over possibility as, perhaps, to have held this very view. At the moment, I am not confident in attributing antiexemplarism to any major figure, except to emphasize that for Aquinas there are *rationes* for whatever God can do, but exemplars only for what he makes.

315

might, otherwise, have been.[2] This story turns out to be false and to distort God's power.

First, set-theoretic modal Platonism is formally inconsistent.[3] This has nothing to do with whether the domains are Platonic realities or Augustinian exemplars. It is because the domains are supposed to be maximal, thus violating the prohibition on maximal sets.

Second, it is inconsistent to postulate an EXTERNAL *real relation* of participation or "exemplification" to account for what makes a thing to be of its kind or to be the individual that it is.[4] Take as an example a human: the very thing that, in order to be at all, has to be a human would have to *be* in order to be *made* human.

Suppose God has, by nature, an idea of a finite imitation of his perfection, say, 'being a human', or 'being Socrates'. There would have to be an *external real* relation of 'sharing in' (or 'exemplifying') by the creature. Socrates is constituted to be a human (or Socrates) by sharing in, exemplifying, that divine idea. Either a "bare particular" is the subject of that relation or we have no subject at all, because Socrates is the product of the sharing relation. The idea that a *monadic real* relation (to F) is constitutive of something that is not identical with F, but *only* shares in F, is inconsistent.

The problem here is not that the sharing relation is essential to me and not to the exemplar. It is that the sharing is real and between distinct realities, one of which, Socrates, has to *be* in order to share. To the reply "being," for a contingent thing, is "sharing," I say no; for then either the exemplars and God have no being (because they do not "share") or "being" is used purely equivocally. Besides, that makes "sharing" both the explanation and the result (the outcome).

Third, two-name accounts of predication that "reduce" modally quantified propositions to assertions about named universals (kinds or natures) and individuals are mistaken about predication and fail to

2. Augustine held to a neoplatonism like that; so did Leibniz. Aquinas was an exemplarist but not a "realist" about more abstract kinds nor a "pluralist" about the *antecedent* divine ideas. *One* divine Exemplar, the *Verbum* (God's self-knowing), is the exemplar for whatever might be.

3. Michael J. Loux, ed., *The Possible and the Actual* (Ithaca: Cornell University Press, 1979), p. 53. In effect, this Platonism denies the "power set" axiom, no. 5, of the Zermelo-Fraenkel axioms. See Fraenkel's article "Set Theory" in *Encyclopedia of Philosophy*, ed. Paul Edwards (New York: Macmillan, 1967), p. 424.

Linda Zagzebski, commenting on this essay, points out that Von Neuman/Bernays/Godel set theory, and several others, have universal classes to which the power set axiom does not apply. The fact is that such "universal classes" are not a set of all sets; they are not sets at all. They are just a shorthand device without any commitment to such *objects*, alongside sets. I thank Scott Weinstein for advice on this point.

4. I indicated these difficulties in two unpublished papers, "The Incoherence of the Philosophers" (a 1982 Notre Dame lecture) and "Moderate Realism."

capture what is meant by assertions in natural language.[5] That is mainly because two-name theories do not preserve the multiple predicable relations of natural language and treat intensional logic as a "very big" case of extensional logic. I mean that in "humans are mortal," "humans" and "mortal" are not respectively names, either of classes or of abstractions; nor in "Socrates is human" is "human" the name of anything. Similarly, although you might want to analyze "blue things are colored" as a conjunction about each blue thing (thus, extensionally), we do not want to say that "blue things have to be colored" breaks down to a conjunction about each possible blue thing (that is, a bigger extension).

Although these are not the main considerations of this paper, they cast doubt upon the existence of a domain of exemplars. They also lead to other grounds for doubt.

Present-day modal actualists (as Michael Loux calls them), who postulate universal domains of essences, propositions. states of affairs, and even divine ideas, implicitly deny the force of the set-theoretic exclusion of maximal domains.[6] They do not offer a non-set-theoretic formality or a nonextensional interpretation of quantification or a replacement for current conceptions of propositional functions and predication. They insist on the exhaustive panorama of possibles or representations of possibles (like exemplars).

They also disregard the objection that a thing cannot be made (constituted) to be, say, a human, or to be that very human Socrates, by some contingent real relation to SOMETHING ELSE, say, an idea, that exists necessarily and independently of it. Yet, as I said, for such real "exemplification" to obtain, the subject has *to be* in order to stand in the relation and also has to stand in the relation in order to be. And the latter is *prior* to the former. (And there is no point in identifying "being" with "sharing," as I have said.)

Further, the "exemplification" or "instantiation" relation cannot be the *same* real relation between the resultant being (the being of the nature, say, Socrates) and the exemplar (essence) it shares, and between the resultant individual and the individual essence,[7] haecceity,[8] and so forth, that "contracts" it; for, presumably, the one "sharing" is

5. See P. Geach on Aquinas and G. E. M. Anscombe on Aristotle, in their *Three Philosophers* (Ithaca: Cornell University Press, 1961), and P. Geach, *Logic Matters* (Berkeley: University of California Press, 1972). They describe naive interpretations of predication that treat as one relation what is clearly several with different truth-conditions.

6. Cf. Loux, *Possible and Actual*, pp. 52–54.

7. Alvin Plantinga, *The Nature of Necessity* (Oxford: Clarendon Press, 1974), ch. 5.

8. See Loux, *Possible and Actual*, pp. 43 and 54, and R. Adams, "Actuality and Thisness," *Synthese* 49 (1981).

prior to the other, it can be many–one, and the second is a one–one relation only. Two explanatory "instantiation" relations plus an infinity of eternal *abstracta* make modal Neoplatonism a very expensive and unconvincing account of the ways things might have been.

Furthermore, Adams, Plantinga, Stalnaker, and Wierenga[9] write as if a property, ACTUALITY, were added to or conferred upon a possible world. But actuality would then accrue to a world accidentally, as something inhering in a subject already in being. Possible worlds cannot be subjects of inherence; for instance, they cannot BECOME actual (I take this to be self-evident). Further, the being of things cannot be INHERENT, either accidental to them or to the world "they inhabit," for similar reasons. If "actuality" is not a predicable accident, a constitutive relation, or a real mode of being, then what is it? Calling it a "property" is just an eyepatch for missing insight. One thing is certain: actual being is not a property and is not even predicable of anything. Those who think "Socrates exists" is like "Socrates is tall" simply do not understand.

Although modal Neoplatonists differ on how the "actual world" is related to the changing beings in the cosmos, typically the actual world is a logical shadow of the changing things, not a cause or explanation of them. So, creation is *not* "adding actuality" to a possible world.[10]

Even though God's effective will RANGES over THE REALM OF THE CONTINGENT, omnipotence is FORMALLY not the power to make states of affairs obtain or to actualize the possible. It is the power to *cause being* ex nihilo. There is no need, then, to think that "the realm of the contingent" determinately decomposes into actual and possible individuals and common natures or into exemplar ideas for them. Decomposition into individuals may be a consequence of creation but not an exemplar condition for it (just as dividing the sherbert into those mouthfuls may be a consequence of one's eating it and the means, too, but is not a condition or precedent).

God's power is more awesome. Its domain is realized with its exercise. What is possible *ad extra* is a result of what God does. God's power has no exemplar objects, only a perimeter (that is, finite being) plus a

---

9. See the papers by R. Adams, A. Plantinga, and R. Stalnaker in Loux, *Possible and Actual*. See also R. Adams, "Actuality and Thisness," pp. 9–10; Plantinga, *Nature of Necessity;* and E. Wierenga, "Omnipotence Defined," *Philosophy and Phenomenological Research* 43 (March 1983). For instance, Plantinga says, "Among the properties essential to an object is *existence*" (Loux, *Possible and Actual*, p. 261).

10. There is neither the range nor the actuality to add to it. There is, besides these Platonists, a realist so Meinongian as to make their Platonism ascetic: D. Lewis. His fabrications anticipate most of the major difficulties I rely upon, and he avoids them by mega-actuality and counterparts.

limit (that of internal consistency, compatibility with the divine being). God creates the kinds, the natures of things, along with things. And he settles what-might-have-been insofar as it is a consequence of what exists; for example, you might have been wealthier. Thus, there is no *mere* possibility with content (for example, "there might have been Martisils, silicon-based percipients, native to Mars"); there are only descriptions, actual and potential, that might, for all we know so far, have been satisfied. They do not, however, "pick out" any definite content that, if actual, would satisfy them. All content *ad extra* is caused by God. In sum, God creates the possibility, impossibility, and counter-factuality that has content (real situations) involving being other than God.

Thus I make the following arguments in this paper. (1) There is not a universal domain of kinds and a universal domain of things of the kinds (or a universal domain of exemplar ideas) determined by God's nature, from which God must choose what to create, nor are there exemplars for empty kinds and things. (2) There are no merely possible individuals, no empty individual names that name. (3) There are no real kinds without things of those kinds; that is, there are no *universalia ante rem*. (These three arguments have the consequence that there are no merely possible kinds of things.) (4) Just as some possibilities for individuals depend on which individuals God creates, so some possibilities and necessities depend on which kinds God creates. (5) The ways things might have been, as far as content goes, are consequences of what God does.[11]

In addition to these five arguments, which are developed below, I also assert that which interpreted modal logic is true depends on the will of God, with limits Descartes should have adopted.[12] Because of the nature of God, S5 as usually interpreted is not true. Also not true is any system interpreted to suppose a universal domain of kinds and individuals (or exemplars) or interpreted to suppose that every range

---

11. Which counterfactual conditionals have any truth-value at all and which are true depend on God's will (when it is not just a matter of syntactic or semantic inheritance of truth-value from categorical statements). Thus, "if there had been silicon-based life on Mars, it would last forever" is *unrooted;* it does not INHERIT a truth-value semantically and does not EARN one either.

12. Namely, nothing true can require God's not existing, or another inconsistency with God's being, or restrict God's effective will to a subrealm of the consistent. Moreover, there is no "absolute realm" of the consistent, with content. And, as Descartes noted, the fact that something seems inconsistent to us, relative to the conceptual alignment we have made, is not absolute assurance that it is. Cf. also Paul Henle's paper on ineffable truths ("Mysticism and Semantics," *Philosophy and Phenomenological Research* 9 [March 1949]: 416–22).

of possibility is truth-variantly accessible from every other or that "not possibly p" is synonymous with "impossible that p."[13]

No universal domains from God's nature. The usual explanation of how God comes to have universal exemplars is that God knows, exhaustively, every way in which the divine being can be finitely imitated and finitely participated. These intensional objects form a universal domain of exemplars. The purchase of this notion is that either you accept the universal domain (hierarchically tiered), decomposed into maximal compossibilia (possible worlds), or you hold there is some finite imitation of God that God does not represent to himself, even though it is possible only if he knows it—a contradiction. (Cf. Aquinas, Ia, 14, 6c.)

We have to deny that there is an extensive multitude, "every way infinite being can be finitely imitated." We have to deny that God's self-knowledge is by finite REPRESENTATION to himself (a point not developed further in this paper). We have to find the mistake in the ancient idea that the perfection of God can be exhaustively participated by an extensional multitude or even exhaustively represented to God in that way.

Plato's idea that perfect exemplars are logically prior (and prior in being) to imperfect participations was adapted by St. Augustine to make the exemplars dependent in being upon God's nature, not will, preserving the necessity and logical priority of the exemplars without allowing them to be independent of God. That adaptation endured throughout Western thought, with the notable exception of St. Thomas Aquinas (despite John Wippel's interpretation), eventually transforming into Leibniz's "complete concepts" and into Spinoza's infinity of divine attributes expressed, each in a replete infinity of modes. It has reappeared, without God, in applied modal logic and in philosophy of mathematics and metaphysics (like Chisholm's ontology of states of affairs).

Exemplars, exhaustive and replete universal domains, are incoherent (*a*) formally, (*b*) in the way they "explain" being, and (*c*) in their presuppositions about empty kinds and possible individuals. Points *a* and *b* I have developed above; here I elaborate particularly point *c*.

Three things bedevil exemplar Neoplatonism: (*a*) "ALL finite imitations of the infinitely perfect being," unlike "all natural numbers," is not an extensive magnitude and so not a domain of quantification; (*b*)

---

13. I mean here that just because it is not possible that there are Martisils, it does not follow that it is impossible that something satisfy the description "silicon-based percipients native to Mars." So, inaccessibility of alien possibility does not guarantee that whatever is so will make the proposition false.

there is no determinate relation "being-a-finite-imitation-of-perfect-being" to order a universal domain; and (*c*) there is nothing about God's being that could generate an ARTICULATE universal domain, because kinds cannot be exhausted by "instances." Thus, there is no principle to assure "downward" from the perfect being that "every" instance is in the domain. The same holds of the sharable kinds. The last defect traces to merely possible individuals and to empty real natures or kinds.

A domain is *universal* just in case every thing of every kind is in it, as in an extensive magnitude. A domain is *articulate* in case it is exhaustive, exclusive, disjoint (both upward and downward), and replete. To be *exhaustive* is to "use up" the field, say, "finite examples of divine perfection." To be *exclusive* is to contain nothing else. To be *disjoint* is to have nothing share (instantiate or exemplify) more than one segment (nature or kind or kind of kind) at any tier. The domain is *replete* when every segment is fully populated, when another name would only double name something. The absence of a downward principle is the same as failure of a basis in God's nature for a domain's being universal, being exhaustive, and being replete. Further contradictions show that the divine nature does not ground disjointness for a universal domain, either.

An articulate universal domain would be pyramidal, with a bottom layer of individuals, sharing natures but unshareable; above would be a first layer of shareable and fully shared real natures (like "being a human") that share in more abstract "kinds" that share in still broader "kinds," until we reach the kinds shared by everything, including one another (Plato's Great Forms),[14] that do not "share" anything else. They have being from something beyond, God. This is Neoplatonism fully ramified.

Some exemplar theories, like Aquinas's, are not committed, beyond the first-level sharable natures, that more abstract exemplars are real natures, because they do not acknowledge univocal general predicates like "living thing" or "cognitive thing." Besides, Aquinas thinks God's self-knowledge (Verbum) is a single *ratio* that is the exemplar for whatever God makes and that a multiplicity of *rationes* for creatures is not a logical condition for distinct creatures but a consequence of creation. Thus Aquinas, as I understand him, escapes the criticisms mounted here.

What of the "exhaustive finite participation" idea? God's perfection

---

14. See Plato's *Sophist*, and G. E. M. Anscombe, "The New Theory of Forms," in *Collected Papers*, vol. 1 (Minneapolis: University of Minnesota Press, 1981).

could not logically "refract," by increasing intension, into discrete, finite, unsharable units that exhaust the field. First, no kind is exhausted by individuals. Individuals cannot by "logical division," as a result of increasing intension, exhaust the nature to form an extensive magnitude, a well-ordered domain of quantification. (See the argument below regarding merely possible individuals.) For example, pieces of mercury, no matter how many you suppose, would never exhaust (by using it all up) what it is to be mercury, so that there *could* be no more; whereas the "successor" relation does that for natural numbers, purely syntactically.

Second, no nature is exhausted by differentiation. Absolutely speaking, there is no "nearest neighbor" for any human—say, "the one most like me." For then there would be one "separated from me" by the "least difference" of feature that makes a difference of being. But there is no qualitative "least difference" that makes a difference of being.

Third, no nature is exhausted by individuation, whatever the explanation of individuation, unless individuation is itself exhaustible. "Being determinate in an infinity of respects left open by the nature, distinct from every (other) actual thing and APT to have been otherwise" (that is, individuation), can be replicated without end, within any finite nature, assuming material components enough. Since these are the conditions for individuation, a real nature is not exhausted by individuation.

Finally, complete exemplarism would require counterparts, where each difference of feature makes a difference of being in the universal domain (and thus, no thing could have been otherwise than it is [cf. Leibniz]), or would require "haecceities," thisness, to exhaust the realm of individuation. Counterpart theory is false. Furthermore, "actual thisness" would exhaust individuation only if existing individuals are all there could have been. That is false for the same reason: actual things could have been otherwise and are not all there could have been. Therefore, complete exemplarism is false as well.

"Individual essences" beg the question by falling between those two options or by being described with expressions, like proper names ("Socrateity," for instance) and indexicals, "tags," which presuppose individuation of actual things.[15] There is all the difference between

---

15. Plantinga talks of abstractions like "Socrateity" and "Platonicity," which to be different from one another, in the absence of the individuals they differentiate, have to be extrinsically different. That is, *his* saying they are different has nothing to do with whether they are, if they are in being independently of Plantinga's will. What differenti-

"Socrateity," founded in the proper name for Socrates, and "Klee-geity," which ends in the empty name "Kleeg." Thus the coherence of the notion of an individual essence is derivative from actual individuation. If the domain of individual essences is individuated by the NAMES the essences involve, and the individuation of a real thing consists in its exemplifying the essence with *its* NAME on it, what does the name in an unexemplified individual essence name? For these and other reasons, a universal domain cannot be an exhaustive extension of finite participations in perfect being.

Augustine, Scotus, Leibniz, and (mutatis mutandis) Spinoza did not think of "the domain of finite imitations of infinite perfection" as an extensive magnitude, a domain of quantification and instantiation, and certainly not as constituted by units that combine set-theoretically.[16] So they did not consider whether there is a consistent principle to "decompose" undifferentiated perfect being uniquely and exhaustively into finite units. Had they done so, I think they would have said, "No!"

For there to be such a principle, an Achilles tendon and a three-knuckle digit would have to stand, relatively to God, in a definite comparative perfection under an ordering that extends to all possibility. The conditions for such a principle to "generate" a universal domain from God's being cannot be satisfed, as I have indicated. The problem, in the end, is with a universal domain's being exhaustive, disjoint (so that no name picks out two things and no thing is of two kinds), and replete. Yet that is necessary in order for names to exhaust the realm and for there to be empty kind names and empty individual names, as the ultimate logical decomposition into two-name singular propositions requires.[17]

There are no merely possible individuals. The main consideration is that

---

ates them? Certainly not the THINGS they WOULD individuate if individuals exemplified them. Certainly not the mere NAMES?

16. One does not have to accept that all reality is formally set-theoretic; I do not. But that does not absolve the modal Neoplatonists with maximal domains from having to sketch an alternative.

I won't waste time here arguing that an independent and necessary "Platonic heaven" of such exemplars has analogous problems, made worse by the excessive number of things needed to "explain" physical objects and the incoherence of the participation relations. Besides Socrates, in early Plantinga, we have HUMANITY and SOCRATEITY. There seem to be too many objects and too little for God to do—and no way for him to do it!

17. Inconsistencies follow not only from the supposed univocity of being and from the supposed discreteness and exhaustiveness of the classification but also from the fact that all the truths about God cannot be stated in any one language (see my "Mask of God," Lecture 3, Notre Dame, 1982). The predicates of no natural language can be "complete"; therefore, there cannot be an articulate classification, conception, even by God, under which God's infinite being can be finitely imitated.

nothing but actual being can supply the determinancy that is logically required for individuals with respect to an infinity of predicates and with respect to difference from everything else, while allowing the things to have been otherwise than as they are.

The nature cannot individuate. Otherwise, there could be only one thing of the kind, or each difference would make a difference of being, or the kind would be a determinable. But individuals are not determinates under a determinable. Determinates are shareable; individuals are not. Determinates are predicable; individuals are not. Every difference does not make a difference of being, for that would require that individuals could not have been otherwise. And there are no material natures that cannot be shared. So, a real nature cannot individuate.

Individuation—what differentiates a thing from everything else so that it could have been otherwise, and which determines it with respect to an infinity of predicates not determined by the nature—must lie "outside" the nature. It must lie in what is actual, because it accounts for an actual thing's being able, or apt, to have been otherwise. Why does that preclude individuation from being merely possible?

Every individual of a material nature, regardless of its nature, is apt TO HAVE BEEN OTHERWISE, no matter what temporal state you choose for it or whether we regard its whole actual being as one state. At the extreme, it might not have been at all; trivially, it might have coexisted with more things than there are; more significantly, it might have done something else, say, moved on a different path or been struck by a destroying object.

Thus, "being-able-to-have-been-otherwise" in some cases requires that the thing itself be really able to change; in others, that something else be really able to change. Other cases demand that the thing "be able not to have been at all" and "be able to have existed in other circumstances." For an actual being, "not to have been at all" is a definite difference (backward, as it were), while for something merely possible, "being" is not a definite difference forward, as we shall see. So I will treat separately a general "aptitude to have been otherwise," an aptitude that may not, for all we know at the moment, require actual ability to change.

Some being-apt-to-have-been-otherwise requires that a subject really be able to change, to BECOME (for example, I might have been a murderer; that would require that, at some time, I would change from nonmurderer to murderer, there being no possible world in which I am a murderer without going from moral goodness to moral evil). Sometimes, being-apt-to-have-been-otherwise requires that some other subject be really able to change (for example, when I, standing still, become farther from you as you move away).

Real ability to change cannot belong to a merely possible thing. At most, a merely possible thing is a thing that WOULD be really able to change if actual. Real ability to change requires actual being in its subject. I mean that saying " 'being really able to change' CONSISTS in 'a thing's being different in different possible worlds' " is just false. That may be a consequence of being able to change; it is certainly not what it consists in.

In addition, nothing can be an individual of a material nature—a tiger, a carbon atom, a snake, or a saint—that is not really able to change. That is a logically necessary condition for being OF-A-MATE-RIAL-NATURE. It is de re necessary of every natural thing. No merely possible thing can change, except in the shadow sense that it has different features at different times. As a result, there are no merely possible things of any real nature. Thus, there are no really possible individuals at all, because there can be no individual that is not of a material nature. (Pure spirits, God, angels, devils, and so forth are not, strictly, individuals).

Suppose not all real natures require things capable of change or that other things be able to change. Consider "being-able-to-have-been-otherwise" in general. A thing-in-being is, on the whole, apt to cease to be, but a thing-not-in-being is not APT to be. (Leibniz thought that mere possibles had aptitude—even tendency—toward being, and A. Kenny says in his book on Descartes that many medievals thought possibles had aptitude to be.[18] That, surely, is typically Neoplatonist and a minority view.) For those who deny that there is some kind of "possible being" (*esse possibile*), or an *esse essentiae* of Henry of Ghent, the merely possible lacks any real aptitude at all, including the ability to change and *conatus* to be.

Now, I know modal Neoplatonists offer analyses to cover this by describing the OUTCOMES of every aptitude, whether real ability to change, passive aptitude to have things happen, or more ghostly ones, like being apt-not-to-have-been. They describe those outcomes as arrays of what would obtain were other possible worlds to be actual. However, those outcomes follow (on the supposition that the "possible worlds talk" has a consistent interpretation) from the aptitude in ques-

18. See John Wipple, "The Reality of Nonexisting Possibles according to Thomas Aquinas, Henry of Ghent, and Godfrey of Fontaines," *Review of Metaphysics* 34, no. 4 (1981): 729–58; also in J. Wipple, *Metaphysical Themes in Thomas Aquinas* (Washington, D.C.: Catholic University Press, 1984).

tion but do not explain or constitute it. Nor do those outcomes even require the aptitude, since those conditions could be satisfied for sets of worlds without change or aptitude. That is evident from the ringing difference of meaning between "that table is apt to have been otherwise, that is, it might have been painted, damaged, crushed, or not have been made at all" and "something merely possible is apt to have been instead." The latter does not even *suppose* a subject of aptitude.

Real counterfactual aptitudes can no more be analyzed as an array of OUTCOMES than my real ability to speak English can be analyzed as an array of my actual and possible utterances. (For one thing, we know that a thing could produce the same array of utterances without having the ability to speak English.)[19] To describe ability to BECOME as traits possessed in "other" worlds it to substitute output for capacity and to provide no subject of real *becoming*. Such analyses are not only incomplete, they are false.

Real aptitude, like real disposition, logically requires a causing subject in being. There can be no merely possible individual that is a causing subject in being.[20] Therefore, there are no merely possible individuals. A similarly basic consideration underlies the argument below that there cannot be empty real natures, because natures are capacities subsisting ONLY in their realizations.

There is nothing, outside the actual, to account for the bivalence of infinite (but not all) predicates that are not de re necessary from the nature but that apply to an individual, depending upon what (else) is actual.[21] That contrasts with imaginary things that are indeterminate even to predicates that must apply disjunctively, as "ancestors" of what is immediately so, regardless of what is actual. Something determines WHICH of two predicates, say, "traveled through Idaho, or not," applies to a given person. It belongs to the actual (for example, whether he did or not) and in a way that requires an infinity of determinateness that transcends what is said. The imaginary can be indeterminate to both

19. There is also an argument that 'being intelligent' cannot be the same as any pattern, even of infinitely dense infinite arrays—say of judgments or statements or actions—because such an output can be 'mimicked' by a mimetic machine. The intelligence has to ORIGINATE the pattern. Capacity to do that does not even require exercise, but it does require actual being. That origination is just what the reduction of ability to exercise leaves out.

20. I think R. Adams argues to the same effect in "Actuality and Thisness."

21. Bivalence of an infinity of features is not the same as bivalence of all properties. Individuals are essentially dense in features (as the discussion of transcendent determinacy shows) and yet also essentially hazy, especially counterfactually. So I don't think it is determinate, say, that I either have or have the opposite of the property "successful salesman, if I had not been a philosopher."

and has no "transcendent determinacy." So, too, with the merely possible.[22]

The real truth-conditions for any contingent truth are continuous and dense, "transcendently determinate" in a way that mere possibility, requiring articulate domains as it does, cannot supply. Contingent reality, when what we say is true, is always more determinate than whatever we can contrive to say. In order for it to be true that Jones traveled through Idaho, some infinity of things, *not* included in what is meant, must obtain (but not just the one that does obtain). This is "transcendent determinacy."

Nothing about the merely possible (or the imaginary) can supply the transcendent determinacy that infinitely exceeds what we mean, as is required for the concrete truth-conditions for what we say. Thus, nothing "merely possible"—whether states of affairs, propositions, situations, change, or being—is determinate enough to be. Whatever is "merely possible," as a situation, is logically indefinite, so that differing "transcendent infinities of the concrete" could realize it. Thus, no description or "name" of the "merely possible" succeeds in "picking out" what can REALLY be. The domain of the merely possible is empty of content.

Look again at how individuation, (*a*) "being determinate with respect to an infinity of predicates not included in the nature," (*b*) "being different from every distinct thing that is actual," and (*c*) "being ABLE, APT, to have been otherwise," is not satisfied by the merely possible. Someone will say individuation has analyses, like "the very same thing has distinct traits in other worlds." But where "being-apt-to-have-been-otherwise" requires something to be really able to change, no merely possible thing has that aptitude. Besides, BEING-ABLE-REALLY-TO-CHANGE is a de re necessity of everything of a real, finite nature. No merely possible subject has that ability. So there is no merely possible subject that has a real finite nature. That means there are no merely possible humans.[23]

---

22. Empty names are a great logical embarrassment that exemplars are supposed to remedy. But exemplars make it worse; they increase the number of necessary existents, they provide no account of the "exemplification" relations, no account of how God generates them, of how individual essences differ absolutely from one another, or of what the role of God is in creation. The result is to step from logical embarrassment into religious catastrophe.

23. Oversimplifying for rhetorical effect, the only way I could have been otherwise would have been to BECOME otherwise, say richer. No merely possible thing can BECOME at all. So I could not have been a merely possible thing. Further, an auxiliary argument: to be actual and to be merely possible are incompatible. (This is not just a sophism.) Neither the real natures nor the real things could have been merely possible. That's just

The only subjects of becoming are individuals. There are *no* subjects of individuation. Nothing BECOMES individuated by standing in some relation (say, to an individual essence or haecceity). That would require "deeper individuals," *bare nominata*, neutral to kind and to individuation. That would only repeat the problems with fewer resources to resolve them.

IF THERE CANNOT BE MERELY POSSIBLE INDIVIDUALS, THERE CANNOT BE IDEAS FOR THEM EITHER. In one sense, that is obvious, the sense in which "idea of" is like "picture of" or "name of"; in another, it is not, where "idea of" is like "so-and-so picture" or "picture-for." Why cannot God have an exemplar-for, a picture-for, an individual, the exemplar being as determinate as the thing would be itself? In one sense God's knowledge of himself, the *Verbum*, is the exemplar for any creature whatever (see both Bonaventure and Aquinas). But that's the sense in which W. C. Fields is the exemplar for any imitator, and equally for all imitators, regardless of differences among them, because they can be "W. C. Fields impersonators" only to the extent that they do imitate him. Thus, a single exemplar can be the exemplar for a nonquantifiable infinity of diverse "imitations." In that sense, which is the exemplarity doctrine I attribute to Aquinas, I have no objection to exemplar theory; there is, antecedently, nothing about the exemplar that "generates" the domain of finite imitations. Rather, there is something about each imitation that picks out the exemplar.

For the exemplarist's purposes, it would not do for God to have an exemplar for one or only some individuals in a way that is conditional upon his having made some actual thing (as Aquinas explicitly holds in Ia, 15). He must be able to have a complete idea for any and all individuals, irrespective of whether there is any actual finite being at all. But a complete exemplar would include every feature of the thing, including every INDEXED de re necessity (for example, "son of John and Mary"). For without those, the other features could be satisfied by things that differ in INDEXED de re necessities, and thus the idea would not be "for" a unique individual. If, however, God can have exemplars of all individuals with all INDEXED de re necessities without any actual finite being, then what do the indexes indicate? This is what refutes, inter alia, Leibniz's "complete concept" hypothesis. Indexicality requires actuality.

Because no exemplar is tied to any particular thing, even though all, perhaps, form an interindexed network (James, son of John and Mary,

---

because the merely possible *cannot* change and the actual must be *able* to. So the domain of the merely possible—what might have been actual—is empty, and necessarily so.

made HAMLET in paper from Bengal in the year after the eighty-ninth atomic attack, and so forth), still it is not determined WHICH individual each is. Things that differ in INDEXED de re features could satisfy such exemplars. To say they could not have had "any more" indexed features than the exemplars include is to require that they be actual individuals. For if not actual, then on being made actual, each acquires "being this" individual, related to THAT John and Mary, and so forth. That is, each acquires de re indexed necessities by being made actual. So the only way a divine exemplar could include EVERY indexed de re necessity of its object is to be the exemplar of an actual thing. And if the exemplar is not of an actual thing, then it CANNOT, consistently with being an exemplar of what can be, contain every de re necessity of its object. As a result, God cannot have complete exemplar ideas of what is not actual.

In short, relative indexicality is an immediate consequence of coactuality for things.[24] That cannot belong to mere exemplars. Therefore, there is not a domain of exemplar ideas of individuals.[25] Indexing without a root in actual being is like pointing without a context.[26]

Another reason there are no merely possible individuals is that actual being is prior to what-might-have-been, as far as that has content. (This, of course, is a consequence of the position I am developing, not a premise of it.) Although the individual has to be definitely determined in an infinity of ways not specified by the nature, some ways it MIGHT HAVE BEEN—from its aptitude for real becoming—are indeterminate, apart from God's will applied to a thing in being. This conclusion requires support from the reasons why there are no empty real natures

24. That is another feature D. Lewis incorporated nicely; because for him actuality is relative, so is indexicality. It is interesting to see how many of these and earlier difficulties Lewis anticipated and avoided with his counterpart hypothesis. He adroitly replaced messy reality with neat madness.

25. The basic idea is that all individual exemplars would have to include the indexed de re necessities of each, but would not be indexed to any actual reality. Diverse indexing to actual reality (e.g., "NOW!" commands of the creator) would yield diverse real individuals (more accurately, counterparts), all satisfying the exemplars, yet *not* having all their de re necessary features in common, depending, in a word, on which "NOW" caused them to be. And if the exemplars are not entirely networked together with interlocking indexicals, so that one's being actual requires all the others (the way your existing requires the existence of all your ancestors), then alternate worlds of individuals, as exemplified in the ideas, could be satisfied by distinct transworld individuals. To avoid that, the exemplars would have to have indexed features in a world and across worlds to what is actual.

26. Divine exemplars, even so detailed, would not determine actual being, because they would either not index to actual creatures or would exist consequently upon the actual world. Therefore, there are none.

and why "how-things-might-have-been" *supposes* things in being, whose
being and determinacy come from God's will (see below).

There are no real kinds without things of those kinds. A description that
purports to name a "merely possible kind" (say, "laser telephone") is
satisfied by things that DIFFER in de re necessary features not indexed to
the bearer.[27] Therefore, it does not pick out a real kind. Things of the
same real nature do not differ in what is nonindexically de re necessary
of each.[28] Empty kinds (for example, fish-that-thinks) cannot be real
kinds because they are, however specified, indeterminate to things that
differ in (nonindexed) de re necessities, such as "with dorsal fins,"
"without dorsal fins." Without "naming" realizations, there is nothing
for "kind names" to pick out that is sufficiently definite to count as a
real nature.

That argument shows that we cannot pick out empty kinds by descriptions or names, not that there cannot be any. But that deepens
suspicion, especially conjoined with the earlier observation that WHAT a
thing is cannot be explained by an EXTERNAL "sharing" relation to
something that exists independently. For it makes us ask what *is* the
"relationship" of a real nature (a real kind, like "human," "water,"
"gold") to the resultant thing-of-the-nature? (It makes no progress to
say the common natures are platonic objects, as Donnellan, Kaplan,
and Salmon do.)

Let us distinguish (*a*) kinds that had members but have none now

27. "Necessary features not indexed to the bearers" is a key notion, to be understood
as follows: F is a necessary feature of N, not indexed to N, just in case, without F, N does
not exist (for any world you choose), and $(\exists x)(Fx)$ does not entail Fn, though of course Fn
entails $(\exists x)(Fx)$.

28. For now, I skip over disjunctives, such as gender, and also treat natures only as
shared contemporaneously. The notion "nonindexically necessary" is broader than "not
indexed to the bearer" because it covers alio-relative indexing too, e.g., to parents. To
accommodate evolution, "is of the same real nature as" is not coextensive with "is the
offspring of." After enough steps individuals cease to have necessarily true of them
something that was necessarily true of ancestors, and they acquire necessities, not necessities of ancestors. Merely possible kinds are not "real" kinds, not simply because individuals with differing nonindexical necessities might belong, but rather because the
specification, no matter how complete, can never determine, for all candidates so differing, whether they belong or not.

The idea is that some real kinds, by their relationship to other natures, are transformational, so that the necessities required for membership alter over time (but not enough to
preclude successor kinds, by becoming fluid kinds). Persons, for instance, may have
various natures. At the extreme, because God determines the de re necessities of things,
Jesus satisfied both the necessities of humanity and divinity, like a person's being both
spatial and temporal, when many things are one or the other and not both. (Of course,
to-be-divine is a real nature only by analogy, because strictly, it is not sharable by distinct
beings.) Natures do not alter, strictly. What natures are realized is what alters. Natures
are transformational, being themselves realized in the potentialities of prior things.

(say, mastodons)—*a real nature*, (*b*) kinds that are no more than descriptions derived from kinds that have or had members but are themselves physically impossible (say, babies with feet on their heads, dragonflies with lizard snouts)—the *antikinds* of medieval illustrators, and (*c*) *apparent* kinds (say, griffins and unicorns, phlogiston, caloric, and ether)— things that some people thought were real though, in fact, there is no such sort actually or potentially in nature. The apparent kinds and the antikinds are necessarily empty. That's not because they have the anti-ontological predicate "merely fictional" but because whatever they can pick out is indefinite in a way a real kind cannot be. They do not differentiate all candidates by (nonindexed) de re necessities exclusively into membership or lack of it. Clearly, a real nature does that by constituting the "resultant" to be of the nature and everything else not.

None of this decides the issue. Only an account of the relationship of the nature to the resultant thing will do. But at least we need consider for now only natures realized in individuals. There can't be empty real natures because *the nature of a thing is to the thing as capacity is to realization, where the capacity does not subsist in the condition of something else*, as the ability to play a C-major scale subsists in the potentialities of a pianist. Rather, the active capacity that is a real nature (say, "being human") subsists in the realization—the individual—but it is not identical with it because it can subsist in ANY realization or active potentiality to realization (however remote), but it cannot subsist without realization, actual or potential.[29]

In brief, *real natures are active capacities for realization (as de re necessities of individuals) subsistent in their realizations alone*. No wonder there cannot be empty real natures. As Abelard thought, when the last rose dies, there is no longer such a thing as "being a rose"; only the name remains.[30]

It would be a mistake to regard this account of real natures as a "tailored replacement," designed merely to escape the difficulties I mentioned for modal actualism. Moderate realism is a hypothesis that stands on its own explanatory power: its elegance, parsimony, and coherence with what we know of the real natures of things, especially synthetics, and its economy in dealing with natural necessity, predica-

29. See my unpublished paper "Moderate Realism." It is too complex here to try to show that this is what a real nature must be if it determines all the de re, nonindexed necessities of individuals. Reflection in this new context, however, may suddenly disclose that.

30. Cf. Umberto Eco, *The Name of the Rose*, trans. William Weaver (San Diego: Harcourt Brace Jovanovich, 1983).

tion, counterfactuality, and modality. I forgo illustrating that with an account of synthetic natures[31] to sketch, instead, two of its theologically salient consequences.

Just as some possibilities for individuals depend on which individuals God creates, so some possibilities and necessities depend upon which kinds God creates. First, there are simple and uncontroversial cases of both sorts. Whether it is possible that I marry a certain person depends on whether that person actually exists (tenselessly). Had she not, it would not have been possible that I marry her; there would have been no "subject in a possibility." There would have been no definite impossibility either. HER not having existed at all is *not* a possible situation, except relatively to the world in which she actually exists. In part, that is because the "transcendent determinacy" for the situation that determines WHICH situation it is, is in the actual. Had some "other world" obtained, it would not have been determinately so but only so by default that *she* did not exist; no state of affairs whose constituent is picked out by her names would *not* have obtained.

Many sorts of individual possibility and necessity depend on the very things that happen to exist, for instance, my being a human, my not being invisible, our disagreeing about this. So, too, with the kinds of things. What things CAN be is, partly, parasitic on what things there are. Burpee's hunt for the white marigold presupposed flowers that by breeding could be color varied to white. Kinds by transformation require prior kinds.

Whether antilichts repel gravitons depends on what they are, and that, surprisingly, depends on whether there are any. (I count remote natural potentiality as "being" for this purpose.) Whether caloric was misdescribed (as jadeite was) depends on whether caloric is real. There are no counterfactual EARNED truths or falsities whose subjects are unrooted kinds. "Antilichts repel gravitons" has no earned truth-value. Are antilichts photon-annihilating particles or light-absorbing regions of space? If there are some, there may be an answer. Otherwise, "the former," "the latter," "both," and "neither" would do. An unrooted, truly alien kind has no realizations. (Alien, unrooted kinds are not really kinds. Real kinds can have realizations. These "kinds" cannot.) Because "antilichts repel gravitons" also does not nest semantically in our discourse (though it could easily be made to), the utterance has no truth-value at all, neither earned nor inherited, whereas "phlogiston resists ether drag" has no EARNED truth-value, but it can in various ways INHERIT a truth-value (see the argument below).

---

31. I expect to discuss this in a forthcoming paper, "Synthetic Natures from Natural Necessities."

There are possibilities and impossibilities for things according to their kinds. Most birds can fly; humans cannot. So, if the kinds of creatures were different, the real possibilities of things—and real impossibilities—would be different, as would what might have been, too. Thus, "humans might have landed on Mars by now" is parasitic for content on the actual being of humans. We cannot name any real kinds there might have been instead of any of the kinds there are. So we have no access to what might have been instead; but that is not just epistemic, it is ontological.

More deeply, what necessities intertwine into the de re necessities that a nature imposes depend upon the will of God. At bottom, that is why alien kinds are inaccessible; they depend for reality upon an exercise of the divine will that did not occur.

Whether all species of rational animals (I assume that whales might, for all we know, be rational animals) divide into two genders, only one of which can bear offspring, is from the will of God. Whether humans are naturally immortal or not is a de re necessity, also from God's choice; what, in effect, that choice was is hotly disputed, as is whether God chose that we have genuinely free will or not. Whether homosexual tendencies are incidental to human nature or a natural necessity is a matter of God's will. Whether no human can be water breathing as well as air breathing also seems to depend on God's will. In fact, all a posteriori de re necessity (lying outside systems of inherited truth-value) depends on the will of God.

Some counterpossibilities depend on kinds humans have made, transformational kinds: capital letters, alphabets, quarter notes, neumes, castling in chess, summary judgment in law, and architraves and pediments in fifteenth-century archirecture. Humans made margerine, linoleum, vinyl, acrylic, polyurethane, penicillin, Demerol, Novocaine, and heroin. Each involves real possibilities and impossibilities. In contrast, there is no state of affairs "humans are aquatic creatures" that does *not* obtain: inheritance relationships are enough to provide the needed truth-values. Whereas "antilichts absorb caloric" has neither earned nor inherited values. There is no definite situation that is not rooted in real natures or things that does not obtain.

The ways things might have been, as far as content goes, are consequences of what God does. This point differs only in emphasis from saying that all de re necessities (lying outside systems of inherited truth) depend on God's will. On the general picture I offer, we can still account for the truth-values of the counterfactuals we are quite certain have values (for example, "if I had gone to Newark yesterday, I'd be tired now") and can dispose of the greater number of such conditionals as lacking earned values (for example, if I'd been a woman, I'd have wanted children"), with a very large portion having no truth-values at all, except purely formally, even ones with names of real things (for example, "if I'd been a woman I'd have married an Oriental").

Counterfactual statements, of course, INHERIT truth-values syntactically when treated either truth-functionally or under varying principles of implication. They can also inherit truth-values if embedded in the semantic relations of unbound or craft-bound discourse. Thus, we might say, "If a mutual fund were open-ended, it would redeem its shares," because that is what the words mean in law. We might say that "if I became a neutron, I would see monads" is true because the antecedent is necessarily false, basing that on the meaning relationships of the English expressions "I" and "neutron," and on the logical principle that a conditional with a necessarily false antecedent is true. We might also take the whole meaning into account and say it is false because neutrons have no power of sight. Or we might say it is false because monads cannot be seen. In each case, a value is ascribed on the basis of meaning relationships and a selected "inheritance" (logical) relationship from other statements. In contrast, we might, if bold enough, go beyond meaning and say the statement has an EARNED negative truth-value because there cannot be monads. But "if martisils had vision problems, they would have evolved glass eyes" cannot have an earned truth-value for failure of reference, and it cannot have a definite semantic truth-value because it is not (yet) embedded deeply enough in meaning relationships, still it can have various syntactic truth-values, depending upon how it is treated.

The general principle is that what there is accounts for WHAT MIGHT HAVE BEEN, as far as that is determinate. The only compliant reality from which truth can be earned is what is actually so, involving actual and potential—not merely possible—being. Truth can be earned only from real situations. The only real situations are actual and potential, involving real natures and things as constituents.

Finally, one should not think that every system of inherited truths has to terminate in a stratum of earned truths. There can be truth by inflation as well; an abstract system can as a whole be true just because its objects satisfy *all* its statements and no condition of reality can disconfirm any of them.[32] This matter of "truth" has to be left for now, just begun. I addressed it to indicate the broad sweep of the consequences of saying the real natures of things depend on the will of God. One gets into a very long story by finding there are no *universalia ante rem*.

---

32. There are various "satisfaction" relations. For now, "does not comply with a contradictory negation of any of it" will do.

Contributors

Marilyn McCord Adams is Professor of Philosophy at the University of California, Los Angeles. She received her A.B. from the University of Illinois in 1964, her Ph.D. from Cornell in 1967, and Th.M. from Princeton Theological Seminary in 1985. Her principal publications include numerous articles on medieval metaphysics and theology, and a forthcoming two-volume book on the philosophy of William Ockham.

Robert Merrihew Adams is Professor of Philosophy at the University of California, Los Angeles. A Presbyterian minister, he studied theology at Oxford and at Princeton Theological Seminary, and philosophy at Princeton and Cornell universities. He has published papers on metaphysics, ethics, and the history of modern philosophy, as well as on philosophical theology. He taught philosophy at the University of Michigan before going to UCLA.

Robert Audi is Professor of Philosophy at the University of Nebraska. He received his B.A. from Colgate University in 1963 and his Ph.D. from the University of Michigan in 1967. His main research interests are in epistemology, the philosophy of mind (especially action theory), ethics, and the philosophy of the social sciences. His principal publications have been in these fields, and he is currently writing books in epistemology and the philosophy of action.

Kenneth Konyndyk received his Ph.D. from Wayne State University in 1970 and is chairman of the Philosophy Department at Calvin

College. His publications include articles in the *International Journal for Philosophy of Religion, The New Scholasticism, Philosophical Studies,* a chapter in a book on Jacques Ellul, and numerous reviews in various journals.

Ralph McInerny is Michael P. Grace Professor of Medieval Philosophy at the University of Notre Dame, where he has taught since 1955. *Being and Predication,* a collection of his articles, will soon appear from Catholic University Press. He is editor of *The New Scholasticism,* has just completed a book on Boethius and Aquinas, and has begun research on the history of Thomism.

George I. Mavrodes is Professor of Philosophy at the University of Michigan. He was educated at Oregon State College (B.S.), Western Baptist Theological Seminary (B.D.), and the University of Michigan (M.A., Ph.D.). He is the coeditor, with Stuart Hackett, of *Problems and Perspectives in the Philosophy of Religion* (1967) and the editor of *The Rationalty of Belief in God* (1970). He is the author of *Belief in God: A Study in the Epistemology of Religion* (1970) and of numerous articles.

Nelson Pike is Professor of Philosophy at the University of California, Irvine. He received his B.S. from Carroll College in 1953, his M.A. from the University of Michigan in 1955, and his Ph.D. from Harvard in 1962. Before going to Irvine, he taught at Cornell University. He is the editor of *God and Evil* (1963), and his edition of David Hume's *Dialogues Concerning Natural Religion* (1970) includes an extensive commentary. He is the author of *God and Timelessness* (1970) and of numerous articles on topics in the philosophy of religion.

Alvin Plantinga is John A. O'Brien Professor of Philosophy at the University of Notre Dame. He was educated at Calvin College (A.B.), the University of Michigan (M.A.), and Yale University (Ph.D.). He previously taught at Wayne State University and Calvin College and is a past president of the Western Division of the American Philosophical Association. He is the author of *God and Other Minds* (1967), *The Nature of Necessity* (1974), *God, Freedom, and Evil* (1974), and *Does God Have a Nature?* (1980).

Philip L. Quinn is John A. O'Brien Professor of Philosophy at the University of Notre Dame. He was formerly William Herbert Perry Faunce Professor of Philosophy at Brown University and has also taught at the University of Michigan, the University of Illinois at Chicago, and The Ohio State University. He is the author of *Divine Commands and Moral Requirements* and of papers and reviews in the areas of philosophy of religion, metaphysics, value theory, philosophy of science, and philosophy of mathematics.

James F. Ross is Professor of Philosophy at the University of Pennsylvania. He received his A.B. and A.M. from the Catholic University of America in 1953 and 1954, his Ph.D. from Brown in 1958, and his J.D. from the University of Pennsylvania in 1974. He is the author of *Philosophical Theology* (1969), *Introduction to the Philosophy of Religion* (1969), *Portraying Analogy* (1982), and the forthcoming *Creation*.

William L. Rowe is Professor of Philosophy at Purdue University. He received his B.A. from Wayne State University in 1954, his B.D. from Chicago Theological Seminary in 1957, and his M.A. and Ph.D. from the University of Michigan in 1958 and 1962. He is the author of *Religious Symbols and God: A Philosophical Study of Tillich's Theology* (1968), *The Cosmological Argument* (1975), and *Philosophy of Religion* (1978). He is coeditor, with William J. Wainwright, of *Philosophy of Religion: Selected Readings* (1973).

William J. Wainwright is Professor of Philosophy at the University of Wisconsin–Milwaukee and previously taught at Dartmouth College and the University of Illinois at Urbana. He was educated at Kenyon College (B.A.) and the University of Michigan (M.A., Ph.D.). He is the coeditor, with William Rowe, of *Philosophy of Religion: Selected Readings* (1973). He is the author of *Philosophy of Religion: An Annotated Bibliography of Twentieth-Century Writings in English* (1978) and *Mysticism: A Study of Its Nature, Cognitive Value, and Moral Implications* (1981) and is currently writing a book on the philosophy of religion.

Nicholas Wolterstorff was educated at Calvin College (A.B.) and Harvard University (M.A., Ph.D.). He has been in the philosophy department at Calvin College since 1959 and has also taught at Yale University, Haverford College, University of Chicago, University of Texas, University of Michigan, Notre Dame University, Temple University, Free University of Amsterdam, and Princeton University. He is the author of, among other books, *On Universals* and *Works and Worlds of Art*, and editor, with Alvin Plantinga, of *Faith and Rationality*.

Index

Library of Congress Cataloging-in-Publication Data
Main entry under title:

Rationality, religious belief, and moral commitment.

Includes index.
1. Religion—Philosophy—Addresses, essays, lectures.
I. Audi, Robert, 1941–   . II. Wainwright,
William J.
BL51.R295 1986   200′.1   85–48200
ISBN 0–8014–1856–9
ISBN 0–8014–9381–1 (pbk.)